A HISTORY OF PLAYING CARDS AND A BIBLIOGRAPHY OF CARDS AND GAMING

BY

CATHERINE PERRY HARGRAVE

*Compiled and Illustrated from the Old Cards
and Books in the Collection of The United
States Playing Card Company in Cincinnati*

NEW YORK
DOVER PUBLICATIONS, INC.

To
JOHN OMWAKE
Whose pleasure and interest it has been for nearly forty years to gather together these old records of the past five centuries concerning his ancient and honorable craft of playing-card making, and whose kindness and understanding and coöperation have made the arranging of these things and the writing of their story a happy task

63468

Published in Canada by General Publishing Company, Ltd., 30 Lesmill Road, Don Mills, Toronto, Ontario.
Published in the United Kingdom by Constable and Company Ltd., 10 Orange Street, London W. C. 2

This Dover edition, first published in 1966, is an unabridged republication of the work originally published by Houghton Mifflin Company in 1930. This reprint is published by permission of the United States Playing Card Company.
The thirty-one full-color plates from the original edition are here reproduced as black-and-white halftones. In addition, this volume contains four newly prepared color plates, showing cards from sixteen different packs.

Standard Book Number: 486-21544-X
Library of Congress Catalog Card Number: 66-15935

Manufactured in the United States of America
Dover Publications, Inc.
180 Varick Street
New York, N. Y. 10014

PREFACE

'If it be true that good wine needs no bush, 'tis true that a good play needs no epilogue: yet to good wine they do use good bushes; and good plays prove the better by the help of good epilogues.' Even so this story seems to demand a foreword, not because of its excellence or lack thereof, but because of the unusualness of the subject.

Thirty years ago a large part of this collection was bought from George Clulow, F.R.G.S., an Englishman who was an authority on the subject, and whose group of both the cards themselves and books pertaining to them and their use is acknowledged to be one of the most complete and scholarly that has ever been gathered together, containing many examples that are unique. Additions have been made from time to time, until the collection now numbers more than a thousand different examples of cards, and nearly as many books.

Aside from their interest to artists and craftsmen who can appreciate the virtue of these things as rare and often lovely examples of early printing and etching and engraving, there is a very human appeal.

They are a gay and intimate little by-road into the past. Their mission has been to seek and dispense pleasure and there is little of grimness or tragedy in their story. It leads from the far-away Venice of the Doges with its busy port, through soldiers' camps, pausing at feudal courts, and at a snatch of Romany song, wandering through the countryside with a gypsy band. And if occasionally it strayed before a frowning cathedral where a somber monk demanded that all tric-tracs and dice and cards and other worldly vanities be consigned to the flames, it was only that a gentle brother in the monastery on the hill or the patient craftsman in the village below might furnish them anew. It found its way to ancient seats of learning and aided and abetted many a roving mountebank at the crossroads. In the palace of the queen where the court played at games with strange names, often with cards of rare delicacy, a little silk-clad prince learned his lessons from other cards, especially made for him. And if an excessive duty depressed the card-makers, it led to the delightful adventure of smuggling their wares over the Pyrenees into waiting Spain, or across the rivers into the Low Countries.

The excellent Christopher Sower at his press in Germantown made religious playing cards in 1744 — three hundred and eighty-one to a set — for his good brethren. And an ennuied and storm-bound and, alas, backsliding citizen of Nantucket, despairing of getting cards from the manufactory in Boston, was reduced to making his own.

PREFACE

The trail goes on and on. The old cards are to be found in the historical societies in this country, just as they are in the print collections throughout Europe, usually as examples of early printing or engraving rather than as cards. There are, besides, card collections at the Librairie Nationale, at the British Museum, at Dresden, Munich, Nuremberg, and Vienna, and at our own National Museum in Washington. Of private collections there are many in Europe; the Queen of Spain is said to have one, and we know of three in this country, one of which was recently given to Harvard.

On a cold March morning in New York, the trail seemed to have ended despairingly among the towering walls and in the rush of the city. Yet just around the corner were Alexander Anderson wood blocks that he had made for card wrappers, and which had waited more than a hundred years to be discovered — a pre-cigar-store Indian, a state seal, an early American version of Harry VIII, and the sea fight of the gallant Decatur. There are small Spanish cards stenciled in yellow, made in the fifties, that might be part of a Mark Twain story, and Thackeray made cards for himself, with a story or verse for each one. It is a long tale, to quote 'Alice,' that grows 'curiouser and curiouser,' a good game, and a joyous and sun-dappled road to yesterday.

In our search for records of American playing cards and their makers, we have received valuable help from Mr. U. A. Slade, the Library of Congress; Dr. Charles Moore, formerly of the Division of Manuscripts, the Library of Congress; Mr. Fred G. Floyd, Hingham, Massachusetts; Mr. George L. Dow, the Society for the Preservation of New England Antiquities, Boston; Mr. Frank C. Ayres, the Business Historical Society, Boston; Mr. Henry W. Royal, the Pilgrim Society, Plymouth, Massachusetts; Mr. H. M. Lydenberg, Dr. F. Weitenkampf, Mr. Strippel, the New York Public Library; Miss Anna A. MacDonald, the Pennsylvania State Library and Museum; the Pennsylvania Museum, Fairmount Park, Philadelphia; Mr. Asa Don Dickinson, the University of Pennsylvania; Mr. G. M. Abbot, the Library Company, Philadelphia; Mr. Bunford Samuel, the Ridgway Library, Philadelphia; Mr. Mantle Fielding, Philadelphia; the Historical Society of Pennsylvania; Mr. W. D. Appleyard, Mr. John H. Pratt, New York; the Cincinnati Public Library; Miss Belle Hamlin, the Historical Society of Cincinnati.

CONTENTS

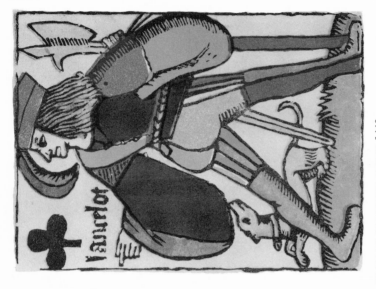

PLAYING CARDS FROM WOOD BLOCKS, MADE IN PROVENCE ABOUT 1440

These are the earliest printed playing cards of Europe that have ever been found

ILLUSTRATIONS

ILLUSTRATIONS

ILLUSTRATIONS

ILLUSTRATIONS

ILLUSTRATIONS

COLOR PLATES

facing page 70

facing page 71

facing page 98

facing page 99

A HISTORY OF PLAYING CARDS

.·.

CHAPTER I

INTRODUCTORY

THE history of playing cards is not only the record of the persistence of a fifteenth-century craft, practically unchanged in its essential aspects, but the story of the universal trait of human nature, the allure of chance, which is as characteristic of the Far East as it is of our own country, and was as alive thousands of years ago as it is to-day. And for its gratification throughout the centuries it has employed the artists and craftsmen of all lands and times — painters, and makers of missals and beautifully illuminated manuscript, workers in wood block and engravers of metal and stone and finally the printer and his press; so that its story embodies the romance of all of these, and makes them intimate and understandable things which bring the old past very, very near.

Just how far back into the past the history of playing cards goes, no one can say with certainty. But we are indebted to Mr. Stewart Culin, Director of the Brooklyn Museum, for the most interesting researches on this subject. He believes that both chess and cards are derived from the divinatory use of the arrow, and that they represent the two principal methods of arrow divination. The basis of the divinatory systems from which games have arisen is the classification of all things according to the Four Directions. This method is universal among all primitive peoples in Asia and America. In order to classify objects and events which did not in themselves reveal their proper assignment, resort was had to magic. Our present games are the survivals of these magical processes. The identity of the games of Asia and America may be explained because of their common object and the identity of the mythic concepts underlying them which appear to be universal.

As an example, we may take the national game of Korea, called Nyout, which is played by moving objects used as men, around a circle, according to throws made with sticks about eight inches long, used as dice. On the fifteenth day of the first month, this game is still used for divination. Early in this month, a small book is sold in the markets of Seoul, 'Correct Planet Rule,' which carefully explains the meaning of all combinations of numbers thrown, in Chinese characters and Korean text. The names of the throws are neither Chinese nor Korean, however, but belong to the language of the mountain peoples to the west. This very fact opens long vistas of possibilities into the dim past. It does not seem improbable that those earliest men, whoever they may have been, who crossed those vast plains of Mongolia and camped beside its lakes, ages before the beginning of history, may have used the same method for 'making magic' and determining their course in that ancient world, so fraught with great and terrible dangers. Primitive man tossed his arrows into the magic ring which he had drawn on the ground with the proper rites and incantations. And who can say that some power higher than the stars did not direct their flight, and bring him in safety to his journey's end?

KOREAN BOYS PLAYING NYOUT
From 'Korean Games,' Stewart Culin

Our American Indians used their arrows in the same way, and in many instances the gaming sticks, which supplanted them, are still feathered. Pachisi of our childhood, backgammon, the Game of Goose, which first flourished in sixteenth-century Florence, and even chess, are direct descendants of these old rites.

Coming down many, many centuries from those most high and far-off times, we find the Egyptian civilization. In the sculptures of Beni Hassan, on the east bank of the Nile, are pictured players at draughts and at mora, a game which is still played in the East. These sculptures were made in 1740 B.C., at the time of Joseph. And from the tomb of Tut-anhk-amen has recently come an inlaid and ivory gaming board of practically the same period.

Following the Biblical narrative through the Exodus, we come again to the old, old idea: 'And the Lord spake unto Moses, Aaron shall cast lots on the two goats, and the one on which the lot falleth, he shall be the scapegoat.' And later, on the threshold of the promised land, 'Joshua cast lots for them before the Lord.' There is no trace of ordinary games of chance or hazard among the Hebrews, and it was not until after the Exile that the Greek games were introduced by the Herodian princes.

Both Herodotus and Plutarch mention dice repeatedly, and in the British Museum are draughtsmen and dice of the Roman period, so simple in design that they must have been copied from those in use at a much earlier time.

In 1694, the learned Thomas Hyde, Professor of Arabic at Oxford, and librarian of the Bodleian, wrote his important work on Oriental games and the history of chess. Much of this is a direct translation from the Oriental writers who were his authorities, and there are many quotations in the original languages. In spite of the difficulty of the text, it is a most interesting and enlightening volume, and there are delightful plates showing the variations of the chess board and men in Arabia, Persia, India, and China. The very name of the book, 'Mandragorias,' or 'Mandrake Play,' is the Indian name for chess. According to Dr. Hyde, chess was the invention of Nassir Daher in India, about the year A.D. 500, and was first played in Persia at the court of the great Cosru, in the middle of the century. It reached China at about the same time. From his preface we infer that he had in preparation a 'Historia Chartiludii,' and it is unfortunate that nothing more is known of this proposed treatise. Such an Oriental view of the history of playing cards would be of the greatest interest to-day.

A little over a hundred years after the publication of Dr. Hyde's book, Mr. Christie, of London, wrote his equally scholarly series of essays concerning 'An Inquiry into the Antient Greek game supposed to have been invented by Palamedes, antecedent to the Siege of Troy; with Reasons for believing the same to have been known from remote antiquity in China, and progressively improved into the Chinese, Indian, Persian and European Chess,' in which he shows, with many quotations from the classics and from the work of Dr. Hyde, that chess, instead of being the invention of one man, was a gradual development throughout many centuries of a game played by the shepherds of western Asia before the days of Homer. It was played with pebbles in a square divided by certain lines. In the center of the square was a small figure of a sheepfold, in which the pebbles were kept. He shows how the later Greek game of Petteia was played on a

OF THE

ANTIENT GAMES OF SKILL.

OF THE

Πετ]εία, Τρ:όδ:ον, and Ludus Latrunculorum.

FRONTISPIECE OF CHRISTIE'S 'INQUIRY INTO THE ANTIENT GREEK GAME
SUPPOSED TO HAVE BEEN INVENTED BY PALAMEDES'

(4)

board similarly marked, and how like its moves were to those in the game of chess. This is the game which is supposed to have been played by the Grecian leaders at the siege of Troy.

The Ludus Latrunculorum of the Romans was a much later form of Petteia, which, like many other things which passed from Greece to Rome, lost much of its ingenuity and luster. This Roman game was a form of draughts, and it is thought that the Roman soldiers took it into Germany and France and Spain. More detailed accounts of this and other games of the Romans are to be found in 'Itali ed altri Strumenti Lusori degli Antichi Romani, descritti da Francesco de' Ficoroni,' a vellum-bound volume published in Rome in 1734, and 'Monumenta Latina Postuma Josephi Averani,' Florence, 1769.

Meanwhile, the game of pebbles, Petteia, seems to have flourished in Asia through many centuries. Very gradually its form changed somewhat, and the sheepfold became a mound, or barrier, or dividing line, and the game assumed a military aspect; while the idea of shelter or inviolability that had attached to the sheepfold became an attribute of one of the pieces used in play, a characteristic of the king, in chess to-day.

It is supposed that the game was taken into China by an outcast race of Hindus who settled in the provinces north of the Hoang-ho. South of the river lived the Tartars, and the struggles between the two seem to have been pictured in the game they played. Certain it is that the river dividing the opposing forces is still shown on the Chinese chess board.

CHAPTER II

CHINESE AND JAPANESE PLAYING CARDS

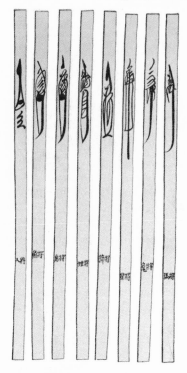

KOREAN PLAYING CARDS

THE earliest playing cards were undoubtedly Chinese. Again it is Mr. Culin who alone speaks authoritatively on the subject. He says: 'Playing cards existed in China in or before the twelfth century, were introduced into Europe from China in the thirteenth century and were spread quickly from Europe over the civilized world. Certain Chinese cards which have come down to the present time were imitated from Chinese paper notes which bore pictorial symbols of their value. These pictures furnished the suit marks of the Chinese pack, and, copied again in Europe, without knowledge of their true significance, gave rise to the suits of coins, clubs, swords and cups of the early European game. . . . All games appear to have their roots in more or less primitive conditions, and to have so grown up from these conditions that it is impossible to say that any individual was their inventor.'

In this connection it is interesting to note that the Korean playing cards always bear a pictured arrow on their backs, flaunting their lineage from the ancient rites of the feathered arrow and the magic ring. The Korean cards are narrow strips of oiled paper about seven and five eighths inches long, and half an inch wide. There are ten cards in each of the eight suits, men, fish, crows, pheasants, antelopes, stars, rabbits, and horses. Mr. Culin believes these Korean cards to be the ancestors of the Chinese ones.

BACK OF A KOREAN PLAYING CARD

These Chinese cards were copied from Chinese notes, paper money which originated in the Tang Dynasty (618–908), some of which still survives. It is said that the gamblers sometimes played with and for the actual bank

notes. This is confirmed by a Chinese encyclopedia of 1678 which describes 'leaves,' an early Chi-
nese card game, as 'Sung
money.'

The old Chinese money-
derived game, as it exists to-
day, is made up of one hundred and twenty cards composed of four identical sets
of thirty cards each. These
cards are narrow, flexible
strips of cardboard not more
than three eighths of an inch
wide. There are nine cards to
each of the three suits, coins,
strings of coins, and myriads
of strings of coins; and three
extra cards, the red flower, the

VARIOUS STYLES OF THE MONEY-DERIVED CARDS
OF CHINA

A CHINESE PLAYING CARD IN THE
STAATLICHES MUSEUM FÜR VOL-
KERKUNDE, BERLIN

Found in 1905 by Dr. A. von Le Coq
with fragments of manuscripts of the Uigur
period in the glen of Sangim near Turfan,
Chinese Turkestan. This card, which corresponds to the Red Flower of the present
Chinese pack, presumably is not later than
the eleventh century A.D., and probably is
the oldest known playing card.

The seal over the man's head denotes
money, three fan, and the characters at the
top and bottom give the maker's name.
(From Stewart Culin, in 'The Game of
Ma Jong.')

white flower, and old thousand which are
distinguished from the others by seals
and inscriptions. The white flower shows
a highly conventionalized picture of a
mountain rising from the waves, and the
red flower and the suit
of myriads of coins, por-
traits of characters, in
the old Chinese folk
tale 'The Story of the
River's Banks.' This
story relates the adven-
tures of an emissary of
the emperor to the Tem-
ple of the Taoists on
the Mountain of Dra-
gons and Tigers, where
dwell the genii of the

A VARIATION OF
THE WHITE FLOWER

Showing the stag or
deer, instead of the
more usual stag flower.

one hundred and eight stars of ill omen.
The Japanese version of the story was

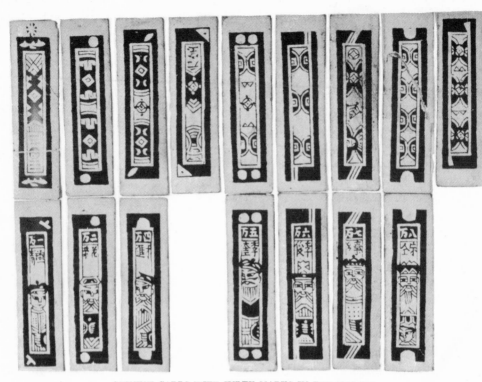

CHINESE CARDS WITH INDEX MARKS IN THE MARGIN

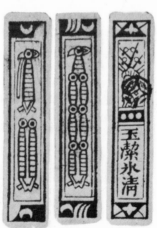

MÁ TSÉUK FROM KIU-KIANG

The indices are survivals of Korean numerals

(8)

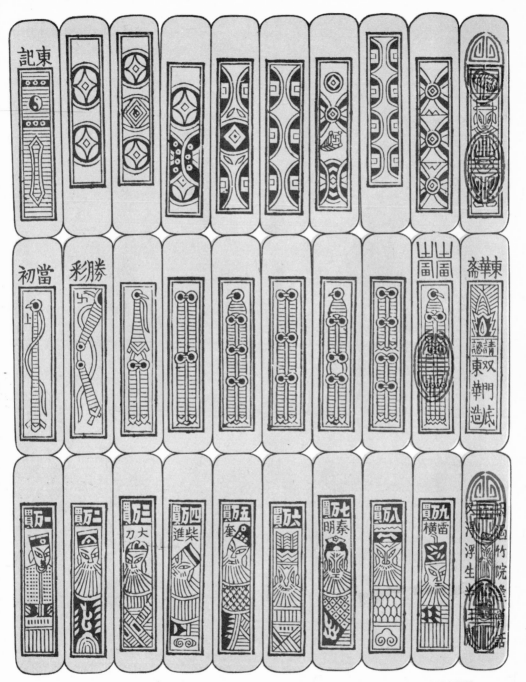

A PACK OF KWAN P'AI, CHINESE PLAYING CARDS WHOSE SYMBOLS ARE BORROWED
FROM THE OLD CHINESE PAPER MONEY

The top row is the suit of coins, the second, the suit of strings of coins; and the third, the suit of myriads of strings of coins. The last card in each row is the honor card of the suit. In the suit of coins it is called Red Flower; in the suit of strings, White Flower; and in the suit of myriads, Old Thousand.

CHINESE DOMINO CARDS, SHOWING SOME OF THE CHARACTERS FROM THE STORY OF
THE RIVER'S BANKS

delightfully illustrated by Hokusai. His portrayal of the robber band, with their flaming torches, and of the red palace, with its sealed doors, among the black pines of the mountain-side, give it a charm all its own.

To the Chinese, these cards with the curious little portraits are known as the 'thirty-six celestial generals and the seventy-two earthly malignants,' and they are believed to bear so powerful and magic a charm that they are placed on the coffins of their dead.

Mr. Culin says that the terminology of Chinese games is made up of slang, and is highly elusive. These little money-derived cards are called 'kwan p'ái,' 'stick cards,' or 'má tséuk,' 'hempen birds' or 'sparrows.' These cards are used to play two types of games; in one, the cards form certain winning combinations, and in the other, the higher cards take the lower.

In the south of China are similar money-derived cards. Here, however, a pack consists of four sets of thirty-eight cards each, and the cards themselves are wider, usually about two and three quarters inches long and one and one eighth inches wide. There are four suits: coins, strings, myriads, tens of myriads, and three extra cards. The last two suits and two of the extra cards bear the curious little portraits from the old folk tale and carry as potent a charm as their neighbors in the north. These cards of the south country are called 'lut chí.' Mr. Culin believes that it is probable that European playing cards were copied from some such pack with four suits.

MONEY-DERIVED CARDS WITH FOUR SUITS FROM FUH CHAN, CHINA

The nine of each suit and the three extra cards are shown

We have many sets of the kwan p'ái, varying ever so little from each other according to the localities from which they come. There are also two slightly differing forms of the lut chí.

Then, too, there are the domino cards. There is no essential difference between dominoes and cards in China, and the two are used inter-

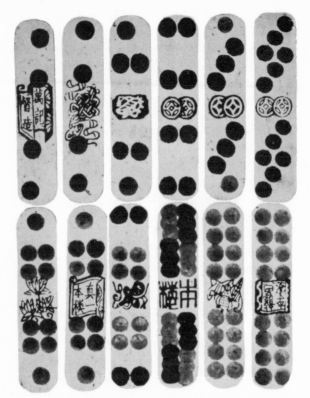

DOMINO CARDS WITH COINS, SCROLLS, AND SYMBOLS

There are five sets of twenty-one cards each in this series. The coins, scrolls, and symbols are emblematic of the blessings of life.

CHRYSANTHEMUM, PLUM, AND BAMBOO

THE BAT, SYMBOL OF GOOD FORTUNE

(10)

changeably. In Shanghai, Mr. Culin tells us, the first street within the wall is given over to the making and selling of dominoes, the designs usually being copies from cards. In one set of domino cards the decora-

THE FIVE BLESSINGS

The five Blessings — Fuk, Luk, Shau, Hí, Ts'oi (Happiness, Promotion, Long Life, Posterity, Wealth) — are extra cards, or jokers, often found with packs of the money-derived cards as well as with the domino cards.

tions are delightful little line drawings, in red and green, of the bamboo and plum and chrysanthemum; in another, they are scrolls or coins in black; and there are many variations of a delightful series having one suit of twenty-one cards, each bearing a butterfly, a second with very Oriental little crabs, and a third with charming little full-length figures of the characters in 'The Story of the River's Banks,' including the tiger and the dragon. There are also usually six figure cards without the domino marks. As regards both line and color these cards are the most delicate and lovely little prints, in spite of the fact that chess has always been the game of the educated people, and cards have always been frowned upon as a disreputable form of gambling.

CHINESE CHESS CARDS

Bearing the symbols of the chess pieces

Long ago, dominoes were used for fortune-telling in China, which may explain the fanciful markings but the ancient symbolism and traditions are lost.

There are also the chess cards which come in gay little Chinese paste-

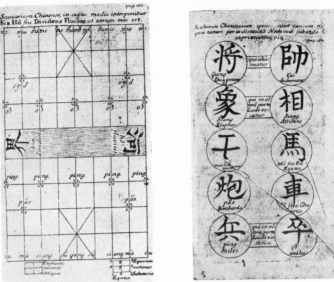

THE CHINESE CHESS BOARD AND THE NAMES OF THE PIECES
From Hyde's 'Mandragorias' (1694)

board boxes. There are four suits to a pack; one of twenty-eight red cards with Chinese symbols, and line drawings of the familiar little full-length figures, in black; a suit of twenty-eight white cards, in which the markings are flowers in addition to the symbols; a suit of twenty-eight yellow cards, in which the marks are animals; and thirty-three green cards, twenty-eight with birds and butterflies upon them, and five figure cards, jokers or honors, with no other markings.

THE FIVE BLESSINGS FROM A SET OF CHESS CARDS
The five little men are more often found than the three with the dragon and the tiger in all Chinese card games.

A game of Tséung K'i, or Chinese chess, is so different from the form of the game which was brought into Europe, and fits so perfectly the descriptions of Dr. Hyde and Mr. Christie, that it seems too bad not to mention it, just because it is not a card game.

The board is made of paper, marked into sixty-four squares by green

THE JAPANESE FLOWER GAME: FIRST THREE MONTHS

The Flower Game is really the calendar of Old Japan. There are four cards for each of the twelve months. These are the first three months: first month, the pine; second month, the plum blossom; third month, the cherry blossom. The first two cards in each month count one apiece. The third shows a Tanjaku, or little verse, fluttering in the frosty pines, and among the windy plum blossoms, and from the gay cherry bough. This card counts five points. The fourth card is the honor card, and counts sometimes ten and sometimes twenty. It bears the emblem of the flower festival of each particular month, or of the old legend connected with it. The first is the pine and the stork, the second the plum and the singing bird, and the third the cherry and the curtain.

(13)

THE JAPANESE FLOWER GAME: FOURTH, FIFTH, AND SIXTH MONTHS

Fourth month, the wisteria; fifth month, the iris; sixth month, the peony. The honor cards are the wisteria and the cuckoo, the iris and the firefly, and the peony and the butterfly.

(14)

THE JAPANESE FLOWER GAME: SEVENTH, EIGHTH, AND NINTH MONTHS

Seventh month, the clover; eighth month, the eularia; ninth month, the chrysanthemum. The honor card of the seventh month is the clover and the wild boar. The eularia is a beautiful wild grass of the moors that beckons to travelers plodding along the road. The first two cards in some of the later sets show the hillock in the moors quite bare, and, because it looks like a silhouette of a priest's shaved head, it is called Bohzu, or priest. There is no Tanjaku. Instead, the third card shows wild geese flying over the moorland and counts ten points. The honor card shows the full moon rising over the moor and the seductive silver eularia and counts twenty points. The honor card of the ninth month is the chrysanthemum and the wine-cup.

(15)

THE JAPANESE FLOWER GAME: THE LAST THREE MONTHS

Tenth month, the maple; eleventh month, the willow; twelfth month, the paulownia. The honor card of the tenth month is the deer in the autumn wood; in the month of the willow, the Tanjaku is the second card, the willow and the bird the third, which counts ten points, and the honor card is the willow and the rain and counts twenty points. In the newer packs of cards the willow and the rain shows the adventurous frog of the fairy tale and the traveler with his parasol. But in the older sets the traveler wears the time-honored straw coat, and the frog does not appear at all, as why should he? for the pelting rain and the wind in the willows were made for frogs, and it is the frog who makes this story, as every one knows. The twelfth honor card is the paulownia and the phœnix. There is no Tanjaku for this month.

(16)

lines. These are separated into two parts by a blank space in the center, labeled in Chinese characters 'Kià Ho,' or 'The River.' Four squares in the middle of each side of the board in the first and second rows, nearest the edge, are crossed with two diagonal intersecting lines marking an enclosure, which is called the 'Palace.' The pieces are placed at the intersection of the lines instead of in the squares. They are made of wood and look like our checkers, except that they are inscribed on either side with the Chinese characters for their names, distinguished by the colors red and blue.

VARIATION OF
THE WILLOW
AND THE RAIN

On each side there is a Tséung, or general, corresponding to our king; two Sz' or Councillors, which are our bishops; two Tséung or elephants; two Má or horses, which are our knights; two Ch'e or chariots, which are our castles; two P'au or cannon; and five Ping or Tsut, foot soldiers, which are our pawns.

A full description of this game is to be found on pages 863–66, of

THE WINTER CHERRY

A game borrowed from sixteenth-century Portuguese adventurers. There are four suits of twelve cards each and the Portuguese suit signs of cups, swords, coins, and batons are plainly discernible. The cards shown are the five of cups, the two of swords, the nine of coins, and the six of batons. The three court cards of each suit — the sota, caballero, and rey — on the lower line are not so easy to distinguish.

Mr. Culin's catalogue of 'Chess and Playing Cards' in the 'Report of the
United States National Museum' for 1896.

In Japan the cards are soft-colored and lovely little prints, as whimsical
and engaging as the names of the games they are used to play. There
are the poetry games, founded on the old romances; the flower game, with
the twelve flowers, by whose names the twelve months are known in Japan;
this is one of the most common games, as well as one of the most charming.
A pack consists of forty-eight cards, showing the flower for each mont.
in four different phases; usually these cards are about one and three fourths
by one and one fourth inches, though we have a set that are only one inch
long and half an inch wide, but are charming and perfect miniature
prints. Each print is mounted on heavy black cardboard.

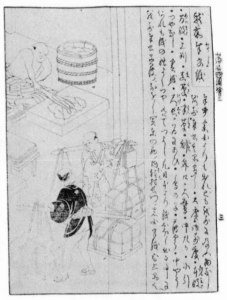

PAPER-MAKING IN OLD JAPAN

The Winter Cherry, with its suit marks of red balls, is the gambling
game of Japan; there is also the game of Ancient Plays, with portraits of
seventeenth-century actors from the rare and famous old prints; and the
Song Game.

As early as the seventh century they were making wood-block prints in
the Buddhist monasteries in Japan, and pilgrims to the shrines were given
small ones as mementoes of their journeyings. So slips of that wonderful
early paper with its mystic markings, 'like ripples on the surface of a
stream,' may have been used then as now to play those games which have
come down unchanged through the centuries. Certain it is, that no people

CARDS FROM THE JAPANESE GAME OF HANA AWASE, OR FLOWER-MATCHING

HINDOO PLAYING CARDS OF THE PERSIAN EIGHT-SUIT TYPE

west of those great barrier mountains have ever been able to approach the whimsical grace and loveliness, the charm and serenity and joy, that the Chinese and Japanese have from time immemorial put into their playing cards as into everything that pertains to their everyday life.

CHINESE AND JAPANESE PLAYING CARDS IN THE COLLECTION OF THE UNITED STATES PLAYING CARD COMPANY

55 sets of Chinese money-derived cards	1650 cards
4 sets of Chinese chess cards	165 cards
33 sets of Chinese domino cards	693 cards
19 sets of Japanese Flower Game	912 cards
2 sets of Japanese Winter Cherry	96 cards

Total: 113 editions, 3516 cards

CHAPTER III

PLAYING CARDS OF INDIA

ONE of the oldest theories as to the origin of European playing cards was that they were brought from India by wandering fortune-telling gypsies, and in substantiation of this claim are pointed out interesting analogies between the Indian game and the Spanish game of Hombre, and between the Indian suit signs, and those of the Italian and Spanish cards. Mr. Culin, however, who is our best authority on the cards of these Eastern countries, feels sure that the Indian cards were inspired by those of Europe.

They are round painted or lacquered discs of thin wood or cotton fiber paper or ivory, and are used to play a game called 'Ganjifa.' They are curiously different from the cards of any other country.

We know that Godfrey of Bouillon, returning from the First Crusade, brought with him chess which had found its way from India into the Holy Land. And it has been suggested that the Indian cards were possibly first used upon chess boards, instead of the usual chess men, to play chess, a game of pure skill. And that later games of chance evolved.

We have a set of these lacquered cards from Jaipur, in a lacquered box, which might have been so used. They are only an inch in diameter, and from their workmanship are probably of the eighteenth century.

Another early series is unusual in having the background of all of the cards of the same color, a soft buff. Usually a different color is used for each suit, vivid reds, greens, yellows, and shades of orange, rich browns and blacks, and deeper tones of red and green.

There are either eight or ten suits in a set of these Indian cards; twelve cards to each suit, consisting of numerals from one to ten and two court cards. One of the court cards of each suit represents one of the ten Incarnations of Vishnu, and the other shows some incident connected with this particular incarnation; while the suit signs are symbols of the incarnation represented.

The ten Incarnations and usual suit marks are:
1. Matsya the Fish, which towed the ship containing Menu (Noah), his family, and the creatures saved from the Deluge. Suit of Fish.
2. Kourma the Tortoise, on which rested the mountain that, revolved by the serpent Sesha, greatly disturbed the sea, and produced the Fourteen Gems. Suit of Tortoises.
3. Varah the Boar, who came to destroy the giant Hiranyakcha. Suit of Boars.

HINDOO CARDS OF THE PERSIAN TYPE HAVING EIGHT SUITS

This shows the ten and two court cards of the four superior suits — Taj or crowns, Soofed or moons, Shumsher or sabers, and Gholam or slaves. These are from Jaipur.

(21)

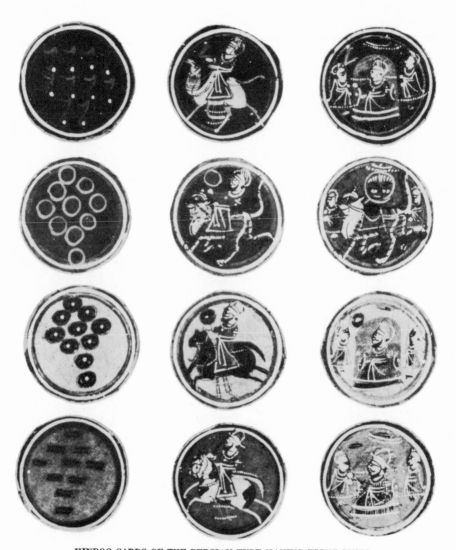

HINDOO CARDS OF THE PERSIAN TYPE HAVING EIGHT SUITS

The ten and two court cards of the four inferior suits — Chung or harps, Soorkh or suns, Burat or diplomas, and Quimash or merchandise.

(22)

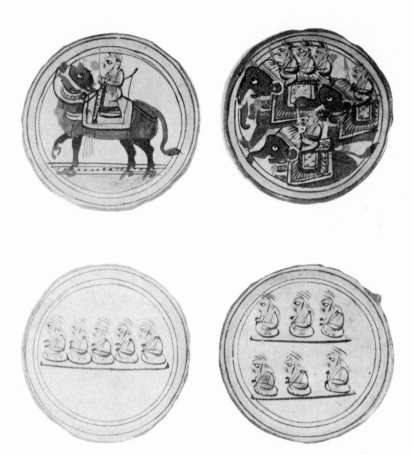

EIGHTEENTH-CENTURY HINDOO CARDS HAVING A BUFF BACKGROUND
IN ALL THE SUITS
These are the court cards and the five and six of the suit of dwarfs

(23)

HINDOO PLAYING CARDS WITH TEN SUITS PICTURING THE TEN AVATARS OF VISHNU

One of the numerals and court cards of the first three incarnations:

I. Matsyavatara the Fish. The human part of the body is colored blue, symbolic of its divinity. He holds the Chakra, or flaming wheel, emblematic of the living force behind all things, and the Castrala or magic jewel which illuminates all things and is a perfect mirror of the world.

II. Kourmavatara the Tortoise. The head is blue.

III. Varahavatara the Boar. The body is blue, but not the head. He holds the Chakra, and wears the jewel on his breast.

(24)

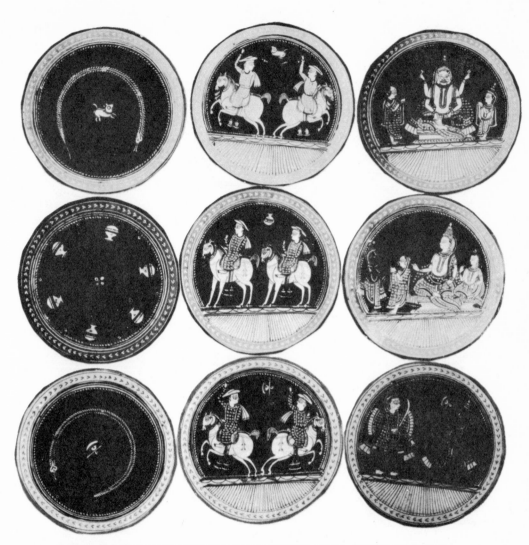

HINDOO PLAYING CARDS WITH TEN SUITS: FOURTH, FIFTH, AND SIXTH AVATARS

IV. Narasinhavatara the Lion holds the two sacred symbols aloft, and in his lap rests the divine child. The Child is blue.

V. Vamanavatara the Dwarf. Vishnu is the Dwarf, painted blue, and the emblem of the incarnation is a water-jar.

VI. Paracu Rama, the Bramin with the Axe. He is the militant little figure bearing the axe, and is painted blue.

(25)

HINDOO PLAYING CARDS WITH TEN SUITS: SEVENTH, EIGHTH, AND NINTH AVATARS

VII. Rama Chandra, who won his wife Sita in a contest of arrows. Vishnu is seen bending his bow. He is painted blue. Compared to his dizzy feat, William Tell's was as nothing. The suit sign is an arrow.

VIII. Krishna the Black, seated upon a throne and holding aloft his two emblems. He is painted blue. The suit sign is a thunderbolt.

IX. Buddha seated on his shell throne, in meditation.

(26)

4. Nara-Simha the Lion, who came to destroy the giant Hiranycas-yopa. Suit of Lions.
5. Vamanavatara the Dwarf, who came to save men from the giant king, Bali. Suit of Dwarfs or of Water Jars.
6. Paracu Rama, of the Axe, who came to punish the military caste and destroy their power. Suit of Axes.

HINDOO PLAYING CARDS WITH TEN SUITS: THE TENTH AVATAR

X. Kalki, the White Horse, the incarnation to come, when Vishnu with his sword will sweep triumphant through the world, dispelling the powers of darkness. The suit sign is a sword, and Krishna, all blue, leads the white horse.

7. Rama Chandra, the Gentle Rama, like the Moon, who avenged men and gods for the iniquities done by Ravana, the demon king of Ceylon. He won his wife Sita in a contest with arrows. Suit of Arrows. We have a series in which the suit sign for this Avatar is monkeys, perhaps because of this monkey king of Ceylon, who built the bridge across the sea from the mainland to his island.
8. Krishna the Black, the most popular of all the Incarnations, and believed to be the perfect manifestation of Vishnu, whose emblem is the Chakra or quoit of lightning which he hurled at his enemies. Suit of Quoits. Sometimes this is the suit of Cows, because the youthful Krishna lived with the cowherds.
9. Buddha the Enlightened, who sits upon his shell-shaped throne in meditation. The suit of Shells. In several series the suit sign is umbrellas, emblems of kingly rank.
10. Kalki, the White Horse, the Incarnation to come, when, with sword in hand, Vishnu will sweep triumphant through the world, destroying all the powers of darkness. Suit of Swords, sometimes Horses.

There are many variations of these suit signs and they are often exceedingly hard to recognize. It is interesting to see how many of these are symbols in similar stories of the Scythians, which persisted in the legends and rites in Greece.

Most of these Indian cards come in wooden boxes as gayly lacquered and as elaborately decorated as the cards themselves, with pictures of the Incarnations on the sides and lid.

HINDOO PLAYING CARDS OF THE PERSIAN TYPE WITH EIGHT SUITS
These are the two court cards and the one of sabers

Some of them are quite large, to accommodate the later cards which are from three to three and three quarters inches in diameter, and decorated with intricate borders.

An incomplete series of early painted cards which we have lack all the usual detail, but more than make up in interest because of the unusual animation of the honors. Vishnu appears variously upon a white horse, on a gayly caparisoned black elephant, on a golden lion, and on a piebald camel. These cards are one and seven eighths inches in diameter and the only ones we have without the bright lacquer finish.

We have a late series, which bear the European suit signs of hearts,

HINDOO PLAYING CARDS USING THE EUROPEAN SUIT SIGNS OF HEARTS, SPADES, DIAMONDS, AND CLUBS

There are four suits of thirteen cards each. These are the ace and the court cards of spades.

(29)

PERSIAN PLAYING CARDS PAINTED ON IVORY
From Singer's 'Researches into the History of Playing Cards,' London, 1816

spades, clubs, and diamonds, in addition to the Indian suit signs. These are probably cards which were made by Camoin et Cie. of Marseilles, late in the nineteenth century.

Then, too, there are the Persian cards, which come with a great variety of interesting suit signs and designs, and are used to play the game of Ganjifa. Often these cards are veritable little miniatures of exquisite workmanship and coloring, sometimes being painted on ivory. There is no mention of these cards in the 'Arabian Nights' and it is impossible to say just when they made their advent into Bagdad.

HINDOO PLAYING CARDS IN THE COLLECTION OF THE UNITED STATES PLAYING CARD COMPANY

2 sets of Hindoo cards with ten suits	240 cards
3 sets of Hindoo cards with eight suits	288 cards
1 set of Hindoo cards with eight suits, buff ground, eighteenth century	96 cards
3 sets of Hindoo cards with eight suits, eighteenth century	296 cards
1 set of Hindoo cards with European suit signs	52 cards

Total: 10 editions, 972 cards

CHAPTER IV

PLAYING CARDS IN FRANCE

HOWEVER playing cards may have found their way into Europe, and whatever country may first have used them, it is in France that their actual history begins. For in 1392, in the register of the Chambre des Comptes of Charles VI of France, there is an entry of the royal treasurer of moneys paid one Jacquemin Gringonneur, painter, for three games of cards 'in gold and diverse colours, ornamented with many devices, for the diversion of our lord, the King.' Seventeen of these strange old painted cards survive in the Bibliothèque Nationale at Paris. They are atouts from a pack of tarots, as this early European game of cards was called. These atouts or high cards are believed to have been brought from the East by fortune-telling gypsies, outcast tribes of India who made their way through Persia and Arabia and Egypt into Italy. This would seem a plausible theory, excepting that these gypsies did not appear in Europe in considerable numbers until the fifteenth century, while these cards are known in France and Flanders and the Low Countries, in Germany and in Italy, before 1350. In a tarot series, in addition to the customary fifty-two cards, there are four cavaliers or mounted valets besides the twenty-two high cards. These last are supposed to have been taken from an Egyptian book of hieroglyphics containing the principles of an ancient mystic philosophy in a series of emblems and symbolic figures.

Many explanations and interpretations have been written of these strange cards; the best known and most elaborate working out of their meaning and origin is in a book written by Court de Gebelin in 1781. It is an infinitely involved theory, but is interestingly commented upon by Singer in his 'Researches into the History of Playing Cards and Printing.' Curiously enough the titles of these atouts even in the Italian and German packs are always in French, and often the spelling is execrable. This is another mystery, because France was the first country to discard them, and it is only in Italy and Germany and Switzerland and Austria and Bohemia and Hungary that they are found to-day.

The names on these cards are usually:

1. Le bateleur	9. L'ermite	16. La maison Dieu
2. La papesse	10. La roue de fortune	17. L'estoile
3. L'impératrice	11. La force	18. La lune
4. L'empereur	12. Le pendu	19. Le soleil
5. Le pape	13. La mort (often this	20. Le jugement
6. L'amoureux	title is omitted)	21. Le monde
7. Le chariot	14. La tempérance	22. Le mat (usually un-
8. La justice	15. Le diable	numbered)

THE DESIGNS OF THE TAROT CARDS PAINTED FOR CHARLES VI IN 1392

These are greatly reduced in size

THE USUAL DESIGNS OF THE ATOUTS OF A TAROT SERIES

Very much reduced in size

(33)

THE ATOUTS OF A FRENCH TAROT PACK OF THE EARLY EIGHTEENTH CENTURY

Le Pape and La Papesse are supplanted by Le Grandprêtre and La Grandprêtresse. Hebrew letters or numbers were sometimes painted on the atouts of early Italian tarot packs. These characters were in themselves symbolic, their significance being the same as that of the picture on the card.

(34)

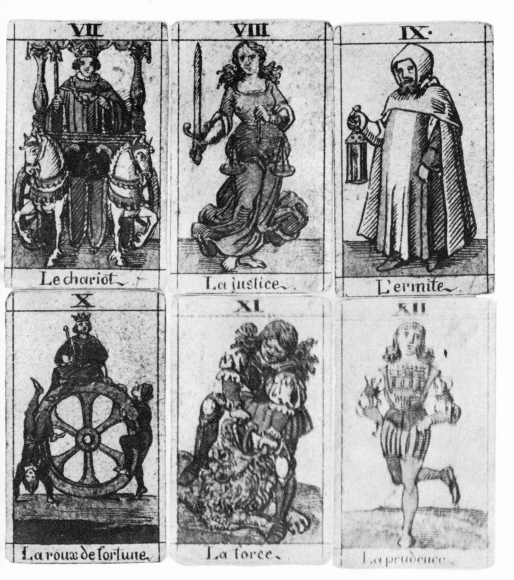

THE ATOUTS OF A FRENCH TAROT PACK OF THE EARLY EIGHTEENTH CENTURY

The ninth, L'Ermite, is almost an exact copy of a little German woodcut of 1550 picturing Saint Jude. The meaning ascribed to this card is protection and kindliness. The Hebrew letter corresponding to it is Teth, meaning a shelter, or place of safety. The twelfth atout, La Prudence, takes the place of the usual Le Pendu, and it is rather interesting to know that prudence is one of the attributes of that most uncomfortable card.

(35)

THE ATOUTS OF A FRENCH TAROT PACK OF THE EARLY EIGHTEENTH CENTURY

The fifteenth is usually Le Diable, typifying everything evil. The eighteenth, La Lune, lacks the mystic and sinister quality of the conventional design, and looks more like an illustration for an Æsop fable.

(36)

THE ATOUTS OF A TAROT PACK OF FRENCH CARDS OF THE EARLY EIGHTEENTH CENTURY

These tarot cards are always quite large. There are beautiful facsimiles of these Charles VI atouts in 'Jeux de Cartes Tarots et de Cartes Numérales' published in Paris by the Société des Bibliophiles Français in 1844. Only thirty-two copies of this book were issued, and these illustrations are hand illumined.

We have twenty-one of the atouts of a tarot series, presumably of the early eighteenth century. They are conspicuous because of their small size, being only one and seven eighths by three and three eighths inches. The designs, which are from copper plates and the coloring which is done by hand, are typically French. There is a light-

TAROTS OF BESANÇON, 1800
Jupiter and Juno replace the usual Pape and Papesse in most of the tarots of southern France

ness and grace about the little figures which is not characteristic of the tarots of any country. The two, instead of being La Papesse, is Le

CARDS OF A FRENCH MINCHIATE PACK

These are the twenty-first, twenty-eighth, thirty-first, and thirty-sixth atouts, the six of cups, and the six of batons.

Grandprêtre, and the three, La Grandprêtresse. Seven, Le Chariot, shows only a fleur de lys where often the maker's initials are given. The four and five are Le Roy and La Royne, and twelve instead of being the uncomfortable Le Pendu, becomes La Prudence, pirouetting in a truly Gallic manner on the foot from which he usually hangs. Fifteen, Le Diable, is a traveling mountebank in jester's clothes, with a lion biting at his leg, the design which is usually Le Mat in a French tarot pack.

We also have a complete pack of seventy-eight tarots of the old Italian designs and of the usual size, five by two and one half inches. They are

LE PAPE

ONE OF THE TAROT CARDS PAINTED FOR CHARLES VI OF FRANCE
IN 1392

CONJUROR'S CARDS, PROBABLY USED BY A FRENCH MOUNTEBANK IN THE
SEVENTEENTH CENTURY

coarse stenciled wood blocks. On each court card and atout is the name of
the maker, and his country, 'France, J. Jerger.' He was a card-maker at
Besançon at the beginning of the nineteenth century. The suit signs are
Italian, which is a characteristic of the French tarots, perhaps because
most of them are sent to Italy to be used. The titles of the atouts are:
Le Bateleur, Junon, L'imperatris, L'empereur, Jupiter, L'amorex, Le
Charior, La Justice, Le Capucin, La Roux de Fortune, La Force, Le Pendu,
Death (unnamed), Temperance, Le diable, La Maison Dieu, L'Etoile, La
Lune, Le Soleil, Le Jugement, Le Monde, Le Fou. This is the listing
peculiar to southeastern France.

There is another series, an Italian variation of the tarot game called
'Minchiate,' with the usual Italian designs. We have only thirty-eight
cards of the pack of ninety-six. Fourteen are brightly colored by hand, the
rest are uncolored proofs. Each card has a dotted border after the Italian
manner, and each bears
the water mark of the
fleur de lys, adopted by
the French Government
for paper made for play-
ing cards.

To go back to the
fourteenth century,
there is a manuscript,
'Le Roman de Renard
le Contrefait,' which
seems to have been
written between 1328
and 1341, in which the
following line appears:

'Jouent aux des, aux
Cartes aux tables.'

Again in the 'Chron-
icle de Petit Jean de
Saintre,' who was a
page at the court of

A MINIATURE IN 'LE ROMAN DU ROI MELIADUS DE
LEONNOYS,' BY HELIE DE BORRON
Latter half of the fourteenth century

Charles V, the governor of the pages rebukes them for playing at cards;
and in a poem by one Guillaume de Guilleville, written in 1350, the
line, 'Jeux de tables et de cartes,' is found; while the earliest known print of
persons playing at cards is a miniature in 'Le Roman du Roi Meliadus de
Leonnoys,' by Helie de Borron, which was probably written some time in
the latter half of the fourteenth century. A king and three attendants

PAINTED PLAYING CARDS OF FIFTEENTH-CENTURY FRANCE

play, while three others look on, and the cards themselves bear the old suit marks of batons and coins. So that the antiquity of French playing cards is well established.

Certain it is that in 1397 they were so plentiful that a Paris decree forbade working people to play at 'tennis, bowls, dice, cards or ninepins, on working days.'

It seems reasonable to suppose that all the earliest European cards must have been similar to those painted for the king, their cost making them

PAINTED PLAYING CARDS OF FIFTEENTH-CENTURY FRANCE

prohibitive to any but the nobles. The demand for cards by other people brought about the making of them with stencils, and it is very possible that they were made from wood blocks before 1423, the date of the Buxheim Saint Christopher, which is generally accepted as the date of the beginning of printing.

There are other painted cards of the early fifteenth century which first show the suit signs of Cœurs, Carreaux, Trèfles, and Piques which are characteristic of the French cards of to-day. The suit signs of the old tarots had been Cups, Swords, Coins, and Batons; the French suit signs are supposed to have been introduced by a famous knight, Étienne Vignoles, or Lahire, as he is called. He is said to have invented the game of piquet, which was the game of knights and chivalry, in contrast to the old game which had come out of the East, which had its inception in chess, the game of war. Lahire is said to have had the help of his friend, Étienne Chevalier, who was secretary to the king and a clever draughtsman and who may have been responsible for the new designs. The suit of Cœurs denotes the church; Carreaux, the arrowheads or diamonds, are symbolic of the vassals, from whom the archers and bowmen were drawn; Trèfles, or clover (clubs) signifies the husbandmen, and Piques, or points of lances (spades), the knights themselves.

For piquet there were only thirty-six cards used, and the old emblematic atouts of the tarot series were dispensed with, together with the two, three, four, and five of each suit, and the fourth court card, the cavalier. At the beginning of the eighteenth century the sixes were also left out, so

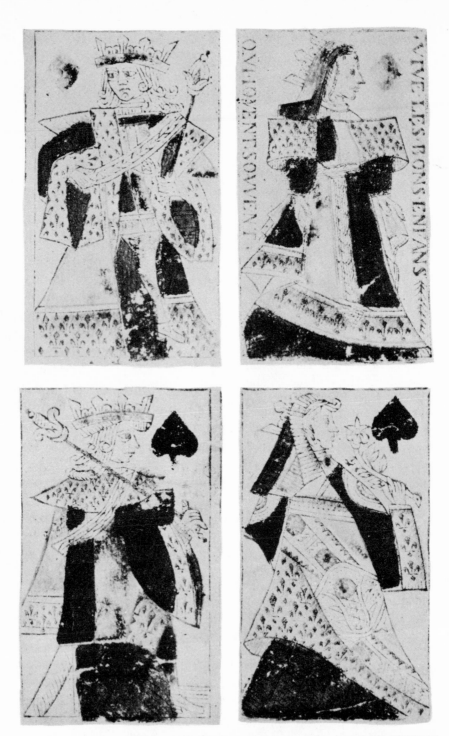

PLAYING CARDS MADE BY FRANÇOIS ARNOUX, LATE IN THE FIFTEENTH CENTURY

His motto is on the Reine de Carreaux

(42)

that to-day a piquet pack has only thirty-two cards. Écarté was another French game, perhaps the same as la Triomphe, which is listed in the Maisons des Jeux of the middle of the seventeenth century, and was played with a piquet pack; from this game the French colonists in America evolved euchre.

It is about 1440 that we first find the named court cards, another characteristic of French cards of to-day. These are the earliest known cards from wood blocks which have survived. We have two of these, and the others are in the British Museum. They are knaves, or valets as they are called in France, and bear the names of famous knights, Lancelot, Hogier, Rolant, and Valéry. In the annals of Provence, where they are thought to have been made, the knaves were known, as early as 1361, as 'Tuchim,' the name of a band of robbers who infested the neighboring forests. This name had probably been brought from the East by the Moors, for the Arabian word for darkness and evil was 'tu'chan.'

These cards were found in 1841, making up the boards of the binding of a fifteenth-century book. When it was found early in the century that the oak boards used for binding bred bookworms, which destroyed the pages the boards were meant to protect, the binders began using paper of sufficient thickness to be a protection. Paper in itself was very scarce, and many a valuable manuscript was used to give body to the vellum and calf bindings of those early days.

We have two other sheets of fifteenth-century cards which were pre-

PLAYING CARDS OF ANTOINE BONNIER, CARTIER À MONTPELLIER, 1703

PLAYING CARDS OF ALEXANDRE LIONNET, CARTIER À MONTPELLIER, 1730–1750

served in the same way. They bear the name of their maker, François Arnoux, and his motto, 'Vive les bons enfans qui jouent souvent.' These are all court cards, and the borders of their costumes are decorated with fleur de lys. Both the motto and these same borders appear again two hundred years later in early eighteenth-century cards made in Montpellier. M. d'Allemagne, the French authority on playing cards, is of the opinion that François Arnoux must have worked in the same locality and that his designs were handed down unchanged through the years, which is typical of playing-card history. No other example of his work is known. His designs are quaint and pleasing and his colors, old blue and rose, so soft and lovely that they have all the charm of a scrap of old tapestry.

PLAYING CARDS MADE BY FULCRAND BOUSCAREL, CARTIER À MONTPELLIER, 1745–1750

In a report addressed to the Intendant of Languedoc on the ninth of November, 1693, it is written, 'The Hospice of Montpellier whose revenues are not sufficient to take care of poor strangers asks the two privileges of the making of playing cards and the sale of glass in all the diocese.'

The characteristics of the Arnoux cards are to be found in the eighteenth-century ones of Montpellier made by Antoine Bonnier, Alexandre Lionnet, and Fulcrand Bouscarel. There are the same fleur de lys trimmings, and Bonnier uses the same motto. Lionnet's Reine de Carreaux bears his name and the motto 'En Dieu son Esperence,' while his valet bears the arms of Montpellier. The court cards are of the Provence type and the gowning of the queens is most delightful. They are the fifteenth-century costumes of François Arnoux, but the faces lack the charm of his early ones.

A fifteenth-century print of Rouen has as its title 'Le Revers du Jeu des Suisses,' and shows a number of royal personages and their followers about a card table. This time the cards are those of France. Still another is a

LE REVERS DU JEU DES SUISSES

1. Le roi de France; 2. Le Suisse; 3. Le Duc de Venise; 4. Le Pape; 5. L'Empereur; 6. Le roi d'Espagne; 7. Le roi d'Angleterre; 8. Le Duc de Wurtemberg; 9. Le Comte Palatin; 10. Le Seigneur Jean-Jacques Trivulce; 11. Le Duc de Milan le More; 12. Le Duc de Lorraine; 13. Le Duc de Savoie; 14. Le Marquis Montferrat; 15. Dame Marguerite.

The tradition is that Henri Picard rashly entertained five kings at one time at dinner, and tactfully smoothed over an awkward situation when one of his royal guests began to lose his temper at play.

miniature in a manuscript at Paris, a French translation of the 'Civitas Dei' of Saint Augustine, by Raoul de Presle. It shows two ladies wearing stately hennins playing at cards with a gentleman, and again the cards have the French suit marks.

Antoine Janin was a card-maker at Lyon in 1516. We have a complete pack of fifty-two of his cards. The court cards are slim, debonair little figures that might have stepped from the retinue of Francis I. The valets lean nonchalantly on their halberds, and two of them bear Antoine Janin's name in Gothic letters. The plain backs of the cards were used, possibly a hundred years later, by an artist who has painted a different variety of bird on each one, and the result is most colorful and picturesque.

It is interesting to follow these old French 'cards for playing' through the centuries; in the early cards from wood blocks, widely varying types of

Anthoine Janin

PLAYING CARDS OF ANTOINE JANIN, CARTIER À LYON, 1516
Showing the decorated backs

(47)

court cards are characteristic of different parts of France — Auvergne, Lyon, Rouen, Lorraine, and all the rest — and their individuality persists until the Revolution. An instance showing how carefully this individuality is guarded is shown by a card wrapper of Grenoble, on which the maker

A PLAYING CARD WRAPPER OF GRENOBLE, 1731

explains the uncomfortable position of King David, pictured thereon, by saying that he has been obliged to change him, because he had been copied by several persons.

The custom of naming the court cards persisted variously in different parts of France; often the names were in honor of local heroes, or were those of characters in the old legends and myths. In the collection at Paris is a sheet of fifteenth-century cards which for the first time bear the names Alexander, Cæsar, Charlemagne, and David, which later on under Henri IV were adopted as the names of the four kings. Rachel, Argine, Pallas, and Judith became the queens, and Hector, Lancelot, Roland, and Hogier, the valets.

A valet of trèfles, made in Thiers about the middle of the seventeenth century, is a stocky and defiant person, as different as possible from the valets of Antoine Janin. Ancient Thiers was the greatest paper-making city of the realm, and by the sixteenth century the renown of the playing

A VALET OF TRÈFLES FROM THIERS,
c. 1680

A VALET OF PIQUES BY PHILIPE MONET,
CARTIER À THIERS, 1637–1685
The lion of Thiers is on his breast

cards of Thiers was well established and in many a family the craft descended from father to son for generations. They made quantities of Spanish cards as well as many of the French type which were used throughout Guyenne.

Bordeaux was an important seaport, and shipped many cards to Spain. It was not until 1665 that a cartier of Limoges suggested that cards be made there, as a source of revenue for the Hospice. In 1669, the royal authorization came, Bordeaux being the twelfth city in the kingdom to be granted this right. Their cards are very like those of Thiers. Jean Valet and Jean Vianey were among the early makers.

The story of print-making at Chartres is typical of that in many a French town. It still treasures some of its fifteenth-century religious prints, Mary and the Holy Baby, on very early paper; a quaint little palisaded garden where Saint Catherine and Saint Barbara and Saint Mary walk among the stiff little flowers; and Saint Martin, giving his cloak to a beggar.

A little later are found prints of a king speaking to his soldiers on the eve of battle, and a victorious army entering a walled city. Several times

A VALET OF CARREAUX BY FRANÇOIS PHILIPOU, CARTIER À THIERS, 1690–1701

the advent of a king inspires ballads describing the royal cortège, with the royal portrait above, and toward the end of the eighteenth century, the prints of the Wandering Jew and Pyramus and Thisbe are popular.

Side by side with the old prints are the old playing cards of Chartres, the card-maker and the print-maker often being one and the same. In 1702, Guillaume Chesneau, cartier, won renown for himself and for Chartres by using for his cards a special paper which bore as a water mark the arms of his king. With the coming of the Revolution, which frowned alike upon religion and royalty, even as personified on playing cards, the sale of both prints and cards was forbidden, so the art of the print-maker fell into disrepute and his press was stilled. It was in 1805 that the last print-maker of Chartres opened his shop under his sign 'Aux Quatre As,' and again produced the little royalties with the great names that had been familiar to all of France for more than two hundred years.

The Revolution at the end of the eighteenth century dethroned these royal families as well as the one at Versailles. It substituted on the cards, not very cleverly, philosophers, emblematic personages, and sans-culottes.

In 1808, at the height of his victories, Napoleon desired to replace the bizarre old figures of the court cards with others of 'extreme elegance and purity.' Accordingly, at his command, Gatteaux submitted designs in the classic manner. We have uncolored proofs of these. Gatteaux's name, with the date, 1811, is on the shield of the valet of trèfles.

There are also uncolored proofs of the cards offered by David, the painter. They are engraved by Andrieu whose name is on the knave of hearts. These are the designs that Napoleon accepted. As might be ex-

VALET OF CARREAUX AND VALET OF CŒURS BY JEAN VALET I, CARTIER À BORDEAUX.
1690–1695

VALET OF CARREAUX BY JEAN VIANEY, CARTIER À BORDEAUX, 1690

(51)

VALET OF PIQUES AND VALET OF TRÈFLES BY PIERRE BAUDARD, CARTIER À BORDEAUX, 1701–1711

He served his apprenticeship from 1692 under Jean Valet I

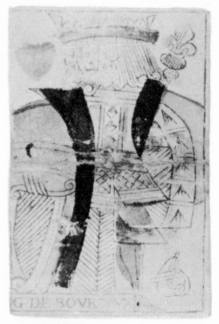

ROI OF CŒURS, PROBABLY BY JEAN VALET II

The mark in the lower right-hand corner is that of Nicolas de la Garde, to whom the card industry was leased in Bordeaux from 1716 to 1719. Cards made during this period are lettered 'Généralité de Bordeaux.'

PLAYING CARDS OF ÉTIENNE PETIT, CARTIER À LYON, 1635

(53)

PLAYING CARDS MADE BY JACQUES COISSIEUX, CARTIER À ROMANS, 1792–95

PLAYING CARDS DESIGNED BY GATTEAUX AT NAPOLEON'S COMMAND IN 1811

(54)

PLAYING CARDS DESIGNED BY DAVID AT NAPOLEON'S COMMAND IN 1811

FRENCH COURT CARDS OF 1813

VALET OF TRÈFLES OF A FRENCH PACK OF 1816

VALET OF TRÈFLES, PARIS, 1827
From a very early double-head pack

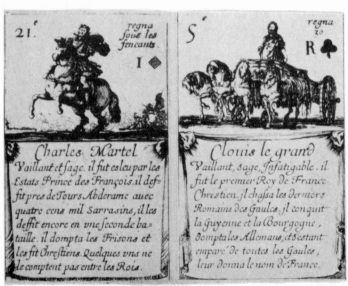

CHARLES MARTEL, THE ACE OF DIAMONDS, AND CLOVIS, THE KING OF CLUBS, FROM LES ROYS DE FRANCE, 1644

pected, the drawing is excellent and each statuesque little personage carries the pomp and dignity of conquering Rome.

The artistic merit of these was not appreciated, however, for in 1813 they were replaced by the old familiar cards that had been in use before the Revolution, and which are being made with but little variation to-day.

The date of the nineteenth-century cards — and sometimes the maker's name — is often to be found on the valet of trèfles. We have a pack dated 1827, which are unusual because they are double heads. Most cards have the full-length figures until a considerably later date. Their backs are a marbled design in pink, and this is also a characteristic of French and German cards of this time.

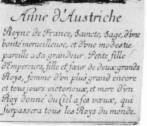

LE JEU DES REINES RENOMMÉES, PARIS, 1644

Many cards were made in France besides these usual ones 'for playing.'
When at the accession of Louis XIV, who in 1643 came to the throne under
the regency of his mother, Cardinal Mazarin was charged with the com-
pletion of his education, he devised a series of card games to interest the
young king in his studies. This is not strange, considering the tremendous
vogue of cards at court. Jean Desmarests, a member of the Académie
Française prepared these games, and in 1644 published an explanation of

LE JEU DE GÉOGRAPHIE, PARIS, 1644

them which bore the title 'Les Jeux de Cartes, des Roys de France, des
Reines Renommées, de la Géographie, et des Fables, cy devant dediez à
la Reine Régente, pour l'instruction du Roi.' Each game in this series contains fifty-two cards and a title card. Each card bears a finely designed
and engraved full-length figure, with a description below. The kings begin
with Pharamond and Clodion, long before the days of Clovis, and end with
young Louis himself. On several of the cards it is necessary to group as

many as five kings, to get them all in. Each king is numbered, from one to sixty-five, and the number of years of his reign is given.

The queens begin with Martesie, queen of the Amazons, and end with Anne of Austria, the mother of the king. They must have been played like our game of authors, for they are separated into groups, with dreadful but amusing finality, by a single adjective at the upper right-hand corner — pious, clever, cruel, unfortunate, celebrated, saintly, good, wise, brave, happy, and capricious. We have them in different states of the proof, some with suit signs in the upper left-hand corner, and some without.

Le Jeu de Géographie shows similar little figures on each card, each emblematic of the country described below. We have one series in which the cards are colored by hand, and others uncolored, one with suit signs in the corner of each card. The title card shows two hemispheres au travers, lettered, 'Géographie: A Paris, chez Henry le Gras, libraire au 3ᵉ pilier de la grande salle du Palais.' All the title cards bear Le Gras's name as publisher.

Le Jeu de Fables have delightful small delineations of the Greek myths on each card. We have all of these games, both in the form of packs of cards, and in small calf-bound books. They are all extremely interesting and of much rarity, and from an artistic standpoint are of value as the work of the famous Florentine engraver, Stefano della Bella. There is a reprint of the whole edition at Paris in 1698.

LE JEU DE FABLES, PARIS, 1644

FROM A MYTHOLOGICAL SERIES OF
1680

THE ARMS OF THE POPE, CLEMENT IX
From the De Brianville heraldry, 1665

HERALDIC PLAYING CARDS OF C. ORONCE FINE DE BRIAN-
VILLE, 1655
The Roi de Trèfles, showing the arms of the Pope, Alexander VII,
and the Prince of Carreaux, with the arms of Castile and Leon

(60)

About 1680, another series of mythological cards was issued, similar to those of Della Bella. The style of the engraving in the small illustrations is that of Sebastien le Clerc, though some of them are hardly as good drawing as is usual in his designs. These cards have the French suit signs, and the court cards are marked R (roi), D (dame), P (prince), and C (chevalier), this last taking the place of the ace.

In 1655, the famous series of heraldic cards, designed by C. Oronce Fine

JEU DE CARTES DU BLASON, BY PÈRE F. C. MENESTRIER, PUBLISHED BY
THOMAS ALMAURY AT LYONS, 1692
The King and four of Fleur de Lys, the two of Lions, and the two of Eagles are shown

de Brianville, were issued. In those days 'pour apprendre le Blason' was a
very necessary part of the education of a gentleman. The arms of the
states of Europe are shown; the suit of hearts bears those of France; spades,
those of Germany; clubs, the Italian; and diamonds, the Spanish and
Portuguese. The court cards are designated in the same way as those in
the mythology series just described. The king of trèfles shows the papal
arms of Alexander VII (Chigi). A little book of explanation went with
these cards. We have an edition of 1659, one of 1665, and an eighth edition,
with no date, all published at Lyons; so they must have been much in
demand.

A beautifully engraved series of heraldic cards followed these in 1692,
'Jeu de Cartes du Blason, publié à Lyon.' The suit signs are the fleur de
lys for France, the eagle for Germany and Flanders, the rose for Italy, and
the lion for Spain and Portugal. On the pavillon, or ace, of fleur de lys are
the arms of the Duc de Berri. Armorial bearings are shown on each card,
and the court cards are portraits of the European rulers.

Still another 'Jeu Heraldique' was issued 'à Paris chez Daumont, rue
St. Martin.' Our edition is an uncut sheet of the fifty-two cards, bearing the

JEU HERALDIQUE OF DAUMONT, PARIS, 1698

usual suit signs and the coat of arms of noble families. The court cards
have full-length figures upon them in addition to the bearings. The
'Reglemens du Jeu Heraldique' are given at the top, and there is a card of
dedication 'A Monseigneur le Comte d'Artois.' These were printed from
copper plates, about 1698.

SORTIE.

Sortie est l'attaque que font
les assieges en sortant de
nuit sur les assiegeans pour
les combattre, pour ruiner leurs
trauaux ou pour enclouer leur
canon. Pour se defendre des
Sorties on a soin que les tran-
chees soient flanquees dans
leurs detours et fortifiées par
des redoutes de distance en
distance.

MONTER LA TRANCHÉE.

Monter la Tranchée, c'est monter
la Garde a la tranchée : ce qui se
dit des Fantassins qu'on dispose
dans la tranchée pour soutenir
les trauailleurs et empescher
que les ennemys ne fassent des
Sorties et ne comblent leurs
trauaux on dit pareillement
releuer la tranchée lorsque de
nouvelles troupes viennent
prendre la place des premieres
dans la tranchée.

L'Héroïque valeur que ce grand Roy couronne
N'estime dans ces prix que la main qui les donne.

LE JEU DE LA GUERRE, PARIS, 1660

(63)

LE JEU DU NAINE JAUNE

(64)

Another of the so-called educational games is the 'Jeu de la Guerre.'
This is also an uncut sheet of fifty-three cards from copper plates intended
to teach military science. Each bears an illustration of a military operation
with a description below. The game was played with dice and a lively account of it is given in the Académie des Jeux of 1668. It is dedicated by
Daumont, the publisher, to the Duc de Berri, the son of Louis XIV. It
was invented and the designs were drawn by Gilles de la Boissière, and
engraved by Pierre le Pautre. A later edition of this game is listed in the
British Museum Catalogue.

There are, besides, the Jeu des Cartes Militaires of Desmartins, published in 1676, and 'Le Jeu des Nations' of 1684. In a 'Dictionnaire des
Jeux,' published in Paris in 1792, there are large engraved plates of many
games that may or may not have been educational. There is the 'Poule de
Henri IV,' the old 'Jeu de l'Oie,' the 'Jeu de Marine,' the 'Jeu de Mappe
Monde,' the 'Jeu du Lindor ou du Naine Jaune,' and the 'Jeu de l'Hymen,' which are among the most picturesque.

About 1760, a number of 'Jeux des Cartes Historiques' were published by
Vanackers in Lille. The author's name is given on the case as E. Jouy. In
a circle at the top of each card is a portrait head of some famous person,

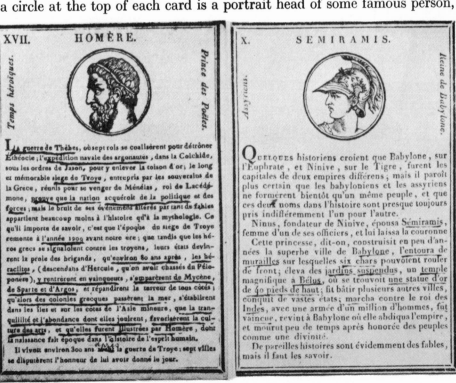

JEU DES CARTES HISTORIQUES, LILLE, c. 1760

whose biography occupies the rest of the card. The leaflet of 'Avis' says that this is the troisième jeu of the series. We have four cards of a similar series showing heads of famous Romans, and three of another which is a Grecian series. The cards of each series are numbered one to forty-eight,

JEU MYTHOLOGIQUE, LILLE, c. 1760

and there are no suit signs. They are printed from wood blocks, and are chiefly interesting because each little portrait head is taken from an old coin or medal.

The quatrième jeu, of which we have the complete set, is 'Histoire Mythologiques' and the mythology is that of Greece and Rome.

The early nineteenth century brought a number of games which are the most delightful little French color prints imaginable. These are round, three inches in diameter, at the top of the card. Below is the story of the print, and at the bottom is a moral in verse. They are evidently intended as a game for children, for on each card, in the corners, are four letters of the alphabet. The first series recounts the adventures of M. Calicot, a rascal, and the lovely but foolish Mlle. Percale, and the tragic dénouement through the dramatic interference of her stern father, M. le Rond.

In the second series the subjects are not a continuous story. The titles are: 'L'amour enchaîné,' 'L'hiver,' Le café tortonnie'; while the last three are street musicians.

In the third series the letters are small ones, instead of being capitals as in the preceding two. Again the prints are not a continuous story. The subjects are: 'Baisé à la capucine,' 'Famille anglaise en promenade'; the next three are dances, and the last, three fashionable gentlemen, with the title, 'Prenez garde. Il existe un différence du Calicot au Casimir et Pékin.'

There is also a 'Jeu Géographique et Mythologique,' the title being on the roi de trèfles, with which the series begins. There is a miniature playing card at the top of each card, a symbolic figure representing some country beside it on the left, and a figure out of Greek mythology on the right. The rest of the card is taken up with a description of these two. The ten of trèfles, which is France, gives the boundaries as they were at the height of Napoleon's conquests.

A complete piquet pack of thirty-two small cards, two and one fourth by one and one half inches with the usual French suit signs, was also undoubtedly meant to have an educational value. On the ace of diamonds, which is also the title card, is lettered, 'Jeu Français et Anglais et Portugais.'

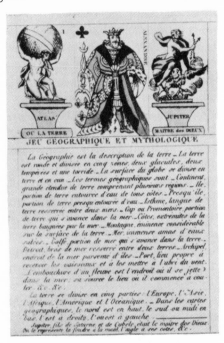

FROM 'LE JEU GÉOGRAPHIQUE ET MYTHO-
LOGIQUE'

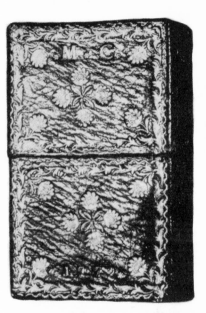

TOOLED-LEATHER CARD-CASE CONTAIN-
ING LE JEU DE SOCIÉTÉ, 1772

SMALL EDUCATIONAL PLAYING CARDS FOR THE ACQUIRING OF FOREIGN LANGUAGES,
c. 1800

There is a French phrase at the top of each card, the Portuguese equivalent in the middle, and the English translation at the bottom. The spelling is often amusing; the French is not that of the Academicians, and the king's English is ruthlessly slaughtered; the whole pack is carelessly printed and colored, on the cheapest of paper. From the court cards, they are evidently of the early nineteenth century, but we have never found them listed in any book on playing cards. Small cheap cards were often distributed among the soldiers of an army, however, and we have wondered if this might not have been an idea of Napoleon's to unite his men. This surmise is given still more weight because we have three other games of these small cards, a 'Jeu Français et Allemand et Italien,' a 'Jeu Français et Russe et Polonais,' and a 'Jeu Français et Espagnol et Hollandais.'

'Le Grand Jeu de la Géographie avec costumes colorées' is a series of twenty-four of the most decorative and delightful little color prints. Two thirds of each card is taken up by a print showing the inhabitants of some country. The rest of the card is the description. Number one begins auspiciously, 'La France est la pays le plus agréable de l'Europe. . . . Napoléon Premier en a augmenté la splendeur par la magnificence des monumens qu'il y a fait élever. Ses brillants conquètes ont enrichi ses muséums et bibliothèques par les objets les plus précieux. Les Français sont humains, généreux, leur courage est admiré généralement. Les Françaises sont aimables et spirituelles.' The inhabitants of even the most far-away countries, as depicted on these cards, are French to their fingertips, and are utterly charming.

At the end of the nineteenth century, this old idea of educational cards still survived. A game consisting of eight packs of cards in a wooden box, 'Le Magistre Nouveau Jeu de Géographie pour instruire les enfants tout en les amusant,' seems a little complicated for any children. The cards contain coats of arms and questions and answers concerning the departments, cities, and towns of France. A similar series to teach the history of France is the 'Nouveau Jeu Histoire.'

The making of Spanish playing cards was an important industry in France by the latter half of the seventeenth century. The great demand for cards in Spain kept many makers busy in Gascony and Aquitaine, Languedoc and Auvergne. These cards were quite different from the French ones. They were usually Hombre packs, of forty cards, with Spanish suit signs. Jehan Volay was a well-known maker of Thiers. His cards are hand-colored wood blocks, gay with red and blue and yellow, and his name usually appears on several of the cards of each pack, and the Spanish arms on one. We have very similar cards 'fechas en Bordeaux,' which is lettered on the two of swords. There are many examples of Spanish cards made in France during the nineteenth century, and they are

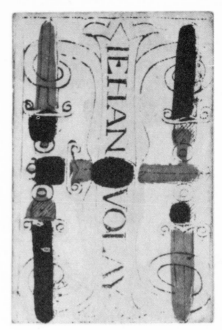

SPANISH PLAYING CARDS MADE BY JEHAN VOLAY OF THIERS, c. 1680

(69)

chiefly interesting because of the exactness with which they follow the standards of their Spanish users. This is equally true of the French cards made for the English market, which are large and substantial, and bear no trace of the French characteristics, except the maker's name, and even this conforms to English usage and appears on the ace of spades. There are also French cards made for export of the Bavarian type, and other cards for export to Turkey and Roumania, Austria and South America.

About 1870, decorated aces were very popular. A pack of playing cards

SPANISH PLAYING CARDS MADE IN BORDEAUX, 1691

THE TWO OF COINS, THE ONE OF COINS, AND THE VALET OF CUPS

Cards from Un Jeu d'Allouette, an old Breton game mentioned by Rabelais and played with cards with Spanish suit signs. The court cards are the old designs of Jehan Volay, the Valet of Cups having the Lion of Thiers upon his breast. The coins are also like his, the two showing the arms of Thiers in one circle, and the one showing the arms of Spain, lettered like Volay's 'Rex Carolus Hispaniarum Dei Gratia.'

Top left: Chinese (see p. 8B); *top right:* Indian (see p. 18B); *bottom left:*
French, 1392 (see p. 38A); *bottom right:* Japanese (see p. 18A).

Top left: French, *c.* 1440 (see p. vi); *top right:* French, 1692 (see p. 38B);
bottom left: French, 1856 (see p. 72A); *bottom right:* German, early 18th century
(see p. 108B).

for export to South America shows views of South American cities on each ace, and some for Trieste show pictures of Paris, while some patience cards with fancy suit signs, which are nevertheless recognizable as the French cœurs, carreaux, trèfles, and piques, show scenes from 'Lohengrin' on each ace.

Among the most interesting of all the cards we have is an evidently incomplete series of twenty-two cards from copper plates, colored by hand. The diagonal division line on many of the cards suggests that they were used by some mountebank, and the costumes of the few figure cards are those of the court at the end of the seventeenth century. The subjects shown include an ostrich, a pipe, a goblet, a violin, a rooster, a bagpipe, a courtier, a cavalier, a parrot, a guardsman, a lobster, a lady of the court, the mountebank himself, a monkey, a lion rampant with a parasol, and a sinister person with a ladder. Both the drawings and coloring are delightful, and it is to be regretted that they cannot tell their own story. There are no suit signs nor lettering, and the backs are plain. An even less complete series is in the British Museum.

There is also a series of leger-de-main cards of the early nineteenth century, but, in spite of their beautiful coloring, they hold none of the charm of the early cards.

A LEGER-DE-MAIN CARD, *c.* 1800

The cards in the latter series are completely taken up with grotesque figures having enormous heads and two faces.

Still another series of about this same time are great grotesque heads, facing both ways, and which may be looked at either way, from either end of the card. Later in the century this same idea was used, and the cards were called 'Binettes.'

We have a group of etchings, which show what delightful things might be done with the figures of the court cards. These are by Benner, a miniature painter who studied and worked with Isabey. They are full-length figures in the costume of the fifteenth century, and are very Flemish, and rather suggestive of the court cards of the famous round series of Cologne. A

half-century later a pack of cards with the usual French suit signs have court cards dressed in the costume of the period. They are well drawn, and printed from copper plates and colored by hand. The roi de trèfles is lettered, '1848, Paris, Rue Richelieu 102.' The backs are a design of branching coral in yellow.

A pack designed in 1856 has for its court cards in the suit of piques, Charles VI, Odette, and a page with a falcon; in cœurs, Louis Quatorze, the Duchesse de la Vallière, and a page with a salver; carreaux, Henri IV, Gabrielle d'Estrées, and a page of the chase; trèfles, François I, the Duchesse d'Estampes, and a knight's page. They are most pleasing little designs, and we have the artist's proofs, beautifully hand-colored. These cards were reprinted about 1891.

A PLAYING CARD DESIGN FROM AN ETCHING BY BENNER, c. 1810

Other cards with court cards showing contemporary costumes were made about 1878 by O. Gibert, Paris, whose name appears on the valet of trèfles. These cards are hand-colored lithographs.

About this time there was also issued a pack with court cards showing

FRENCH COSTUME CARDS OF 1848

COURT CARDS FROM LE JEU DE CARTES HISTORIQUES, PUBLISHED IN PARIS IN 1856

TWO CARDS FROM LE GRAND JEU DE GÉOGRAPHIE, PUBLISHED IN PARIS ABOUT 1800
A CARD FROM A FORTUNE-TELLING SERIES DESIGNED BY MANGION ABOUT 1830
AND A CARD FROM A CHILDREN'S ALPHABETICAL GAME OF ABOUT 1800

COSTUME CARDS, PARIS, 1873

LE JEU LOUIS QUINZE

(73)

various rulers of France. Cœurs, being the Roman occupation; piques, Henry of Navarre; carreaux, Napoleon; and trèfles, Louis Philippe; and in addition each suit sign bears a symbol of the reign.

There are many beautifully decorated and lithographed series in the later years carrying out this idea of fancifully costumed court cards.

JEU DE WHIST INDIENNE

Among the most pleasing of these is a pack of patience cards with court cards in Dutch costume, a 'Jeu Louis XV' with appropriate costumes and decorations, and a pack called 'Indian Whist' which has real artistic merit and is an interesting example of most beautiful and unusual designing, lithographing, and color. The court cards are in Indian costume, the numerals being decorated with appropriate flower designs, forming a pleasing background.

LE JEU DE DRAPEAUX, PARIS, 1814

A pack of cards that does not belong to any of these groups is the rather famous 'Jeu des Drapeaux' which was issued under the Restoration in honor of Napoleon's return. It is a piquet pack with a title card, bearing the name on a flag, carried by one of the Old Guard. On a pillar beside him are the names of all the great victories from Ulm to Moscow. The cards themselves picture Napoleon's soldiers, the suit signs being on the flags they carry. The heart suit shows the French soldiers, and the king carries the famous motto, 'La garde meurt et ne se rend pas.' They are spirited and delightful little prints, hand-colored.

About this time there are a number of alphabet games for children. Besides the letters, each card bears a whimsical little full-length figure; there are knights, harlequins, jugglers, etc. Each card is divided into three parts by two horizontal black lines. Perhaps they are meant to be cut

apart on these lines so that they may he put together in different ways. They are good little color prints. Another similar series has pictures of birds and animals upon the cards, and in a third, the figures are tumblers, jugglers, and musicians; while a fourth has figures with enormous and grotesque heads.

CHILDREN'S CARDS, FRENCH COLOR PRINTS OF THE EARLY NINETEENTH CENTURY

There are four other series of these cards, presumably for children, because there are four letters of the alphabet at the top of each one. The rest of the card is taken up by a circular color print. The subjects are most sophisticated caricatures with such titles as M. des Sorbets, Marie à la Coque, M. Double Croche, Mme. La Joie, etc.

MUSICAL CARDS OF 1830

A much pleasanter series is one giving the music of a popular dance on each card, the waltz, the cotillon, and the contradance. This is a series of fifty-two cards with the usual French suit signs. The heads of the court cards appear at the very top of the card, while on the numerals more than half the space on the card is given to showing the suit signs in the usual manner. The court cards are original and pleasing designs from copper plates, hand-colored. They were made about 1830.

Fortune-telling and divination, the oldest of all uses of games of chance, has many examples among the French. 'Le Passetemps de la Fortune des Dez' was published at Paris in 1634. It is a calf-bound volume with the arms of its original owner stamped in gold in the center of both covers. There is a greeting to the reader in the form of a rondeau, and at the end of the book the Biblical prophets are explained in a long series of couplets. The space between explains all possible combinations of throws, and also pictures in full-page engravings the signs of the zodiac, with most interesting decorative work all around them, evidently deeply and darkly symbolic. This has foretold many an event in its day, judging by its marginal notes.

Many a little book gives equally valuable and mysterious directions for fortune-telling with cards; also for interpreting dreams, and explaining signs and portents.

CARDS FROM THE TAROTS D'ETTEILLA, THE MOST FAMOUS OF THE EIGHTEENTH-CENTURY FRENCH FORTUNE-TELLING CARDS

The most famous of all the French cards for fortune-telling are the 'Tarots d'Etteilla.' Late in the eighteenth century, a wig-maker named Alliette read the book of Court de Gebelin on the old tarots, and their mystic symbolism. Thereafter he designed several sets of fortune-telling

Voyage 24

Bon Voyage par Mer 25

Procès Chicane 26

Richard corrupteur 31

Jalousie 32

Fausse Amie Femme dangereuse 33

FRENCH FORTUNE-TELLING CARDS OF THE LATE EIGHTEENTH CENTURY

(78)

cards, based on de Gebelin's theories. He used his own name, backwards, as a name for his cards. The little Paris perruquier enjoyed a great vogue for many years, both at the court and throughout France. His cards ran through many editions, and the designs changed, but the original characteristics are kept. The first atout bears the name Etteilla at the top. Also each card is lettered 'Droit' in the upper margin, and 'Renversé' in the lower. The meaning of the card, its suit, and numerical value are lettered in the side margins. Many of the old traditional designs are recognizable in his atouts, and the other cards bear the Italian suit signs arranged in the Spanish manner. Our Cartes d'Etteilla are wood blocks, hand-colored, and as in the old tarot series there are seventy-eight cards.

There was also a series of forty cards, the Petit Etteilla, and there are several imitations of these pretty little hand-colored cards, printed from copper plates.

It is hard to put much credence in the many stories that have been told of Napoleon's belief in these things, but we have a series of cards for fortune-telling published during the Restoration, in the hope that the star of his destiny might once more be in the ascendancy.

A very clever series of fifty-two cards is the 'Jeu de la Sybelle des Salons.' There is a card of explanation, showing how they are to be dealt, to yourself, to your house; to what you do expect, and to what you don't expect. Practically the entire card is taken up with a whimsical illustration, the subjects varying greatly. The designs are by a well-known caricaturist of the time, Mansion, and each card is signed. Though they were issued in good faith as fortune-telling cards, you can't help but feel that their author is laughing at their users. They are hand-colored lithographs, with infinite charm, and were printed by Gaudais in 1830.

FROM A SERIES OF FORTUNE-TELLING
CARDS OF ABOUT 1840

There were also published at Paris many transformation cards, which were popular for a number of years. In these the suit signs form part of a fanciful design, and the thing was done with varying degrees of cleverness and success many times and in many places. The court cards are travesties

TRANSFORMATION CARDS, PARIS, 1873

of the usual ones. They have little value as 'cards for playing' and they are not as amusing as you might expect them to be.

We have a pack of thirty-four 'Kolibri Cards' of about 1860, consisting of twenty-one pictorial cards and thirteen numerals. The pictorial cards are from copper plates, hand-colored, and show pictures of dancers in different countries. These were designed by Geiger, a Viennese card-maker, and were used as the atouts in a costume tarot series in Vienna, a few years later.

Our group of French cards ends with the 'Cartes Souvenirs' of the Paris Exposition, a photograph on each of the fifty-two cards.

There were silver playing cards at court in the days of Louis XV, and packs painted by the famous miniature painters in those gay days when gaming had become a madness at court; when 'La Maison' or 'Académie des Jeux' appeared each year laying down the laws and conventions for playing those games with the strange names which had become of such vast importance. Our first 'Maison des Jeux,' is dated 1657, and it is a 'nouvelle édition.'

It was a Frenchman who wrote the first

KOLIBRI CARD, PARIS, c. 1860

history of playing cards, the 'Bibliothèque Curieuse' of Père Menestrier in 1704. And it was a Frenchman who two hundred years later gave us the most authoritative and detailed account of the story of cards in his own country in his 'Cartes à Jouer du XIV au XVIIIeme Siècle.' This is by M. Henry René d'Allemagne.

FRENCH PLAYING CARDS IN THE COLLECTION OF THE UNITED STATES PLAYING CARD COMPANY [1]

*Painted tarots of Charles VI, 1392 (facsimiles)	17 cards
Small tarots, c. 1720	21 cards
Besançon tarots, J. Jerger, c. 1800	78 cards
*Minchiate cards, early nineteenth century	38 cards
*Provence knaves, 1440	2 cards
*Cards of François Arnoux, fifteen century, Montpellier	16 cards
*Cards of François Arnoux, early sixteenth century, Montpellier	20 cards
Cards of Antoine Bonnier, Montpellier, 1700	8 cards
Cards of Alexandre Lionnet, Montpellier, 1730–1750	50 cards

[1] The starred items are from the collection of George Clulow, F.R.G.S.

Cards of Fulcrand Bouscarel, Montpellier, 1745–1750	35 cards
Cards of Jean Valet, Bordeaux, 1690	2 cards
Cards of Jean Vianey, Bordeaux, 1690	1 card
Cards of Jean Valet II, Bordeaux, 1699	1 card
Cards of Pierre Baudard, Bordeaux, 1701–1708	8 cards
Cards of Bordeaux, 1713	10 cards
Cards of Antoine Janin, Lyon, 1516	52 cards
Cards of François Philipou, Thiers, 1672	2 cards
Cards of Philippe Monet, Thiers, 1637	1 card
*Cards by Gatteaux, for Napoleon Bonaparte, 1811	12 cards
*Cards by David, for Napoleon Bonaparte, 1811	12 cards
Cards of 1813, patron de Paris	12 cards
*Cards of 1816, patron de Paris	52 cards
*Cards of 1827, patron de Paris	52 cards
*Des Roys de France, Paris, 1644	40 cards
Des Roys de France, Paris, 1644	40 cards
*Les Reines Renommées, Paris, 1644	53 cards
Les Reines Renommées, Paris, 1644	52 cards
Les Reines Renommées, Paris, 1644	38 cards
*Jeu de Géographie, Paris, 1644	53 cards
Jeu de Géographie, Paris, 1644	53 cards
Jeu de Géographie, Paris, 1644	45 cards
*Jeu de Géographie, Paris, 1698	9 cards
*Jeu des Fables, Paris, 1644	53 cards
*Jeu de Mythologie, 1680	52 cards
De Brianville Heraldry, 1655	48 cards
De Brianville Heraldry, 1665	28 cards
*Menestrier, Heraldry, 1692	29 cards
*Daumont, Heraldry, 1698	53 cards
*Jeu de la Guerre, 1680	53 cards
Jeu des Cartes Historiques, Lille, 1760	47 cards
Jeu des Cartes Mythologique, Lille, 1760	48 cards
Jeu des Cartes Historiques, 4th edition	7 cards
Jeu des Cartes Historiques, 3d edition	38 cards
Alphabet Game, c. 1800	6 cards
Alphabet Game, 1800	6 cards
Alphabet Game, 1800	6 cards
Jeu Géographique et Mythologique	32 cards
4 piquet sets of soldier cards (foreign languages)	128 cards
Grand Jeu de Géographie	25 cards
Le Magistre Nouveau Jeu de Géographie	480 cards
Le Magistre Nouveau Jeu d'Histoire	480 cards
*Jehan Volay cards, 1680	42 cards
*Spanish cards of Bordeaux, 1691	34 cards
Jeu d'Allouette	48 cards
6 packs of nineteenth-century Spanish cards, 48 cards each	288 cards
4 packs of nineteenth-century English cards, 52 cards each	208 cards
3 packs of nineteenth-century cards, Bavarian type	156 cards
1 pack of nineteenth-century cards, for export to Turkey	52 cards
1 pack of nineteenth-century cards, for export to Roumania	52 cards
1 pack of nineteenth-century cards, for export to Austria	52 cards

1 pack of nineteenth-century cards, for export to South America	52 cards
1 pack of nineteenth-century cards, decorated aces, South America	52 cards
1 pack of nineteenth-century cards, decorated aces, Trieste	52 cards
*1 pack of nineteenth-century cards, decorated aces, Lohengrin	52 cards
*Conjuror's cards, 1692	22 cards
Leger-de-main cards, early nineteenth century, complete piquet pack	32 cards
Leger-de-main cards, early nineteenth century, complete piquet pack	32 cards
Playing card designs by Benner, c. 1815	16 cards
*Costume cards, 1848	52 cards
*Costume cards, 1856	52 cards
*Costume cards, 1873	52 cards
*Costume cards, 1878	52 cards
Jeu de Louis XV	52 cards
Whist Indienne	52 cards
*Jeu des Drapeaux, complete piquet pack, 1814	32 cards
Jeu des Drapeaux, complete piquet pack, 1814, and title card	33 cards
*Five Alphabet card games, complete, each 12 cards	60 cards
4 Caricature card games, complete, each 6 cards	24 cards
*Musical cards	25 cards
Tarots d'Etteilla	78 cards
Tarots d'Etteilla	78 cards
Le Petit Etteilla	40 cards
*Jeu de la Sybelle	52 cards
Fortune-telling cards, 1830	40 cards
Transformation cards, 1840	52 cards
Transformation cards, 1873, complete piquet pack	32 cards
Kolibri cards, 1860	31 cards
Cartes Souvenirs, Paris Exposition	52 cards
French piquet cards, 1868	32 cards
Dutch costume patience cards, 1890	52 cards
French patience cards, 1900	52 cards

Playing cards of Provence, probably of the late fifteenth century. Hogier, the valet of spades, the valet of hearts, unnamed (this may be because the left-hand side of the card has been cut off); the queen of clubs, Hélène, and fragments of twelve numerals. The cards are very large, $4 \times 2\ 7/8''$, from wood blocks, hand-colored.

Court cards by Christophe Bertoin, cartier à Romans-sur-Isère, 1715–19. Le roi des cœurs is barefooted and stands with drawn sword and upraised left hand. Le roi des carreaux wears high boots, with a dog's head at the top of each. The valet of carreaux is barefooted, but a curious little human face looks out from the cuff of each trouser leg, below the knee. The cards are from wood blocks on paper of a chamois-like texture. The color, which is hand-work, reds predominating, is exceedingly soft.
                                                                    6 cards

Another valet des carreaux of Christophe Bertoin, printed from the same block as the former. The outline is much clearer, however, and the color — red, black, and yellow — harsh. The strange little faces at the knee are very much in evidence.

Playing cards by Jacques Coissieux, cartier à Romans-sur-Isère, 1725–43. A valet of spades which bears his name, printed in blue, and colored yellow and a curious brown and black, and a reine de trèfles, also in somber colors and bearing the mark of the three fleurs de lys in a circle.

Cartes de révolution by Jacques Coissieux, cartier à Romans-sur-Isère, 1792–95. The kings wear red caps instead of crowns and are each lettered 'Génie.' The queens are lettered 'Liberté,' and the valets, 'Égalité.'   16 cards

Cards by Jacques Coissieux, just after the Revolution, returning the crowns and the familiar names to the kings and queens.   6 cards

Court cards from La Rochelle, roi et valet des piques, reine des trèfles, et deux valets, l'un rouge, l'autre, noir. On the plain backs of the cards have been listed Italian books, titles, and number of volumes, the dates running from 1764 to 1796. Except for the valet of piques, all of the cards have been cut down on two sides. The mark on the red valet is a full-blown poppy, on the black one, a lion and a fleur de lys.   5 cards

Reine des piques et reine des trèfles, each marked 'Société.' On the back of each is a note 'À madame veuve.' Perhaps they were made by La Veuve Pavie, La Rochelle, 1784–87.

Valet de piques, Pierre Desvignes à Lyon, 1760. Un roi des carreaux, named 'Cezar,' bearing the filigrane of Rennes, 1746, a large and ornate fleur de lys.

Une reine de cœurs, 'Judic,' with the fleur de lys filigrane of Dijon of 1763.

Cards by François Carrajat à Chambéry, his name on the valet des trèfles, four court cards and four numerals, 1794.

Valet des trèfles by Jean Baptiste Mitoire, La Chapelle Rue d'Anjou au Marais, à Paris. His mark is the flying bird. 1746–70.

Three valets des trèfles by Guillaume Mandrou, Paris, 1754–1808, each showing his mark, 'The King of Siam.'

Valet des trèfles, Soumard, Paris. His mark shows two birds facing each other, and is lettered 'Aux 3 Colombes.'

Valet des trèfles, his mark lettered 'Vachias,' Lyon (for Antoine Vachat?), 1745. The mark of the bee on his breastplate.

Valet des trèfles, lettered 'Ducrost.' D. G. Paris. His mark shows the stork and fox of the fable and is lettered 'A la sigogne.'

Valet des trèfles of Mathieu Raisin, Paris, 1747–72; his

mark bears his name and address surrounding a gnome and a battlemented tower.

The court cards of Le Jeu Impérial engraved by Andrieu after designs of Jean Baptiste David, at Napoleon's command, 1810. These are crudely colored with stencil.

The court cards designed by Gatteaux at Napoleon's command, 1811. Colored with stencil.

Court cards of the First Empire by Danbrin of Paris, 1809. Beautifully hand-colored, named in the old manner. The valets bear the crowned eagle on their breastplates and shields.

Court cards by Jean Minot, cartier à Paris, 1767–1808. These are the usual named court cards, the mark on the valet des trèfles showing an Indian with drawn sword, and lettered 'Au Grand Gustave de Paris.'   8 cards

Court cards of the Revolution by Jean Minot, à Paris, the kings and queens *sans* crowns, but the queens and valets retaining their old names. There is no address on the maker's mark.   9 cards

Court cards by Valentin Minot, cartier à Paris, 1781–90. These are revolutionary ones, similar to those of Jean Minot.   7 cards

Complete set of named court cards by Guillaume Mandrou, à Paris, 1754–1808, with the mark of the King of Siam.   12 cards

Court cards, three queens, and three valets, by J. Pinaut, cartier à Paris, 1791–94. The usual suit sign is repeated in miniature in the lower right-hand corner of each card and there are Roman numerals at the side of each, II on the queens and III on the valets.   6 cards

Court cards of 1816, stenciled in color and named. There are two aces of trèfles, one a fleur de lys, the other the usual trèfle in a circle of small fleur de lys.   14 cards

Court cards, stenciled and named, the king of trèfles shows the crowned eagle of the Empire. 1813.   7 cards

Playing cards, presumably of the seventeenth century, 2 5/8 × 1 1/2″. The backs are decorated with an all-over conventional design. The cards are wood blocks, hand-colored in soft reds and blues. The kings are very animated; the queens are in the gowns of the early seventeenth century, and wear their crowns at a precarious angle. The valets sport unnaturally long plumes. The numeral cards are bordered with a conventional design half an inch wide, colored in blue and yellow. The ace of trèfles shows the lion and the unicorn with the crown, from which a tree bearing large and luscious blackberries grows amazingly. The ace of carreaux shows two stags, also holding a crown, from which sprouts a luxuriant plant with yellow flowers. These cards are interesting to compare with those of Delêtre, cartier à Paris, 1672, shown by M. d'Allemagne (vol. II, page 70). There is no clue to the maker of these of ours. The valet des trèfles carries a blank scroll, and a mark of a highly conventionalized flower is below. 14 cards

Three valets des piques, stenciled in color, blue and yellow predominating, named Hogier. The little dog of the fifteenth-century designs paws at his gallant master. These are by Charles Cheminade, cartier à Grenoble, 1747–68. There were five generations of card-makers in the family. 3 cards

Valet des piques, Hogier, from the same design used by Cheminade, by Barthélemy Mazet, à Grenoble, 1773–86. 1 card

Complete set of court cards with the old French names, made by Barthélemy Mazet à Grenoble, 1773–86. The valet of trèfles bears the mark of the three flowers, and the bee on his breastplate. 12 cards

Valet of piques, 'Brave M. Scævola,' defying the king with his hand in the flame. Cards by J. Minot, 1793, for the Revolution, with kings, classic sages, the queens, virtues, and the valets, four heroes, Hannibal, Horatius, Scævola, and Decius Mus. 1 card

Playing cards of the Revolution by Claude Vial à Grenoble, 1774–98. The kings wear red liberty caps, the queens, veils on their heads, and the valets, tricornes. They are unnamed. 11 cards

Three extra valets des piques by Jean Minot, à Paris, during the Revolution. One of them is lettered 'Force.' 3 cards

A valet of piques, Hogier, made by Charles Guillot, cartier à Paris, 1742–88. 1 card

Two queens of hearts, two of diamonds, two of spades, eight of clubs, and seven of hearts, probably by Pierre Desvignes, Lyon, 1760. The numerals are stenciled, the queens printed from wood blocks and hand-colored in scarlet, yellow, and black, with ermine bands of blue. The skirt flares up stiffly and shows a large and firmly planted right foot.

Court cards of Lyon, from wood blocks and stenciled in red, blue, black, and yellow. The king of carreaux bears the mark of the golden sun with the fleur de lys in the center. The valet of piques smokes a pipe, like that of Pierre Desvignes, c. 1750. 8 cards

Complete set of court cards of Lyon (c. 1750); the king of carreaux and the valet of trèfles bear the mark of the sun, the former showing the fleur de lys, the latter a face in the center. The feet of three of the queens are in evidence, and the valet of piques smokes a pipe. 12 cards

Complete set of court cards of Lyon. The king of carreaux and the knave of trèfles both bear the mark of the golden sun with the face in the center. The queens wear short gowns that show their large buckled shoes, the smoke curls luxuriously from the pipe of the valet of trèfles, which is lettered 'Man J. B.,' and the valet of trèfles is lettered 'Lyon,' c. 1740. 12 cards

Valet of piques of Lyon, smoking a pipe. A wood block hand-colored in browns and blue, c. 1750. 1 card

Reine de trèfles, possibly of the time of the Revolution. It is from one of the old blocks of Jacques Coissieux of Romans, seemingly, but the crown is removed and yellow curls put in its place. The card is also shorter than those of Coissieux, and the bottom of the gown of the original queen has been cut off.

Playing cards of Étienne Petit, cartier à Lyon, 1635.   25 cards

Playing cards of Jacques Coissieux, cartier à Romans-sur-Isère, 1792–95.   6 cards

Jeu de Société, gold-edged cards, on each of which is written a Bible verse, not all in the same handwriting. They are in a red morocco case, tooled in gold and lettered 'M.C. 1772.' The same thing was done in England at about this time by the Wesleys, who printed their game and interspersed it with verses from their hymns. The good Methodists played it by drawing a card and using it as a conversational text. But it seems soon to have taken on the old significance of cards for divination, and many decisions were made according to the guidance of these little scraps of paper. This French game was doubtless used in this way, also.   61 cards

Total: 156 editions, 5077 cards

CHAPTER V

PLAYING CARDS IN GERMANY

A PECULIAR interest attaches to the story of German playing cards, partly because of the assiduity with which the early makers plied their craft, so that their cards flooded the markets of other countries; partly because of the eminence of some of the artists whose beautifully designed and executed cards have come down to us, rare and fragile and lovely old prints of the fifteenth and sixteenth centuries; and partly because Germany was the scene of that momentous invention, the printing press, and of the first European prints from wood blocks. The probability that these very first prints were playing cards, as many authorities believe, leads us into long and devious lanes of conjecture.

FROM 'DAS GULDIN SPIL,' OF INGOLD, A DOMINICAN MONK, 1472

In a book printed in 1472, 'Das Guldin Spil,' of Ingold, the assertion is made that cards were brought into Germany very early in the fourteenth century, probably by soldiers returning under the Emperor Henry VII, after depredations upon Rome. Cards are mentioned in the archives of Nürnberg, between the years 1380 and 1384. From 1392 there are certain and many references to playing cards in the guild books and registers of the German towns. Particularly in Nürnberg, Augsburg, and Ulm are recorded early in the fifteenth century both the names of card-makers and card-painters. A Kartenmacher (card-maker) is frequently on the same page with a Kartenmaler (card-painter), showing that there was a distinction between the two branches of the art, though, like the barbers and surgeons of those days, both belonged to the same guild. The names of many women occur in the town books of Nürnberg as card-painters, between 1423 and 1477.

THE PAINTED CARDS OF STUTTGART, 1440
The queen of hounds and the under valet of ducks

Perhaps the very earliest German cards we know are some that were painted at Stuttgart not later than 1440. They are very large, 7″ × 4″, and are a hunting series with dogs, stags, ducks, and falcons for suit signs. This was a typically German idea, and it recalls a story of the homesick young Florentine who was serving as secretary to Frederick at the German court. He complained that the people of this north country were barbarians, who cared only about the chase, and for poetry, not at all. Nevertheless, there is more than a little of the feeling of the Renaissance in these lovely old cards. The ten of each suit is a banner, bearing the suit sign. In the suits of stags and dogs, the court cards are all ladies, charming little figures in the costumes of the early fifteenth century. She who corresponds to the under valet (this is a pack of fifty-two cards, ten numerals, and three court cards to each suit, like ours of to-day) stands in a garden, in one instance with a fawn, in the other with a hound. She who takes the place of the upper valet is a very great lady, indeed. She caresses her fawn in one suit and the great leaping dog in the other. The queens are seated upon stately thrones, but are young and utterly lovely.

THE PAINTED CARDS OF STUTTGART, 1440
The banner and king of falcons

In the suit of ducks the under valet is a prince dressed in rich velvet and feeding a duck in the pond. The upper valet is a young prince, too, with broad lace collar, and he holds up triumphantly the ducks he has killed. The king is mounted and carries a banner, bearing his suit sign. The king of falcons is also young, and rides proudly with his falcon on his wrist. The upper valet is a knight talking to his falcon, and the under valet is the falcon itself.

It does not seem possible that cards could have been produced in the quantities they were, by painting and stenciling alone. Early fifteenth-century records in the guild books of Ulm tell of the exporting of cards in hogsheads. In 1441, we find the card-makers of Venice appealing to the Senate against the importation of playing cards 'whereby our art is brought to total decay.' In looking about for another and quicker medium for our busy German Kartenmacher, prints from wood blocks naturally present themselves.

German authorities believe the first wood engravers were Karten-machers; that the monks, observing the wide distribution of cards, adopted the same size and form and printed the beloved and revered 'Little Saints' and sacred symbols, which are among the very earliest prints that have

THE PAINTED CARDS OF STUTTGART, 1440
The two and queen of stags

come down to our day. Perhaps this is the explanation of why the name of wood engraver does not appear upon the burgess books until the middle of the fifteenth century, while that of card-maker is common thirty years earlier.

It has been said that the Germans learned of wood-block printing from merchants who came from China to Russia by way of Arabia and the Red Sea. The Chinese process bears an exact resemblance to that of the early German wood engraver. Marco Polo describes the making of paper money in Chambulu, 'some of the value of a small penny, some of a Venetian silver groat.' He tells how 'the principal officer of the great Cham smears with cinnabar the seal consigned to him and imprints it upon the money so that the figure of the seal, coloured in cinnabar, remains impressed upon it.'

Among the early German cards of great artistic merit that have come down to us is a series of 'Cartes à Ensignées Animées,' which are described by both Bartsch and Passavant and attributed variously to the Master of 1466, to the Master of the Playing Cards, and to the Master of the Monogram E.S. There were doubtless several sets of these, for the cards vary greatly in size and shape. In one series the suit signs are bears, lions, stags, birds, and flowers and leaves, the leaves being little faun-like creatures; scattered remnants of similar series are frogs, dogs, rabbits, leopards, dragons, and other mythical monsters. The numeral cards of these series are thought to have run from one to nine in each suit, besides which there were three court cards, either a king, queen, and knave, or else a king and

CARTES À ENSIGNÉES ANIMÉES
A nine of birds is shown

SAINT JOHN THE BAPTIST, SUPPOSED TO BE ONE
OF A SERIES OF PLAYING CARDS OF A GERMAN
MONASTERY, 1450–1460

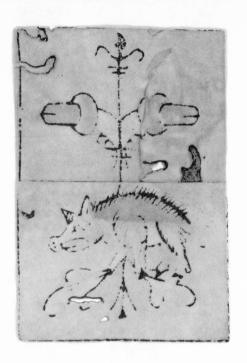

GERMAN PLAYING CARDS PRINTED FROM WOOD BLOCKS AT AUGSBURG NOT LATER
THAN 1460

The two of acorns, the six of hearts, the ten or banner of bells, and the under valet of leaves
are shown.

an upper and a lower knave. The diversity of the suit signs is explained, since cards were made by hand in those days according to the desire of the purchaser, who had put upon them any signs that pleased his personal

fancy. The court cards are in the costumes worn at court, and in one series, in which there is a suit of escutcheons, the king, with three fleurs de lys on his banner, is said by Passavant to represent Charles VII of France. There is also a suit of helmets, which from its size would seem to belong to this set of cards. These are all engraved from copper plates, and the animals on each card show not only a variety of attitudes, but different types.

The Round Cards of Cologne are another famous series which Passavant describes under 'Le Maître des Cartes à jouer de forme ronde': 'The originals of these cards are to be ranked among the finer engravings, au burin, of the fifteenth century.

CARTES À ENSIGNÉES ANIMÉES
A king of fleur de lys, who is supposed to be
Charles VII

The inscription, "Salve Felix Colonia," accompanied by three crowns which is on the titled wrapper, informs us that these cards had their origin at Cologne. We must conclude at the same time that they appeared between the years 1461–83, if we accept the figure of the mounted king of columbines as representing Louis XI of France, who reigned at that period. Up to the present time we have re-

THE ROUND CARDS OF COLOGNE, 1470
The queen of parrots, the valet of roses, and the king of columbines, who is supposed to be Louis XI

mained in ignorance as to the master who executed these engravings, and, further, it is almost impossible to point out any other engraving which could be safely attributed to him. His manner resembles that of John of Cologne, from Zwolle, though it cannot be said to be identical with it in details.'

There are five suits, hares, parrots, pinks, columbines, and roses. It is supposed that the fifth suit was intended to replace one of the others at the owner's desire. There are thirteen cards in each suit, the king, queen, and valet, and ten numerals. There is an inscription in Latin on the ace of each suit. The kings and queens are richly caparisoned little figures on horse-back, while the valets are men-at-arms. They are much more Flemish in character than German.

There is a third series of cards, some of which are attributed to Israel von Meckenen and others to Schöngauer. The pack consists of fifty-two cards, with the Italian suit signs of cups, swords, and batons, but with a suit of pomegranates replacing the usual one of coins. They are engraved from copper plates with a goldsmith-like technique. The designs on the two of batons and the three of swords are described by Bartsch as Schön-gauer's work. The honors of each suit are king, queen, and valet. The pomegranate is supposed to be in honor of Philip the Fair, who, after his marriage to the daughter of Ferdinand and Isabella of Spain, and his sub-sequent victory over Granada, adopted it as his emblem. The figure cards are much better in design and execution than the others. The kings sit on impressive Gothic thrones, the queens are slender and regally gowned, and the valets are mounted. The ten of each suit is a banner.

The most beautiful cards of all are those of Vergil Solis, a goldsmith of Nürnberg; these are very rare, and ours is said to be the only complete series known. Again, there are fifty-two cards in a pack, and the suit signs are lions, monkeys, peacocks, and parrots. Each ace bears the monogram of the artist. The honors are king, queen, and valet. The cards, particu-larly the numerals, are examples of most exquisite conventional design.

There is also a series of engraved cards, attributed to Hans Beham, and one by Jost Ammon, a delightful series published in a small volume, 'The Book of Trades.' There is a moralizing verse below each card design. The four suits are books, printers' balls, wine-pots, and drinking-cups, and the humor for which the artist was famous is discernible in almost every one.

We have also a complete set of thirty-six small trappola cards, one and three quarters by one and a half inches, printed from silver plates early in the seventeenth century. The suit signs are hearts, bells, acorns, and leaves, with whimsical arrangements of animals and little figures on each one, very reminiscent of Jost Ammon. An early German monogram is on the six of leaves, and the court cards are king, queen, and knave. The tens

CARDS ATTRIBUTED TO VON MECKENEN AND SCHÖNGAUER, 1500

The three and nine of swords, the valet of cups, the two and ten of batons, and the
ace of pomegranates are shown.

(95)

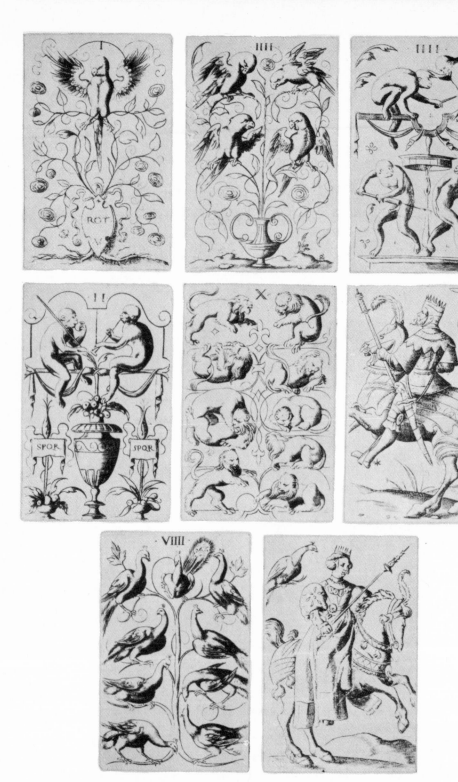

PLAYING CARDS OF VERGIL SOLIS, EARLY SIXTEENTH CENTURY

Ut quondam Amphion fera traxit carmine saxa
  Grata movens homini gaudia, grata Deo:
Haud aliter facimus. Tu vivas mœstus in ævum,
  Munera qui spernis nostra, Melancholice.

Weil ich dien den kunsten frey
Mit Bucher binden mancherley,
Hoff ich man werd mich schatzen gleich
Ein Gliedlein in dess Phoebi Reich,
Hut dich, veracht nicht schlechtes ding,
Schaw vor was es für nutzung bring.

Du hast gewonnen edler Hort,
Ich will nun dein sein hic und dort.
Da lebet Gott, wo Mann vnd Weib
Zwen menschen sein, ein Seel, ein Leib.

PLAYING CARDS FROM 'THE BOOK OF TRADES,' BY JOST AMMON

(97)

are banners, and there are in addition the two, six, seven, eight, and nine of each suit. Trappola came out of Italy, a better game of chance than the old tarots, just as piquet followed them in France.

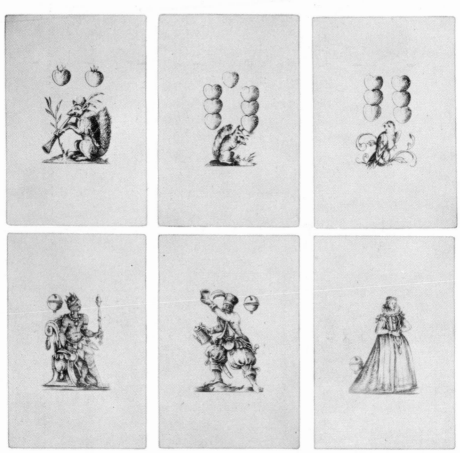

PLAYING CARDS, FROM SILVER PLATES BY GEORGES HEINRICH BLEICH
SEVENTEENTH CENTURY

It is interesting to see that all of these early German cards are numeral series, all, with the exception of the last, packs of fifty-two, and not the old tarots. These, of course, were not the cards made in great quantities, but were *de luxe* editions for the chosen few.

The cards that called forth such protest in Venice, without doubt had Italian suit signs and in all details conformed to the Italian standards.

We have forty-five cards of a pack of fifty-two, of the ordinary playing cards of the fifteenth century, with the conventional German suit signs of hearts, bells, leaves, and acorns. These must have been made in very large quantities, and were correspondingly cheap, and therefore not treasured,

Top left: Bohemian, 1664 (see p. 146A); *top right:* German, 18th century (see p. 124B); *bottom left:* German, early 17th century (see p. 124A); *bottom right:* German, *c.* 1750 (see p. 146B).

Top left: Italian, 1664 (see p. 232A); *top right:* Italian, early 18th century (see p. 226B); *bottom left:* Russian, 1830 (see p. 272B); *bottom right:* English, 1678 (see p. 176B).

so that to-day they are almost the hardest of all cards to find. A similar but less complete series were found by a Dr. Stukeley, and are in the Schreiber collection of cards in the British Museum. There are also some stenciled cards of this time in the British Museum collection, and thirty-one similar cards from wood blocks in the Royal Library at Berlin. Ours were found recently in the original binding of a Concilienbuch von Konstanz, Ulrich von Reichenthal, Augsburg, Sorg, 1483.

The binding had a typical Ulm appearance, and so we presume that our playing cards were printer's waste from some Ulm card-maker. The aces and the three, four, and five of hearts and the four of acorns are missing, and there are two fives of bells. Singer, in his 'Researches into the History of Playing Cards,' says: 'In the library of the Stadt house at Ulm was an old manuscript chronicle of that city finished in 1474, under the rubric of which was written the following memorandum, "Playing cards were sent in large bales into Italy, Sicily, and other parts by sea, getting in exchange spices and other merchandise." By this it may be seen how numerous the card-makers and painters dwelling here must have been.'

Our cards are from wood blocks, on early paper, slightly wormed. The two of each suit shows a boar each in a different attitude. In the other packs, the Stukeley, and the one in Berlin, there is a unicorn, or white hart couchant, as Singer calls it. He refers to it as the emblem of Richard II and infers some sort of connection. On these other packs, besides the animal, there are a crossed hammer and axe, which may have been a sort of coat of arms or crest, for later cards often carry the crests of the towns in Saxony. The six of hearts of our series shows a smiling fox with an unfortunate gosling in its mouth, and the nine a long-tailed and ferocious cat, while falcons perch upon the banners in each suit. These banners are interesting to compare with those of the Stuttgart cards and the equally decorative ones of the later series with the pomegranate suit. All the other fifteenth-century German cards from wood blocks have ten spots instead of banners.

The upper and under valet of each suit in our series is a knight, sometimes with a sword, sometimes with a swashbuckling cloak. In the Stukeley cards the knave of acorns is shooting a crossbow. Singer suggests that he is after the white hart on the two; also the archers were drawn from the peasantry, of which the suit of acorns is emblematic, though after all it may have been merely a happen-so and a vagary of the old-time maker. At any rate, it is a pleasing little variation.

The kings are seated on thrones in the Italian manner. This is true of the other series from wood blocks and stencils, as well as of the pomegranate cards and the Cartes à Ensignées Animées. In the round cards of Cologne and the Stuttgart cards, the kings are on horseback. In all of

these fifteenth-century packs from wood blocks, the aces are missing, yet
all the more carefully made cards of the time show them in packs of fifty-
two cards. For trappola there were thirty-six cards to a pack, one, two,
seven, eight, nine, ten, and three court cards to each suit, and it was not
until the eighteenth century that the aces were generally omitted, making
a pack contain only thirty-two cards. There is no game that we know of
calling for forty-eight cards and no contemporary description of any such
pack or game, yet we find many cards in the next century, seemingly without aces.

Our little fifteenth-century cards are hand-colored, in pinks and greens
that have faded in the long years that have passed.

Early sixteenth-century cards printed from wood blocks and colored
with stencils were found, like the earlier French cards, making up the

LANDSKNECHTS PLAYING AT CARDS
From a print by Anthony of Worms, 1529

boards of a sixteenth-century book.
These have the German suit signs
of hearts, for the Church; hawks
or bells, for the nobles (the hawks
were emblematic of the chase, and
the bells were a favorite decoration on court costumes); leaves for
the husbandmen or citizens, and
acorns for the foresters or peasants.
There are three court cards to
each suit, king, upper and under
knave, and nine numerals, making
forty-eight cards in all.

The national game of lansquenet
is played with trappola cards, or
thirty-six of the usual pack of
fifty-two. It is a very simple game,
and a print by Anthony of Worms,
dated 1529, shows two soldiers
playing it. Its name comes from
Landsknecht, a foot soldier with
a lance, and it is supposed to have
originated among the soldiers of
the disbanded troops who were
wandering about the provinces of Upper Germany toward the end of the
fifteenth century. The card on the table looks more like a five of the
French suit of carreaux than like a five of hearts, which, of course, might
be either French or German.

Another is a print of the year 1500, entitled 'Le Grand Bal.' In one corner it shows the Duke and Duchess of Bavaria, who have retired from the gayety into a recess, where they sit at a table playing cards. Each one keeps a chalked score on the table.

'LE GRAND BAL,' 1500

A print by Israel von Meckenen shows a very animated card game between a lady and a gentleman. They both have on the long pointed shoes that were worn at court at the end of the fifteenth century.

Then there is one which has a lengthy title — 'In the year 1452 in consequence of a sermon delivered in the public place opposite the chapel of Our Lady of Nürnberg, by Cardinal John Capistran, 76 shovel boards, 2640 tric-tracs (which were checker boards), 40,000 dice, and a great heap of packs of cards, as likewise a variety of trinkets and objects of vanity, were burnt in the market-place.'

From all of which it seems that the Germans were card-makers for other countries, as well as making cards for their own with their national suit signs of hearts, bells, leaves, and acorns, which perhaps came into being about the time the French evolved their cœurs, piques, trèfles, and carreaux.

Besides being the great early makers of 'cards for playing,' they have the distinction of having the most ancient of all the educational games at

cards. It was devised by a Franciscan monk, Thomas Murner. He was
born at Strassburg, and taught philosophy, first at Cracovie, then at Fribourg, at the beginning of the sixteenth century. An interesting account

AN EARLY PRINT OF ISRAEL VON MECKENEN

of this game is given in the 'Mémoires de Dom Calmet, abbé de Senones,'
published in 1728. He says: 'This monk, teaching philosophy at Cracovie
and then at Fribourg in Switzerland, perceived that his young pupils had
great difficulty in understanding the writings of a Spaniard that were given
them to study. He resolved to try a new method, by pictures and figures,
in the form of a game of cards, so that the pleasure of playing would make
the pupils surmount all the difficulties of this intricate study. This he did
with such success that the great doctors of the University of Cracovie
said that in the beginning this Father was suspected of employing magic
because his pupils made such extraordinary progress. And to justify himself he was obliged to produce this new game for the eyes of the great doc-

tors themselves who not only approved but greatly admired the method of the good monk.'

These cards come in book form. Our copy, which is from the Didot Library, contains the fifty-two full-page wood cuts of these cards, and is excessively rare. The full title of the book is 'Logica memorativa Char-

JOHN CAPISTRAN DENOUNCING WORLDLY VANITIES
NÜRNBERG, 1452

tiludium logice, siue totius dialectice memoria: & nouus Petri hyspani textus emendatus: Cum iucundo pictasmatis exercitio: Eruditi viri.f. Thome Murner Argentini: ordinis minor: theologie doctoris eximii.' Below this on the title-page is the printer's device on a shield, between the Eagle of Saint John and the Lion of Saint Mark. The printer's name occurs at the very end of the book; 'Nobis quoque quam plurimam gratiam referes: Necnon Joanni Adelpho: viro fecundum cor nostrum: huius operis castigatore: quod Argentine industrius vir Joannes Gruninger impressit. Anno a Cristi saluatoris natiuitate M.D.IX. Ipsa die diui Thome Cantuaeiensis.'

On the fly-leaf of our copy is written, 'Jeu de Cartes inventé par Thomas Murner, professeur de l'Université de Cracovie, pour servir à l'enseignement de la Logique: Strasbourg, 1509, 2me édition non moins rare que la Ière qui est de Cracovie, 1507. Rien de plus bisarre peut-être, et toutefois, rien de plus curieux que cette fantaisie doctorale, dont l'auteur faillit d'être brûlé comme sorcier. C'est la plus ancien exemple connu de l'application du jeu de cartes à l'instruction élémentaire.

Logica
memoratiua

Chartiludiũ logice/ſiue totius
dialectice memoria:& nouũs Petri hyſpani tex
tus emendatus:Cum iucundo pictaſmatis
exercitio:Eruditi virt .ſ.Thome
Murner Argẽtini: ordi
nis minoꝝ:theolo
gie doctoris
eximij.

TITLE-PAGE OF THE 'LOGICA MEMORATIVA' OF THOMAS MURNER
STRASSBURG, 1509

(104)

'Mes Nouvelles Etudes historiques sur les Cartes à jouer. Paris. 1842.'

There is a prologue dated 1508, an exordium, and the signs of the tractatus or suits, which are sixteen, and are bells, lobsters, fish, acorns, scorpions,
caps, hearts, grasshoppers, suns, stars, birds, moons, cats, shields, crowns,
and serpents. Then comes the 'Modus
ludendi' and 'Noticia materie,' and
then the 'Typus Logice,' a full-page
allegorical wood cut; then a 'Modus
Practicandi' of four pages, and then a
full description of each card and its
significance; then an 'Exercitium Se-
cunda pars'; and finally a sort of epilogue by Master Joannes de Glogovia
of the University of Cracovie, and Canon
of Saint Florian at Clepardia, testify-
ing to the usefulness of Murner's work
and how highly it has been approved,
and telling, besides, that the author had
received from the Université a gift of
twenty-four Hungarian florins. The
fifty-two quaint little engravings are
boldly done and most curious and interesting wood cuts. The type is exceedingly beautiful.

ONE OF THE CARDS FROM THE 'LOGICA
MEMORATIVA' OF THOMAS MURNER
STRASSBURG, 1509

One hundred and twenty years after
the publication of Murner's cards a new
edition was published at Paris by Jean
Balesdens, a French advocate, who
dedicates the book to the Cardinal de
la Valette. The prints of the cards are reduced in size, and some of the
costumes are altered to be in keeping with contemporary styles. In the
'conclusio operis' the printer's name is given as Thomas Vandvoot in
Bruxelles, 'Anno a Christi Saluatoris natiuitate 1509. Ipsa die diui
Augustini Episcopi.'

There must, therefore, have been three editions of these cards, the first at
Cracovie in 1507, the second at Strassburg, and the one at Brussels from
which the Paris edition was taken.

In 1518, Murner published another set of cards, also in book form, this
time to teach the Institutes of Justinian. The title is 'Chartiludium Institute summarie,' printed at Strassburg by Johannes Priis, at the expense
of Johannes Knoblauch. The form is similar to that of the first game, but
there are twelve suits of ten cards each in this game. The first card of each

suit is the figure of some German ruler. The suit signs are falcons, bells, combs, acorns, hearts, crowns, buckets, church bells, bellows, beads, shields, fish, and knives.

'Das Geistliche Deutsche Carten Spil,' of Andream Strobl, was published in Sulzbach in 1603, with many approvals by high church digni-

A CARD FROM THOMAS MURNER'S 'CHARTILUDIUM INSTITUTE SUMMARIE, STRASSBURG, 1518

taries. Each of the eight cards of the four suits of hearts, bells, leaves, and acorns are represented in Biblical illustrations with a decorative border, and the suit sign unobtrusively but unfailingly shown. They are finely engraved from copper plates, and there are nearly three hundred pages of text for each suit. The book is on beautiful early paper and bound in oak boards covered with pigskin, and has clasps.

A series of astronomical cards, published in Nürnberg in 1656, is interesting. We have only seven of these. They are uncolored wood-block prints, and show the orbits of the sun, the moon, the earth, and Venus, Saturn, Mars, and Mercury. The astronomical drawing occupies most of the card,

THE UPPER VALET OF LEAVES, FROM THE BOOK OF BIBLICAL
PLAYING CARDS OF ANDREAM STROBL, SULZBACH, 1603

but there is an explanation in German below each one. There is a little book of instructions, which has one curious little illustration, two separate little engraved discs, one representing the earth and the other its orbit, loosely sewn to the page in a space left for it.

There is a later astronomical series of Nürnberg designed by Johann Philipp Andrae, a mathematician, in 1719. There is a title card and a frontispiece card, the other fifty-two having the usual German suit signs in addition to a conventional representation of a constellation, and its de-

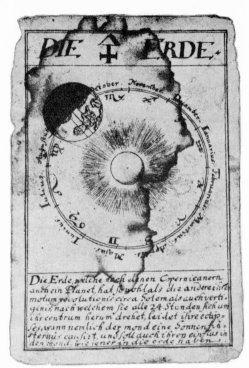

AN ASTRONOMICAL PLAYING CARD, FROM A
SERIES MADE IN NÜRNBERG IN 1656

GEOGRAPHICAL CARDS OF NÜRNBERG, SHOWING MAPS OF THE WORLD, 1640

CANIS MINOR ET MONOCEROS.

Der Hund hat ü. Stern. deren 1. der ersten 2. der dritten . 1. der fünfften . 8. der sechsten grösse . das Einhorn bestehet aus 21. Sterne. davon 2. der dritten. 10. der vierten . 5. der fünfften . 4. der sechsten grösse zu sehen .

PEGASUS ET EQUULEUS.

Hat 23 Sterne. deren 3. der andern . 3. der dritten . 6. der vierten. 3. der fünfften . 8. der sechsten grösse zu sehen . Equuleus ist zu beschauen mit 6. Stern. der vierten grösse .

DER ☉ KÖNIG.

♉ DER STEINBOCK

Hat ♑ 38 Sterne, deren 5. der dritten grösse . 2. der vierten. ü. der fünfften: 15. der sechsten. und 3. Nebulose . hin und wieder an dem Leib ausgetheilet zu ersehen. ist das Winter Gestirn an welchem sich die ☉ am weitesten von uns gewendet .

DAS ☽ DAUS.

ORION.

Gebildet durch 63. Sterne deren 1. der ersten . 4. der andern, 4. der dritten . 16. der vierten. 20. der fünfften 17. der sechsten grösse zu bemercken.

ASTRONOMICAL PLAYING CARDS MADE AT NÜRNBERG, 1719

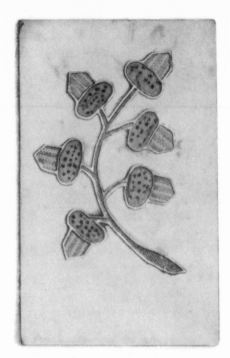

TRAPPOLA CARDS OF THE EARLY EIGHTEENTH CENTURY, THE PRINTED DESIGN
EXQUISITELY COVERED WITH SILK APPLIQUÉ

scription according to the Copernican system, but with German names instead of the usual Latin ones. The cards are colored by hand.

We have another copy of this game in which the title card is missing. Mr. Clulow dates this series 1685.

GEOGRAPHICAL CARD OF NÜRNBERG, SHOWING MAP OF EUROPE, 1678

There are two series of geographical cards from Nürnberg in the last half of the seventeenth century. They are both packs of fifty-two cards with French suit signs which occupy the upper margin of the card. The rest of the card is taken up with a map. The first series are maps of different parts of the world, and no other example of these cards is known.

They are so similar in form to the second series, which are maps of countries in Europe, that they were probably made by the same maker. There is a Mercator's Projection on the ace of spades and the signatures, 'J. H. Seyfrid delineavit. Wilhelm Pfann sculpsit.' Pfann's name is also on the ace of clubs and diamonds. They were printed in Nürnberg by Johann Hoffmann in 1678, and they are said to have been invented by Johann Pretorius.

There is a series of cards made in Augsburg in 1685 by Johann Stridbeck, the suits being warriors, philosophers, celebrities, and poets. There is a portrait head in a round medallion at the top of each card, and a description in German below. There are, besides, French suit signs, the designating numeral or initial being placed within the mark itself. The cards are from copper plates, uncolored.

FAMOUS PERSONAGES
An historical card game by Johann Stridbeck, Augsburg, 1685

Almost a century later nearly the same thing is done again, but this time

GERMAN HISTORICAL CARDS, 1765

the portraits are of characters in German history. They begin with Charlemagne and end with Joseph II. The cards are very large and the portraits are roughly engraved.

There is also a German edition of the 'Reines Renommées' of della Bella, in which the description is in German. They lack the delicacy of the French series and the suit signs are also a departure from the originals. They were published in Germany about 1655.

An heraldic series of Nürnberg cards of 1693 show the arms of the reigning families in Europe. The descriptions are in German, while the suit signs are French. The arms on the chevalier of spades indicate the relation of Germany to Spain at the time, for they bear the legend, 'Die Spanischen Reiche in Italie.'

There is an Augsburg edition of the Daumont heraldry, an uncut sheet duplicating the Paris edition, except that the Reglemens du Jeu are also given in German. A later edition of these cards, issued in 1719, are separate cards, with the text on the court cards in German. The designs of the originals are exactly reversed in this series and the results as to the heraldry are rather absurd.

CALLIGRAPHIC PLAYING CARDS MADE BY JOHANN CHRISTOPH ALBRECHT NÜRNBERG, 1769

HERALDIC PLAYING CARDS, NÜRNBERG, 1693

(111)

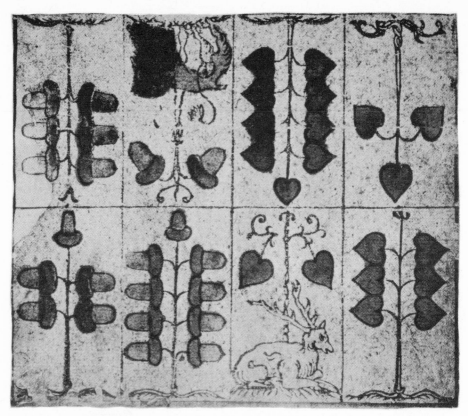

UNCUT SHEET OF PLAYING CARDS FROM SOUTH GERMANY, 1556

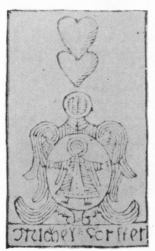

PLAYING CARDS OF MICHAEL FORSTER
SOUTH GERMANY, 1610

VALET OF HEARTS BY MICHAEL
FORSTER, OF MUNICH, 1723

(112)

Cards with the German suit signs show an infinite variety of designs and arrangement. We have an uncut sheet of early stenciled cards which are typical of those in common use. On the two of leaves is a stag, on the two of acorns a lion, on the two of bells a boar, and on the two of hearts a bear. This is a trappola series of thirty-six cards, and the decoration of the two spots is still a characteristic of the cards made for that game. The date, 1556, is on the three of hearts.

UNCUT SHEET OF PLAYING CARDS FROM FRANKFORT, 1585

There are also uncut sheets of cards printed in blue outline from ancient wood blocks. The two and six of hearts bear the name 'Michael Forster.' The designs are very crude and they were probably made early in the seventeenth century. Later designs of court cards, more approaching the French standards, also bear the name of 'Michael Forster in München.' Perhaps two generations or more elapsed between the making of the first sheet and the second ones. The latter are doubtless the work of the Michael Forster who plied his craft early in the eighteenth century.

Another sheet of card proofs in heavy blue outline contains forty-eight little cards two and one eighth by one and five eighth inches. The court cards are king and two knaves, the upper and the under being distinguishable by whether the suit sign is turned up or down. The drawing is childishly simple, and yet there is an animation about the little figures that the German cards often lack. The ace of each suit is a banner flaunting the suit sign, and there is also a flying bird on each one. There is a wild boar on each two spot and a crouching dog on the eight of hearts. The cards were probably made in the last quarter of the seventeenth century.

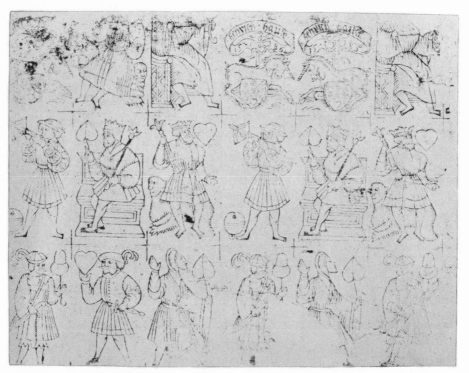

PLAYING CARDS OF HEINRICH HAUK, INNSBRUCK, 1586

A pack of trappola cards of the early eighteenth century have their printed design exquisitely covered with silk appliqué. The colors are so delicate and harmonious and lovely that the little court cards, a king with flowing robes and two knaves to a suit, are quite regal in spite of wretched drawing. The decorative flowers on the numerals, as well as the suit signs themselves, are charming.

A card sheet of the middle of the eighteenth century, with one of the

MUNICH PLAYING CARDS, *c.* 1680

kings lettered 'Im Regensburg,' shows court cards carefully worked out to the smallest detail. There are kings, queens, cavaliers, and knaves. The queens are particularly interesting, being in the costume of the time.

These are followed by many sheets of proofs of cards made by Andreas Benedictus Gobl, a most prolific card-maker of Munich during the second half of the eighteenth century. There is an amazing variety of types among his court cards. Sometimes the queens are homely German house-wives with a crown stuck dowdily and at a precarious angle at the back of their heads. And the knaves are stolid and staid German youths. There are several examples of double head cards among these eighteenth-century ones. Often the cavaliers are almost Oriental-looking, with Indian turbans, long drooping mustaches, and loose jacquard coats.

PLAYING CARDS BY SEBASTIEN FOJA, AUGSBURG, 1721

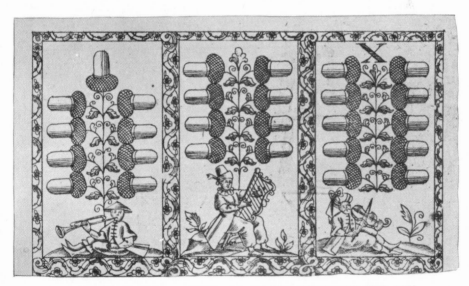

TRAPPOLA CARDS MADE AT MUNICH BY ANDREAS BENEDICTUS GOBL, 1750

Most of the styles are elaborately copied from those in vogue at court, to the smallest detail, and the little figures, though wooden, are not conventionalized as in the French cards. Some of the court cards have profiles amusingly like those of the House of Hapsburg. The numeral cards are all decorated with strange little figure groupings, evidently borrowed from the idea of Jost Ammon, but rarely with any of his whimsical touch, though with great diversity of subjects. The high powdered head-dresses of the French

TRAPPOLA CARDS BY CONRAD JEGEL, NÜRNBERG, 1800

court are shown in one series, and in many the stiff little queens carry equally stiff and absurd little parasols or flowers or fans.

A pack of trappola cards of 1805 are square, and are wood blocks colored with stencil. The coarse paper and the crude workmanship make them noticeable.

A trappola series of Conrad Jegel in Nürnberg at about the same time is much more entertaining. There is animation in the knaves and in the little figures on the numerals, and the stenciled colors are vivid and gay.

Another square series containing twenty-four cards, king, two knaves, two, nine, and ten of each suit, are also wood blocks, brightly stenciled.

NÜRNBERG TRAPPOLA CARDS BY J. E. BACKOFEN, 1813

On the two of leaves, beneath two ridiculous red birds is the date, October, 1813. On the two of acorns is the maker's name, J. E. Backofen, and beneath it a sedate and soulful lion who must be kin to the king, their expressions are so exactly the same. The lion holds the Nürnberg coat of arms.

Similar cards come from Dresden, Altenburg, Augsburg, and many another German town; none precisely alike, but with differences not individual or interesting enough and much too numerous to enumerate at length. Many have a local interest. The cards of Gratz often resemble the Swiss cards, and a series made in Goslar in 1872 show pictures of the surrounding mountain country on each numeral. The upper knaves are hunters, and the lower, serving men.

In Jena in 1876 was issued a pack of trappola cards, the suits being glands, sunflowers, leaves, and acorns of fanciful design. The two of glands shows the arms of Maximilian, the king is Maximilian himself, and the two valets his herald and one of his foot soldiers. The same idea is followed in

TRAPPOLA CARDS BY F. A. LATTMANN, GOSLAR, 1872

TRAPPOLA CARDS BY DR. T. SCHROETER, JENA, 1876

(120)

the other suits. The suit of sunflowers belongs to Rudolph of Hapsburg with an attendant bowman and squire with a falcon, and below the coat of arms is lettered 'Dr. T. Schroeter, Jena.' The suit of leaves belongs to Frederick Barbarossa and two crusaders, and Charlemagne is the king of acorns with a wandering minstrel and a trumpeter. These are lithographed cards, excellent in design and workmanship.

There are some interesting trappola cards designed in 1897 by Jules Diaz, with excellent illustrations in the manner of Jost Ammon. They are

CARTES DE FANTASIE BY JULES DIAZ, MUNICH, 1897

PLAYING CARDS OF HANS BOCK, VIENNA, 1583

(122)

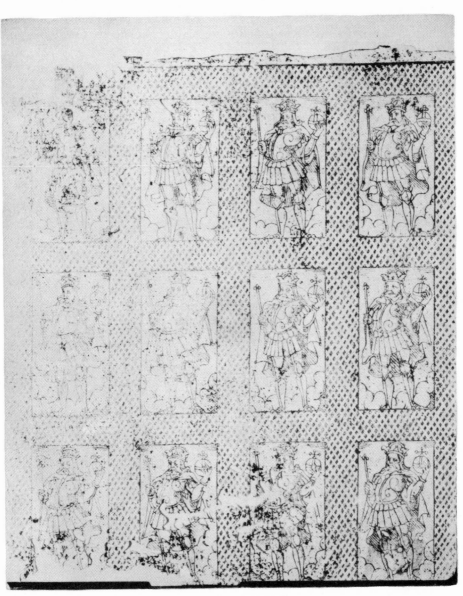

VIENNESE CARDS, 1550

(123)

done by surface printing in four colors and a rather remarkable effect is secured by using a broad line. The drawing is vigorous and the four kings are quite different, an astrologer, a jester, a fat and jovial monarch, and a lean and irritable one, and all of the eight knaves are beggars, lame and halt and blind.

Another pictorial series was lithographed in Leipzig about 1885. The cards were designed by E. Burger; the heart suit is emblematic of love, with cupids and troubadours, etc. Bells illustrate industry and commerce, leaves, the chase, and acorns, war, all in medieval Germany.

In the later German cards for trappola and skat, which are double heads, the whimsical designs on the numerals are dispensed with.

The Viennese cards are pretty much a repetition of the German ones. Many of the Bohemian packs which are made here are extremely crude in design and the colors are almost barbaric. The effect of the whole is very

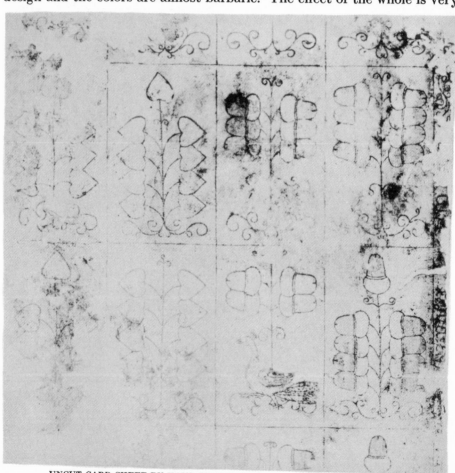

UNCUT CARD SHEET BY HANS ZELLER, KARTENMACHER ZU WIEN, 1540

PLAYING CARDS FROM THE EARLY SEVENTEENTH CENTURY, PICTURING THE CHASE
BY AN UNKNOWN GERMAN ENGRAVER

GERMAN TAROT CARDS OF THE EIGHTEENTH CENTURY

The two upper cards are atouts from an Oriental series made at a time when Chinese Chippendale was in favor. The two lower cards are from a series of Animal Tarots.

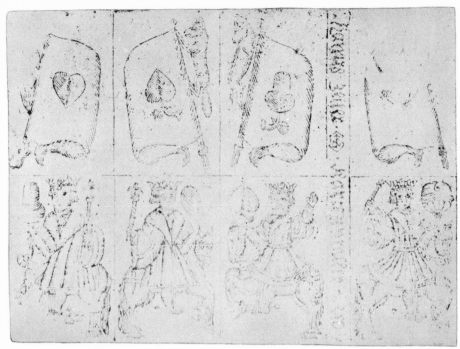

UNCUT CARD SHEET BY HANS ZELLER, KARTENMACHER ZU WIEN, 1540

striking, and seems somehow very appropriate. The court cards are almost invariably local types. Many of these cards bear the name of J. Nejedly, who was a Viennese card-maker in the middle of the nineteenth century. There is one pack of trappola cards picturing Augsburg quite delightfully, and among the cards and proof-sheets of Josef Glanz, another Viennese maker of about 1860, there are many examples of Swiss cards as well as the Bohemian with the German suit signs.

Of cards with the French suit signs in these German lands, there are many. The earliest one we have is a pack of fifty-two cards, from copper plates and colored by hand, and most of them bear the monogram of an unknown artist. Besides the suit signs arranged in the usual manner they picture a day's hunting across the field and through the forests of early seventeenth-century Germany. The kings and valets are debonair gentlemen and the queens gracious little ladies. No other example of these cards is known to exist.

By the middle of the eighteenth century we find great numbers of tarot packs being made in Germany. Curiously enough, the suit signs of the numeral cards are invariably French. The character of the atouts is quite changed, and, instead of the old emblematic designs, anything that appeals to the maker's fancy seems to be used. Animal tarots were very popular.

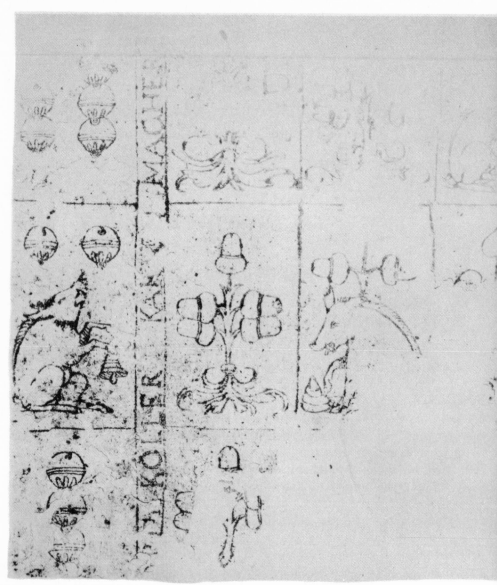

UNCUT CARD SHEET BY KOLLER, KARTENMACHER ZU WIEN, 1550

(126)

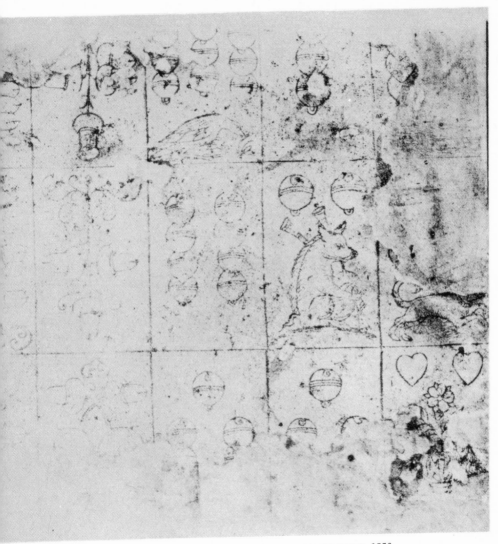

UNCUT CARD SHEET BY KOLLER, KARTENMACHER ZU WIEN, 1550

(127)

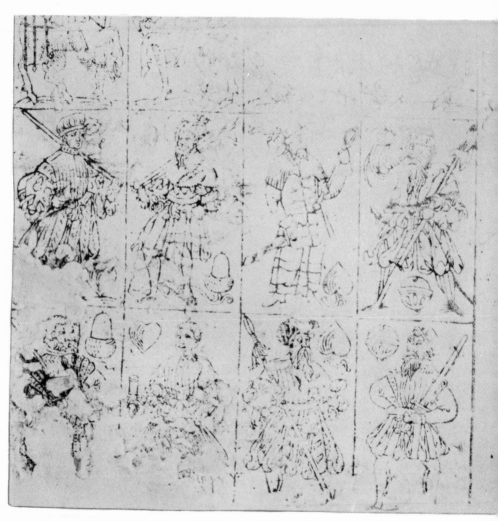

UNCUT CARD SHEET BY HANS BOCK, KARTENMACHER ZU WIEN, 1560

(128)

UNCUT SHEET, DESIGN FOR CARD BACKS, VIENNA, 1550

Most of these are legendary beasts, and an invariable palm tree in the background and the coloring gives them an Oriental flavor. They are not named — perhaps because words failed when their makers tried to do it, but they are numbered with large Roman numerals, often at both top and bottom. Only the mat or fou of the old atouts keeps something of his original design and is still unnumbered. The court cards, king, queen, cavalier, and knave for each suit, are affable little German families. Andreas Benedictus Gobl, of Munich, made a great variety of these tarot series.

Some of the series of animal atouts are interspersed with elephants with howdahs and gentlemen on camels elegantly carrying parasols, which still further add to the Eastern atmosphere. Some of these atouts are double heads, with most uncomfortable-looking results. Sometimes the atouts picture a chase and show hunters with horns and falcons and dogs and horses.

There is a series of animal tarots of about 1770 in which the outline is printed so vaguely from wood blocks as to be negligible. The colors are stenciled and are very soft. The cards are probably the work of some South German card-maker.

There is a little decorative border around each of the cards of a tarot

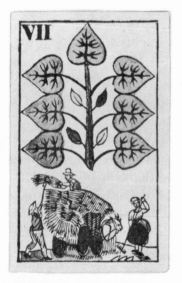

BOHEMIAN TRAPPOLA CARDS BY J. NEJEDLY, VIENNA, 1855

TYPICAL COURT CARDS OF EIGHTEENTH CENTURY GERMAN TAROTS, MADE BY ANDREAS
BENEDICTUS GOBL, OF MUNICH, 1750

MUSICAL TAROTS BY P. F. ULRICH, LEIPZIG, 1780

series made by Joseph Fetscher, of Munich. The cards are double heads, and the design and the coloring are both very nice.

The most beautifully done of all these curious little series is one printed from copper plates and colored by hand. With their little Oriental figures they are reminiscent of Chinese Chippendale which was having its vogue just at this time.

There is a series of musical tarots of 1780 in which the atouts show music and scenes from the popular operas of the day. The court cards are characters from the operas, and on the valet on foot of trèfles is the name of the maker, P. F. Ulrich, of Leipzig.

A pack of tarots with court cards of the Bavarian type, which are said to have belonged to Marie Louise, the wife of Napoleon, have very amusing animal atouts. The IV is a camel with two blue legs and two brown ones, which give him the effect of wearing leggings; V is the fox of the fairy story with the nine handsome tails, each a different color, VI is a wolf, also in leggings eating a bright blue lamb; and XIII is a crocodile with red spots on his green armor, devouring an unhappy victim, whose blue trousers and red legs are still to be seen. This pack is from wood blocks and the designs are very crude. They must have distressed Napoleon, and it seems odd that such a thing should have found its way to court. Delightful things were being done by card-makers at this time. A beautifully engraved series, hand-colored, by Andreas Benedictus Gobl, of Munich, has atouts which picture a wedding party, gay little horsemen and flower-decked coaches, with explanatory verses, a couplet on each card.

WEDDING TAROTS BY ANDREAS BENEDICTUS GOBL, MUNICH, 1780

There is a pack of fifty-two cards with the French suit signs, but with court cards of the German type, with queens who carry fans and parasols. These were made about 1800 by 'Lauretz Ummer in München,' whose name is on the knave of spades.

A sheet of hand-colored proofs of court cards, for a pack commemorating the battle of Leipzig, curiously enough have the French suit signs, though the kings are medallion portraits of the kings of the allied countries, and the knaves are the marshals at the battle. The queens are Pomona, Flora, Diana, and Ceres, but in the costumes of 1813.

PIQUET CARDS OF LAURETZ UMMER, MUNICH, 1800

COURT CARDS COMMEMORATING THE BATTLE OF LEIPZIG

(133)

A second series also made in Leipzig, with the same idea in mind, show the portraits in more conventionalized card form. They are nicely engraved and the color is soft and pleasing, but they have not the charm of the earlier cards. The queen of hearts is lettered, 'Industrie Conytoir in Leipzig,' 1813.

A curious animal tarot series was made by Peter Schachner in Wels in 1816, the most curious cards being the cavaliers who ride spotted wooden hobby-horses. Ten years later, there is a series as delightful as it is unusual. The court cards and atouts are quaint little figures in Turkish costume. Every one is pictured, dervishes and dancing girls, Janissaries and porters, soldiers and sailors. The maker was H. Müller, whose name is on the knave of clubs.

Animal tarots, made in Nürnberg in 1830, show fine upstanding camels and sea serpents, defiant deer, who gaze with hauteur at the hunter's gun, and amazing porcupines with many-colored quills rampant. These are by Johann Math Backofen. There is a similar series of Franz Fasolt, of Brunn, of about the same time.

A tarot series, issued in Frankfort in 1879, pictures historic scenes and personages of all lands and times in its atouts. The court cards are also celebrities, Gordon and Louis Quatorze, Kepler, Leopold I, Charles I, Marlborough and Shakespeare. The titles of the atouts are in French. A later edition of these bears the Italian duty stamp lettered, 'Venezia.'

A series made by a rival card-maker in Frankfort at about the same time shows the typical German tarots of that time. The atouts picture domestic scenes in German life of the day, and the court cards are the conventional Bavarian ones.

During the nineteenth century the French piquet packs of fifty-two cards grow more and more numerous. In a pack of 1825, the only clues to the maker are the initials 'G. B.' in script on the knave of diamonds. The court cards are not attractive.

A series issued in 1834 have scenes of the Portuguese insurrection on each of the four aces. A similar pack made in Frankfort in 1868 pictures scenes from the lives of Peter the Great, Frederick the Great, Napoleon, and Wellington on its aces.

Another pack is a piquet series of thirty-two cards. The cards are very thick and heavy and are coarsely engraved and colored with stencil. The court cards are peasants, the kings being bowmen or men-at-arms, and the aces are each upon a shield. At the bottom of each card are two bars of the music and the accompanying words of a Thuringian folk-song. These cards were made just about the time of the French musical series.

A piquet pack of fifty-two cards, made in Württemberg about 1850, has the name of the makers, Susz and Kunze, on the knave of clubs. The

GERMAN PLAYING CARDS OF 1834, COMMEMORATING THE PORTUGUESE INSURRECTION

GERMAN MUSICAL CARDS — A TRAPPOLA PACK CONTAINING A FOLKSONG, 1840

numeral cards are stenciled and the court cards of curious design are from wood blocks.

In 1860 a maker in Hamburg, H. Rubcke, issued a series of fifty-two cards with fancy suit signs recognizable as French ones. Besides the suit signs each card pictures a scene in or near Hamburg, and the court cards are people in native costume, with the exception of the kings of spades and hearts, the former being Carolus Magnus and the latter Carolus XII.

A departure from the usual cards is an oval series made in Leipzig about 1865. The court cards are in historical costumes and there is a decorative border, a repetition of the suit sign about each one.

The court cards in all of these series retain their German character, in spite of the French suit signs. In a pack made in Frankfort about 1870,

OVAL CARDS, LEIPZIG, 1865

TAROT CARDS BY H. MÜLLER
The national costumes of Turkey, 1826

both the mien and costume of the court cards are reminiscent of the Rhine legends.

A pack, made in Frankfort about 1878, have court cards emblematic of Asia, Europe, Africa, and America. Ferdinand and Isabella and the Spanish ambassador are the American ones. The numeral cards are decorated with designs of people and incidents in the quarter of the world to which each suit is attributed.

At the end of the century the German card-makers are noted for the many beautifully lithographed series with court cards not at all conventionalized in court costumes of various lands and times. These are very similar to the French Jeu Louis XV. A series made at Goslar has genuine artistic merit and a great deal of originality. The court cards are most delightful little figures of medieval days, ladies with wimples and hennins

CAVALIER, QUEEN, AND KING OF A VIENNESE TAROT SERIES MADE IN 1820 BY MATTHIAS KOLLER

VIENNESE TAROTS BY MATTHIAS KOLLER, 1820

VIENNESE THEATER TAROTS BY UFFENHEIMER, 1827

(138)

REBUS TAROTS, BUDA-PESTH, 1832

VIENNESE POLITICAL TAROTS, 1848

(140)

MILITARY TAROTS BY T. ALBRECHT, INNSBRUCK, 1750

AN ATOUT FROM A PACK OF
KAISER TAROTS, VIENNA, 1870

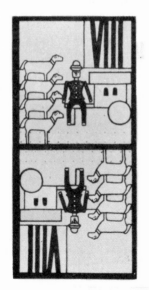

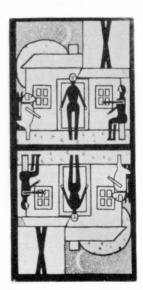

TAROTS BY DITHA MOSER, VIENNA, 1906

(141)

and kings and knights and huntsmen out of the romances of Frederick
Barbarossa and Otto of Saxony.

There are Viennese tarots as early as 1820, with court cards of a distinct
type, neither French nor German; sometimes the atouts picture scenes in
Vienna, and sometimes incidents from Sir Walter Scott's novels, when the
court cards become the best-known characters from these stories. A tarot
series from Buda-Pesth with these court cards pictures the names of the
novels in rebus form on each atout.

There are also theater tarots with atouts picturing scenes from popular
plays and operas. Many of these Viennese tarot series contain only fifty-
four cards, four numerals and four court cards to each suit, besides the
twenty-two atouts. They are known as 'Coffee-House Tarots,' and seem
to have been a local development of the old game.

A number of Viennese card-designers were noted as masters of their
craft and there are hand-painted proofs of court cards, sometimes in classic
costume, sometimes in the half-barbarous splendor of the Russian court,
sometimes lords and ladies of Vienna, veritable little miniatures — El-
finger, Pausinger, and Gigerl are three of these artists.

About 1848 a series of atouts picture a scathing political satire against
the government, and about ten years later the Crimean War is pictured.
A series from Pressburg of about the same time has atouts definitely
Chinese in character, and another pictures the wanderings of Blondel in
search of his king.

An animal tarot series by Pausinger in pen and ink are good little
studies. The variety of subjects seems inexhaustible. Viennese types in
caricature are shown in a pack of about 1860, and historical cards picturing
kings from Rudolph to Joseph II are side by side with military tarots in
which Franz Joseph and his generals appear. The so-called 'Kaiser tarots'
picture the chase in all lands and a series by Gigerl of about the same time
are caricatures of Viennese persons of fashion. A most original and delightful series was designed by Ditha Moser for the benefit of a Viennese
charity at Christmas-time, 1906. Only one hundred packs were printed.
The atouts are double heads, stiff little Noah's Ark people, animals, houses,
and trees. The court cards give the effect of stained-glass windows and
picture medieval knights, Egyptians, Assyrians, and royalties of the
sixteenth century. The numeral cards are cross-barred and bordered in
black.

The first Viennese whist cards we have are of about 1850. Two packs
come to a box, and the cards are smaller than ours of to-day, and both the
court cards and the designs of the numerals are dainty and pleasing. A few
years later the usual size piquet cards appear. We have a set of these
made of iron, in the usual colors. Presumably they were inspired by the

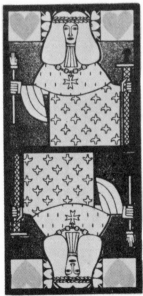
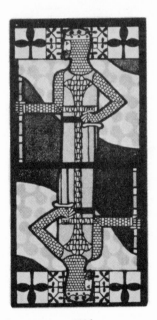

TAROTS BY DITHA MOSER, VIENNA, 1906

(143)

PIQUET CARDS BY LÖSCHENTIOHL, VIENNA, 1806

silver cards which had been used at the French court in the reign of Louis XV.

Vienna is well represented among the beautifully lithographed cards with the fancy court cards, which are found in both France and Germany. These come in all sizes, from the smallest of patience cards to the large-size piquet packs.

Among the cards with French suit signs is a pack on each numeral of which some variety of flower is daintily and carefully engraved. The suit signs are also engraved and colored by hand, and on the ace of clubs is the name of the artist, 'Chez Löschentiohl à Vienne, 1806.' He was a gold-smith whose work won him great favor with the royal family during his lifetime. The court cards are also from copper plates, full-length figures of famous personages, and two of them, the queen of hearts, Mary Stuart, and the queen of spades, Iphigenie, are signed 'Mayer,' who was a co-worker with Löschentiohl. Only two other sets of these cards are known to be in existence.

To Germany belongs the honor of the first and most famous transforma-tion cards, as are called those in which the suit signs are made to form part of the humorous design. Late in the eighteenth century it became the custom to give little pocket almanacs as New Year's gifts. These are usually bound in red morocco and contain a number of prettily engraved copies of famous pictures, sentimental anecdotes and poems, and almost invariably some of the pages, which are just about the size of a playing card, are given to designs for these transformation cards, which are some-times very clever and witty, and show great ingenuity.

In 1805, J. G. Cotta, a bookseller of Tübingen, issued a complete pack of these cards, in which the court cards picture characters from Schiller's 'Jeanne d'Arc,' while the numerals are the transformations of all sorts of subjects with no continuity or reference to each other or to the court cards.

CARDS OF 1805, ILLUSTRATING SCHILLER'S 'JEANNE D'ARC'

These were so successful that for the five succeeding years he issued other packs. In 1806 the court cards are Ulysses and other classical figures; in 1807, characters from Schiller's 'Wallenstein,' in 1808, Arabian cos-tumes; in 1809 he seems to have skipped a year; in 1810 he comes back

PIQUET CARDS, VIENNA, 1809

with court cards with mythological and comical figures, the comical ones being caricatures of Napoleon and other famous people. These are cleverly drawn and are said to be the work of Osiander. The last series, Knightly Orders, was issued in 1811. They are all beautifully engraved and hand-colored.

In Vienna the same thing was done. A series was designed by H. F. Müller in 1809, with court cards fancifully costumed, the designer's name being on the knave of diamonds. A pack of 1814 is very similar. There is an infinite variety of subjects, the designs are whimsical and interesting, and the workmanship is excellent. The court cards and the suit marks are colored by hand. The name of the artist, Johann Neidl, is on the ace of hearts, and the government stamp with the date.

A third Viennese series with court cards in classical costume is also by H. F. Müller; the spade suit illustrates a Viennese story, 'Beatrice,' and the cards originally appeared, a few at a time, in the 'Repository of Arts' for 1818–19.

Among the German cards, especially those made in Bohemia and Hungary, are many with Italian suit signs. In the early cards these suit signs are brightly stenciled in red and blue, and the cards are large, five and a half by two and a quarter inches. A trappola pack of thirty-six cards from wood blocks are interesting in design. There is expression in both the faces and attitudes of the court cards. The horses of the cavaliers are spirited and a very natural little dog barks at the heels of the ones in cups and coins. 'Prag' is lettered on the cavalier of swords. On the two of swords, after the Venetian manner, is a couplet, in German instead of Italian, and the date, 'Die Karten Ist Drum Nicht Erdacht Das Man

ABOVE: THE FIRST TWO ATOUTS OF A TAROT SERIES

BELOW: THE CAVALIER AND THE TWO OF SWORDS OF A TRAPPOLA PACK MADE IN
PRAGUE IN 1664

THE WITCH, THE CAT, THE BIRD, AND THE HORSE
From a pack of cards for 'Bird's Play,' an old game of the Rhine country, *c.* 1750

VIENNESE CARDS, 1814

(147)

TRANSFORMATION CARDS BY H. F. MÜLLER, VIENNA, 1818

These cards were very popular. They are delicately colored by hand. A set of these was given by Lafayette to one of his aides, the Marquis de Calmes, and they are still in the possession of his family, in America.

Zanck und Hader Nacht. 1664 H.S.' The maker's name is on the one of batons, 'Augustin Z. Mahler in Prag.' A series made in Prague a hundred and fifty years later, except for the discontinuance of the old couplets on the twos, and a substitution of double heads as court cards, shows practically no changes, and is another example of the persistence of the old forms in this craft.

The many later examples of these trappola cards, made in Trieste and Vienna, conform more and more to the modern Italian type. There are also occasional tarot series having the old emblematic atouts, and these are always accompanied by the Italian suit signs. In these, too, the old order does not change. They are always printed from wood blocks and colored with stencils, and the maker's initials are usually to be found on the seventh atout, Le Chariot.

These old symbolic figures always suggest the fortune-telling cards. Germany produced many of these. 'Zeit Kurtzende Lust und Spiel Hausz,' a fat little vellum-bound book of 1372 pages which was published in Kunstburg in 1680, describes many of these, as well as contemporary games as played in different countries. There are interesting engraved plates.

'Vier Farben,' written in Leipzig in 1829 by Susanna Rumpler, explains the legend and lore attaching to the ordinary German 'cards for playing' and shows how they may be used with infallible results for the telling of fortunes.

NÜRNBERG FORTUNE-TELLING CARDS MADE BY
J. E. BACKOFEN, 1820

Among the fortune-telling series is one of pictorial cards, the title of each being given in French, German, and English. They come in a gay little box lettered, 'Sibille, the fortune-telling gypsy mother.' There are a num-

GERMAN FORTUNE-TELLING CARDS, c. 1840

ber of variations of the 'Le Normand' fortune-telling cards. Mlle. Le Normand was high in favor at the French court early in the nineteenth century, as a diviner, and the tales told of the credence put in her utterances are almost past belief.

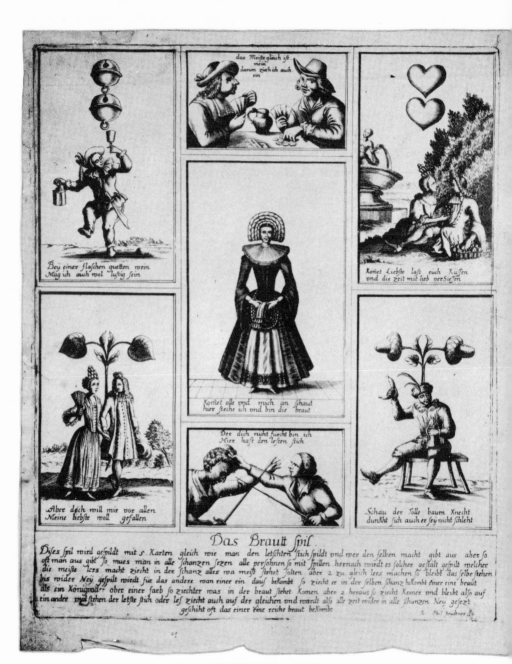

BRAUTT SPIL, c. 1700

(150)

An uncut engraved sheet of the late seventeenth century, by Jo. Phil. Steÿdtner, gives directions for playing the game of Brautt Spil. There are seven pictorial cards, the four at the corners bearing the suit signs of hearts, bells, acorns, and leaves.

The cloister cards, another curious card game, were made at Augsburg in 1753. At the top of each card is lettered the name of one of the German suit signs, and the rest of the card is taken up with religious text in German. These were the only cards permitted by the Pope to the ecclesiastics and the monastic orders at the time.

An old game, called variously 'Birds' Play' in the Rhine country and Switzerland, 'Cucu,' in Italy, and 'Gnau,' 'Cambio,' and 'Kille' in the north countries, Norway and Sweden and Denmark, where it is still played, consists of two series of picture cards of ten cards each, and two series of Roman numerals of twelve cards each. The picture cards of a hand-colored

HARLEQUIN ET PIERROT, A VIENNESE CARD GAME, 1806

eighteenth-century series are quite as amusing as the animal tarots of those days.

There is a delightful little game of German proverbs. It contains

twenty-four cards, numbered one to twenty-four, a German proverb written on each, and another twenty-four, similarly numbered, illustrating these proverbs with little hand-colored engravings. The designs are much in the style of Chadoweicki and are printed from copper plate. Several are signed, 'H. F. Müller.'

Another game of about this time, also having charmingly engraved and colored little cards, is 'Harlequin et Pierrot, nouveau jeu de société avec 32 cartes enluminées et 60 cartes contenant des Numéros.' On each of the 'cartes enluminées' is an amusing little full-length figure in the costume of the early nineteenth century. There is also a harlequin on a green ground and a Pierrot on an orange ground, and two sets of numeral cards numbered from one to fifteen. On the back of the Pierrot is written, 'This pack of playing cards came from Lieutenant Kaminski, a young Pole serving in Regiment Beaulieu in billet during the

A VIENNESE DOMINO CARD

Other domino cards are listed in various card collections, but none so whimsical as these.

march of the G. P. corps, in the year 1815.' There are directions in both French and German for playing with these cards, which were published in Vienna in 1806.

GERMAN PLAYING CARDS IN THE COLLECTION OF THE UNITED STATES PLAYING CARD COMPANY [1]

The painted cards of Stuttgart, facsimiles, 1440	52 cards
*Little Saints, facsimiles, 1440	3 cards
*Cartes à Ensignées Animées, 1466	45 cards
*Round cards of Cologne, 1470	65 cards
*Cards attributed to Von Meckenen and Schoengauer, 1500	40 cards
Cards attributed to Von Meckenen and Schoengauer, reproductions by Ottley	47 cards
Cards attributed to Von Meckenen and Schoengauer, reproductions by Ottley	47 cards
*Cards from silver plates, Georges Heinrich Bleich	36 cards
*Vergil Solis cards, 1540	52 cards
Jost Ammon cards, 1564	52 cards
Ulm cards from wood blocks, 1460	46 cards
Uncut sheet, wood blocks, Hans Zeller, Vienna, 1540	21 cards

[1] The starred items are from the collection of George Clulow, F.R.G.S.

Uncut sheet, wood blocks, Hans Zeller, Vienna, 1540	16 cards
Uncut sheet, wood blocks, Hans Zeller, Vienna, 1540	15 cards
Uncut sheet, wood blocks, Hans Zeller, Vienna, 1540	16 cards
Uncut sheet, wood blocks, Hans Zeller, Vienna, 1550, design for backs	
Uncut sheet, wood blocks, Italian kings, 1550	12 cards
Uncut sheet, wood blocks, Koller, 1550	14 cards
Uncut sheet, wood blocks, Koller, 1550	16 cards
Uncut sheet, wood blocks, Koller, 1550	18 cards
Uncut sheet, wood blocks, Hans Bock, 1560	18 cards
Uncut sheet, wood blocks, Hans Bock, 1560	16 cards
Uncut sheet, wood blocks, Hans Bock, 1560	17 cards
Uncut sheet, wood blocks, Hans Bock, 1580	21 cards
Uncut sheet, wood blocks, H. H., Vienna, 1580 (Heinrich Hauck)	21 cards
Uncut sheet, wood blocks, Heinrich Hauck, Innsbruck, 1585	
Three uncut sheets, wood blocks, South Germany, 1556	36 cards
Uncut sheet, wood blocks, Frankfort, O. H., 1585 (Heinrich Hauck?)	24 cards
*Logica Memorativa, Chartiludium, Thomas Murner, 1509	52 cards
Logica Memorativa, Chartiludium, Thomas Murner, Paris edition, 1629	52 cards
*Chartiludium Institute summarie, Thomas Murner, 1518	
*Carten Spil, Andream Strobl, 1603	32 cards
Astronomical cards, Nürnberg, 1656	7 cards
*Astronomical cards, Nürnberg, 1685	53 cards
*Hunting series, 1610	52 cards
*Nürnberg geography of the world, 1640	51 cards
*Reines Renommées, 1680, German edition	12 cards
*Famous personages, Augsburg, 1685	52 cards
*Nürnberg geography of Europe, 1680	52 cards
Nürnberg geography of Europe, 1680	38 cards
*Nürnberg heraldic cards, 1693	38 cards
Nürnberg heraldic cards, 1693 — reprints	38 cards
Trappola cards from wood blocks, Michael Forster, Munich, 1610	18 cards
Trappola cards from wood blocks, Michael Forster, Munich, 1721	12 cards
Uncut sheet from wood blocks, 1680	48 cards
The Game of Brautt Spil, 1700	5 cards
Circular card game, c. 1650	
*Appliqué cards, 1710	31 cards
*Daumont heraldry, Augsburg edition	53 cards
Astronomical cards, Nürnberg, 1719	54 cards
*Regensberg card proofs	15 cards
*Uncut sheet, military tarots, J. Albrecht, Innsbruck, 1750	
*Uncut sheet, tarot proofs, Gobl of Munich, 1750–80	38 cards
*Uncut sheet, tarot proofs, Gobl of Munich, 1750–80	38 cards
*Uncut sheet, hunting tarots, Gobl of Munich	22 cards
*Jeu du Lindor, Gobl of Munich	5 cards

*Cucu, Gobl of Munich	
*Uncut sheet, animal tarots, Gobl of Munich	65 cards
*Five uncut sheets, trappola cards, Gobl of Munich	90 cards
Complete pack, animal tarots, Gobl of Munich, hand-colored	78 cards
*Seventy uncut sheets, court cards, tarots, and trappola cards, Gobl	1400 cards
Uncut sheets, trappola cards, Gobl	
Eleven uncut sheets, trappola cards	392 cards
Six uncut sheets, tarots	218 cards
Complete pack, wedding tarots, hand colored, Gobl of Munich	78 cards
*Complete pack, animal tarots, stenciled	78 cards
Trappola cards, hand-colored	30 cards
Munich tarots, c. 1780	65 cards
Birds' Play, hand-colored, c. 1760	32 cards
Cloister cards	32 cards
Tarot cards, Italian designs, stenciled	22 cards
German historical cards, 1765	57 cards
*Calligraphic cards, 1769	52 cards
Tarot cards, 1770, South Germany	75 cards
Bavarian tarots, Joseph Fetscher	78 cards
*Musical tarots, 1780	46 cards
Trappola cards, Graz, 1782, Leopold Milchram	36 cards
Trappola cards, Graz, 1790, Anton Herrl	36 cards
Bavarian animal tarots, 1790	78 cards
*Proverb game, H. F. Müller, 1791, hand-colored	47 cards
Piquet cards, Lauretz Ummer, Munich, c. 1800	33 cards
Trappola cards, Conrad Jegel, Nürnberg	36 cards
Trappola cards, South Germany, 1805	32 cards
*Cotta cards, Jeanne d'Arc, 1807	52 cards
Cotta cards, Jeanne d'Arc, 1807	43 cards
Cotta cards, Wallenstein, 1807	52 cards
Cotta cards, Arabian costumes, 1808	52 cards
Cotta cards, Ulysses and other classical figures, 1806	52 cards
*Cotta cards, caricatures of famous people, 1810	52 cards
Cotta cards, knightly orders, 1811	52 cards
Cards commemorating the Battle of Leipzig, 1813	12 cards
Cards commemorating the Battle of Leipzig, 1813	52 cards
Trappola cards, Johann Backofen, Nürnberg, 1813	36 cards
Fortune-telling cards, Johann Backofen, Nürnberg	36 cards
Animal tarots, Peter Schachner in Wels, 1816	53 cards
Turkish tarots, H. F. Müller, 1826	54 cards
Animal tarots, Backofen, Nürnberg	46 cards
Animal tarots, Franz Fasolt, 1830	54 cards
*Piquet cards, Portuguese Insurrection, 1834	42 cards
Sibille, fortune-telling cards, 1840	32 cards
Musical cards, Thuringian folk-song, 1840	32 cards
Piquet cards, Susz and Kunze, Württemberg, 1850	52 cards
Uncut sheet trappola cards in color, Dresden, 1850	
Uncut sheet tarot cards in color, Dresden, 1850	
Whist cards, H. Rubke, Hamburg, 1860	52 cards
Trappola cards, J. G. Rollwagen, Augsburg, 1856	36 cards

Piquet pack, brown fortune-telling cards	52 cards
Oval piquet cards, by F. Gunthel for A. Tweitmeyer, Leipzig, 1865	52 cards
Trappola cards, Pitner in Gratz, 1867	36 cards
Piquet cards, historical aces, Dondorf in Frankfort, 1869	52 cards
Zeko piquet cards, C. L. Wüst, Frankfort, 1860	52 cards
Piquet cards, stenciled court cards, 1870	49 cards
Caricature cards, Dondorf in Frankfort, 1870	52 cards
*Comic Karte, Fromme and Bunte, Darmstadt, 1870	52 cards
Bavarian piquet cards, 1870	51 cards
Piquet cards, court cards in costumes of the Rheingold legends, Dondorf, Frankfort	51 cards
Piquet cards, Altenburg, 1870	52 cards
Le Normand fortune cards, 1870	32 cards
Historic trappola cards, F. A. Lattmann, Goslar, 1872	35 cards
Piquet cards, F. A. Lattmann, Goslar, 1874	52 cards
Piquet cards, Ludwig and Schmidt, Halle, 1874	52 cards
Trappola cards, C. L. Wüst, Frankfort, 1875	32 cards
Trappola cards, Stralsund, 1875	32 cards
German arms cards, T. Schroeter, Jena, 1876	36 cards
Piquet cards, Stralsund, 1877	32 cards
Geographical cards, designed by Haussmann for Dondorf, 1878	52 cards
Trappola cards, Altenburg, 1878	32 cards
Costume tarots, Dondorf, 1879	32 cards
Cards for the blind, Braille system, Stralsund, 1884	52 cards
Three packs of trappola cards, humorous, by Jules Diaz, Munich, 1897	108 cards
Trappola cards, Altenburg, 1880, by Schneider	32 cards
*Medieval German cards by Burger, 1885	36 cards
Tarot cards, C. L. Wüst, Frankfort, 1885	53 cards
Historical tarots, Dondorf, 1887	78 cards
Skat cards, Germany, 1890	36 cards
Piquet cards, Eduard Buttner, Berlin, 1895	52 cards
Piquet cards, Hamburg American Line, 1895	52 cards
'Impressionist' cards, C. L. Wüst, Frankfort, 1899	32 cards
German fortune-telling cards, 1900	32 cards
Piquet cards with costume court cards, Dondorf, 1900	52 cards
Piquet cards with costume cards, Dondorf, 1900	52 cards
Piquet cards with costume court cards, Dondorf, 1900	52 cards
Piquet cards for export to Rangoon, C. L. Wüst, Frankfort, 1900	52 cards
Lithographed whist cards, fancy court cards, 1900	52 cards
Lithographed patience cards, fancy court cards, 1906	52 cards
Historical costume cards, Goslar, 1906	52 cards
Trappola cards for fortune-telling, Dondorf, 1908	36 cards
Whist cards, geographical whist cards, Dondorf, 1910	52 cards
Trappola cards, Augustin Z. Mahler, Prag, 1664	36 cards
Domino cards, Vienna(?)	1 card
Löschentiohl Whist cards, Vienna, 1806	52 cards
Harlequin et Pierrot cards, 1806	92 cards
'Transformation' whist cards, Johann Neidl, Vienna, 1814	52 cards

'Transformation' whist cards, H. F. Müller, 1818	52 cards
'Transformation' whist cards, H. F. Müller, 1809	52 cards
Viennese tarots, 1820, Matthias Koller	39 cards
Viennese cards, 1820	41 cards
Bohemian trappola cards, 1820	36 cards
Sir Walter Scott tarots, 1827, Vienna	54 cards
Bohemian trappola cards, 1828	31 cards
Rebus tarot cards, 1832, Buda-Pesth	39 cards
Tarots of Johann Georg Steiger, Wien, 1836	42 cards
Theatre tarots, Max Uffenheimer, Wien, 1838	50 cards
Tarots by Carl Holdhaus, Wien, 1842	54 cards
Trappola cards, Uffenheimer, Wien, 1844	36 cards
Original water colors by F. Ferasch, for court cards, 1845, Wien	12 cards
Original water colors by F. Ferasch, for court cards, 1855, Wien	12 cards
Seven card wrappers, Ferdinand Fellner in Agram, 1830	
Court cards, Ferdinand Fellner in Agram, 1830	12 cards
Court cards, Johann Norbert Hoffmann, Wien, 1830	12 cards
Four card wrappers, A. Aulich, Wien, 1830	
Hungarian trappola cards, 1840	32 cards
Court cards, Johann Georg Steiger, Wien, 1850	12 cards
Court cards, Johann Georg Steiger, Wien, 1850	12 cards
Court cards, Christian Spielvogel, Wien, 1850	12 cards
Court cards, Franz Hajek, Wien, 1850	12 cards
Court cards, Carl Holdhaus, Wien, 1850	12 cards
Court cards, Carl Holdhaus, Wien, 1850	12 cards
Court cards, Carl Gilsa, Buda-Pesth, 1840	12 cards
Hungarian trappola cards, 1845	36 cards
Trappola cards, Carl Titze, Wien, 1850	36 cards
Six sheets of uncut proofs, trappola, tarot, and court cards, c. 1850	
Political tarots, 1848, Wien	54 cards
Geographical tarots, Carl Titze, 1850	52 cards
Viennese tarots, Piatnik in Wien, c. 1850	49 cards
Author's tarots, Carl Titze et Josef Glanz, Wien, 1851	54 cards
Whist cards, two packs in one box, Josef Glanz, 1851	104 cards
Sibille, fortune-telling cards, 1852	46 cards
Trappola cards, Johann Nejedly, Wien, 1854	30 cards
Trappola cards, Johann Nejedly, Wien, 1855	32 cards
Turkish War tarots, Josef Glanz, Wien, 1855	54 cards
Tarots, Oriental designs, Franz Tinver, Pressburg, 1855	42 cards
Bohemian trappola cards, Wien and Prag, J. Nejedly, 1855	29 cards
Historical tarots, Wien, 1859, Johann Sageder	38 cards
Original water colors, costume court cards, by Elfinger, c. 1860	17 cards
Original pen and ink drawings, animal tarots by Pausinger, 1860	21 cards
Tarot cards, Viennese types, Josef Glanz, c. 1860	54 cards
Whist cards, Nejedly, Wien, c. 1860 (two packs, incomplete)	75 cards

Viennese costume cards in honor of a royal wedding, Josef Glanz, 1862	24 cards
Tarots, showing views in Vienna, Josef Glanz, 1862	54 cards
Historical tarots, E. Knepper, Wien, 1862	38 cards
Military tarots, Wien, 1864, Josef Glanz	54 cards
Iron cards, Johann Nejedly, c. 1850, Wien	25 cards
Uncolored proofs of court cards, after designs of Elfinger, Josef Glanz, 1860	
Twenty-six uncut sheets of playing card proofs by Josef Glanz, Wien, c. 1860	
Costume tarots by Josef Glanz, the first copy from the designs by Geiger, 1864	54 cards
Italian trappola cards, Trieste, 1866	53 cards
German tarots, Johann Nejedly, Wien, 1866	53 cards
Kaiser whist cards, after designs of Elfinger, by Josef Glanz, 1866	52 cards
Original water colors of court cards, Elfinger	12 cards
Skat cards, Trieste, 1870	25 cards
German tarots, Wien, L. Jager & Dobler, 1870	54 cards
German tarots, Ludwig Gigerl, Wien, 1870	54 cards
Italian trappola cards, Trieste, 1870	51 cards
Whist cards, Modiano, Trieste, 1880	52 cards
Whist cards, Conrad Jager, Proschwitz in Austria, 1875	52 cards
Gigerl tarots, Viennese caricatures, Josef Glanz, 1873	54 cards
Kaiser tarots (hunting series), Piatnik, Wien	54 cards
Italian playing cards, Finazzer, Padda et Cie, Trieste, 1875	51 cards
German tarots, Piatnik, 1875, Wien	54 cards
Austrian Military Tarots, F. Piatnik and Sohne, Wien, 1880	54 cards
Bohemian trappola cards, Josef Glanz, Wien, 1885	36 cards
Whist cards, geographical aces, Josef Glanz, Wien, 1886	52 cards
German tarots, Ferd. Piatnik and Sohne, Wien, 1890	53 cards
Kaiser's Jubilee whist cards, Piatnik, Wien et Buda-Pesth, 1898	53 cards
German trappola cards, Piatnik, 1900	36 cards
Tarot cards by Ditha Moser, Vienna, 1906	54 cards
Miniature playing cards, Interlaken	52 cards
Miniature playing cards, Interlaken	52 cards

A sheet of uncut German cards, the date 1570 on the nine of bells. Hand-colored. The backs are printed in an all-over pattern. There is a piper on the four of bells, a stag couchant on the five of bells, a snail on the five of hearts, and on the two of hearts and bells there is lettering; on the former, 'Im Spil Ist Das ein groosse kunst' and on the latter 'Das karten spil' followed by what was perhaps the maker's name, which unfortunately is so wormed and discolored as to be illegible.

Neye Welt. Geographical playing cards of Asia, Africa, and America. The pack of fifty-two cards and the book explaining them. Nürnberg, Johann Hofmann, 1710. The book is bound in stamped vellum 16mo. On the title-page is the monastery stamp 'Ad Bibliothec ——' the name of the monastery being blotted out. Each card is a map, the French suit signs being in the margin at the top. The cards and book are both in a case of the stamped vellum. Slightly wormed.

Europa. Geographical playing cards of Europe. The pack of fifty-two cards and the book explaining them. As in the other series, each card is a map. The frontispiece shows Europa, an impressive dowager sitting at a table, on which is a globe and an atlas, and handing Mercury the geographical cards. The second frontispiece shows Mercury flying above a card table surrounded by nine gentlemen, showering them with the cards. These engravings are both by Hirschman. Nürnberg, Johann Hofmann. They are also from a monastic library, and, like the former set, are bound in stamped vellum.

Total: 360 editions, 11,013 cards

CHAPTER VI

PLAYING CARDS IN BELGIUM AND HOLLAND

THE story of playing cards in Flanders begins very long ago. There is a little book, 'Cartes à Jouer en Belgique, by Alexandre Pinchart, chef de section aux Archives Générales du Royaume à Bruxelles.' It is really a compilation of excerpts from the old archives, but the events of every day are recounted so simply and so vividly that it reads like a diary of those high and far-off times.

In 1355 there reigned in Brabant, Wenceslas and Jeanne. Their generosity was known throughout the world; their court was much visited and very sumptuous. Poets gathered there; the duke himself dabbled in poetry. Not a week passed but some notable minstrel found his way there. Among the French ones were Guillaume de Machault and Eustache Deschamps, his pupil, from the court of Charles V, and Jean de Malines and Jean d'Ivoix. Among the Flemish ones were Augustin de Dordrecht, Jean Dille, Jean Fisier, and Godefroid de Tricht.

These recounted daily the occupations of the duchess and the duke. Often they went to attend fêtes and jousts in neighboring countries. There is a long list of tourneys which took place in various parts of these ancient duchies. In 1379 at a fête at Bruxelles, it is written that cards were played.

On the fourteenth of May, Renier Hollander, receveur général de Brabant, gave to Monseigneur and to Madame four peters and two florins to buy some games of cards. On the twenty-fifth of June of the same year he paid yet other monies to Ange Van der Noel for a game of cards that the duchess had bought from him.

On the twenty-eighth of August, 1380, there is paid by order of Jeanne to a certain master who had delivered 'three pairs of cards' a sum of two old half crowns. The twenty-first of November following, one of the servitors of the duchess received a florin for the purchase of a similar game. For these cards is used the Flemish word 'quartspel,' so that by then cards must have been well known in the countryside and played in the taverns.

A little later, the duchess, being at Ivoix, in the duchy of Luxembourg, sent two of her servitors to Bruxelles to buy two packs of cards which cost a peter and a half in gold. There are many entries to both the duke and the duchess for monies with which to play at cards. One of these seems to have been given the duchess when playing with her husband.

There are records of these old games and the gains and losses incurred.

Many notables of many different courts played at the game which happened to be the favorite. When its popularity waned, it was replaced by another.

In 1427 there were two master card-makers in Tournai, Michel Noël and Philippe du Bos. They formed a guild and upon its records each registered the mark he chose as his own. One was a rose, the other a wild boar. Each master card-maker had as his helpers those who prepared the colors, les broyeurs; those who applied the colors, les bruneteurs; and those who prepared the paper, les carteurs. Their duties are clearly defined by the rules of the guild, which also stipulate the colors that may be used. The register contains the names of many women who worked at the making of cards.

Tournai was a center of the arts. It numbered among its citizens painters and makers of missals, workers in bronze, carvers of wood, sculptors, embroiderers of tapestries, goldsmiths, and, later, engravers of wood and copper. Many of these also turned to the making of playing cards and the industry flourished for more than a hundred years.

Before leaving the fifteenth century we ought to mention a painting that has been attributed to Van Eyck, the title of which is 'Philip le Bon consulting a card fortune-teller.' Whether or not Van Eyck painted it, the costumes are those of the reign of Charles VIII, and it is interesting as showing cards once more in their old, old character of divination.

FROM HOLBEIN'S
'DANCE OF DEATH'

Fifty years later there are also the famous prints of Holbein, 'The Dance of Death.' One of them shows a gambling party interrupted by Death and the Evil One. On a table is the five of diamonds, and the ace is on the floor.

In 1533 there is a volume of Latin dialogues on games, printed at Antwerp, and we find the French cards used. About the same time, Vives, a Spaniard, wrote a similar book, in which he says that both the French and Spanish cards are used in the Netherlands, to play both French and Spanish games.

In 1522, Robert Péril, an engraver of wood from Liège, came to Antwerp, and became the first card-maker there. He enjoyed a great reputation as a pattern-maker, and was also listed as a haberdasher. He was followed by Jean Maillart from Rouen, who was inscribed as a printer in the guild of Saint Luc. Card-making throve in Antwerp, and for more than a hundred years cards were exported to London and France, recognizable always, because the maker's name appears, as well as his mark, which is sometimes a red pig, sometimes a wild boar, and sometimes a rose.

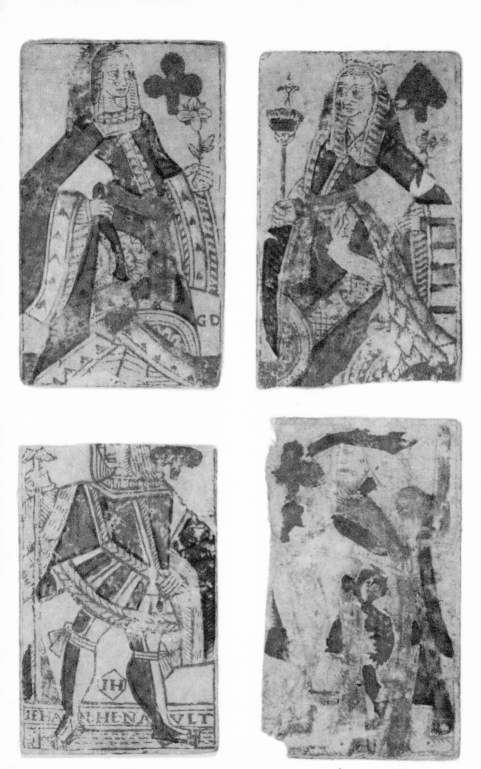

PLAYING CARDS MADE BY JEHAN HENAULT, CARTIER À ANVERS, 1543

THE SCHOLER'S PRACTICALL CARDS, LONDON, 1656

We have some of these old cards, of a pack of fifty-two. The knave of clubs bears the maker's name, Jehan Henault, his initials appearing in a hexagon above, and also on the king of clubs. The cards have been so much used that it is impossible to distinguish the maker's mark. Other cards very similar to these bear the initials 'G. D.,' probably standing for Guillaume Daret, another maker of the early sixteenth century. Daret, however, is of Tournai, while Henault is a cartier at Antwerp.

During the seventeenth century cards were also made at Liège, at Namur, at Gand, and at Bruxelles, 'as fine as might be desired.' The cardmakers at Bruxelles used a paper specially made at Liège and acquired a great reputation. They imitated the English and Swiss cards, and 'strangers of all lands admired their beauty and fineness.'

A tarot series with the old emblematic atouts bears the initials 'P. M.' on Le Charior. This may be for Pierre Mainet (his name sometimes also appears as Mannet, Meniet, Mainnet, and Minet), cartier at Tournai.

The claims that have been put forward in favor of many cities of the Low Countries, as the scene of very early printing — Haarlem, Utrecht, Louvain, Deventer, Alost, Bruxelles — add to the interest of these old cards from wood blocks, as well as to that of those early records which show that cards were not only painted for the court, but produced by some other and cheaper method for the populace.

There is a fat little book, five hundred and twenty-eight pages thick, 'The Spiritual Card Game with Hearts Trumps, or the Game of Love, by the Reverend Father Joseph of St. Barbara, a barefoot Carmelite. Illustrated and adorned with many copper plates. The Third Edition. Antwerp.' There is a dedication, followed by six ecclesiastical approvals, dated 1666.

There is an engraved title-page and full-page engravings of the thirteen cards of the heart suit. There is more of symbolism in this game of the good Flemish father than is found in similar German games, and there is the gentleness and the reverence of a Fra Angelico in the pictured designs. The king shows saints and the great of the earth, kneeling before God the Father; the queen shows two saints in adoration before Mary, the Queen of Heaven; the knave shows the rich and mighty before the throne of the crucified Christ. The ten shows Moses with the Ten Commandments, each one a heart upon the tables of stone; the nine shows nine choirs of angels; the eight pictures eight Christian virtues; the seven, seven works of mercy; the six, the goals to be striven for in human life; the five, the wounds of Christ; the four, the last ends, being the death and the ordeal, hell and heaven. The three pictures the Holy Family; the two, the worship of God the Father and Mary the Mother; and the one, the Truth which must be in a Christian Heart.

'THE SPIRITUAL CARD GAME OF LOVE,'
ANTWERP, 1666
The Ten Commandments

'THE SPIRITUAL CARD GAME OF LOVE,'
ANTWERP, 1666
The nine choirs of angels

'THE SPIRITUAL CARD GAME OF LOVE,'
ANTWERP, 1666
The seven works of mercy

'THE SPIRITUAL CARD GAME OF LOVE,'
ANTWERP, 1666
The Holy Jesus, Mary, and Joseph

DUTCH PAPAL CARDS, 1719

It is the greatest possible contrast to the card games for which Holland was famous fifty years later, which are satires presented in the vein of the broad Dutch humor of the eighteenth century.

The earliest of these pictorial series is a satire on the Papacy. Besides our copy, there is one at the Bodleian, and one in the Schreiber Collection at the British Museum. All of the papal scandals are raked up and pictured, so that the use of the cards was forbidden to all good Catholics, and all possible copies were burned by the command of Rome. The subjects begin in the heart suit and are continued through diamonds, clubs, and spades, though they do not follow in exact chronological sequence. Pope Joan is on the three of hearts, Luther and Calvin are in the club suit, and the spades tell the story of Pasquier Quesnel of Amsterdam, against whom Clement

XI issued a bull because of his heresies. The little cards are contemporary with these stirring events, which accounts for the great interest in this episode. The title cards, of which there are two, are both scathing satires, and on one it is lettered that the cards may be had 'at Rome, at the Fisherman's Ring, by Peter Waanregt, at the Crowned Constitutions Nun.' Each card, besides the engraved picture with the text below, has the usual suit signs and numerals or initial letter, proclaiming its value, as a 'card for playing.'

The next series, which is similar to these cards, is a satire on John Law and the Mississippi Bubble. Again there are two title cards, the one showing the cock which was on the arms of John Law of Lauriston and the other bearing the name of the game, 'April Kaart of Kaart Spel van

MISSISSIPPI BUBBLE CARDS OF 1720
In the series of 1721 the cat on the four of spades is named 'Madame la Petite'

Momus Naar de Nieuwste Mode.' John Law's Mississippi Bubble scheme started about 1717, was at its height in 1719, and collapsed in 1720, so that Law fled from Paris. There are several allusions to the South Sea Company. On the three of spades, the three companies, the South Sea, the Mississippi, and the West Indian, sit side by side in a swing. On the four of spades, Madame la Petite is supposed to mean the wife of Thomas Knight, the cashier of the South Sea Company, who bought his shares in her name. A booklet issued with these cards describes each one minutely. Below the engraving, which occupies most of the space on each, is a couplet in Dutch verse, and each card has also the usual suit sign and numeral or letter.

A second edition of these cards shows the same designs, but the couplets are all different, and one of the title cards reads, 'Pasquin's Windkaart op de Windnegotie van 't Iaar 1720.' The other title card is the familiar cock.

Still another pack of pictorial cards was issued about 1740. These have the usual French suit signs and in addition a design characteristic of the humor of the time in Holland. The court cards of the four suits satirize the inhabitants of Europe, America, Asia, and Africa. The red suits are printed in red, the black in black, from copper plates. The ace of clubs gives the name of the maker, ''t Amsterd by A. de Winter.'

There is another series, this time of fifty little cards with vignettes of various subjects, fairly engraved. According to the catalogue of the Schreiber Collection in the British Museum, there should be fifty corresponding cards with inscriptions of a fortune-telling character, and also fifty lottery tickets; the three sets being used together, to play the 'lottery game' which was popular in both Holland and Germany about 1720.

Toward the end of the seventeenth century the card-makers of Lyons edited cards with specially designed court cards for export to Flanders, probably to compete with Rouen, which up to that time had been the only town in France to export their cards there. A government report of 1714 says, 'Indeed the reputation of the cards of Rouen is known in Spain, in Russia, in Switzerland, in Denmark, in England and especially in Flanders.' Later, a great many of the card-makers of Rouen, because of the duties imposed, emigrated to Holland, Belgium, and Germany to ply their trade.

The editions of the 'Académie des Jeux,' published early in the eighteenth century at Amsterdam, show pictures of the old Dutch cards. They resemble the French in their suit marks, though the court cards and the atouts are more of the German type. The queen is called Barbara, and the king, though lacking the dignity of the French one, is lettered, 'K. David,' the 'K' presumably being for the German 'Koenig.' The knave looks like a Rotterdam skipper, and is named 'Pieter Mefferdt,' for the card-maker *par excellence* of the time in the Low Countries.[1]

We have a book of games, 'Divertissemens Innocens,' published at The Hague in 1696; there is an engraved frontispiece and the title-page is charming with its red and black lettering, detailing the names of the strange old games. There is a 'Maison des Jeux' of 1702, also published at

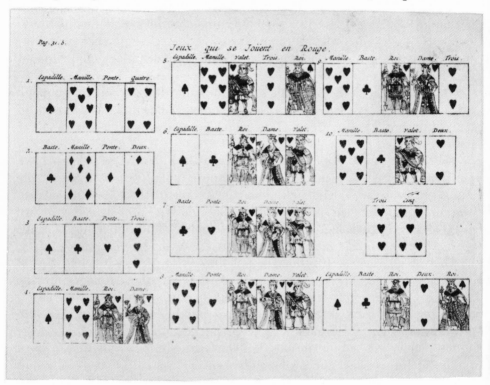

PLATE FOR 'LE JEU DE L'HOMBRE' FROM 'LA PLUS NOUVELLE ACADÉMIE UNIVERSELLE DES JEUX,' LEYDEN, 1721

The Hague, and one of 1721, issued at Leiden. In 1728, a three-volume edition of the 'Académie des Jeux' was published at Amsterdam and from that time on the Amsterdam editions rival the Paris ones in numbers; there is also an edition of 'Hoyle's Games' published at Liège in 1794.

The ever-present controversy concerning the morality of gaming also has a representative at Amsterdam in a two-volume 'Traité du Jeu,' by Jean Barbeyrac, published in 1709. A three-volume edition was also issued in 1733.

Among the Dutch cards are some stenciled ones, roughly done on coarse

[1] *Jeux de Cartes Tarots et de Cartes Numérales.* Paris, 1844.

paper. On the back of each is lettered, 'Made by H. M. Guest, Klerks-dorp, Traansvaal, Feb. 1901, during the Anglo Boer War.' The court cards are rough silhouettes in purple, but they are most amusing pro-traits of the English royal family.

PLAYING CARDS MADE AT KLERKSDORP IN THE TRANSVAAL IN 1901 FOR
THE ENGLISH SOLDIERS

Among the later cards made in Holland and Belgium, the majority have the French suit signs. Sometimes the court cards resemble the French ones, sometimes the German. Often the name of the maker is to be found on the queen of hearts, and the name of the city where he works on the knave of clubs. Very often these packs have the pictorial aces.

Many of the cards of Belgium are made at Turnhout, a little village out-side of Antwerp, where the inhabitants have existed for many years by making playing cards and prayer books, and the old processes are still used. The cards are printed from wood blocks, and the workers take them home to color them. An old motto is retained on the ace of spades, 'Dieu pour Tous.'

BELGIAN AND DUTCH PLAYING CARDS IN THE COLLECTION OF
THE UNITED STATES PLAYING CARD COMPANY [1]

*Piquet cards, Jehan Henault, Anvers, 1543	28 cards
*Piquet cards, Guillaume Daret, Tournai, 1543	10 cards
The Spiritual Card Game of Love, Father Joseph of Saint Barbara, Antwerp, 1666	13 cards
*Tarot cards by Pierre Mainet(?)	8 cards
Papal cards, Amsterdam or Utrecht, 1719	50 cards
Lottery cards, Amsterdam(?), 1720	50 cards
*Mississippi Bubble cards, 1720	50 cards
Mississippi Bubble cards, 1721	53 cards

[1] The starred items are from the collection of George Clulow, F.R.G.S.

*Comic geographical cards, Amsterdam, 1740	52 cards
Piquet cards, Bruxelles, 1870	52 cards
Piquet cards, Bruges, 1880	52 cards
Piquet cards, Turnhout, 1880	52 cards
Piquet cards, Turnhout, for export, 1898	52 cards
Piquet cards, geographical aces, Amsterdam(?), 1900	52 cards
Piquet cards, geographical aces, Amsterdam(?), 1900	52 cards
Stenciled cards, H. M. Guest, Klerksdorp, Transvaal, 1901	14 cards
Piquet cards, Volendam, 1905	52 cards
Theater tarots, 1905	78 cards
Piquet cards, Rotterdam, 1905	52 cards

Total: 19 editions, 822 cards

CHAPTER VII

PLAYING CARDS IN ENGLAND

IT is known that sometime during the twelfth century, chess, which had found its way from India into Palestine, was brought back to England and the Continent by returning crusaders. A manuscript in the British Museum, describing the later crusade under Richard Cœur de Lion says

> 'And Kyng Rychard stode and playe
> At the Chesse in his galley.'

A curious old edict is also preserved there, which shows the state of gaming among Richard's followers. It reads: 'No person in the army is permitted to play at any sort of game for money except knights and clergymen; who in one whole day and night shall not, each, lose more than twenty shillings, on pain of forfeiting one hundred shillings to the archbishop of the army. The two Kings may play for what they please; but their attendants not for more than twenty shillings, otherwise they are to be whipped through the army for three days.'

In the Wardrobe Rolls of Edward I there is a game mentioned, 'Quatuor reges,' which was at first supposed to mean cards. It has been pointed out, however, that Chaucer, a hundred years later, in his intimate description of fourteenth-century England, does not mention cards, but says only that

> 'They dancen and they play at ches and tables'

and the game of King Edward was undoubtedly chess.

It is probable that it was in the early fifteenth century, during the constant fighting in Normandy and Touraine, Anjou and Poitou, that English soldiers brought French cards back with them to England. These cards must have served as models for English makers. For in spite of the fact that paper was not made in England until the end of the century, we find the importation of playing cards forbidden in 1463 upon the petition of the English artificers.

About 1484, they seem to have become an important part of the Christmas festivities, at least among the upper classes, and in 1495 an edict of Henry VII forbade their use to servants and apprentices except during the Christmas holidays.

Henry apparently knew only too well the fascination of this new game, 'cards for playing,' for among his private expenses are several entries for money for losses at cards. Perhaps his daughter inherited his taste for gaming, for of James IV and his bride it is written, 'The Kynge came prively to the said castell, and entered within the chammer with a small company, where he found the Queene playing at Cardes.'

The costumes of the English court cards, or 'coate cards' as they used to be called, are of the time of Henry VII. The queens wear the queer lappets over their ears which were worn by the ladies of Henry's court, but their way of wearing their crowns on the very backs of their heads did not come into vogue until Elizabeth's time. The knaves, with their flat caps 'Broade on the crowne like the battlements of a house,' are like the figures pictured in the paintings and tapestries of that far-off day, and their 'striped stockings, red greene and yallowe,' [1] are to be found on many an old figure in the early wood cuts. A 'knave' in those days was used in the same way as the French 'valet,' and merely meant a son. Later, it came to mean a rogue, and from that meaning our present term, 'jack,' is supposed to have come. Originally it was 'Jack a napes,' which in its turn was from 'Jack a naipes,' 'naipes' being the Spanish word for cards.

In each country the old cards endure, unchanged through the centuries, the favored colors and characteristics persisting, as individual and faithful a mirror of the taste and temperament and traditions of the people as other branches of their arts.

It is curious to see how from the very first cards made for export have conformed with the accepted idea of the country for which they were made, and what small favor has been vouchsafed foreign cards. An early English advertisement reads persuasively: 'Spanish cards lately brought from Vigo. Being pleasant to the eye by their curious colors and quite different from ours, may be had at 1s. a pack at Mrs. Baldwin's in Warwick Lane.' But this effort to introduce Spanish cards failed utterly, as did many others. So, too, have all attempts to improve the bizarre old figures with which we are familiar. Many innovations have been offered from time to time, but they have been popular only as novelties, which is also true of the many educational, historical, and fanciful cards which reflect entertainingly the sentiments, the outstanding events, and the styles of their times. But for serious card-playing the unchanging old conventional cards have always been preferred.

By 1628 there were so many card-makers in London that they formed themselves into a company under the protection of a royal charter. The title of the company of card-makers was 'The Master, Wardens and Commonalty of the Mistery of the Makers of Playing Cards of the City of London.' The archives of the company record the entry of many marks that their owners wished to protect, and it is interesting to note that two of these, the rose and the wild boar, were identical with the marks registered two hundred years earlier at Tournai.

[1] Samuel Rowlands: *The Four Knaves*. London, 1611.

In 1706 there was entered the mark of King Henry VIII; in 1714 the mark of the Merry Andrew, and in 1741 the Great Mogul and the Valiant Highlander; and these survived for almost two centuries. In the latter half of the nineteenth century they seem to have become the property of any maker who chose to use them, and they indicate quality in the following order: Great Mogul, Henry VIII, Valiant Highlander, and Merry Andrew.

An early writer inveighing against gaming says: 'The Playe of Cards is an invention of the Devill, which he found out, that he might the easilier bring in ydolatrie amongst men. For the Kings and Coate Cards that we use nowe, were in olde time the images of idols and false gods: which since they that would seeme christians, have changed into Charlemaigne, Launcelot, Hector, and such like names, because they would not seeme to imitate their idolatrie therein, and yet maintaine the playe itself.'

Satires and epigrams were the most fashionable form of writing for a while, and cards hold a conspicuous place as a popular subject. In 'The Four Knaves,' which Samuel Rowlands wrote in 1611, the knaves plead for a change in the fashion of their attire, which even then was out of date. There are numerous allusions to amusing tracts and pamphlets that have gone before; when a wit or gallant 'wore a pair of velvet breeches, with panes or slashes of silk, an enormous starched ruff, a gilt handled sword, and a Spanish dagger; and played at cards or dice in the chambers of the groom porter, and smoked tobacco in the tilt yard, or at the play house'; when an astrologer from the sacred precincts of Cambridge dares make dire prognostications that fill the kingdom with concern, and when the kingdom seems not only to have ears for astrologers, but for all 'Couzening Knaves.' How one of these is brought to grief is amusingly told in 'How Maister Hobson Bayted the Divell with a Dog.' It reads: 'Not farre from Maister Hobson's house there dwelled one of the cunning men, otherwise called fortune tellers, such cossening companions as at this day (by their crafts) make simple women beleeve how they can tell what husbands they shall have, how many children, how many sweethearts, and such like: if goods bee stole, who hath them, with promise to helpe them to their losses againe: with many other like deceittfull elusions. To this wise man (as some terms him) goes Maister Hobson, not to reap any benefit by his crafty cunning, but to make a jest and tryall of his experience; so causing one of his servants to lead a mastif dog after him, staying at the cunning man's doore with the dog in his hand, up goes Maister Hobson to the wise man, requesting his skil, for he had lost ten pound lately taken from him by theeves, but when and how he knew not well: the cunning man, knowing Maister Hobson to be one of his neighbors and a man of good reputation, fell (as he made showe) to conjuring and casting of figures, and after a few words of incantation, as his common use was, he tooke a very large faire looking glasse, and bade Maister Hobson to looke in the same, but not to cast his eyes backward in any case; the which hee did and therein saw the picture of a huge and large oxe, with two broad hornes on his head, the which was no otherwise but (as hee had often deceitfully shewd to others) a cossening fellow like the cunning man himselfe, clothed in an oxe hide, which fellow he maintained as his servant, to blinde the peoples eyes with-all, and to make them beleeve he could shew them the Divell at his pleas-ure in a glasse: this vision Maister Hobson perceiving, and guessing at the knavery thereof, gave a whistle for his dog, which then stayed below at the doore in his man's keeping, which whistle being no sooner heard, but the dog ran up stayers to his maister as he had beene mad, and presently fastened upon the poore fellow in the oxe hide, and so tore him as it was pittifull to see: the cunning man cried For the passion of God take off your dog: No (quoth Maister Hobson) let the Divill and the dogge fight: ven-ture thou thy Devill, and I will venture my dog. To conclude, the oxe hide was torne from the fellow's backe and so their knaveries were dis-covered, and their cunning shifts layd open to the world.'

Good Maister Hobson's exposé did not do away with the desire for fortune-telling, for there are many subsequent fortune-telling series of cards published in old England, and the chap-books are mute evidence of the popularity of the subject with their titles, 'The Dreamer's Oracle,' 'Fortune-Telling by Cards,' and 'Napoleon's Book of Fate.' There is a fortune-telling series of fifty-two cards, with two cards of explanation, published in 1665. In the upper left-hand corner of each card is the usual suit sign, and the cards in each of the four suits are numbered I to XIII. The cards bearing the odd numbers each have a circle with signs of the zodiac upon them, the even numbered cards each holding thirteen num-bered answers. The court cards are variously named — Cupid, Semira-mis, Wat Tyler, Holophernes, Mahomet, Proserpina, Nimrod, Hewson, Clytemnestra, and Pharaoh appearing as full length figures. On each king are five numbered questions, such as 'whether the person is beloved or not.' According to the directions, 'When any person is desirous to try their fortune, let them go to one of the four kings and choose what ques-tion they please,' and the elaborate process involving the other cards is described at length. The explanation ends, 'The stars foretell, they love you well.'

During the troubled years succeeding the fall of Charles, the demand for cards could not have been great. There is a curious little alphabet game of this time, each card having two rows of letters upon it and through the space in the middle runs a couplet, such as

'Od cypherd year are Leap yr. never
Even cyphered yr. are Leap yr. ever.'

FORTUNE-TELLING CARDS PUBLISHED IN 1665

The usual suit signs are placed diagonally on each card, and its value designated by Roman numerals, while the court cards and aces are marked by the letters *L, C, D,* and *M.* It is hard to tell whether they are meant for a children's game or as a sort of ecclesiastical calendar, which many of the couplets seem to imply. They are probably the 'Scholer's Practicall Cards' published by F. Jackson, M.A., in 1656. A little book of instructions tells how to spell, write, cipher and cast accounts by means of the cards. Several games might also be played with them, among them Saunt, an early English name for piquet.

With the accession of Charles II, cards were again in favor. An heraldic series, not unlike the French heraldic cards of de Brianville, were issued about 1675 by Richard Blome. On the three of hearts is a dedication of the cards to the second Duke of Albemarle, signed 'Ric. Blome.' The suit of hearts has the armorial bearings of ten different persons of rank, from the

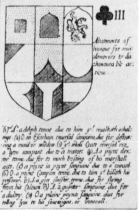

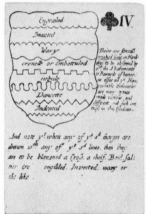

HERALDIC CARDS OF RICHARD BLOME, 1675

king to a squire, and the other suits are given to the depiction of the
various 'charges' used in heraldry.

Another pack of fifty-two cards is that of 'The Arms of the English
Peers in 1684.' They are uncolored, each card bearing the usual suit sign
and number, the court cards having initials for prince, queen, and king.

One of the most famous, certainly one of the rarest of all the series of
heraldic cards is 'The Blazoning of the Ensignes Armorial of the Kingdoms
of Scotland, England, France and Ireland and of the coats of arms of the
Nobility of Scotland. As they are Illustrate upon the Cards Armorial.'
This is their full title as it appears in the supplement to the second edition
of Camden's 'Description of Scotland,' which was published in Edinburgh
in 1694. The cards are from copper plates, colored by hand, the work of
Walter Scott, an Edinburgh goldsmith. They are the only known cards
with a directly Scotch origin and are of the greatest rarity. In the com-

THE ARMS OF THE ENGLISH PEERS IN 1684

plete set there are fifty-two cards and two extra ones, one bearing the title beneath the arms of Edinburgh, 'Phylarcharum Scotorum Gentilicia insigna illustria a Gualtero Scot Aurifice Chartis Iusorijs Exepressa Sculpsit Edinburgi Anno Dom: 1691.' The other bears the seal of the Lyon office impaled with the arms of Sir Alexander Erskine of Cambo.

Sir Walter Scott is said to have had one of these packs of cards at Abbotsford, on which he noted that one Walter Scott, goldsmith, of Edinburgh, was admitted into the fraternity of his craft in 1686, and another Walter Scott in 1701.

The English geographical cards begin with a series issued in 1675, each with the usual suit signs stenciled in color, and the numerals numbered from I to X. The king of each suit shows a portrait head of Charles II, and the queen, that of Catherine of Braganza. Most of the space on each card is taken up with a map of one of the counties of England. The card of explanation reads: 'The four suits are the four parts of England, the 13 northern counties are clubs, the western are spades, the eastern are hearts, and the southern are diamonds. In each card you have a map of the county with the chiefe towns and rivers, a compass for the bearings and a scale for mensuration, there is also given the length, breadth and circumference of each county, the latitude of the chiefe citty or towne, and its distance from London, first the Reputed, and then the Measured Miles by Esquire Ogilby. By his leave we have inserted, there is also the road from London to each Citty or Towne, the Great Roads are drawn with a double line, the other roads a single line, as also the hills and other Remarks. The use of these cards are the same with the common cards in all respects only useing the numbers of these instead of the spots on the other.'

An edition five years later gives the same little maps and statistics, but the sequence of the counties is changed. The 'chiefe cittys' are marked in

Middlesex.

Length ___ 24.
Bredth ___ 18.
Circumference ___ 95.
Londons Lattitude ___ 51: 30:

Huntington S.

Length ___ 27.
Bredth ___ 18.
Circumference ___ 65.
Huntington { D from Lon: 58: 57.
{ Lattitude ___ 52: 17:

Rutland

Length ___ 14
Bredth ___ 12.
Circumference ___ 42
Okeham { D. from Lon: 72: 90
{ Lattitude ___ 52: 45:

The Explanation of these Cards.

The four Suites are the 4 parts of England, the 13 Northern Counties are Clubs, the Western are Spades, the Eastern are Hearts, and the Southern are Diamonds, in each Card you have a Map of the County, with the cheife Townes and Rivers, a Compas for the Bearings, and a Scale for Mensuration, there is also given the Length Bredth, and Circumference of each County, the Latitude of the Cheife Citty or Towne, and its Distance from London, First the Reputed and then the Measured Miles, by Esq Ogilby, with his leave we have Incerted, there is also the Road from London to each Citty or Towne, the great Roads are drawn with a double line, the other Roads a single line, as also the cheif Hills and other Remarks The use of these Cards are the same with the Common Cards in all respects only useing the Numbers in these insted of the spots in the Other. IIII

Northampton Sh. I

Length ___ 55
Bredth ___ 26
Circumference ___ 125
Northamp { D from Lon: 55: 66:
{ Lattitude ___ 52: 14:

Stafford Sh: IX

Length ___ 45.
Bredth ___ 23.
Circumference ___ 142.
Lichfeild { D. from Lon 94: 116.
{ Lattitude ___ 52: 50.

Shrop Shire. X

Length ___ 38.
Bredth ___ 30.
Circumference ___ 135.
Shrowsb. { D from Lon. 124. 155.
{ Lattitude ___ 52: 47.

THE MAPS OF THE COUNTIES OF ENGLAND, 1675

(176)

♣ King

Armes of England

Gules three Lyons passant in pale, or Armed & langued azure all within the Garter

♥ King

Armes of Scotland

Or a lyon Rampant Gules armed & langued azure within a double tressure flowred & counterflowred with flowr de lis of ye within the order of Scotland

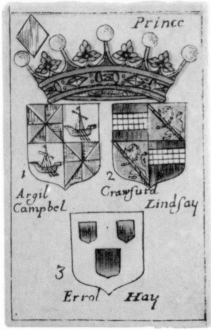

♦ Prince

1 Argil Campbel

2 Crawfurd Lindsay

3 Errol Hay

♠ 9 Earles of

23 Strathmore Lyon

24 Abercorne Hamilton

25 Lothian Ker

'THE BLAZONING OF THE ENSIGNES ARMORIAL OF THE KINGDOMS OF SCOTLAND ENGLAND, FRANCE AND IRELAND AND OF THE COATS OF ARMS OF THE NOBILITY OF SCOTLAND,' EDINBURGH, 1693

The court cards of each suit are king, queen, and prince. The arms of the four kingdoms are shown on the four kings, the arms of dukes are on the queens, and those of marquises on the princes. The numeral cards show the arms of earls, viscounts, and barons.

ENGLISH COURT CARDS MADE BY L. HEWSON, LONDON CARD-MAKER, 1678

red, and there is a red border around each card of the red suits. We have
Esquire Ogilby's 'England Exactly Described, or a Guide to Travellers,' a
book of folding maps, the originals of those on the cards. As in the cards,
where the maps are only a sixth of the size of these, each county is shown
alone. They show the high roads that led, as all high roads did, to London,
with the taverns marked and the times for changing horses; the little roads
and the little rivers that meander pleasantly down from the 'chiefe hills'
that soar in line after line; there are cathedral towns with their spires, and
castles with their battlements and best of all, the forests, thick clumps
of little Kate Greenaway trees, Sherwood, and Arden and Windsor and
all the rest.

A less interesting game, because it lacks the cunning maps, is 'The
Geography of England and Wales, accurately delineated on fifty two
cards, including the boundaries, extent, products,
manufactures, etc., of each county, with directions for playing an entertaining game. Published
September 20, 1799, by J. Wallis, 16 Ludgate St.,
London.' As in the earlier games there is a card
for each county, but the information is simply
listed on each one.

A geographical series of the world, published
in 1678, devotes the heart suit to Europe, the
diamonds to Asia, the spades to Africa, and the
clubs to America. The court cards are distinguished by medallion portraits, hand-colored,
mostly of contemporary rulers in the part of the
world described. The ace of each suit serves as a
tabular classification, and the most of each card
is taken up with a description of that part of the
world the name of which appears at the top.
For Americans, particularly, the club suit is

THE QUEEN OF CLUBS FROM
THE ENGLISH GEOGRAPHICAL
CARDS OF 1678

most entertaining. The king is John IV of Portugal, and the card is
appropriately given to a description of Brazil, which was part of his do-
main. The queen shows Queen Elizabeth, presiding over the 'English
Plantations on or near the continent of America,' presumably because
'Virginia' had been named for her. The jack is a 'Cannibal' and the
West Indies are described as the Cannibal Islands, while the divisions
shown on the nine remaining numerals are 'The Artick or Polar Land,'
the Western Coast of Southern America, Mexico or New Spain, Florida,
Canada or New France, the Chief Islands, Paraguay, New Mexico, and
Terra Firma, which is Panama, Central America, and the northern shore
of South America.

GEOGRAPHICAL CARDS, H. WINSTANLEY, LITTLEBURY

(178)

An even more enlightening series is the one published in 1665 by H. Winstanley, at Littlebury, whose name is on the ace of hearts. His cards not only describe the far lands and their inhabitants, but picture them as well. Again, hearts represent Europe, diamonds Asia, spades Africa, and clubs America. They picture and describe most vividly 'Jamestown and the Verginians,' 'Boston and the New English,' 'Bearford and the Greenlanders,' 'Witsborg and the Australes,' 'Saint Iago and the Chilians,' 'Saint Salvador and the Brasilians,' 'Assumption and the Paraguys,' 'Lima and the Peruvians,' 'Saint Foy de Bogota and the Castellans,' 'Santa Fé and the Californians,' 'Mexico and the Mexicans,' 'Quebec and the Canadians.' The text, particularly about the Spanish settlements, is so surprising that it is a temptation to quote many of these little cards. We have thirty-seven cards of this series, and six which are reprints from an incomplete pack in the British Museum. We have seen a most delightful uncut edition, presumably unique; the title-page reads 'All the principall Nations of the World, presented in their Habits or Fashions of Dressing with a Prospect of Their Capital Citys and a Geographycal Description of the Provinces and Citys and Remarkable Places in and Belonging or Depending to Ech Government with an observation of their Fruitfulness, Trading, Religions, and as Much of History of all as Could be Contained in so Small a Space. And which is most Humbly Presented and Dedicated to the Honourable Herbert Esq. not for his Improvement But that it was Part of his Studys and from Whom I must own to have Received most of my Instructions in the Composing of these Cards. And therefore they haveing so Honourable a Birth I shall not use many Arguments to Perswade how advantageous they may be to all Persons that will bear in mind whay is said in few words of so great a subject. H. Winstanley, Littlebury, fecit.'

A little book covered in cherry-colored silk contains 'A brief explanation of The Countries, & represented by the New Geographical Cards. London: Published by C. Hodges Stationer, 27 Portman street. 1827.' The cards are beautifully made from steel plates and colored by hand, with much gold. The heart suit is carmine, the clubs are green trefoils, the diamonds gold, and the spades blue pike heads. Besides these suit signs, arranged in the conventional way, each numeral card bears a map of some part of the world, those in the heart suit being European countries, spades American, clubs African, and diamonds Asiatic. The court cards are attempts at full-length portraits of contemporary rulers, for the most part. But the American suit has George Washington, as a young man and without powdered hair, for the king, while the queen and jack are Indians.

Of the seventeenth-century 'cards for playing' there are some which were made by L. Hewson, whose name is on the knave of clubs, in the

GEOGRAPHICAL PLAYING CARDS OF 1827

The spade is supposed to be a portrait of young George Washington

French manner. This Hewson, the card-maker, was a son of Hewson, the cobbler, one of Cromwell's generals who was caricatured mercilessly in numerous satires. The cards are printed from wood blocks and colored with stencil, and are cut very unevenly. Neither the texture of the cards nor the workmanship compares with that of the educational cards of the same time. Perhaps it was because of the poor quality that the cards from the Continent were preferred, or possibly the French and Belgian ones were cheaper or more pleasing in design. Hewson's cards certainly do not compare with French cards of that time, in any respect. At any rate, in spite of the law against their importation, the foreign cards were most used at the gay court of Charles II.

Following a petition of the Company of Card-Makers, a proclamation was issued in 1684 strictly forbidding their importation and threatening seizure, whenever they were found. The Company on their side established an office for sealing all playing cards of English manufacture, and regulating the price at which they were to be sold. An advertisement of this time explains how many poor persons are deprived of a way of making their living because of the unlawful importation of cards from other lands. An advertisement of the next year states that a surveyor has been appointed to approve the quality of the cards before sealing.

Mr. H. D. Phillips, an English card-maker of the late nineteenth century, in the catalogue of his collection of playing cards, makes the following interesting observations concerning English cards:

'For determining the periods at which certain packs of English cards were issued, something must be said, which, up to the present, has not been definitely stated. A hint on the subject was given by Cavendish in "Card Essays," London, 1879; "Duties on Playing Cards," pages 85–102; but the means of ascertaining an approximate date for the particular pack issued at any time between the years 1712 and 1862 has never been set forth in clear terms. Cards issued before 1712 must be judged by pattern and make, by historical references contained within the pack or by such outside references as may be found in the advertisements of card-makers — as the well-known Lenthall advertisement — or in the newspaper notices of the period.

ENGLISH 'CARDES FOR PLAYEING,' 1705

Yet nevertheless for that period of one hundred and fifty years there has been within all packs of cards, published according to law, a complete evidence of the period of issue hitherto unexplained, but denoted by the duty marks, taken together with the name of the sovereign in whose reign they were issued, the duties varying from 6*d.* to 2/6 in an ascending scale, and then falling from the highest point to 3*d.*

Duties on cards were imposed for two reasons: first, to prevent the importation of foreign cards, and second, as a means of revenue, made by Act of Parliament.

In order to show briefly the means resorted to under these two heads, the main points of the Letters Patent, Orders of Council, and Acts of Parliament are here recited:

1615. July 20th. Letters Patent granted by James I to Sir Richard Coningsby for the 'imposition of five shillings upon every grosse of Playing Cards that shall be Imported into this Kingdom' and an office created of 'Inspector of all Playing Cards imported.'

This was an easy means of paying off a debt due from King James to Sir Richard Coningsby.

1616. The card-makers remonstrate against Coningsby's patent.

1628. October 22nd. Worshipful Company of Makers of Playing Cards incorporated by Charter of the 4th, Charles I, with powers to seize foreign cards, or 'cards defectively made or unsealed,' on condition that the company thus incorporated should pay two shillings on every gross of packs 'made and sealed as thereafter appointed' and 1/— to the officer appointed to receive the same.

1631. The Commons complained of the duty on cards as 'arbitrary and illegal, and being levied without the consent of Parliament.'

1638. Proclamation 14th, Charles I, 18th June. No one to 'seal cards' but his Majesty's officer, and no cards to be imported or if imported, the said officer to seize same. All foreign cards seized to be 'put into English Binders.'

1643. July 11th. Orders to seize all imported cards and proceed against the importers.

1684. November 7th. Charles II orders all foreign playing cards imported to be 'Seized and condemned.'

Next is an enactment of duty by legal means:

1710. 9th Queen Anne, c. 23, XXXIX. That from and after 11th June 1711, for a period of 32 years, 'all playing cards made in or imported into Great Britain' shall pay a duty of 6d per pack. Cards not to be removed from the maker's premises until the 'seal upon the paper and thread enclosing every pack of cards' was approved by the Commissioners appointed to receive the 'vellum parchment and paper duties.'

After long series of protests by card-makers, paper-makers, and importers, and the working, or 'Poor Card-Makers,' against the duty:

1711. 10th Queen Anne, c. 19, CLX–CLXII. Cards that were made and finished before the 12th June 1711, were to be sealed for 1/2d per pack if taken to the Stamp Office for the Vellum, Parchment and Paper Duties. But from and after August 12th, 1712, no cards were to be exposed for sale, or used for play in any public gaming house unless the wrapper was 'sealed and stamped or marked' and one of the cards 'stamped or marked on the spotted or printed side.'

1719. 6th Geo. I, c. 21, LVII–LX. A 10 pound penalty imposed on any one re-issuing or using old stamps or seals, and other provisions against frauds on the Revenue.

1756. 29th Geo. II, c. 13. That from and after the passing of this Act, there shall be paid 'For every pack of such cards the sum of 6d over and above the duty of sixpence payable for the same.' Also that the Commissioners shall cause to be made 'a seal, stamp or mark to be used to denote the additional duties hereby granted.' That cards

for exportation shall have a special wrapper, and that one card in
each such pack shall be specially stamped as for export.

1765. 5th Geo. III, c. 46, IX–XVII. That from and after 5th July, 1765,
'Every maker of playing cards in Great Britain shall send to the
Commissioners for the Stamp Duties on vellum, parchment and
paper, in order to have as many several aces marked or impressed
thereon as such maker shall desire. . . .' also to send 'jews or wrappers for inclosing cards in order that the same may be stamped and
delivered again. . . .' and that the Commissioners shall and may denote one of the sixpenny duties charged on playing cards in Great
Britain on such 'jew or wrapper.'

ENGLISH PLAYING CARDS, 1765

1776. 16th George III, c. 34, VI–XVII. That from and after June 1st,
1776, sixpence extra duty be imposed and that in order to 'prevent
the multiplication of stamps upon such pieces of vellum, or parchment or sheets of paper on which several duties are by several Acts
of Parliament imposed, it shall be lawful for the Commissioners to
cause one new stamp to be provided to denote the said several
duties, and the duty granted by this Act on every piece . . . charged
with the said duties.'

1789. 29th Geo. III, c. 50. That from and after August 1st, 1789, sixpence extra duty be imposed, and a similar clause was inserted to that in the act of 1776 about 'one new stamp.'

1800. 39–40th Geo. III, c. 67. This is the 'Act for Union of Great Britain and Ireland.' By and under schedule B. the duty on cards imported into Ireland from Great Britain was fixed at 1/5 per pack with an additional 2 1/4d per lb. weight.

1801. 41st Geo. III, c. 86. An extra sixpence duty and regulations relating to the exportation of cards which were not to be moved from the maker's premises until after ten days' notice had been given. The Commissioners were to put in force any former law respecting the manner of denoting the duty on cards, and the 'sealing, stamping or marking' of the wrappers, and to have power to 'alter or renew' the manner of denoting the duties imposed by law.

1804. 44th Geo. III, c. 98. 'Whereas the several rates and duties on stamped vellum, parchment and paper and upon other articles and things ... are become very numerous, intricáte and complicated' ... that from the 10th October, 1804 all such duties were to determine and cease except such as were granted by the act of 39–40 George III, i.e., The Act of Union. Nevertheless in spite of such a preamble cards were set down in the schedule as liable to a duty of two shillings and sixpence.

1815. 55th Geo. III, c. 101. 'The label or wrapper shall be so contrived and shall be so fastened on the said wrapper as that the said several stamps, marks or seals shall appear on the sides of each pack of cards in such manner as the Commissioners shall direct.' ... No cards to be deemed waste for the purpose of sale unless the corners were cut off.

1828. 9th Geo. IV, c. 18. All previous Acts concerning the duty on cards and regulations as to their manufacture and sale were repealed. A new duty of one shilling per pack was imposed, which was to be 'denoted on the ace of spades of each pack of cards.' Every maker was to send a sufficient quantity of paper to the Commissioners of Stamps to have the aces marked and impressed thereon, and also patterns intended for wrappers, for the approval of the Commissioners.

1862. 25th Victoria. Duty reduced to 3d per pack to commence from the 1st of September, the duty to be denoted on the wrappers.

It will be observed that the foregoing acts of Parliament enforcing the payment of specific duties do not give any details as to the stamps to be employed for denoting the duties levied, but they supply very important evidence which is almost always missing in old packs of cards, that for many years one sixpence of the duty was levied on the wrapper, a point which up to the present seems to have been entirely missed, no doubt owing to the fact that so few wrappers have been preserved.

The following notes will form a 'circa' of issue for cards dating between 1712 and the present day:

1712–1714. A red stamp on the ace of spades, a crown above the monogram A.R.

1714–1765. A red stamp on the ace of spades, a crown above the monogram G.R. Some existing packs do not bear these duty stamps because they were issued illegally to evade payment of duty. In others the stamp has completely faded away. Most are so faint that they can only with difficulty be seen, and it is difficult to find any distinguishing feature in the stamps used, as to which of the three Georges they belonged.

DUTY ACE, 1765–1776

1765–1776. Duty one shilling. The ace of spades is surrounded by the Garter wreathed at each side with a crown above, and motto, 'Dieu et mon Droit,' below, on a ribbon. Beside the crown, 'George III, Rex.' On these aces there is no statement as to the amount of the duty; the stamp itself counted as sixpence (which must hereafter be borne in mind), the other sixpence was levied on the wrapper.

DUTY ACE, 1806

1776–1789. Duty one shilling and sixpence. Same ace of spades as used from 1765–1776, but above it 'Sixpence Addl. Duty.'

1789–1801. Duty two shillings. Same ace of spades as used from 1765–1776, but above it, 'Sixpence Addl. Duty,' and round the sides, to the left, 'Sixpence'; to the right 'Addl. Duty.'

1801–1820. Duty two shillings and sixpence.

PLAYING CARDS OF THE FRENCH TYPE, FOR EXPORT, 1810

Same ace of spades as used from 1789–1801, but added below the ace, 'Addl. Duty Sixpence.' Some time about the end of George III's reign, there was another ace of spades used, to all intents and purposes the same in appearance as the foregoing, but with a different lettering: above the ace, 'Duty,' to the left, 'One shilling,' to the right, 'and Sixpence'; this 'One shilling and sixpence' being obviously an easier way of denoting the extra duty. The other shilling was made up by two sixpenny impressed stamps on the wrapper, one on the front, and one on the back, so that the ace itself no longer counted as having a 6*d* value.

1820–1828. Duty two shillings and sixpence. Same ace of spades as that for the latter part of the 1801–1820 period, with 'Duty One Shilling and Sixpence' and 'Geo. IV.' Here again were two sixpenny impressed stamps on the wrapper.

DUTY ACE OF 1830

1828–1862. Duty one shilling. A new duty ace now appears, known subsequently as 'Old Frizzle' on account of its intricate pattern and flourishes, after the manner of bank note engraving. The ace itself contained the royal heraldic quarterings, and is otherwise distinguished as being supported by a lion and a unicorn. Above all 'Duty one shilling.'

1862. Duty three pence, levied on the wrapper only. No duty ace, but for a time most makers used a fanciful ace of spades.

The idea of a fanciful duty ace was probably borrowed from a card-maker's device, for several very early makers used these; perhaps the nearest approach to the duty aces was the one used by Ludlow and Company, about 1700, a black ace within the Garter of the Thistle surrounded by rays of light supported by the lion and unicorn, above the maker's name, 'Ludlow & Co. Patent Knight's Cards.'

Our only example of English 'cards for playing' of the eighteenth century, previous to 1712, have a plain ace of spades and no mark of either maker or of duties imposed. These are, of course, from wood blocks, with stenciled colors. They are interesting to compare with the handiwork of Hewson's cards of 1678. His retain many of the characteristics of the French cards from which they were copied. These later ones are truly British, larger, with more solid and substantial court cards. The same type appears unchanged in the cards of Gibson and Osborne, which from the ace must have been made in 1765. These cards are an uncut sheet, and there are two others so similar that they must be of the same time, but the cards, though they are of the same pattern as these first ones, are of a much smaller size, one series being two and a quarter by one and a half inches, and the other two and a half by one and a half inches. The surface of all of these sheets is waterproofed, and the cards have been printed from wood blocks, and the colors added by stencil. The sheets are only partly made, being two layers in thickness instead of three, and the back is coated with black to secure opacity, before the final third layer of paper is put on.

Among the makers whose aces prove them to be of this time are Yates and Barnes; Henry Hart, who made cards for export to America; and Stopforth and Son, whose cards for export to France are small and have the named court cards of the French type.

Toward the end of George III's reign there are cards of Josiah Stone, Hall and Son, and Hunt and Sons, the court cards sturdy Britishers all. A second pack by Hunt and Son are cards of the usual size, but the designs, both of the court cards and numerals, take up only two and a quarter by one and three eighths inches leaving a plain border all around each card. The court cards are rather delicate and seem to be copies of seventeenth-century patterns.

For the period between the years 1828 and 1862, with the new duty ace, we have a number of makers. Bancks Brothers, successors to Hunt and Son; Hardy and Sons, with cards whose backs are stained yellow, instead of being the conventional plain white; Reynolds and Sons, the backs of whose cards are a pattern in red and white in a pack of about 1845, and a few years later show a design in white and gold with a harp in the center.

We have a pack of de la Rue's cards of about 1860, possibly a few years earlier, with court cards of a slenderer and more delicate type than is usual.

The backs of these cards are decorated with a bunch of violets. The colors are soft and pleasing both in the face cards and in the decoration of the backs. Other cards made at about this time by de la Rue are double heads of the conventional English type, but the backs are beautifully decorated with conventional designs.

This decoration of the backs has been a special feature of the playing cards manufactured in England in the last seventy-five years. It had its first really artistic development under de la Rue and Company in London. Mr. Owen Jones was their artist, and he drew on all that was best from all countries and times for his inspiration. We are fortunate in having the book of his original designs. Each one is a gracious and lovely thing, reminiscent of a piece of Chinese porcelain, or a Persian tile, or old French needlework, a magical weaving of line and color. His flower designs are exquisite little arrangements that leave nothing to be desired, and breathe the fragrance of long-ago gardens.

After 1862 we find a great diversity in the type of the aces of spades. There are also other innovations. Perry and Company issue cards with a waterproof surface, and de la Rue makes his with round corners and indices. Bancks Brothers present double-head cards in 1867, and soon after advertising packs, one an advertisement of a London hotel, and the other of a shop. Goodall succeeds de la Rue as a maker, but keeps up the

THE ACE OF SPADES WITH A PORTRAIT OF PRESIDENT GRANT, AND
THE KNAVE OF HEARTS, 1874

tradition of the well-designed cards. In 1874, a pack of cards was issued in honor of the marriage of the Duke of Edinburgh with court cards of a less conventional type, while the aces hold portraits of Queen Victoria, President Grant, the Russian Czar, and the German Emperor.

Woolley and Company is another English maker. In 1884 he experiments with indices, putting the lettered value of each card in one of the suit signs.

James English and Company in 1880 makes cards called 'Anglo-American Squeezers.' 'Squeezers' was the name used for indexed cards by the Consolidated Card Company of New York at the time.

There are political playing cards made by Deakin and Company in 1880, with caricature portraits of the leading political figures in England for the court cards. These were evidently so successful that they were followed by a second similar series the next year.

A pack of the usual fifty-two cards, but with the aces and twos of fanciful design were published by Fitch and Company in 1883, to play a game called 'Heartsette.'

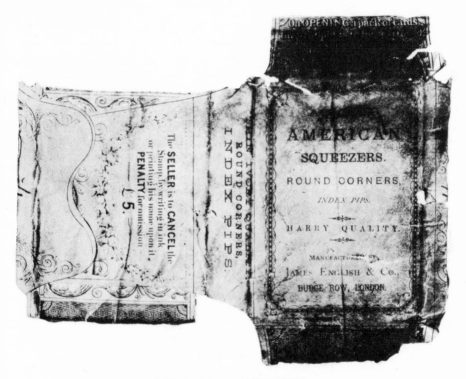

ENGLISH CARD WRAPPER, 1880

There are also cards for export of about this time with the popular decorated aces, showing pictures of the land in which they are destined to be used.

The joker, which was an American institution of about the fifties, first appears in Canadian cards made by the Union Card and Paper Company of Montreal in 1887. There are other Canadian cards made by the Canada

Bank Note Company at about the same time, and a few years later there are fancy patience cards made by Mitchell in Toronto.

There are quite beautiful historical playing cards published in London, similar to the Jeu Louis XV, but with court cards depicting costumes of four English reigns, Plantagenet, Tudor, Stuart, and Hanover.

PLAYING CARDS IN HONOR OF QUEEN VICTORIA'S DIAMOND JUBILEE, 1897

In 1897, Queen Victoria's Diamond Jubilee is marked by a beautifully designed pack of cards, with appropriately decorated aces, period court cards, and an excellent portrait of the Queen on the back of the cards. These are by Goodall.

A much more modest and less elaborate pack for the same purpose was issued by Kimberley at Birmingham under the name of Royal National Patriotic Playing Cards.

Goodall published a card game called 'Manx,' an ordinary pack of fifty-two cards, with two extra picture cards to each suit.

We have also the artist's proofs of Australian cards of 1915, whose court cards are very clever war-time caricatures.

AUSTRALIAN PLAYING CARDS, 1915

Late seventeenth-century England was notable for the many historical series of cards which followed one another, depicting in their quaint little cuts and accompanying lines of description many events of great moment in contemporary English history. The first, the Spanish Armada, was not contemporary except in the sense of being a protest against the leanings toward the Church of Rome which James II had shown while he was Duke of York. There are fifty-two little prints, picturing the attempted invasion and the events connected with the dispersing of the great fleet. The cards, which bear the usual suit signs and Roman numerals, do not seem to follow any order in their delineation.

This is followed by 'The horrid Popish Plot, lively represented in a pack of cards,' as an advertisement of 1679 reads. The sequence of events begins

THE HORRID POPISH PLOT, POLITICAL PLAYING CARDS OF 1679

Bulstrod and Whitlock present to
Oliver the Instruments of Governm.

A Covenanting Scot & an English In-
dependent differ about ye things of this
world.

The Army entring the City
persuing the Apprentices.

Oliver seeking God while the K.
is murthered by his order.

Huson the Cobler entring
London.

The Rump and dreggs of the house
of Com remaining after the good
members were purged out.

Bradshaw in ye High Court of
Justice insulting of the King.

THE RUMP PARLIAMENT, POLITICAL PLAYING CARDS OF THE REIGN OF CHARLES II
Hewson, the Cobbler and General, father of L. Hewson the card-maker, is seen on the nine of hearts,
proudly entering London at the head of his troops.

(192)

on the ace of hearts with 'The Plot first Hatcht at Rome by the Pope and Cardinalls' and ends on the four of clubs with 'The Tryall of Sir G. Wakeman, and 3 Benedictine Monks.' These were very popular, for some of the prints are from much-worn plates. We have both a set of the cards and another set of the little prints bound in a tiny book. These have not the suit signs.

'The Rump Parliament,' satirizing all that happened under the Commonwealth, follows this. It is thought that this series must have been engraved in Holland by some of the adherents of Charles II, as Cromwell would certainly not have allowed them in England.

There is an animated recording of the Rebellion of the Duke of Monmouth. In this series the story begins on the ace of clubs, and seems to end with the eight of hearts. It is thought that the spirited little engravings are Faithorne's work.

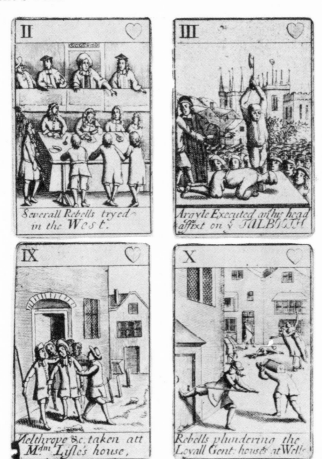

POLITICAL PLAYING CARDS PICTURING MONMOUTH'S REBELLION

IX ♠
The Prince and Princess of Oring
Receve the Memoriall and
Inuitasion from England

X ♠
The Irish Soldiers are promised
of London befor they came
Over and ye estats of ye Protestant

♦ KING.
The Kings Artilary going
to meet the Prince.

VI ♦
The King Expeckting ye Dutch in
the North sends forces ye way

VII ♦
The Dutch Fleet sail betwixt
Dover and Calis so ye French as
well as Inglish might see them
pasby so 7 Overs toogether

VIII ♦
The prince of Oring with his
Armey landing in ye West at
tor bay

THE REIGN OF JAMES II

THE REIGN OF QUEEN ANNE

(195)

KNAVE

Not only Cologn but Bavaria too
Tho'knaves in grain are reckon'd S^ts to you
A^trust we get sweet forgery and deceit
W'cant he do w^t mischiefs not compleat. ?

I

the French Kings breath

The fat Cat denotes ẏ Parti/ans flatterd with ẏ
Substance of ẏ Nation ẏ lean Cat ẏ People of Fra
nce Exhausted by heavy Impo/itions. &c ẏ Blind
Cat ẏ K^s Coun/el, who are at their wits end.

II

the Reward of forgery

The Duke of Anjou Whipping Cardin
Portocarero for forging a Will of the
Late King of Spain.

V

the Devil speaks   theirs
How ist frend Lewis Brother pope what
Both drunk wth bloud Im Glad to see you here
The Fistula in Ano, nay the Pox
and Purgatorys feigned holes and locks
for all but Bawbles in Infernal Stocks
and then their heads he Knocks.

VI

Our Money gone wee passive French submit
And let a Tyrant take our Goods for it
Taxing's ẏ Devil where there's nought to pay
and is to Misery the Shortest Way.

VII

Thus all my Spongey Officers I serve
Squeeze out their ill got Wealth & let 'em
Starve

MARLBOROUGH'S VICTORIES

(196)

Next comes 'The Reign of James II.' The inscriptions are very badly spelled, but the engravings are delightful. The story begins on the ace of spades and ends on the eight of diamonds, with the arrival of the Prince of Orange in London in 1688.

'The Reign of Queen Anne' appropriately follows. Besides the usual suit signs and Roman numerals, an Arabic numeral above the illustration on each card indicates the sequence of events. These begin on the ace of hearts and end on the four of clubs. On the ten of diamonds is the name of the engraver, R. Spofforth.

The most elaborately engraved of all of these are the cards called 'Marlborough's Victories.' They tell the story of the disputes concerning the Spanish succession and other events of the reign of Queen Anne, between 1700 and 1708. Some of the cards have portraits of important persons, Queen Anne, Charles III of Spain, Eugene of Savoy, and several others. The spade suit is a scathing satire of the reign of Louis XIV.

The Bubble Cards appear in 1721, quite different from the Dutch series. There is a miniature playing card in the upper left-hand corner of each card, while most of the card is given to the illustration. These satirize the South Sea Bubble scheme. Ladies play a large part in these small pictures and the social life of the day and its occupations are interestingly shown. In these illustrations, the characters speak

ADVERTISEMENT FOR THE PROVERB CARDS

as they do in our 'funny pages' of to-day, the words coming from their mouths. Below each picture is a quatrain of doggerel verse. These were sold by Carington Bowles, No. 69 in Saint Paul's Church Yard, London.

Other cards printed for Carington Bowles have each one of the lyrics and the music of one of the airs of the 'Beggar's Opera,' which was written by John Gay in 1728. They are delightful little melodies with words worthy of Gilbert and Sullivan and they enjoyed vast popularity both in England and America. We have a little book published in London in 1791, giving the lines and lyrics of the entire opera 'regulated from the prompt book,' and at this time it was even more of a favorite than when it had first come out.

ADVERTISEMENT FOR THE BUBBLE CARDS

Alexander Pope and Jonathan Swift were both at the opening performance in 1728, and Pope wrote later of the opera: 'The vast success of it was unprecedented and incredible. It was acted in London sixty-three days uninterrupted, and renewed the next season with equal applause. It spread into the great towns of England, was played in many places to the thirtieth and fortieth time, at Bath and Bristol fifty, etc. It made its progress into Wales, Scotland, and Ireland, where it was performed twenty-four days together. It was lastly acted in Minorca. The fame of it was not confined to the author only; the ladies carried about with them the favorite songs of it in fans, and houses were furnished with it in screens. The person who acted Polly, till then obscure, became all at once the favorite of the town. Her pictures were engraved and sold in great numbers, her life was written, books of letters and verses to her published, and pamphlets made even of her sayings and jests. Furthermore, it drove out of England for that season, the Italian opera, which had carried all before it for ten years. That idol of the nobility and people which the great critic, Mr. Dennis, by the labors and outcries of a whole life, could not overthrow, was demolished by a single stroke of this gentleman's pen. This remarkable period happened in the year 1728.' Lavinia Fenton was the first Polly Peachum and she was

Here South-Sea Ladies flush'd with Lucky Spouses,
With some for Coaches, some for Country Houses:
Says one, whose Gouty Husband limps on Crutches,
Give me a Brisk Gallant, take you your Coaches.

An Old Welch Justice mounted on a Goat,
Is ask'd, which way his Worship means to Trot;
To London hur is Travelling, quoth he,
To sell Welch Copper, and to Buy South-Sea.

A certain Good Old Worthy Rich in Land,
Keeping his Servants Wages in his Hands,
Bought South-Sea Stock, when they knew nothing of,
Sold it when High, and gave to them the Profit.

A Jobber, for Stock-difference in a Bubble,
Is by another Bite Ketch'd into Trouble;
The Serjeant grumbles, till he gets Restoration,
Or else a Jayl must be the Prisoners Portion.

A certain Lady when the Stocks ran high,
Put on Rich Robes, to Charm her Lover's Eye;
But South-Sea falling, Pawn'd her fine Brocade,
And now appears like other homely Jade.

Three Reverend Teachers, mutually agree,
To venture joint in Sharestock in South-Sea;
Their Stock they bought, by tythe, turn'd into Gold,
And fear will sink them, but a high when sold.

SOUTH-SEA BUBBLE CARDS, LONDON, 1721

(199)

THE BEGGAR'S OPERA, LONDON, 1728

(200)

also the first English actress to marry a duke. The opera has been played almost everywhere throughout the English-speaking world. For more than a hundred years it was all the rage. Then it seems to have been forgotten until a revival last year brought it back with all its eighteenth-century charm and freshness. After such a gallant history, it is no wonder that it appeared on these little cards of 1728. This particular series of musical cards we have never seen listed in any other collection.

PLAYING CARDS OF 1700, 'LOVE MOTTOES'

There is another prettily engraved series of pictorial cards, 'Love Mottoes,' each card bearing a verse as well as the illustration, and both reminiscent of Lovelace. There is a miniature playing card in the corner of each card, and the red suit signs are colored. The Hercules on the ace of clubs is copied from Goltzius. The cards were made about 1700.

FROM THE PLAYING CARD SERIES 'WITTY SAYINGS'

Another series in which the ladies wear the Fontange head-dresses as in the 'Love Mottoes,' is one called 'Witty Sayings.' The subjects are not so pastoral as the last, but are infinitely more amusing. Above the quaint little illustration on each card is its title and they are amazingly varied. The old English duty stamp, in red, is on the ace of spades. The story describing the picture and supposedly containing the witty saying is below each picture.

A PROVERB SERIES OF PLAYING CARDS, 1710

A proverb series of about this time shows the same arrangement, a well-known proverb appearing at the bottom of each card, with the illustration of it, above. These are about 1710.

FROM A PROVERB SERIES OF
1720

A second series follows this, about 1720, illustrating entirely different proverbs; these are more sophisticated, and the proverb appears in both French and English. In 1759 there is a delightful set of little cards, 'Æsop's Fables.' These are little etchings, with the fable and its moral beneath, and must have delighted little Londoners of that time. The name 'I. Kirk' is on several of the cards, and an advertisement in the 'Public Advertiser' for December 17, 1759, reads 'Æsop's Fables' exactly copied after Barlow, with fables and morals in verse, to be had of the proprietor, I. Kirk at the Grotto Toy Shop in St. Paul's Churchyard.' The excellence of the design and the technique are strongly suggestive of Hollar, who etched a set of hunting and fishing designs after Barlow in 1671.

Barlow issued, in 1665, an edition of 'Æsop's Fables,' etched after his own designs. There is no other known example of these little cards.

The FOX and CROW

The Crow with laden beak to th' tree retires,
The Fox, to get her prey, her Form admires;
While she to shew her gratitude not small,
Offering to give her thanks, her prize lets fall.
MORAL.
Shun faithless flatterers, Harlots jilting tears,
They are fool's hopes, & youth's deceitfull snares.

The sick LYON.

The Lyon sick sold, the Beasts aggree,
Each to take Vengeance for past Injury;
He bears with Royal Patience, till he feels,
The dull Ass spurn him with his sawcy heels;
MORAL.
Then dying cry'd let the proud Great be warnd,
For when they're falln, by Knaves & Fools they're scornd

The TAILESS FOX

The Fox who lost her Tail, perfuades ye reft
To bob their trains, as moft commode & beft,
When one replyd, we more difcreet difdain
To buy conveniences with publick fhame;
MORAL.
He that grave Council for your good pretends
Fifty to one promotes his private ends.

the DOLPHIN & TUNIS

The Tunis to escape the Dolphins Shock,
Flying for safety to a fatal Rock,
There lay insnar'd, as was her foe beneath,
Who to Behold him perish, welcome's death
MORAL.
The injur'd innocent is pleas'd to see,
His treacherous friend opprest, as well as he.

The FOX in the WELL.

The Fox in a deep well implores the aid,
Of a grave Wolfe, who many questions made,
How he came there, the Fox half drown'd replyes
Oh cease vaine words & help thy friend that dyes;
MORAL.
Men oft good counsell can bestow in grief,
But with no reall goodwill bring relief.

The BEAR & TWO TRAVELLERS

A Bear approach'd two Travellers, one fled,
To a safe tree, th' other lay still as dead,
The Bear but smelling to his face, retir'd;
The friend descends & laughing thus inquir'd;
MORAL.
What wast he whisper'd in thy ear quoth he;
He bad me shun a treacherous friend like thee

ÆSOP'S FABLES, LONDON, 1759

(203)

CARDS BY ROWLEY AND COMPANY, 1765

There are fancy suit signs, and the court cards are portraits of members of reigning families

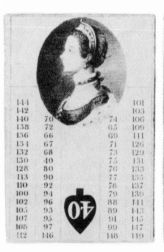

AN ARITHMETICAL GAME, *c.* 1780

(204)

In a pack of cards of 1780, the spade suit sign is replaced by a blue pike head, clubs by a green trefoil, hearts, red chalices, and the diamonds are yellow and faceted. The duty ace bears the maker's name, Rowley and Company, and the court cards are the reigning sovereigns of Great Britain, France, Spain, and Prussia. These are engraved from copper plates.

An arithmetical game of about this date, in spite of having spade suit signs and three court cards, is evidently intended as a children's game, as there is no duty ace. The court cards are very interesting in themselves. The king is a well-engraved medallion portrait of George III, the queen is quite a lovely head of Queen Charlotte, and the knave seems to be the well-known teacher of mathematics, Master Cocker, who wrote several arithmetics, which were used for many years. He may have been the author of this game, which we have not found listed in any other collection of cards.

The doctrines of chance, for which there was such a demand during the seventeenth and eighteenth centuries in England, are many of them written by teachers of arithmetic and professors of mathematics. One by A. de Moivre, F.R.S., in 1718 is dedicated, by permission, to Sir Isaac Newton. Most of them are rather good-sized books, to have room for the many lengthy tables of calculations. And within the calf-bound volumes of most of them are many marginal notes of long ago owners, making them still more invincible 'guides to the Turf, Cock pit, the Card table and other species of public Diversion, either in the Parlour or the Field.'

Early in the seventeenth century a fever of gaming possessed the court and was reflected in the coffee-houses and in private homes. Richard Seymour, in his preface to one of the 'Court Gamesters,' sums up the situation calmly and without exaggeration when he says, 'Gaming is become so much the fashion among the Beau Monde, that he who in Company should appear ignorant of the games in Vogue, would be reckoned low bred & hardly fit for conversation.'

The rows upon rows of volumes on gaming of those days are mute witnesses of the truth of his statement. In a day when printed books were not common, there are often two editions in a single year, seemingly made necessary by slight changes in the rules of the games, or because the first edition was exhausted. The Gamesters start in London in 1674, 'The Compleat Gamester,' 'The Court Gamester,' 'The Gamester's Companion,' and 'The Polite Gamester,' hailing from Dublin. Many bear the amazing title-page: 'The Court Gamester: or, full and easy Instructions for Playing the Games now in Vogue after the best method: as they are Play'd at Court, and in the Assemblies, viz. Ombre, Picquet, and the Royal Game of Chess. Wherein the Frauds in Play are detected, and the

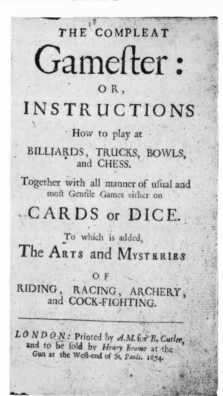

THE COMPLEAT GAMESTER, LONDON, 1674
The frontispiece and the title-page

Laws of each Game annex'd to prevent Disputes. Written for the Young Princesses, etc.' A London paper of 1753 says, 'There is a new kind of tutor lately introduced into some Families of Fashion in this Kingdom, principally to complete the education of the Young Ladies, namely a Gaming Master; who attends his Hour as regularly as the Music, Dancing and French Master; in order to instruct young Misses in Principles of the fashionable Accomplishment of Card playing. However absurd such a conduct in Parents may appear to the Serious and Sober minded, it is undeniably true that such a Practice is now introduced by some, and will it is feared be adopted by many more.'

'Mr. Hoyle's Games' begin in 1743 in Bath, and continue to be published in London for more than a century. All of the earlier editions are autographed. In 1790, goff, or golf, is first included in the list of games that have gradually been added to the original treatises on games at cards. At the beginning of the century cocking and horse-racing still further swell the list. In the very first 'Gamester,' 'The Arts and Mysteries of Riding, Racing, Archery and Cock fighting,' are added to the 'Instructions How

The Explanation of the Frontispiece.

Billiards *from Spain at first deriv'd its name,*
Both an ingenious, and a cleanly Game.
One Gamester leads (the Table green as grass)
And each like Warriors strive to gain the Pass.
But in the contest, e're the Pass be won,
Hazzards are many into which they run.
Thus whilst we play on this Terrestrial Stage,
Nothing but Hazzard with attend each age.
Next here are Hazzards p'ty'd another way,
By Box and Dice, 'tis Hazzard is the Play.
The Bully-Rock with mangy fist, and Pox,
Justles some out, and then takes up the Box.
He throws the Main, and cries, who comes at Seven ?
Thus with a dry fist nicks it with Eleven.
If out, he raps out Oaths I dare not tell,
Hot, piping out, and newly come from Hell.
Old-Nick o're-hearing, by a Palming-trick
Secures the Gamester; thus the Nickers nickt.
Now t' Irish, or Back-Gammoners we come,
who with their money, with their men safe home ;
But as in war, so in this subtle Play,
The stragling men are ta'ne up by the way.
By entring then, one reinforceth more,
It may be to be lost, as those before.
By Topping, Knapping, and foul play some win ;
But those are losers, who so gain by sin.
After these three the Cock-pit claims a name ;
A sport gentile, and call'd a Royal Game.
Now see the Gallants crowd about the Pit,
And most are stockt with Money more than wit ;
Else sure they would not, with so great a stir,
Lay ten to one on a Cocks faithless Spur.
Lastly, observe the women with what grace
They fit, and look their Partners in the face.
Who from their eyes shoot Cupids *fiery Darts ;*
Thus make them lose at once their Game and Hearts.
Their white soft hands, (when e're the Cards they cut)
Make the men wish to change the Game to Putt.
The women knew their thoughts, then cry'd, Enough,
Lets leave off Whift, *and go to* Putt, *or* Ruff.
Ladies don't trust your secrets in that hand,
who can't their own (to their great grief) command.
For this I will assure you, if you do,
In time you'l lose your Ruff *and* Honour *too.*

THE COMPLEAT GAMESTER, LONDON, 1674
The explanation of the frontispiece

to play at Billiards, Trucks, Bowls and Chess Together with all manner of usual and most Gentile Games either on Cards or Dice.'

The establishment of gaming houses in the cities inevitably brought forth various protests. 'An Essay upon Gaming in a dialogue between Callimachus and Dolomedes' was printed in London in 1713. This controversial form was a favorite among the Italians two hundred years earlier, in attacks on gaming in their own country.

'An account of the Endeavours that have been used to Suppress Gaming houses and of the Discouragements that have been met with, In a letter to a Noble Lord' is another, and 'A Disswasive of Gaming,' by Josiah Woodward, runs through many editions, whether because of its potency or lack thereof, it is impossible to say. These and many others are answered with becoming humility in 'A Modest Defense of Gaming,' whose scholarly author quotes the classics and treats his subject with a subtle humor much more poignant than that found in the many satires of the day.

Sometimes these are in the form of plays. 'A Game at Pickquet, Being acted from the year 1653 to 1658 by O.P. and others; with great Applause.

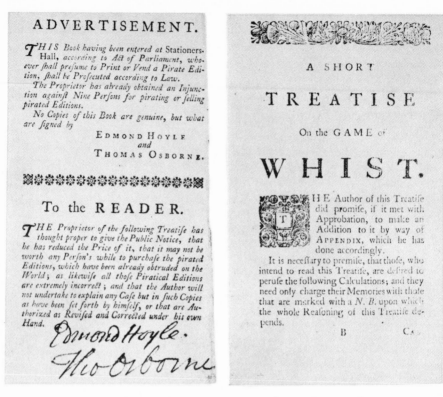

FROM AN AUTOGRAPHED EDITION OF 'HOYLE'S GAMES'

Printed in the Year 1659,' is the earliest we have. 'The Humours of Whist, a Dramatic Satire as acted every day at White's' is another; this same old idea was used by Cavendish the whist authority, in his 'Musical Whist,' a pageant given at an orphanage fête in 1892. Our copy of this is an autographed one, given to William Pole, Musical Doctor at Oxford, who has nearly as many books on whist to his credit as Cavendish, or Hoyle himself.

It is amusing to see how many ex-military men, admirals, lieutenant colonels, majors, etc., write series of books on gaming. One volume of 1814 (which is a tenth edition), written by General Scott, has his own martial portrait for a frontispiece.

In France, many an abbé evinces the same proclivities. 'Le Grand Trictrac, par M. l'Abbé S——, correspondant des Académies Royales des Sciences de Paris et de Toulouse,' is published at Avignon in 1756, 'chez Alexandre Giroud, seul Imprimeur de Sa Sainteté. Avec permission des Supérieurs.' And he is only one of many.

Poetry is largely indulged in, to meet the demand for humor and satire, as well as curious essays and stories. And remembering the books of the learned Thomas Hyde and Dr. Christie, it is an exceedingly entertaining and surprising literature, and it shows besides the wide interest in gaming in those days among all sorts and conditions of people.

The very games have interesting associations and traditions. 'Primero' and 'Gleek' are said by Ben Jonson to be the 'best games at cards for the gallantest company.'

FRONTISPIECE, 'EASY RULES OF WHIST,' 1814

Whist, which was commonly called 'Whisk' (its name comes from 'Hist, be still'), is said to be a very ancient game among us. At the time of Charles II, whist, or the silent game, was played below-stairs in the servants' hall with 'All Fours' and 'Put.' It was in 1736 that it was first 'much studied' by a group of gentlemen who frequented the Crown Coffee-House in Bedford Row. They laid down the following rules:

> To play from a straight suit.
> To study your partner's hand as well as your own.
> Never to force your partner unnecessarily.
> To attend to the score.

Many of the later books on games are sponsored and printed by the English card-makers Bancks Brothers, de la Rue, and Hunt and Sons.

'LONDON CRIES': PLAYING CARDS OF 1795

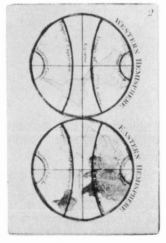

ASTRONOMICAL AND GEOGRAPHICAL CARDS, 1795

(210)

To go back to the pictorial cards, there are two series picturing the familiar London cries. The earlier are charming little prints after the designs by Wheatley. The other is a half-century later, a children's game without suit signs and lacking the virtue of the Wheatley prints.

An educational game of forty cards has the title 'The Elements of Astronomy and Geography explained in forty cards, beautifully engraved and coloured by the Abbe Paris. Published July 15th, 1795, by John Wallis, No. 16 Ludgate St. London.' They are engraved with precision and scientifically, with a diagram, and on the other side of the card is the explanation thereof.

FROM THE KINGS OF ENGLAND'

Another educational game shows full-length figures of the kings of England and gives statistics concerning each one in the suits of clubs, diamonds, and hearts. The heart suit is given entirely to tables of all sorts. On the nine of spades, which is the multiplication table, is lettered, 'Sold at Willerton's Toy Shop, Bond Street.' Magna Charta is another game of 1820. The title-page of the little book of rules for playing it reads, 'Magna Charta or Knight Errantry, a new game for young persons: to which is appended a synopsis of Chivalry by a Lady.'

A series of astronomical cards were issued in 1828. There are thirty-six

ASTRONOMICAL PLAYING CARDS, 1828

cards showing the constellations and four emblematic of the seasons. With them is 'A brief Explanation of the Constellations represented by the New Astronomical Cards. London, published by C. Hodges, 27 Portman

FROM 'THE ROYAL HISTORICAL GAME OF CARDS'

Square.' In a second issue of the cards their number is increased to fifty-two by twelve court cards showing mythological figures. Suit signs are also added, the red chalices, the blue pike heads, the green trefoils, and the golden diamonds, that are used in the geographical series of 1820. The workmanship is beautiful, and the duty ace is lettered Stopforth and Son.

A CARD FROM A SERIES PICTURING FAMOUS PERSONAGES IN 1823

Similar series were published in 1818, 1822, 1824, and 1825

'The Royal Historical Game of Cards' contains forty-five cards, lithographed in gold, the backs a red-and-green plaid. There are nine groups of four cards each, picturing the rulers of England from the time of John in the eleventh century to Victoria in the nineteenth, and for each group, one card giving the chronology of the reigns. Their date cannot be much after Queen Victoria's accession to the throne in 1837.

A children's game, 'Trial by Jury,' has rather amusing caricatures of the personnel of an English courtroom of about 1850 for its court cards, of which there are eleven to each suit. There are also the usual ten numerals with the conventional suit signs, and a card of explanation and rules.

A pack of fortune-telling cards of about this time have the conventional suit signs, and in addition there is an amusing illustration which covers most of each card, with its meaning written below. The red suits are printed entirely in red, the black in black, and their maker was Reynolds and Son.

A CHILDREN'S CARD GAME, *c.* 1820

FROM A HAND-COLORED SERIES
OF ENGLISH BIBLICAL CARDS

ENGLISH LOTTERY CARDS, *c.* 1815

(213)

A SEQUENCE GAME, *c.* 1885

There are 'Amphibological Conversation Cards,' made by Goodall a few years later, and a sequence game of thirty cards with rounded corners bearing a series of amusing little Chinese figures, faintly suggestive of willow ware and printed in the familiar porcelain blue. There is a verse on each card and they were designed by C. E. Eads, about 1870.

A CARD GAME OF 1870

We have the proofs of fifty-two cards for a sequence game, designed, according to Mr. George Clulow, by Miller. The drawings are delightful, and whimsical enough to be Rackham's. When properly put together, they picture a bird wedding and all the attendant activities.

'District Messengers' is a card game whose illustrations bring back London of the nineties, and a pack of patience cards of about this time, issued in Bombay, portray Indian natives of all castes. There are also miniature playing cards three quarters by one half inch, painstakingly made and correct in the smallest detail, even to the gold edges.

The most surprising feature of the English cards is to be found when you examine the transformations or humorous cards in which the suit signs form part of the design. The English, who are supposed to lack a proper sense of humor, have far the cleverest group of these to be found in any country.

Our earliest ones begin auspiciously in 1808 with a series picturing the favorite pantomimes of the time. Some of the numerals show London audiences, and Shylock and Romeo and Juliet are to be found in burlesque.

The king of hearts is Beau Brummel, and the queen, she of the nursery rhyme and the tarts. Mother Goose herself is on the four of spades, and gave her name to a panto-mime at the Haymarket in 1803. The panto-mime of Perouse, pictured on the ace of spades, was produced in 1801; three-fingered Jack on the ace of clubs was in the panto-mime of Obi, which first appeared in 1800, and so was the song of the Spanish guitar, on the four of diamonds.

The next ones are original drawings in pen and ink, on the numerals of two packs of cards; we have forty-nine cards, none of them court cards. They were drawn by Count d'Orsay for Lady Blessington; their humor probably refers to happenings of the day, most of them of purely local interest. But

'THE SONG OF THE SPANISH GUITAR,' FROM A PACK OF TRANS-FORMATION CARDS OF 1808

they are so spontaneous and original and so diversified as to subject that they are a delight even to-day. They must have been a joy in their own time.

ORIGINAL TRANSFORMATION CARDS BY COUNT D'ORSAY

TRANSFORMATION CARDS PUBLISHED BY REYNOLDS

(216)

A well-known series of 1828, whose ace of clubs is lettered 'E. Olivatte, 6 Leigh Street, Burton Crescent,' resembles the German series of Cotta. The court cards are classical figures, and the cards are from copper plates, and hand-colored.

A series of artist's proofs which we have not found listed in any other collection, from the duty ace belongs to the end of George III's reign. The maker's name, Jos. H. Reynolds, is also on this ace. This is a quaint and charming little card game and it would be fun to puzzle out the reason for many of the well-drawn designs. The four of diamonds shows Falstaff and the basket, with Mistress Ford and Mistress Page, but the other cards seem to be merely delightful whimsicalities. The court cards are the usual ones, only the suit sign masquerading as a red owl or a buffoon, a black turkey cock or a knight, on a coal-black charger.

A COURT CARD FROM THE TRANS-
FORMATION SERIES BY I. L. COWELL

FROM A PACK OF TRANSFORMATION
CARDS BY ALFRED CROWQUILL

Another series of the first quarter of the century are etchings by I. L. Cowell. The court cards are full-length figures surrounded by a border of fluttering playing cards. John Tenniel must have remembered these when he did his illustrations for Lewis Carroll's 'Alice.' One of these court cards is Puss in Boots, with an expression reminiscent of the Cheshire Cat, and another is the ass of the 'Midsummer-Night's Dream.'

A later series by Alfred Crowquill are a departure from the usual transformations. The red suits are in black outline on a buff background, and the black ones on a blue. In each pip is an amusing little face, delightfully done. The court cards are travesties of the usual ones. At about this same time a series of 'Picture Cards' were published by William Tegg. Each card of the diamond suit bears the monogram 'J.B.' They are printed on

Dandy Jim from Souf Caroline

TRANSFORMATION CARDS BY WILLIAM MAKEPEACE THACKERAY

(218)

four sheets, one for each suit, and, from the verses at the top, are evidently meant for children, though the subjects are rather sophisticated. These were copied in Vienna and Munich, and in America, where they were made into a pack of transformation cards by Samuel Hart, of Philadelphia.

Another very cleverly designed series was done by Chapman for Reynolds and Sons about 1880.

Last but not least is a series by no less a person than William Makepeace Thackeray. There are twenty-one of these, and they are published in a book of Thackeray's things, 'The Orphan of Pimlico.' These were collected by Miss Thackeray after her father's death, and concerning the cards, she explains that, while he made no pretense to being an artist, so many of his drawings had been published that she thought his audience should know what he could do when he tried. Instead of the crude and vivid little sketches that are interspersed through so many of his letters and writings, we have in the cards finished and charming little drawings, just as vivid and altogether delectable as the things we all know.

The title of the three of spades is 'Mr. Gibbon, Mr. Boswell, Mr. Johnson'; the two and five are 'American Notes and Reminiscences'; and the ten of clubs 'An Assyrian bas-relief. See Herodotus.' Others are excerpts from Shakespeare and Byron, Cooper and Mother Goose, and delicious nonsense rhymes of his own, which he has illustrated. Miss Thackeray says of these: 'The Playing Cards were originally intended to form a completed pack, but only a certain number were ever finished. They amused my father very much at the time he drew them. He was specially pleased with the likeness to Mr. Gibbon which he discovered in the three of spades. I think this is almost the trump card of the whole hand as it is dealt out here.'

This group of unexpectedly varied and colorful card games is a curious and an amusing thing to have come out of staid old England. There is an equally amusing and very British attempt to explain the psychology of this, at least in part, in the foreword, or 'Epistle to the Reader,' at the beginning of 'The Compleat Gamester' of 1674. It says: 'Certainly there is no man so severe to deny the lawfulness of Recreation; There was never any Stoick found so cruel, but at some time or other he would unbend his mind, and give it liberty to stray into some more pleasant walks, than the miry, heavy ways of his own sowr, willful resolutions.... Now what Recreation this should be I cannot prescribe, nor is it requisite to confine any to one sort of pleasure, since herein Nature taketh to herself an especial Prerogative, for what to one is most pleasant, to another is most offensive; Some seeking to satisfie the Mind, some the Body, and others both in joint motion. To this end I have laid before you what variety of Pastimes I could collect for the present leaving the rest (as you like these) to be suppli'd hereafter. . . . To conclude, let me advise you, if you play (when your business will permit) let not a covetous desire to win another's money engage you to the losing your own; which will not only disturb your mind, but by the disreputation of being a Gamester, if you lose not your estate, you will certainly lose your credit and good name, than which there is nothing more valuable.'

ENGLISH PLAYING CARDS IN THE COLLECTION OF THE UNITED STATES PLAYING CARD COMPANY [1]

*Scholer's Practicall Cards, F. Jackson, 1656	45 cards
*Fortune-telling cards, 1665	46 cards
*Geographical cards, the counties of England and Wales, 1675	52 cards
Geographical cards, the counties of England and Wales, 1680	50 cards
*Playing cards by L. Hewson, 1678	24 cards
Geographical cards, the world, 1678	48 cards
*The Horrid Popish Plot, 1679	52 cards
*The Rump Parliament, 1680	52 cards
*Heraldic cards, Richard Blome, 1675	52 cards
*Arms of the English peers, 1686	52 cards
*Monmouth's Rebellion, 1686	52 cards
*The Reign of James II, 1690	41 cards
*Geographical cards, H. Winstanley, 1665	43 cards
*Arms of the Nobility of Scotland, 1693	38 cards
*Love Mottoes, 1700	52 cards
*Stenciled cards, 1705	52 cards
*The Reign of Queen Anne, 1706	43 cards
*Marlborough's Victories, 1708	52 cards
*Witty Sayings, 1710	52 cards
*Proverb cards, 1710	52 cards
Proverb cards, 1720	52 cards
Bubble cards, 1721	52 cards
*Æsop's Fables, 1759	52 cards
*The Beggar's Opera, 1728	52 cards
Lottery cards, 1730	47 cards
History of England on cards, 1760	49 cards
Biblical cards	8 cards
*Six card sheets by Gibson and Osborne, 1765	
*The Rulers of Europe, cards for playing, Rowley, 1765	31 cards
Arithmetical cards	13 cards
*London cries, 1795	9 cards
Astronomy and geography cards, the Abbé Paris, 1795	40 cards
The Geography of England and Wales, 1799	52 cards
Duty aces, Yates and Barnes, 1765, Ludlow and Company, 1800, T. Wheeler, 1803, Hall and Son, 1804, 1806, Hardy, 1804, Hunt and Son, 1806	11 cards
*Transformation cards, 1808	51 cards
Arithmetical cards, c. 1800	7 cards

[1] The starred items are from the collection of George Clulow, F.R.G.S.

The Mystic Oracle, *c.* 1800	6 cards
The Happy Family, *c.* 1820	19 cards
Nipatitwitch, the Bellman, *c.* 1820	17 cards
Famous personages, 1818, G. Smeeton, 17 St. Martin's Lane, London	7 cards
Playing cards by Stopforth for export, 1810	38 cards
Playing cards by Josiah Stone, 1815	52 cards
Playing cards by Hall and Sons, 1817	52 cards
Playing cards by Hunt and Sons, 1818	52 cards
Playing cards by Hunt and Sons, 1818, small stenciled cards	
Educational cards, kings of England, etc., *c.* 1800	36 cards
Geographical cards, 1820	52 cards
Three uncut sheets of playing cards, *c.* 1820	
Transformation cards, 1822	49 cards
Famous persons, 1822, William Darton, 28 Holborn Hill, London	14 cards
Famous persons, 1824, William Darton	5 cards
Famous persons, 1823, William Darton	9 cards
Mental Amusement, C. Gill, printed for J. Souter, London	40 cards
History of England, Darton and Harvey, 1807	50 cards
*Astronomical cards, C. Hodges, 1828	40 cards
Astronomical cards, C. Hodges, 1829	52 cards
*Transformation cards, E. Olivatte, 1828	52 cards
*Playing cards, Bancks Brothers, 1830	52 cards
Transformation cards, Joseph H. Reynolds, 1830	50 cards
The Royal Historical Game of Cards, 1840	45 cards
Playing cards by Hardy and Sons, 1840	52 cards
*Transformation cards, I. L. Cowell, 1812	10 cards
Playing cards, Reynolds and Sons, 1845	52 cards
Picture cards, transformations, published by William Tegg, 1850	52 cards
Pictorial game	49 cards
Transformation cards, William Makepeace Thackeray	21 cards
Transformation cards, Alfred Crowquill, 1850	27 cards
Trial by Jury	42 cards
The Streets of London	44 cards
*Playing cards, Reynolds and Sons, 1852	52 cards
Playing cards, Walsh, Bailey and Company, 1860	52 cards
*Humorous playing cards, Reynolds and Sons, 1860	51 cards
Playing cards, de la Rue, 1860	47 cards
Playing cards, de la Rue, 1862	51 cards
Amphibological Conversation cards, 1862, C. Goodall and Sons	48 cards
Change for a Sovereign, J. Evans and Sons	55 cards
*Playing cards, Perry and Company, 1867	52 cards
Playing cards, de la Rue, 1867	52 cards
Playing cards, de la Rue, 1862, back design by Owen Jones	27 cards
Playing cards, Bancks Brothers, 1868	52 cards
Playing cards for export, de la Rue, 1870	52 cards
Chinese pictorial game	20 cards
Playing cards, C. Goodall	52 cards

Playing cards, Langham Hotel advertisement	52 cards
*Sequence game, Chinese willow ware design, 1872	30 cards
Sequence game, caricatures	48 cards
Meeting of creditors, c. 1875	26 cards
Playing cards, court cards portraits of contemporary rulers, 1874	52 cards
Playing cards, Willis and Company, 1875	52 cards
*Playing cards, Wooley and Company, 1875	51 cards
*Playing cards, Anglo-American Squeezers, James English and Company, 1880	52 cards
Political playing cards, W. H. Willis and Company	52 cards
The Game of Parliament, Henry Reason	46 cards
Famous persons, William Darton, 1825	10 cards
Mother Goose	22 cards
Canadian playing cards, wrapper Le Trappeur, c. 1880	52 cards
Playing cards, Willis and Company, 1880	52 cards
Deakin's Political playing cards, 1881	52 cards
Playing cards, de la Rue, 1880	52 cards
*Transformations, Reynolds and Sons, 1881	52 cards
Playing cards, James English and Company, 1881	52 cards
Playing cards, Woolley and Company, 1882	52 cards
Playing cards, advertisement for Th. Dupuy et Fils, 1882	52 cards
*Playing cards, James English and Company, 1883	52 cards
Heartsetts cards, Herbert Fitch and Company, 1883	52 cards
Back designs English cards, 1886–1919	14 cards
Playing cards, geographical aces, Goodall, 1883	52 cards
Eureka cards, Wooley and Company, 1884	52 cards
Sequence game, birds, by Miller, never published, 1885	52 cards
Playing cards, The Union Card and Paper Company, 1887	52 cards
National Patriotic Playing cards, 1887, Kimberley Press, Birmingham	52 cards
Playing cards, Canada Bank Note Company, Montreal, 1887	53 cards
Playing cards, court cards, costumes of different English reigns, 1890	52 cards
District messengers, Dalziel and Company	44 cards
Bezique cards, Bancks Brothers	52 cards
Playing cards, with pictures of Indian natives, 1895	51 cards
Victorian playing cards, Diamond Jubilee, 1897	52 cards
Empress playing cards, C. J. Mitchell Company, Toronto, 1897	52 cards
Manx, a card game, Charles Goodall, 1912	60 cards
'The Nation' playing cards. Designed by D. H. Souter, 1915	53 cards
Miniature playing cards, Charles Morrell	52 cards
Forty-eight packs of cards, C. Goodall, beautiful back designs, 1900–20	
Playing cards, souvenir of the Nottingham Spring Races, 1896	52 cards
Tarot cards, modern, by Pamela Coleman Smith, 1916	78 cards

Total: 168 editions, 5215 cards

CHAPTER VIII

PLAYING CARDS IN ITALY

TOWARD the latter part of the fourteenth century, cards appear, it would seem almost simultaneously, in all of the countries of Europe. Perhaps Italy's claim to priority is the best founded, because of the importance of Venice as a seaport. She was visited by many travelers from the East and the Near East, which was not so very near in those days of high-pooped, unwieldy sailing ships. And her own merchants brought back much that was new and strange from those far-away lands.

Whether they were brought by merchants or travelers, by soldiers or wandering fortune-telling gypsies, no one knows, but strange emblematic cards appeared, with a very evident allegorical significance and with a distinctly Eastern symbolism. Their very strangeness has prompted endless and elaborate theories as to their origin and their meaning. It has been variously claimed that they came from Persia and Arabia; while Court de Gebelin, whose book, 'Le Jeu des Tarots,' published in Paris in 1781, and the best known on the subject, traces them most ingeniously and entertainingly from Egypt and connects them with Egyptian mythology and symbolism. Egypt put all of her wisdom and science into her hieroglyphics. For its basis there was an alphabet, in which all the gods were letters, all the letters ideas, all the ideas numbers, and all the numbers perfect signs. From this involved and difficult beginning, he traces the still more complicated symbolism of each of the twenty-two tarots. For us it is interesting to see that the number seven retains all of the magic with which it is vested in the old fairy tales and is represented first by the triumph of Osiris and later by the chariot of the sun god, Le Chariot, of the modern tarots. It has from time immemorial been the mystic number of the East, and the whole game of tarots is based on intricate combinations of seven and its multiples. Also, thirteen, which is invariably Death, retains its early Eastern significance of misfortune.

It is thought that perhaps at first there were no numerals with these strange cards; that they were used in some other way, possibly as a means of divination, but certainly not to play at games of chance or hazard. Somewhat modified, they evidently became a game for amusing and instructing children, and are favorably mentioned in this capacity by several writers.

With its propensity for christianizing everything that came within its grasp, medieval Europe vigorously attacked these Eastern cards, with the result that very early 'Le Pape' and 'La Papesse' appear. It has been said that the Italian suit signs are the four symbols sacred to Hermes, forging another link connecting playing cards with fortune-telling. Those who sought help from Hermes' oracle in the old days first made an offering of silver to the temple priests, and the crossing of a gypsy's palm with silver is a survival of that ancient rite. Of the atouts, Le Bateleur and Le Fou are both said to have originally signified Mercury. Le Pendu symbolizes the universal sun myth, which has been called the basis of religion wherever a dying god is worshiped. Its meaning, of course, is emblematic of the winter solstice and the coming of spring.

La Roux de Fortune can be plainly traced from the earliest sun glyphs, which were wheels. As the fate of the earth is dependent on the sun, so the wheel symbolizes fate and fortune. On one side appears the Egyptian god of good, and on the other the god of evil. Le Diable is symbolic of Saturn and is characteristic of the power of evil over mankind.

It is in 1379 that we first hear of numeral cards in Italy. In his 'Istoria della citta di Viterbo,' Covelluzo writes: 'There were encamped about Viterbo paid troops of the opposing factions of Clement VII and Urbain VI, who did commit depredations of all kinds, and robberies in the Roman states. In this year of such great tribulations the game of cards was introduced into Viterbo, which came from the Saracens and was called Naib.' Covelluzo wrote his history in 1480 and it may be merely his personal opinion that cards came from the Saracens. But it is interesting to know that the Hebrew word for sorcery is 'naibi' and that the Spanish one for cards is 'naipes.' It is rather more likely, however, that these numeral cards were European copies of cards from China, whose original four suits of coins, strings, myriads, and tens of myriads became the batons, coins, swords, and cups of the Italian pack.

It is supposed that the Venetians added these numerals to the emblematic series, to compose the game of tarots, making it a game for grown people, and creating an element of chance.

In 1381, in the records of Laurent Aycardi, a notary of Marseilles, it is related how a certain Jean Jacques, son of a merchant, was an immoderate player of cards. Before leaving the city and embarking for Alexandria on a ship destined for that port, his friends feared that in the course of the voyage, ennuied by the long journey, he would abandon himself to his dominating passion. So two of them made him promise before a notary that he would not touch cards after setting foot on shipboard nor at Alexandria, nor after he had returned to Marseilles and been at home eight days. For any infraction of the contract he was to pay fifteen florins in gold.

In 1393, Jean Morelli, a Florentine, naming the dangers to which young men are exposed, says: 'Play not at games of chance or at dice. Play the games which are for children, les osselets, les fers, les naibis.'

This seems to show that both a game of chance and a child's game were played with them at the time. The so-called tarots of Mantegna, the earliest engraved Italian cards which have come down to our time, are evidently an instructive series. They are very large and on very thin paper,

TEN OF THE FIFTY TAROTS OF MANTEGNA, 1485
The originals are each seven inches long and four inches wide

and would be impossible to shuffle or deal. There were fifty of these and the subjects were all mythological or allegorical. They represent the different states of life, the muses, the virtues, the planets, the liberal arts, and the sciences. They are now ascribed to Botticelli and Baldini, and the feeling of the Florentine school is very evident, though the names are in the Venetian dialect.

Miniature painters and decorative painters of great ability fashioned lovely old cards for the gay and beauty-loving Venetians of the fifteenth century. These were tarots with numeral series for playing at cards as we understand the term to-day. Some of these are still to be seen in Naples and Milan and Venice. There are no names on the atouts of these painted tarots.

The painter, Marziano da Tartona, lived at the court of Filippo Maria Visconti, Duke of Milan, and he painted for his young patron a set of cards containing the figures of the gods and with them emblematic animals and likewise figures of birds. It is further written that the young duke played

THE VISCONTI TAROTS

The cards shown are l'Impératrice, l'Empereur, la Force, les Amoureux, le Jugement, le Chariot, the king of swords, the queen of swords, the king of coins, and le Monde.

a game with these painted figures, and later, that he sometimes played a game of hazard on particular occasions, which seems to show that there was more than one way of playing at tarots in those days. It is also written that Marziano was rewarded with fifteen hundred pieces of gold for these painted cards. This was in 1415. In 1454, fifteen francs is paid for a pack by the Dauphin of France, which seems to show that by that time an easy and satisfactory process for making them had been found.

These beautiful cards which were painted for the Duke of Milan in 1415 are still in the possession of his family. They are said to be a minchiate set. If so, it puts an end to the old tradition which says that the game of minchiate was invented by Michelangelo to teach the children of Florence to think and to count. There were ninety-seven cards in a minchiate set, the usual atouts of the tarot pack being increased by the virtues, the elements, and the signs of the zodiac. These atouts are not named. The coin suit marks usually have heads upon them, and the cavaliers, or mounted knaves, are monsters.

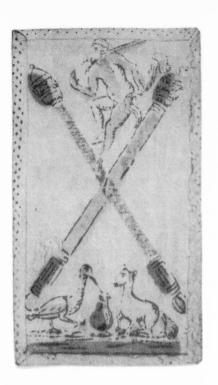

CARDS FROM A GAME OF FLORENTINE MINCHIATE, 1650

The upper cards are the two of batons and the twentieth atout, a sacrificial lamb in a burning bush; and the lower ones are the cavalier of swords and the valet of coins.

COURT CARDS FROM A PACK OF ITALIAN TAROTS OF THE EARLY EIGHTEENTH
CENTURY

The queen of cups, the king of batons, the valet of swords, and the cavalier of coins
are shown.

At this same time Francesco Fibbia, Prince of Pisa, was spending the days of his exile in Bologna. He introduced a new game, known as 'Bologna tarots,' or 'tarocchini,' in which some of the numerals were suppressed, making a pack of sixty-two cards, instead of the original seventy-eight. So delighted was the court with this new game that the author was given the privilege of placing his coat of arms on the queen of bastoni and that of his wife, who was of the Bentivoglio family, on the queen of danari. And there you may see them to this day.

A fifteenth-century manuscript in our library concerns itself in one part with the question of the morality of cards and card games. Its author says that those games are permissible which do not keep people from Mass, and which encourage the heart to good works. A marginal note in Italian lists the atouts of a tarot series in the following order:

1. El Bagatella
2. Imperatrice
3. Imperator
4. La papessa (note referring to those who deny the Christian faith)
5. El papa
6. La Tempentia
7. L'amore
8. La Caro Triumphale
9. La Fortez
10. La Rotta
11. El Gobbo
12. Lo impichato (the hanged)
13. La morte
14. El Diavolo
15. La Sagitta (in place of la maison Dieu)
16. La stella (L'étoile)
17. La lune
18. El sole
19. Lo angelo
20. La justicia
21. El Mondo ave dio padre
22. El mato

TITLE-PAGE OF THE 'DIALOGO DE GIVOCHI,' THE FIRST BOOK PRINTED ABOUT THE GAME OF TAROTS, VENICE, 1575

The earliest printed account of the game of tarots is given in a small volume, 'Dialogo de Givochi che nelle Vegghie Sanesi si usano di fare. Del materiale intronato. All' illustrissima et eccellentissima Signora Donna Isabella de' Medici Orsina Duchessa di Bracciano. Appresso Bertano. In Venetia, 1575.'

All three forms of the game, the original Venetian tarots with seventy-eight cards, Florentine minchiate with its ninety-seven, and the Bolognese

ITALIAN MINCHIATE CARDS
The first twenty atouts

(228)

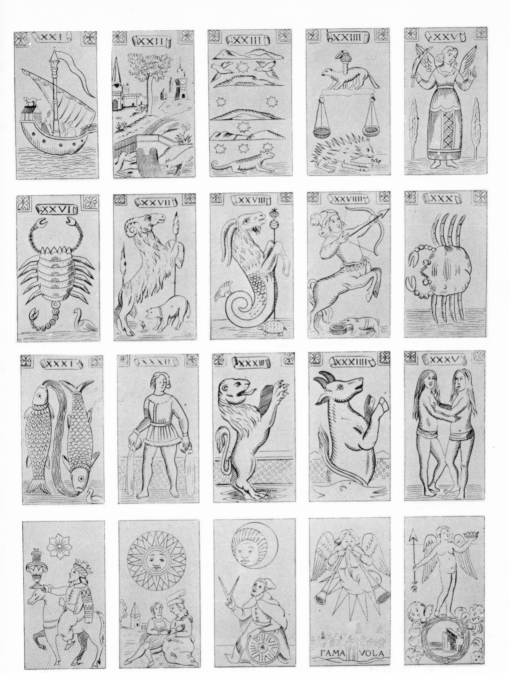

ITALIAN MINCHIATE CARDS

The second twenty atouts

ITALIAN MINCHIATE CARDS

The last two atouts and some of the characteristic court cards and numerals

(230)

with its sixty-two, are still used in Italy, and there are many variations of designs and colors.

An early eighteenth-century series of seventy-eight cards shows the usual designs from wood blocks, pleasingly colored, soft blues predominating. The two of cups bears the name of the maker, 'Francesco Gaetano Ghirardi in Bologna.' We have six other cards of this series in which the coloring is much more crude. These came from the Charlotte Wolter Collection. On the backs of all of these cards is a wood cut, showing a butcher carrying his wares on a pole over his shoulder, and lettered 'Al Mondo.'

The Italian cards have from the first differed from those of other countries in several respects. The backs from the beginning have been decorated with a design from a wood block. Sometimes this is a figure or a flower, sometimes a coat of arms. The cards themselves are often heavy and inflexible, the paper of the back being

ITALIAN CARD BACKS
The one on the right is from a pack of Bolognese tarots the one on the left from a minchiate pack, *c.* 1700

folded over to make a raised border around the face of the card. Often this border is dotted or checkered.

The suit signs are long curved swords or scimitars, for the nobility; cups, which are usually elaborate chalices, for the Church; danari or money for the citizens; and bastoni or clubs for the peasantry.

In both the suits of swords and bastoni, the suit signs interlace most confusingly. The Italian king is always seated.

There is a set of early nineteenth-century tarots which differ in several respects from the conventional packs. They are from copper plates, carefully and delicately colored by hand. The atouts are of the old emblematic character, but are well drawn, and in some instances modernized, il bagatelliere and l'imperatrice (the titles are all in Italian) being in the costumes of the First Empire. The court cards are in the costume of ancient Rome and are very similar in all four suits except for their emblems. Both the suit of swords and the suit of batons are of the Spanish type instead of the Italian, straight short poniards and knotty clubs, placed side by side.

A series, beautifully engraved by C. Dellarocco, bears the stamp lettered

'Milano 1842.' The cards are hand-colored and the atouts are variations of the old designs, with titles in Italian. The name of the maker, Gumppenberg, of Milan, is on the king of bastoni.

The old designs persist even in the lithographed cards of the late nineteenth century. A pack made in Turin have both the court cards and atouts as double heads, with their titles lettered on the side of the card.

The minchiate cards are from wood blocks usually colored with stencil. The designs are curious and archaic, and the dotted backs fold over to make a border around the face of the card. The cavalier of swords is a centaur, and the cavalier of coins has the body of a lion.

The most famous series of the Bologna tarots, or tarocchini, are the designs of Giuseppe Maria Mitelli, in the latter part of the seventeenth century. These are hand-colored etchings. The twenty-two atouts are a complete departure from the old emblematic designs. There are four court cards, the ace and the numerals six to ten of each suit. On the ace of cups are the arms of the Bentivoglio family for whom the cards were made, and who, according to Cicognara, still had the plates in their possession in 1831. On the ace of coins is a portrait medallion with the artist's name below. Reference to the armorial bearings of the family can be traced in several of the cards. The ace of cups and the six of swords show the saw which was their original arms, and there is a suggestion of it in the dress of the queen of coins. We also have these cards as uncolored prints in book form. The title is 'Giuoco di Carte, con nuova forma di Tarrocchini, Intaglio in Roma di Giuseppe Maria Mitelli. Dedicato dall' istesso. All' Illustris: Sig Co: Filippo del gia' Co: Prospero Bentivoglio Illmo Sig^r Co: mio Sig^r e Pron Col:^{mo}' These prints are now very rare.

Very early in Venice, by discarding the atouts of the tarot series, and the queens, together with the three, four, five, and six of the numerals, they

ATOUTS FROM AN ITALIAN TAROT SERIES, BOLOGNA, 1750
VII is the chariot of the sun god, and XIII, death

THE SEVEN OF COINS AND THE VALET OF CUPS OF A TAROT SERIES ENGRAVED AT
BOLOGNA IN 1664

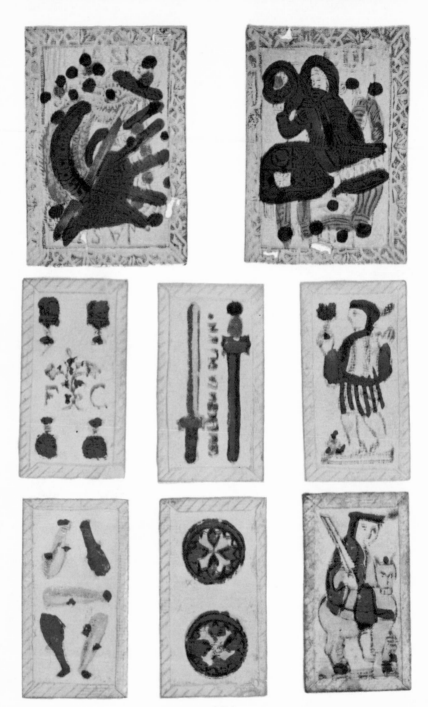

ABOVE: PORTUGUESE PLAYING CARDS OF 1694 — THE ACE OF ESPADAS, OR SWORDS
AND THE CABALLERO OF COINS

BELOW: SIX CARDS SHOWING THE SPANISH SUIT SIGNS, 1617 — THE FOUR OF CUPS, THE
TWO OF SWORDS, THE SOTA OF CUPS, THE FIVE OF BATONS, THE TWO OF COINS AND THE
CABALLERO OF SWORDS

I

Il Bagattelliere

II

La Papessa

III

L'Imperatrice

IX

L'Eremita

X

La ruota della Fortuna

XI

La Forza

ATOUTS FROM A TAROT PACK OF THE EARLY NINETEENTH CENTURY

(233)

had what they called a 'trappola' pack, with which they played the great gambling game which still flourishes, not only in Venice, but in Trieste and Vienna and throughout Hungary. Uncut sheets of early sixteenth-century wood blocks show the kings, cavaliers, and knaves for trappola packs, stenciled in delightful blues.

From the middle of the eighteenth century there are many examples of hombre packs of forty cards, for playing the Spanish game. These usually bear the conventional Italian suit signs, and often the knave is replaced by a queen, which is never found in the Spanish cards. The king is also seated in the Italian manner, and the cards have the familiar Italian border.

A series of these hombre cards of the late seventeenth century are somewhat in the manner of the later minchiate cards. In each suit is a king, a cavalier represented by a horse only, and a knave as a man in armor, to-

CAVALIER, VALET, AND KING OF BATONS, OF AN EDITION OF HOMBRE CARDS MADE FOR THE ALBANI FAMILY ABOUT 1700

gether with the numerals one to seven. On many of the designs the shield of the Albani family appears; it is also on the backs under a coronet with a cross of a Knight of Malta and the name Urbino. The cards are supposed to have been made for the Albani family. They are etchings, uncolored, and on many of them the artist's name is to be found, 'Pietro Leone Ghezzi.'

In the middle of the nineteenth century, these hombre cards are made in Naples, with all the Spanish characteristics, and not resembling the Italian cards in any respect.

There are also many packs of fifty-two cards, sometimes with the Italian

HOMBRE CARDS IN WHICH THE SUIT SIGNS OF SWORDS AND BATONS INTERLACE IN
THE ITALIAN MANNER

A queen, contrary to Spanish custom, also replaces the cavalier in the suits of coins and cups.
Bologna, *c.* 1740

suit signs and the Venetian couplets on the aces of swords and bastoni; sometimes with the French suit signs, when the queen replaces the cavalier, though the cards are still made in the Italian manner with the folded border. Two Florentine series of piquet cards show full-length figures in the costumes of the Middle Ages and those of the sixteenth century, for the court cards.

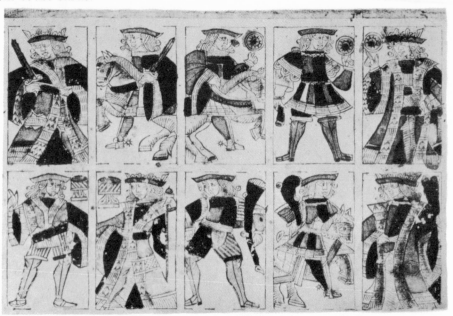

ITALIAN COURT CARDS OF THE EARLY SIXTEENTH CENTURY

Of educational cards, there are many. A seventeenth-century geographical series of fifty-six cards has the greater part of each card taken up with questions and answers concerning geography, in verse. The suit signs are shown in the upper left-hand corner, spades blue, cups pink, coins yellow, and batons orange, a small square hand-colored, and lettered with the name of the card.

Another geographical series is the Italian version of the English geographical cards of 1678. The Italian cards are made with the folded border, and the faces are hand-colored, diamonds green, clubs pink, spades yellow, and the hearts uncolored.

A third geographical series is the 'Gioco Geographice dell' Europa,' a complete tarot series of seventy-eight cards in which the atouts are maps, and the four suits Nord, Sud, Centre, and Isole. The four court cards of each suit are numbered I to IV, and bear the coats of arms of the principal countries with a description of their climates, religions, etc. The other cards are numbered 1 to 10, and describe the divisions of each country.

FROM THE ITALIAN VERSION OF THE ENGLISH GEOGRAPHICAL CARDS OF 1678

They were probably made in Naples, in the second half of the eighteenth century.

The de Brianville heraldry appears in three Italian editions. The first, in 1677, when the cards, beautifully illumined little prints, are found in a tiny vellum-bound book, with the title: 'Giuoco d'Armi dei Sovrani e Stati D'Europa per apprendre L'Armi, La Geographia a l'Historia loro curiosa. Di C Orance Fine detto di Brianville. Tradotta del Francese in Italiano & accrescinto di molte aqquinte necessarie par la perfetta cognitione della Storia Da Bernardo Guistiniana Veneto. In Napoli. Appresso Antonio Bulison all' Inseggna della Sirena.'

The second is an uncolored series of the same prints, with the same title-page, but dated 1681. The binding is a contemporary one of ivory and silver.

The third edition was printed in Naples in 1725 by Paolo Petrini. These are the cards themselves. The arms of the Pope, the king of clubs, are those of Benedict XIII, while in the two earlier series they are those of Innocent XI, and in the original French cards they are the papal arms of Alexander VII. This seems to be the only alteration made in the several editions.

A Biblical series of fifty-two cards show illustrations of Old Testament stories. The strange suit signs at the top of each card are colored by hand. Thirteen of the cards bear an orange circle in which is engraved a bird, animal, or some other emblem, while above is a letter A to NN. Thirteen have yellow diamonds with still other emblems, lettered from O to the end of the alphabet. Thirteen have pink hearts lettered a to nn, and thirteen

IRLANDA

Aria è fredda

Terreno è fertile più di pascoli, che di biade

Governo Politico è foggetta all' Inghilterra, e vi rifiede un'Ufficiale col titolo di Governatore di Irlanda

Religione vi fono in parte Protestanti, e in parte Cattolici.

Ifole 3.

Irlanda

Nell' Oceano

All'ovest della Inghilterra

si divide' in 4.

Parti, che hanno per Capitali

Orientale	Dublino
Meridionale	Limeric
Occidentale	Gallowai
Settentrionale	Londorderi

Dal Nord sino all'Inghilterra è lunga 200 e più miglia Italiane e larga 120

Ifole 5.

Nell' Oceano

All'ovest della Scozia	all'ovest della Inghilterra
Le Vesterne sono	Man
Harrai	Anglesey
	al Sud della Inghilterra
Lewis	
Skie	Vight
Mula	Jersey
Jura	Guernesey
Illay	
Wist	

Dal Nord al Sud è lunga 320 e da un Mare all'altro è larga 240 miglia Italiane.

INGHILTERRA

Aria è fredda

Suolo produce lini, e biade in gran copia

Governo Politico la Monarchia ereditaria dell'Inghilterra gode tutti i vantaggi de' Governi Aristocratici, e Democratici.

Relig. fono pretefi Riformati.

GEOGRAPHICAL TAROTS PROBABLY MADE IN NAPLES IN THE EIGHTEENTH CENTURY

GEOGRAPHICAL TAROTS, BY THE ABBÉ DESPROTTE AT PARMA, 1780

The back of the cards and the II of the suit of Italian maps are shown

CARDS OF THE DE BRIANVILLE HERALDRY, THE ITALIAN EDITION OF 1725

The king of clubs shows the arms of Pope Benedict XIII

(239)

HOMBRE CARDS MADE IN ROME IN 1885 BY VINCENZO TAMAGNINI

(240)

ITALIAN PLAYING CARDS WITH FRENCH SUIT SIGNS, SHOWING FOUR COURT CARDS
A NUMERAL, AND THE BACK DESIGN, *c.* 1750

(241)

lavender jars lettered from *o* to the end of the alphabet. On the last card of each series is a résumé of all that has gone before. On the *y* of jars is the engraver's name, 'A. Visentini, Sculp. 1748.' We have the original drawings of Francesco Zuccarelli, from which these cards were made.

BIBLICAL PLAYING CARDS OF FRANCESCO ZUCCARELLI, 1748

The elaborate use of playing cards for fortune-telling and divination, early in the sixteenth century, is evidenced by a rare and beautiful book published in Venice in 1550. Its title-page reads:' Le Ingeniose Sorte composte per Francesco Marcolini da Forli, intitulate Giardino di Pensieri, Nouamente Ristampate, e in Nouo et Bellissimo Ordine Riformate. M.D.L.' The cards employed by Marcolini are the king, knight, knave, ten, nine, eight, seven, two, and ace of danari. This work is known to iconophilists for the beauty of its wood cuts, after the designs of Giuseppe Porta and Salviati. Besides the frontispiece it contains ninety-nine wood cuts which are emblematic of the virtues and follies, and of the sayings and doctrines of ancient moralists and philosophers. Under each illustration are explanatory triolets, with miniature cards.

A reprint of this book was published in 1784. There is a portrait of Marcolini, as a frontispiece, and on the back of the title-page is an eagle with a banner lettered 'Copia III.' The portrait is signed, 'Ios. Daniotto tot hoc Opus Sculp,' at the lower left-hand corner. But who this engraver was or where the book had its origin is not known. The designs for the illustrations and the playing cards which every page presents are evidently copied from the edition of 1550, but all are engraved from copper plates and the text is in letterpress. At the end of the book there are seven verses

L'Alchimia fa per te, se tu nol sai:
Ne dubitar; che se da che fu'l mondo
Altri perderon, tu guadagnerai.

Grande, le stelle a te ventura danno,
Che per la donna tua, qual la si sia,
Tu non dei sostener punto d'affanno.

S'egli anchora non ha reso a la terra
Il corpo; e l'alma, doue piace a Dio,
Ritornera, ma dopo molta guerra.

Nessun trauaglio mai, nessun'affanno
Ti pungera per la tua donna il core;
E vgial sara il principio e'l fin de l'anno

Se tu sei gentilhuomo; e cerchi honore
Vero e non finto, o per lettere o per arme;
Serui, ch'io te n'essorto ad vn Signore.

Io non ti voglio dar ferma risposta.
Spera pur tu: che la speranza è pasto,
Che nudrisce i meschini; e nulla costa.

Ne dice ben ogni persona tu ma:
Ciascun lo pone in ciel: ciascun vorrebbe
Poter metterli in capo vna corona.

Guardami ben' in fronte quel, ch'io paio:
Se troui, che la fede ti si serbi;
Philosopho non son, ma calzolaio.

Io t'assecuro, che non sara molto,
Che ne la patria tua farai ritorno;
E dentro anchor tu vi sarai sepolto.

Come va il mondo: o pensieracci vani,
Tu pensi, ch'ei sia morto: & egli anchora
Pensa occider te con le sue mani.

Donna non fu qua giu, che buona sorte
Hauesse, come a te destina il cielo
Fino a l'estremo di de la tua morte.

Il Marcolin; ch'ogni mio detto accoglie;
Ha posto nel suo libro de le sorti,
Che tu non sei persona d'hauer moglie.

Lascia costei, segui il consiglio mio:
Che patirai per lei piu doglie e stratio;
Che Santo alcun mai non pati per Dio

Tu non ci tornerai: che la tua stella
Vuol, che peregrinando te ne vadi,
Cercado sepre hor questa parte hor quella

Gioisci ne la fe: dono beato;
Che chi la ti donò, per casi aduersi
Mai non ti mancara, ne t'è mancato.

A par de la noiosa e lunga guerra;
Che dei soffrir, la dolce e breue pace
Fia, come al maggior ciel la picol terra.

Ringratia figliolin la tua ventura
Ch'una sola n'haurai; come si dice,
Fatta proprio a tuo dosso e a tua misura.

Tu sei diuoto di nostra auocata;
E il sabato digiuni in aqua e in pane,
E dubiti, che t'ama la brigata.

Ei viue; & ha ne la sua fronte vn'emme
Congiunto a vn V, che ti dinota ch'esso
Haurà piu vita di Matusalemme.

Ben hai cagion d'hauer letitia e gioia;
Che chi la fe ti die, pone ogni cura
In serbar lei, come si serba Gioia.

La superbia e l'inuidia, che tu porti
Io non lo dico a te, se non sei quello:
Ti fa venir in odio a viui e a morti.

**A PAGE FROM 'LE INGENIOSE SORTE' DESCRIBING FORTUNE-TELLING WITH CARDS
VENICE, 1550**

in triolets eulogistic 'del Gran Daniotto,' and from which it appears that only thirty-six copies of the book were printed.

Another early volume on divination is 'Il Laberinto del Clarissimo Signor Andrea Ghisi; Nel qual si contiene una bellissima & artificiosa tessitura di due milla ducento sessanta Figure, che aprendolo tre volte, con facilita si puo saper qual figura si sia immaginata; Al Serenissimo Don Francesco Gonzaga Prencipe di Mantoua. In Venetia M.DC.VII. Appresso Rampazetto.' The long dedication to the Prince of Mantua is followed by many pages of wood-block prints, each two inches square, evidently emblematic of some vice or virtue. There is a double page of these prints for each letter in the alphabet, the same ones being repeated at times, but their order changed. There is an epilogue in verse, in praise of the author, and the book is in its original vellum binding.

CUCU CARDS, A VERY EARLY ITALIAN CARD GAME

A pack consists of a double set of cards, thirty-eight in all. In each pack the highest card is the Cucu, then Bragon, next the cat, and the inn, the ten numerals, then Nulla, Secchia, Mascherone, and Matto. Cucu is one of the games which is recommended in the directions for playing with the De Brianville heraldry cards, its extreme simplicity not interfering with the educational value of the blazonry, geography, and history that they are supposed to instill into the minds of the players.

There is an old wood block in the Paris collection of prints, which shows Saint Bernardin of Sienna preaching at Bologna against cards and gaming, in 1423. The story is that his hearers were moved to throw their cards into a great blaze in the market-place. There was a card-maker present, who cried out at the sad sight: 'I have not learned, father, any other business than that of painting cards. If you deprive me of that, you deprive me of the means of earning a subsistence, and my destitute family of life.' The saint replied, 'Paint this figure, and you shall never have cause to repent having done so.' Whereupon he drew a radiant sun having in its center the sacred cipher 'I.H.S.'

We find this symbol among the German monastic prints of the fifteenth century. When the card-makers of Venice protest against the importation of cards from Germany in 1441, both painted and printed cards are mentioned, and it is interesting to look back on these old cards of both countries and see what a wealth of ideas and how much real beauty went into their making.

The celebrated Antonio Cicognara, painter of Ferrare, who illumined the beautiful books of the Cathedral of Cremona, designed some exquisite cards, which are in the collection of the Count Colleoni. As in the family of the Duke of Milan, these, too, have been handed down from generation to generation.

In the pastorals which were written by Lorenzo de' Medici in his youth, he speaks of flush and basset as the card games that are played throughout the countryside.

There is a curious little vellum-bound book, published in Venice in 1545, 'The Cards Speak.' The interpretation of the suit signs is that swords recall the death of those who have become mad over gaming; batons or clubs, the chastisement that they merit who cheat; coins or danari, the food of gaming; cups, the wine in which the disputes of the gamesters are drowned.

In the Musée de Hal at Brussels are the first double-head cards known. Surprisingly enough, they have the Italian suit signs. The king of batons bears a round escutcheon, on which is a two-headed eagle and the words 'Carte da Giuoco.' On the two of swords is 'Fabrica di Gaetano Salvotti in Vicenza sul Corso, 1602.'

ITALIAN PLAYING CARDS IN THE COLLECTION OF THE UNITED STATES PLAYING CARD COMPANY [1]

*Uncut sheet court cards in color, early sixteenth century	12 cards
*Mitelli tarots, hand-colored, 1664	62 cards
*Mitelli tarots, uncut proofs	62 cards
*Giuoco d'Armi dei Sovrani e Stati d'Europa, di Brianville, Naples, 1667	52 cards
Giuoco d'Armi dei Sovrani e Stati d'Europa, di Brianville, Naples, 1681	52 cards
*Geographical playing cards, c. 1675	56 cards
Geographical playing cards, 1678	52 cards
De Brianville heraldry, Naples, 1725	52 cards
Geographical tarots, 1725	78 cards
Hombre cards, Ghezzi, 1740	40 cards
Hombre cards, Bologna, 1750, checkered border	40 cards
*Biblical cards, after Zuccarelli, 1748	52 cards
Biblical cards, after Zuccarelli, 1748	52 cards
**Original Zuccarelli drawings for Biblical cards	52 cards

[1] The starred items are from the collection of George Clulow, F.R.G.S.

*Florentine Minchiate, c. 1700	30 cards
Bologna tarots, Ghirardi, c. 1700	61 cards
Bologna tarots, Ghirardi, c. 1700	61 cards
Bologna tarots, Ghirardi, c. 1700	5 cards
Geographical tarots, par M. l'Abbé Desprotte, à Parma, 1780	78 cards
Playing cards, dotted border, French suit signs, c. 1750	52 cards
Italian tarots, c. 1800	78 cards
Milan tarots, 1842	39 cards
Hombre cards, Gumppenburg, Milan, 1842	40 cards
Italian tarots, c. 1850	38 cards
*Hombre cards, Naples, 1853	48 cards
Tarot cards, Naples, 1860	51 cards
Italian trappola cards, 1862	51 cards
Italian trappola cards, 1865	45 cards
Italian trappola cards, 1870, Ottavio Salvotti Riva	52 cards
Playing cards, French suit signs, Milan, 1880	52 cards
Hombre cards, by Eduardo Dotti, 1880	40 cards
Stenciled cards, French suit signs, c. 1880	38 cards
Playing cards, French suit signs, Florence, 1883	52 cards
Costume cards, G. Bonetti, for A. Conti, Florence, 1883	52 cards
Hombre cards, A. Conti, Florence, 1883	40 cards
Cucu cards, P. Masenghini, Bergamo	38 cards
Playing cards, French suit signs, costume court cards, Florence	40 cards
Hombre cards, Tamagnini Pioraco, 1885	40 cards
Italian playing cards, Fratelli Armanino, Genoa, 1888	52 cards
Tarot cards, Serravalle, Sesia, 1893	78 cards
Tarot cards, A. Viassone, Turin	78 cards

Total: 41 editions, 2043 cards

CHAPTER IX

PLAYING CARDS IN SPAIN

THE learned Salvini, who wrote in Florence in the early eighteenth century, believed that it was very possible that the Moors brought cards with them as well as chess when they invaded Europe. The Saracens spread over Asia and Africa and attempted to cross the sea, as early as the seventh century. They had completely conquered Sicily by 832. They were in Spain in 710, and about 731 they penetrated through Languedoc into France as far as Arles, and continued in possession of southern Spain until 1492. About 842 they proceeded from Sicily into Calabria, and a few years later reached Rome and Tuscany. They stayed in different parts of Italy until the tenth century and the Pope and the Italian princes made use of them as soldiers in their incessant warring. They were an enlightened people compared to the Europeans, and it is acknowledged that we are indebted to them for the dawn of science and letters and certainly for chess. The Moors now play hombre, the old Spanish game, which is similar to the Hindoo game of ganjifa in many respects. Whether it was originally their own game, of Eastern origin, or whether they learned it from the Spaniards, it is hard to say.

Bullet, in his 'Recherches Historiques sur les Cartes à Jouer,' which he wrote in 1757, and M. l'Abbé Rive, in his book 'Éclaircissements Historiques et Critiques sur l'Invention des Cartes à Jouer,' published in Paris in 1780, both credit the origin of European playing cards to Spain through this Eastern source.

There is no mention of cards, however, in the 'Arabian Nights,' where they would most certainly have been found had there been any. It is on this fact, and because neither Marco Polo nor Chaucer speaks of them, that Mr. Willshire, who wrote the preface of the catalogue for the collection of playing cards in the British Museum in 1878, credits them with a European origin.

No Spanish cards of a date earlier than 1600 exist, so far as is known, though cards were unquestionably used throughout Spain long before that time. M. d'Allemagne, the latest authority on French cards, thinks that they may have been taken into Spain from France probably in the baggage of some knight in the suite of du Guesclin, going to fight Pierre le Cruel, about 1367.

Another interesting suggestion he makes is that they may have come directly to Spain from Flanders in the trading ships which plied between the two countries laden with wool and other necessaries of life. He adds that this last opinion finds justification in the name itself, 'naipes,' which has always been and still is the Spanish word for cards. In the Spanish dictionary of Fernandez Cuesta, the author says that the Academia of his country thinks possibly 'naip' may come from the Flemish word 'knaep,' meaning paper.

In France at various times cards are mentioned as 'leaves,' 'pages,' or even as 'paper to play with,' 'papier à jouer.' And the fifteenth-century German trappola cards are invariably called 'Trappola Blattern,' meaning 'leaves.'

About 1540 the Flemish author Eckloo, or Pascasius Justus, traveled through Spain. We have his little book 'Pascasii Justi Elzoviensis Philosophiae & Medicinae Doctoris. Alea sive de curanda ludendi in pecuniam cupiditate. Amsterodami, apud Ludovic Elzivirium,' in which he writes that the Spaniards are passionately fond of cards and that he traveled many leagues in that kingdom without being able to procure the necessaries of life, even bread or wine. Yet in every miserable village cards might be met with.

From the fifteenth century, Toulouse and Thiers made a considerable quantity of playing cards for Spain. And Rouen sent her specially made cards for the Spanish market both to Portugal and Spain in the Flemish sailing ships. There was also a brisk trade in Spanish cards with Limoges.

FRONTISPIECE IN THE BOOK OF PASCASIUS JUSTUS

These earliest Spanish cards are quite small, especially those from Limoges and Rouen, and are stenciled in bright yellow and orange and green. Some which we have are only two and seven eighths by one and five eighths inches, and are very rare. They are made in the Italian manner, by folding the paper over from the back of the card, forming a border, marked by faint diagonal lines, about the face of the card. The paper itself is of interesting texture, and the designs are the crudest of wood blocks. On the four of cups are the initials, 'F.C.,' and on the two of swords lettering which seems to be 'Ensconlicencia,' though it is so blurred it is impossible to be sure what it is. Half a century later the cards are larger, particularly from Thiers and Bordeaux, and there is much gay vermilion and blue used, as well as the yellow of which the Spaniards were so fond. We also have cards made by Inferrera, in Portugal, contemporary with these of France. These are also wood blocks, stenciled in orange and black. The paper is similar to that of the Limoges cards, and again the paper from the back is folded over to form a border, this time of quite an elaborate conventional pattern. The border is uncolored. At the top and bottom of each card is the initial of the suit to which it belongs; also the designating numeral, or, in the case of the court cards, an initial showing its rank. The anatomy and costuming of the court cards is very amusing, especially in the gayly caparisoned cavaliers. The aces, which are lettered 'A,' are dragons, with the suit signs in their mouths. Some of these cards in the Librairie Nationale at Paris, which are shown on plate 96 of 'Les Cartes Tarots et les Cartes Numérales,' are entirely different in coloring, being in reds and blues carefully done by hand, similar to that used by Jehan Volay in Thiers.

FRONTISPIECE AND TITLE-PAGE OF 'THE COMPLEAT GAMESTER' OF 1734

The frontispiece, which is after Hogarth, shows a game of Ombre à trois at a triangular table. This old Spanish game was in great favor at the English court. It was superseded by the four-handed form of the game, Quadrille, which was popular until the end of the century.

The national Spanish game of hombre evidently had its origin in the chivalric age, and in the Spanish pack for playing it, there are forty cards. The eights, nines, and tens are left out, and, in accordance with the Oriental custom, there is no queen. Her place is taken by a caballero, or mounted knave. Unlike the Italian kings, the Spanish kings always stand, with flowing, much bejeweled mantles. Because hombre was so often a game à trois, little triangular card tables were made, during the seventeenth and eighteenth centuries, on purpose for playing it.

The suit signs of the Spanish cards are cups, swords, coins, and clubs or batons, but again the designs differ from the Italian ones. The Spanish swords are straight, two-edged rapiers, and the batons are heavy, knotty clubs. These suit signs are always placed parallel to one another, and never interlace as the Italian suits do. The only exception to this seems to be the Inferrera cards.

In 1583 there are records of many card-makers of Lyons emigrating to Spain because of the excessive tax in their own country, but all during the seventeenth century Thiers seemingly furnished cards to all of Spain.

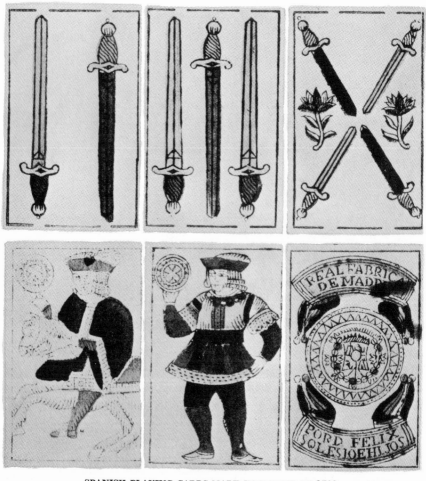

SPANISH PLAYING CARDS MADE IN MADRID IN 1792

We have a complete pack of forty-eight cards, nine numerals, knave, caballero, and king to each suit, which were made in Madrid in 1792. This is told on the four of coins, and the maker's name, 'Real fabricados de Madrid por D. Felix Solesie e Hijos.' These are from wood blocks and are stenciled in red, blue, green, and yellow. The court cards are less Spanish and more French than those of Jehan Volay, of the century before.

A pack of cards of 1801 first shows the numbering of the cards of each suit, from one to twelve, at the upper right-hand corner. The wrapper bears the name of Don Pedro Castillo. This numbering did not become customary until many years later. Stenciled cards made in Cadiz about 1840 do not show it, nor does another pack, dated 1852, whose maker is

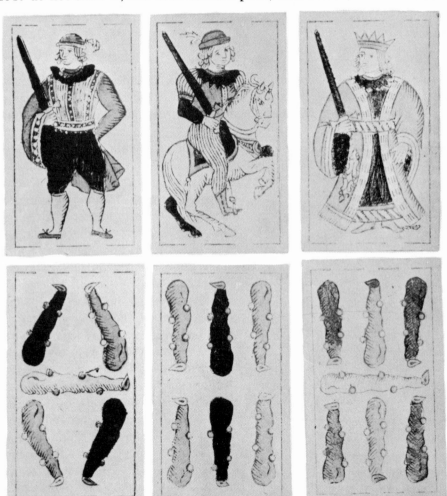

SPANISH PLAYING CARDS OF 1840, SHOWING THE COURT CARDS OF THE SUIT OF SWORDS
AND THREE OF THE NUMERALS OF BATONS

SPANISH COURT CARDS OF 1852

The Sota, Caballero, and Rey of the suit of coins

Don Sanmiarti e Hijo. Nor do those of 'J. B. David en Cadiz y Puebla,' which are dated 1868. However, cards of only a few years later, made in Barcelona by Cristobal Masso, bear the numbers at the upper right-hand corner.

A change from these stenciled cards is found in some prettily engraved

A SPANISH PLAYING CARD WRAPPER

ones made by Fulladosa y Ca., in Barcelona, about 1872. The suit of swords is printed in blue, cups in red, batons in brown, and coins in orange. The court cards are queen, cavalier, and king, and they are all named for Spanish rulers and grandees and ladies, beginning with Pierre le Cruel and the Cid. This is the only instance of Spanish queens that we have, except those in the Portuguese cards by Inferrera, and these are rather a law unto themselves, with their other Italian characteristics.

There are similar stenciled cards of José Bau in Valencia, Leon in Cadiz, Don Segundo Olea in Cadiz, and Camjos e Hijos, G. Villasenor, Juan Codola, Sebastian Comas y Ricart, and Simeon Dura of Valencia. Sometimes, instead of the maker's name, the name of the factory is given, La Flor, or El Ciervo, or El Sol, and the wrappers of the cards are quite as picturesque as their titles.

LEFT: FRONTISPIECE OF THE 'LIBRO Y BARAJA' OF DON FRANCISCO GAZÁN, EXPLAINING
THE MEANING AND USE OF THE CARDS OF THE DE BRIANVILLE HERALDRY,
MADRID, 1748

RIGHT: EL REY DE OROS, BEARING THE ARMS OF POPE CLEMENT XII, OF THIS
SPANISH EDITION OF THESE OLD CARDS

 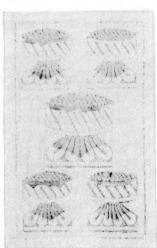 

SPANISH PLAYING CARDS OF 1868
The four, five, and king of cups

(253)

LITHOGRAPHED SPANISH CARDS OF 1900

CARD WRAPPER AND CABALLERO OF SWORDS, MEXICAN CARDS, 1868

NAIPES NACIONALES, MEXICAN PLAYING CARDS, 1896

There are lithographed cards in 1899 made by Rudolfo de Olea, in Cadiz, and these are followed the next year by some of Heraclio Fournier, in Vitoria. In these, the court cards are in costume, the cups swashbuckling noblemen of the seventeenth century, the swords knights templars, the coins courtesans, and the batons Indians.

The Mexican cards begin with some made in 1868 by F. Munguia, whose factory is first La Campana and later La Estrella, in Mexico City, while J. B. Tejeda y Ca. have a card factory at Puebla. Emilio Cuenca y Ca. of Mexico, whose factory is El Sol, have an hombre pack of forty cards, made in 1896, which they call 'Naipes Nacionales,' in which the suit signs become Aztec in character. The kings and knaves are Aztec chiefs, the caballeros conquistadores, the cups are Aztec pottery, and the swords machetes, while the coins and batons are decorated with the Aztec symbols.

There is a great variety of color in these curious old Spanish cards, but very little in design, and it seems a meager story for a nation whose card playing has extended over so many centuries, and been so universal.

SPANISH PLAYING CARDS IN THE COLLECTION OF THE UNITED STATES PLAYING CARD COMPANY [1]

*Stenciled cards, Seville, 1617	22 cards
*Inferrera cards, 1694	16 cards
*Stenciled cards, 1731	48 cards
*Playing cards, Felix Solesjos e Hijos de Madrid, 1792	48 cards
*Playing cards, 1801	48 cards
Playing cards, Barcelona, 1840	43 cards
Playing cards, 1852	48 cards
Playing cards, J. B. David en Cadiz y Puebla, 1868	38 cards
Playing cards, 1838	48 cards
Heraldic playing cards, Don Francisco Gazan, 1748	52 cards
Playing cards, Cristobal Masso, Barcelona, 1872	29 cards
*Historical playing cards, Fulladosa y Ca., Barcelona, 1872	48 cards
Playing cards, stenciled, Barcelona, 1872	47 cards
Playing cards, Fulladosa y Ca., Barcelona, 1872	48 cards
Playing cards, Fulladosa y Ca., Barcelona, 1872	48 cards
Playing cards, José Bau, Valencia, 1875	48 cards
Playing cards, Leon Cristobal Colon, Cadiz, 1875	48 cards
Playing cards, José Bau, Valencia, c. 1875	48 cards
Playing cards, Don Segundo Olea, Cadiz, 1879	26 cards
*Miniature playing cards, stenciled, c. 1880	48 cards
Playing cards, Camjos e Hijos, Barcelona, 1880	47 cards
Playing cards, Torras y Lleo, Barcelona, 1880	48 cards
Playing cards, Heraclio Fournier, Vitoria, 1895	48 cards
Playing cards, Simeon Dura, Valencia, c. 1895	48 cards
Playing cards, made by 'El Ciervo,' Cadiz, c. 1895	48 cards

[1] The starred items are from the collection of George Clulow, F.R.G.S.

Playing cards, made by 'La Flor,' Cadiz, *c.* 1895	48 cards
Playing cards, Rudolfo de Olea, *c.* 1895	48 cards
Playing cards, Juan Codola, Barcelona, *c.* 1895	48 cards
Playing cards, Sebastien Comas y Ricart, *c.* 1895	48 cards
Playing cards made by 'La Flor,' Barcelona, 1896	48 cards
Playing cards, Rodolfo de Olea, 1899 (lithographed)	47 cards
Playing cards, G. Villasenor, Cadiz y Barcelona, 1899	48 cards
Costume cards, Heraclio Fournier, Vitoria, 1900	48 cards
Playing cards, Simeon Dura, Valencia (stenciled)	48 cards
Playing cards, Fulladosa y Ca.	48 cards
Playing cards, Simeon Dura	48 cards
Playing cards, Sebastien Comas y Ricart, Barcelona	48 cards
Playing cards, Heraclio Fournier, 1905, lithographed	48 cards
Playing cards, La Campana, F. Munguia, Mexico, 1868	40 cards
Playing cards, La Estrella, F. Munguia, Mexico, 1882	40 cards
Playing cards, Por J. B. Tejeda y Ca., Puebla, F. Munguia, 1889	40 cards
Playing cards, 'El Sol,' Emilio Cuenca y Ca., Mexico, 1896	39 cards
Playing cards, Naipes Nacionales, Emilio Cuenca y Ca., 1896	40 cards

Total: 43 editions, 1910 cards

CHAPTER X

PLAYING CARDS IN SWITZERLAND

THE story of playing cards in Switzerland begins when one, Joannes, a brother in the monastery at Brefeld, writing in painstaking Latin, 'De Moribus et Disciplina Humane Conservationis,' says, 'Hence it is that a certain game, called the game of cards [Ludus cartarum] has come to us in this year 1377, but at what time it was invented, or by whom, I am ignorant. But this I say, that it is of advantage to noblemen and to others, especially if they practice it courteously and without money.' In the first chapter he treats 'de materia ludi et de diversitate instrumentorum,' and explains how that 'in the game which men call the game of cards, they paint the cards in different manners, and play with them in one way and another' — which would seem to show that they were well known and that they had been in use sufficiently long for more than one kind of game to be played with them.

He goes on, 'As the game came to us, there are four kings depicted on four cards, and each one holds a certain sign in his hand and sits upon a royal throne, and under the king are two "marechali," the first of whom holds the sign upright in his hand, and the other holds the sign downward in his hand.'

These two marshals are represented in the cards of the fifteenth century and later, by the queens and valets, or the two valets or knaves, and it is interesting to see that in the hands of all single-head jacks, even those which are being made to-day in Belgium, the staves in two of them are still help upward and down in the other two. This date also coincides with that in the archives of the court of Jeanne and Wenceslas of Brabant.

He further describes a pack of fifty-two cards by adding that, under these first-named three cards, there are to each king ten other cards, 'on each of which the king's sign is placed, on the first, once, on the second twice, and so on.'

Unfortunately he does not describe these signs and we shall probably never know whether his game came from Italy or Germany, France or Spain, or whether the cards were painted in some neighboring valley with the Swiss suit signs of escutcheons, acorns, roses, and bells. These early Swiss cards had for their court cards the king, chevalier, and knave, which are still used to-day, and the aces which flaunt their signs upon banners. The Swiss game made at Schaffhausen has six numerals to each suit, while that made at Soleure has nine.

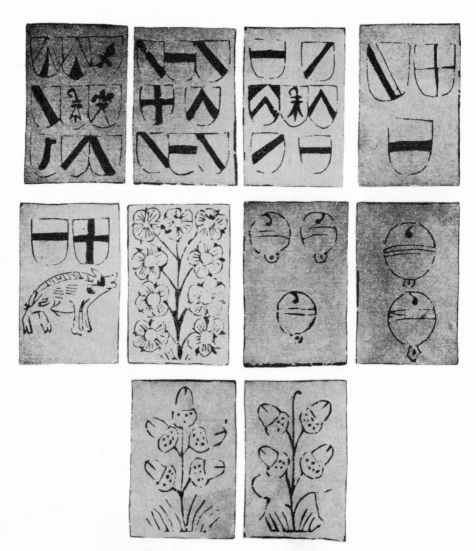

EARLY PLAYING CARDS MADE AT BASLE

Showing the Swiss suit signs of escutcheons, bells, roses, and acorns. The aces are banners.
Sixteenth century

(258)

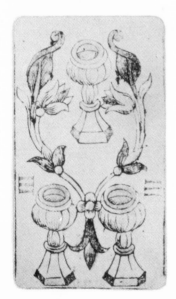
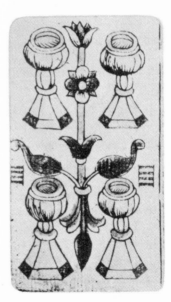

THE QUEEN AND CAVALIER AND THE THREE AND FOUR OF CUPS OF A TAROT SERIES
MADE BY JOANNES PELAGIUS MAYER, OF CONSTANCE, 1680

(259)

THE KING, QUEEN, AND CAVALIER AND THE TWO, THREE, AND FOUR OF COINS OF A
TAROT SERIES MADE BY BERNARD SCHAER EARLY IN THE EIGHTEENTH CENTURY

THE CAVALIER OF COINS, THE KING OF CUPS, AND TWO OF THE ATOUTS
THE SUN AND THE MOON, FROM A TAROT PACK MADE IN CONSTANCE IN 1680

ABOVE THE KING OF SPADES AND THE KING OF HEARTS FROM AN EDITION OF
SWEDISH PLAYING CARDS OF 1880

BELOW: THREE CARDS FROM AN EDITION PRINTED IN SWITZERLAND IN 1878
The aces show views of the country, and the court cards picture the costumes and
the coats of arms of the various cantons.

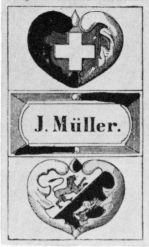
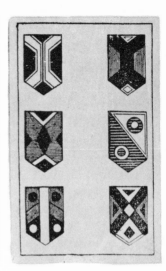

FROM AN EDITION OF SWISS CARDS IN 1874

The ace, two, and six, and the three honors of escutcheons are shown

(261)

It is recorded how an old edict of 1583 at Lyons caused many makers to emigrate to Switzerland because of the excessive duty upon playing cards. This edict, adds an old mémoire, 'terrifying in such a fashion the card-makers, that rather than suffer they preferred to leave the kingdom and their native heath rather than their liberty, taking with them the blocks for the making and the pressing of the card. In such a state which was soon general throughout France, the king revoked the edict, but too late.' However, a record of fifteen years later mentions special patterns used in Lyons for the making of Swiss cards.

Many of the early Swiss cards that have survived are the old familiar tarots. They are wood blocks, very large and very crude in design, but perfectly delightful in their soft old reds and blues. The earliest series we have are tarots of Joannes Pelagius Mayer, of Constance, who was a cartier of the later part of the seventeenth century. A vivacious Juno and Jupiter replace la Papesse and le Pape, and the spelling is as atrocious as the designs are engaging. Cards of the early eighteenth century, by 'Bernard Schaer in Mümliswil im cant. Solothurn,' also have Juno and Jupiter instead of the Papesse and the Pope. The fleur de lys of France is on the two of cups and on every coin in the numerals of that suit.

A third tarot series has both the maker's name and the date on the two of coins, 'Joseph Jagi, M. Cartier a Mümliswil. 1779.' The four of coins bears the three fleurs de lys of France. The coloring of these cards is very effective. A rich blue predominates and the background is a gray blue. In all of these tarot series the characteristics of the tarots made in France

THE QUEEN, CAVALIER, AND VALET OF BATONS OF A TAROT SERIES MADE BY JOSEPH JAGI, CARTIER À MÜMLISWIL, IN 1779

persist; one of these peculiarities is the position of the king of coins. He affects a most unkingly attitude and always sits on the edge of his throne with his legs crossed.

These designs for the most part probably originated in Switzerland, and the fleur de lys may have been added by the French makers during the many years that they supplied Switzerland with cards. There is a plea for protection against an excessive duty, addressed to the syndics in Rouen in 1701, and preserved in its archives. This plea is signed by nearly forty card-makers and reads: 'You are entreated to consider that the city of Rouen is the only city in the realm where with truth can be said there is the most exporting of its manufactures to foreign countries, and it can with truth be said that it does more than all the others together. Indeed, the reputation of the cards of Rouen is known in Spain, Sweden, Russia, Switzerland, Denmark, England, and especially in Flanders. Because of this, in 1648, when the king put a duty on all cards made in the kingdom, he excepted only those of Rouen.'

Even the tarots of the last quarter of the nineteenth century hold to these old designs and traditions. In 1747 there is a long report of the card-makers to the councilors general at Paris, describing at length the success of French cards in various foreign countries, and stressing particularly their popularity in Switzerland, where they were favorites.

Jean Hemau, a card-maker who lived at the end of the seventeenth century, recalls by the attitudes of the figures and their accessories in his cards the wonderful German prints of more than a hundred years before. This old reminder is a sort of adaptation in popular prints of the most beautiful conceptions of those first great master engravers. The church stall in which the king of acorns sits is a veritable Gothic chair of state, ornamented at the sides with the beautiful parchemin paneling, so characteristic of the furniture of the period. The king of roses is on a large low throne, very like those met with in a game picturing the Middle Ages, which was published at Nürnberg. The king of bells wears a flower-decked crown which is also a vestige of a sixteenth-century German game. And the king of escutcheons sits in one of the high stalls that are frequently found in the fifteenth-century German churches.

The acorns grow on stems, without the faintest resemblance to anything in nature, and the roses end in foliage, in the midst of which it is surprising to find an angel's head. The four of bells shows a fortress where hangs the coat of arms of Épinal, where Jean Hemau lived and worked. Many of the old Nürnberg cards show the Nürnberg lion and the coat of arms in the same way.

Most of the characteristics of this old pack of cards have survived in the Swiss cards that are even now being made in Switzerland.

Another vagary of the Swiss cards, in the trappola packs when German suit signs are used, is to have the four designs on the four twos emblematic of spring, summer, autumn, and winter. In such packs the kings are usually mounted, the cavalier is a military officer, and the knave a Swiss hunter.

TRAPPOLA CARDS WITH GERMAN SUIT SIGNS, THE TWO-SPOT OF EACH SUIT PICTURING ONE OF THE FOUR SEASONS

The court cards and two of acorns, which is winter, are shown; *c.* 1885

In one of these, made for Édouard Glantzle at Innsbruck in 1878 by Heinrich Hoffman at Vienna, the court cards are single heads in historical costume, the kings being Rudolph, Frederick, Maximilian, and Francis I, and the numerals picturing historical events and village life during their reigns.

In another series, the two knaves of each suit are named for Swiss heroes, William Tell being prominent.

Another pack, this time of fifty-two cards with the French suit signs, called 'Vues et Costumes Suisses,' by Jean Müller, at Schaffhausen, show the coats of arms and the native costumes of the various cantons on each court card, and the aces show views of the Swiss Alps, with villages nestling between the snowy peaks.

This favorite decoration of the aces is shown in many packs with the French suit signs. The court cards are of an individual type, neither French nor German, except in one series we have, of 1873, which are printed from wood blocks, the designs evidently from the old French ones of Andrieu. The knave of spades of this pack is lettered 'Gassmann à Génève.' We also have a tarot series of about this time by the same maker, in which he departs from the old designs and shows atouts in black and white, small figures in grotesque attitudes, intended to be amusing. The court cards are printed by lithography and they and the numerals are colored with stencil.

There are also miniature packs of cards three quarters by one half inch in tiny slip cases, made at Interlaken and Geneva.

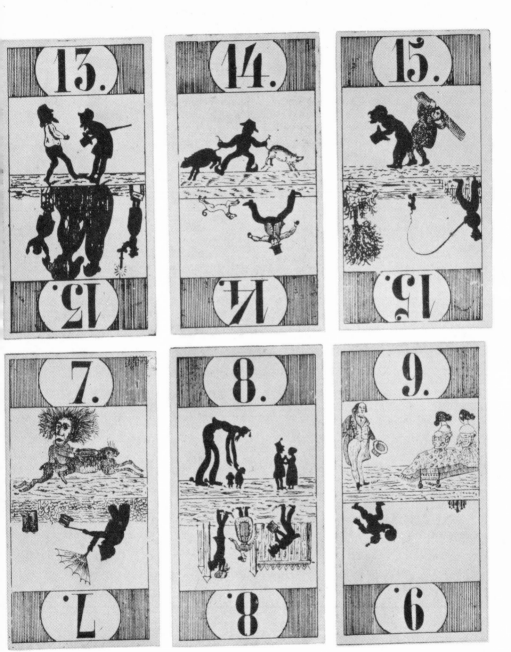

FROM AN EDITION OF SWISS TAROTS PRINTED AT GENEVA IN 1873

(265)

SWISS PLAYING CARDS IN THE COLLECTION OF
THE UNITED STATES PLAYING CARD COMPANY [1]

*Tarot cards, Joannes Pelagius Mayer, Constance, 1680	53 cards
Complete set of wood blocks for printing tarot cards of this period, six blocks, each	15 cards
*Tarot cards, Bernard Schaer, Mümliswil, Solothurn	78 cards
*Tarot cards, Joseph Jagi, Mümliswil	53 cards
Uncolored proofs for atouts, humorous designs, 1873	21 cards
Tarot cards, Gassmann à Génève, 1873	78 cards
Piquet cards, Gassmann à Génève, 1873	52 cards
Swiss playing cards, 1874	36 cards
Swiss playing cards, J. Müller, c. 1880	36 cards
Playing cards, French suit signs, geographical aces, 1878	52 cards
*Costume cards, French suit signs, geographical aces, 1878	52 cards
Costume cards, French suit signs, geographical aces, 1880	52 cards
Playing cards, French suit signs, geographical aces, 1880	52 cards
Tarot cards, Gassmann à Génève, 1883	78 cards
Swiss playing cards, c. 1885	34 cards
Swiss playing cards, uncolored proofs, 1873	32 cards

Total: 16 editions, 774 cards

[1] The starred items are from the collection of George Clulow, F.R.G.S.

CHAPTER XI

THE PLAYING CARDS OF DENMARK AND SWEDEN

THE earliest Danish cards we have are a pack of fifty-two with the French suit signs. The kings and knaves are of the German type, but the queens are charming little ladies of the middle of the nineteenth century, with coiffures, gowns, and bonnets of those days. The knave of clubs bears the maker's name, J. F. Holmblads, Kjobenhavn, and the ace of diamonds, as in the Russian cards, the revenue stamp. These cards are printed from wood blocks and stenciled. A later pack of similar design, though lacking some of the quaintness and individuality of the first one, is lithographed by the same maker.

DANISH PLAYING CARDS MADE IN COPENHAGEN IN 1875

The game of Gnau consists of forty-two cards and is the Danish version of the old game of Cucu. The Bragon of the Italian game becomes a cavalryman with drawn sword in Denmark, and an owl replaces the mascherone. The cards of our game are lithographed in color, and each 'house' bears the name of the maker, S. Salomon & Co., Copenhagen.

In Sweden the Cucu cards are called Kille cards or Cambio, and still further changes appear. Bragon of Italy becomes a soldier with drawn sword, the horse, an armored knight on his charger, and the cat, a boar. We have two sets of these cards, quite unlike in details, but with the same cards, and in each the numeral signs are fleurs de lys. Neither series is colored, and the name of the maker, A. Boman, Stockholm, is stamped on one of the cards of one. The other series is printed on a light green flowered paper.

The 'cards for playing' are the usual pack of fifty-two with the French suit signs. But the court cards have a personality of their own. They are named Gustavus Adolphus, Gustavus I, Gustavus III, and Carl XII.

GNAU CARDS, FROM THE DANISH GAME OF CUCU

They are the horse; the cavalryman, who replaces the Italian Bragon; three of the numerals; the Cucu; the house; the owl, which in Italy is the Mascherone; the cat; and the Harlequin, or Italian Matto

(268)

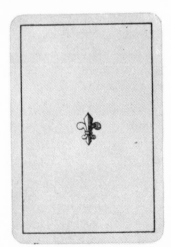

KILLE CARDS, OR CAMBIO, THE SWEDISH VERSION OF THE OLD ITALIAN CUCU

(269)

The earliest series we have are lithographed cards, the portrait court cards beautifully done with careful and precise attention to the details of the costumes. The colors are very soft and pleasing, and the stamp of the maker, Dolabet, Norrkoping, is on the ace of hearts, with the government stamp.

SWEDISH PLAYING CARDS MADE AT ESKILSTUNA IN 1913

A later series, with similarly named court cards, have in addition the title of each card lettered upon it, 'Kung,' 'Drottning,' and 'Knecht.' The maker's stamp on the ace of hearts bears the name, J. O. Oberg, Eskilstuna.

Still another pack shows court cards of a conventionalized Swedish type, but named in the French manner.

PLAYING CARDS OF DENMARK AND SWEDEN IN THE COLLECTION OF THE UNITED STATES PLAYING CARD COMPANY [1]

*Playing cards, L. P. Holmblads, Copenhagen, 1875	52 cards
Playing cards, L. P. Holmblads, Copenhagen, 1875, fine lithography	52 cards
Gnau cards, S. Salomon and Company, Copenhagen, 1870	42 cards
Gnau cards, c. 1880	42 cards
Playing cards by Dolabet, Norrkoping, 1880, lithographed	52 cards
*Cucu cards, A. Boman, Stockholm, 1885	42 cards
Cucu cards, c. 1885	42 cards
Playing cards, Kalmar, 1901	14 cards
Playing cards, J. O. Oberg and Son, 1913	52 cards

Total: 9 editions, 390 cards

[1] The starred items are from the collection of George Clulow, F.R.G.S.

CHAPTER XII

PLAYING CARDS IN RUSSIA

THE earliest Russian cards we have are a geography game, probably of the second quarter of the nineteenth century. They are beautifully engraved and colored by hand. Besides the usual fifty-two cards, there are eight extra ones, each showing a map of a part of Russia. On each of the fifty-two cards is the usual suit sign, a small playing card, occupying the upper right-hand corner. The upper left-hand quarter of the card bears the coat of arms of a Russian province; in the quarter below is a list of the principal towns, and in the lower right-hand corner is a figure in the native costume of the province.

They are richly lovely, these rare little reminders of old imperial Russia. On the excellent little maps, which are faintly tinted in water-color, the distances between the great cities are given in versts, St. Petersburg and Omsk and Moscow, and many others.

So much that is lost and gone is recorded on each little card with its strange Russian words, the vivid symbolism of its gay coat of arms, and its quaint little figure stepping out of a far land and time, that they take on almost the importance of archives.

The hearts are Archangel, with its vast and snowy reaches in the farthest north, symbolized in its device by a Mercury, on a golden ground, like Saint Michael in shining armor slaying the prostrate Lucifer; Viatka, with a crossbow; Kostroma, with its cross, symbolizing its cathedral; Jaro Slav, with its 'bear that walks like a man'; Vladimir, with its crowned lion upon a royal crimson ground, in remembrance of the crowning of the Russian grand dukes in its great cathedral until the middle of the fifteenth century; Orenburg, with Ufa as its capital, showing the double-headed eagle of the imperial family; Smolensk, fortified by Boris in the sixteenth century, showing a cannon; Tver, with the old arms of its mediæval princes; Novgorod 'the great,' harking back to the days of Rurik, with its device showing four fish, two rampant bears, and the candlestick of the church; Pskoff, with its emblem relating to the Hanseatic League; Vologda, with an orb and scepter, and boasting a long list of towns in contrast to most of the sparsely settled provinces; Olonetz, with its emblem of Scandinavian warfare; and lastly St. Petersburg, with the swords and tridents of Peter the Great.

The spades are Voronezh, with the imperial eagle; Livonia, with its capital, Riga, and Esthonia with its capital, Reval, both with devices of

RUSSIAN GEOGRAPHICAL CARDS OF 1830

(272)

RUSSIAN PLAYING CARDS OF 1867

The crest of the government card manufactory appears on the ace of diamonds
shown in the lower right-hand corner. The back design shown in the lower
left-hand corner is a typically Russian one.

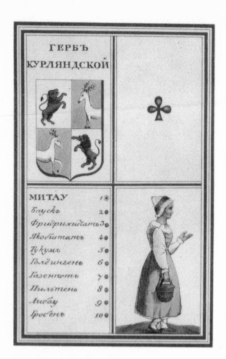

GEOGRAPHICAL PLAYING CARDS PUBLISHED IN RUSSIA IN 1830

the thirteenth-century sword-bearer knights; Irkutsk, with a wolf and lamb, almost Oriental, and probably relating to the dangers of the great road, traveled by the tea merchants; Yeniseisk, with its capital, Krasnoyarsk, and its neighbor, Tomsk, flaunt devices showing the Altai Mountains and white horses, emblematic of the great Siberian road; the device of Tobolsk shows white sails grouped about a golden shrine, and Taurida, in spite of being the stronghold of the Tartars, shows the Russian eagle, as does Kherson; Ekaterinoslav flaunts only the initial of the great Empress and the date of the founding of this province, 1787, by her favorite, Potemkin; Caucasus, with its capital, Stavropol, shows an archer upon a white horse, guarded by the imperial eagle upon a rock; Astrachan, with the sword and crown of Ivan the Terrible, reminiscent of his driving away of the Tartars, while Saratoff shows three little silver fish in cerulean blue.

In diamonds, Perm shows a jeweled icon upon a white lamb against a scarlet ground; Kharkoff, a caduceus and horn of plenty; Kursk, the fire-bearing pigeons of the old legend; Orel, the golden eagle above a castle of Muscovy; Kaluga, a golden crown against an azure ground; Tula, recalling its celebrated makers of arms and keen blades by those crossed on its crimson device; Ryazan, showing one of the mediæval princes; Tamboff, with a beehive and three large bees; Penza, with three sheaves of wheat; Nijni Novgorod, with a vermilion deer which must go back to the time of the Mongol invasion; and Kazan, reminiscent of the Tartars, with a pre-historic black bird with flame-colored wings; Simbersk, with a gold-tipped marble column; and Moscow itself, with a gold-armored knight upon a white horse.

The clubs are Courland, with its capital, Mitau, which harks back to the fourteenth century, with its quartered device showing two rampant lions and two white deer; Bessarabia, with its capital, Kishineff, with the imperial eagle; the three seems to be Byalostok, and there are only three towns listed in this province. Its insignia show an eagle and a mounted Cossack. Pultowa carries on the quarterings of its device a green bay tree, the flag, the Russian eagle, and tents and arms, doubtless in remembrance of Peter the Great's victory over the host of Charles XII of Sweden. Tchernigoff shows a gold-crowned eagle, perhaps relating to its days as an ancient principality; Kieff, whose device shows the angel Gabriel with the flaming sword, symbolic of Saint Andrew's bringing of Christianity to this far port in the first century; Podolia, with its capital Kamenets, and Volhynia, with its capital Zhitomir, both show the imperial eagle; Grodno carries on its device a zebra and a mounted horseman with drawn saber, and Wilna shows the same horseman; Minsk, Mohileff, and Vitebsk all show the Russian imperial eagle, the last two adding a mounted knight.

The gay little costumed figures, the women with their veils and elaborate

RUSSIAN PLAYING CARDS OF 1860, SHOWING THE SEAL OF THE MONOPOLY ON THE
ACE OF DIAMONDS AND THE CHARACTERISTIC RUSSIAN SPADE SUIT SIGNS

(274)

headdresses and full skirts, the men with their long petticoats rich with embroideries and jewels, seem to have stepped directly out of the half barbaric, half Oriental legends of this great vague land.

The Russian 'cards for playing' are either piquet packs of thirty-two or thirty-six cards, or the usual pack of fifty-two, with the French suit signs quite recognizable, but drawn with a certain flowing of line that gives them a very pleasing delicacy. On the ace of diamonds is always the Russian eagle and below it the seal of the card manufactory. This card manufactory was a monopoly under the czars, established by the Empress Marie. The money from it went to the support of a home for the orphans of soldiers and sailors. The seal of this monopoly shows a pelican on her nest, caring for her young who are grouped before her. Very often these seals are printed in gold. The court cards in all of our packs are double heads. They are not entirely conventionalized, and their Russian costumes are very interesting; the work is done with great precision, and the colors

COURT CARDS AND WRAPPER OF A PACK OF RUSSIAN PLAYING CARDS MADE UNDER THE SOVIET, 1928

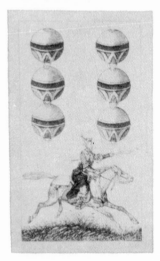

RUSSIAN TRAPPOLA CARDS

(276)

are rich and beautiful. The backs of the cards are reminiscent of the Russian embroideries, conventional designs of great individuality and in excellent taste.

ACE OF DIAMONDS AND COURT CARDS MADE UNDER THE SOVIET, 1928

It is rather interesting to know that in a paper on 'The Origin and Manufacture of Playing Cards,' by George Clulow, F.R.G.S., of London, and read by him before the Society of Arts on May 8, 1889, in London, he says, 'I place America first, and next Russia in the excellence of their materials and their methods of manufacture.'

A pack of trappola cards with German suit signs are almost Oriental. The court cards are full-length figures, and the numerals have the usual groups of little figures at the bottom of each card. The heart suit shows Cossacks riding their horses, the bells are whimsical and delightful little Chinamen and Mongols, the leaves, harlequins, pierrots, and buffoons with court cards in the costume of the sixteenth century, and the acorns show costumes of a century later, with the figures on the numerals, little dogs dressed in cos-

AN ACE OF DIAMONDS
UNDER THE SOVIET

tumes of the same period. The mark of the monopoly is above the elephant on the two of bells.

There is so much individuality and such an Oriental flavor to all of these Russian cards that they seem to be rather the game of the most Western of Eastern peoples rather than that of the most Eastern of Europeans.

RUSSIAN PLAYING CARDS IN THE COLLECTION OF
THE UNITED STATES PLAYING CARD COMPANY [1]

*Geographical playing cards, 1830	60 cards
*Playing cards, 1860, piquet pack	34 cards
Playing cards, 1867, piquet pack	32 cards
Playing cards, 1870	52 cards
Playing cards, stenciled, 1870	52 cards
Playing cards, with German suit signs, trappola pack	36 cards
Playing cards, Russian whist cards, 1875	52 cards
Playing cards, 1880	52 cards
Playing cards, piquet pack, 1884	36 cards
Four packs, piquet cards, 1884	144 cards
Playing cards, whist pack, 1905	52 cards
Playing cards, whist pack, 1913	52 cards
Playing cards, whist pack, 1928, using the designs of Imperial Russia	52 cards
Playing cards, whist pack, 1928, using the designs of the Soviet	52 cards

Total: 17 editions, 758 cards

[1] The starred items are from the collection of George Clulow, F.R.G.S.

CHAPTER XIII
PLAYING CARDS IN AMERICA

THE gaming sticks of the American Indians resemble those of Asia, some of them being marked with the feathered shaftment of an arrow, and others with the symbols of the Four Directions; they are used in a similar way, and their origin is undoubtedly identical.

As to playing cards the first ones were unquestionably brought to America by the Spaniards. Cards of deerskin or sheepskin, painted after the manner of the old Spanish cards of three centuries ago, are still occasionally to be found among the Indians of the Southwest. According to Mr. Culin, the Indians call the four suits 'Copas,' 'Escudos,' 'Espadas,'

PLAYING CARDS WITH THE SPANISH SUIT SIGNS PAINTED ON SHEEPSKIN
Used by the Indians in the southwestern part of the United States

and 'Bastones' or 'Palos.' The names of the king and valet are 'rey' and 'sota,' as in Spanish, but the cavalier, or 'caballo,' they call 'jliv,' or horse. The ace, they call 'as,' but for the other numerals native names are used. Their game they call 'con quien' (with whom?). It is also known by the native name 'daka cunitsnun,' meaning cards ten. The 'rey,' or king, is also called 'inju' or 'inshu,' meaning good.

There is a legend telling how the sailors with Columbus, who were inveterate gamblers, threw their cards overboard in superstitious terror upon encountering storms in these vast and mysterious seas. Later, safe on dry land, they regretted their rashness, and in the new country made other cards for themselves out of the leaves of the copas tree, which greatly interested the Indians. There seems to be more than a probability of truth in this story, for Garcilaso de la Vega in his 'Historia de la Florida,' which was published in Madrid in 1723, tells us that the soldiers of the Spanish expedition of 1534 played with leather cards. Cards were known to the early Mexicans as 'amapatolli,' from 'amatl,' meaning paper, and 'patolli,' meaning game.

Bullet, in his 'Recherches Historiques sur les Cartes à Jouer,' says that the Spaniards carried into the New World their passion for cards. This little book of one hundred and sixty-three pages, published at Lyons in 1757, is the most delightful essay on the subject that we know. The author, as a loyal Frenchman, decides that playing cards had their origin in his own France, under Charles V. His description of the intimate life of four-teenth-century France is as vivid as a snatch of song of François Villon, whom, indeed, he quotes:

> 'Trois Detz plombez de bonne carre
> Et ung beau joly jeu de Cartes.'

He quotes also the old legends and romances, the court records and historians and even la sainte Bible, in explaining the names of the French court cards.

To return to America, we must again quote Mr. Culin regarding the earliest cards made in America which have come down to our time. These cards, naturally enough, are Spanish, and are in the Archives of the Indies, in Seville. There are two uncut sheets of wood blocks, one showing the court cards of the four suits and the numeral cards of the suit of swords, colored in red, blue, and black. The swords are crossed instead of being arranged in the usual Spanish manner, which suggests that some Portuguese adventurers may have had a hand in their making. The back of the sheet bears an inscription in pen and ink: 'Nueva Espana, 1583. Archivo de Indias, No. 117. Dibujo.'

THE BACK OF A SPANISH-AMERICAN PLAYING CARD OF 1583

From *Chess and Playing Cards*, by Stewart Culin, *Report of the United States National Museum*, 1896

The other sheet bears the imprint of eighteen different designs for card backs. Mr. Culin says, 'The devices are all different, and embrace a mixture of Mexican and European subjects, including the Emperor Montezuma, his successor Quahte-motzin, native priests performing various rites, and grotesque figures, apparently of the school of Albert Dürer.'

European cards must have been brought to this new country by the English in Virginia and the Dutch in New Amsterdam. That they also found their way into Puritan New England is proved by a Plymouth Colony record of 1633, when several persons were fined two pounds each for card-playing. In 1656 there is a Plymouth Colony law, fixing the penalty for card-playing at forty shillings for adults; children and servants 'to bee corrected att the discretion of theire parents or masters and for the second offence to bee publickly whipt.'

In the same year, in New Amsterdam, playing at tric-trac during the time of divine service is prohibited. The Netherlanders lived more luxuriously in their houses than any other people, and their Old-World habits came with them into the New, with their carved furniture and tapestries, their velvet and russia leather chairs, their muslin and flowered tabby curtains, their tall clocks and paintings by Antwerp masters.

In the other colonies, too, all manufactured articles that required skill or nicety of workmanship were brought from the old country. In Virginia a ship from England would unload upon the planter's wharf part of its motley cargo of mahogany tables, chairs covered with russia leather, wines in great variety from the Azores and Madeira, brandy, Gloucester cheeses, linens and cottons, silks and dimity, quilts and feather beds, carpets, shoes, axes and hoes, hammers and nails, rope and canvas, painters' white lead and colors, saddles, demijohns, mirrors, books, playing cards — pretty much everything.

As early as 1624 the Virginia Assembly enacted the following·law: 'Mynisters shall not give themselves to excesse in drinking or yette spend their tyme idelie by day or by night, playing at dice, cards or any unlawfull game.'

Likewise, horse-racing was a favorite sport, but it was for gentlemen only. An order of the County Court of York in 1674 reads: 'James Bullocke, a Taylor, haveing made a race for his mare to runn w'th a horse belonging to Mr. Matthew Slader for twoe thousand pounds of tobacco and caske, it being contrary to Law for a Laborer to make a race, being a sport only for Gentlemen, is fined for the same one hundred pounds of tobacco and caske.'

The English introduced horse-racing in New York, and imported playing cards in great quantities. Under the Dutch, the colony had enjoyed more holidays than other parts of America, Saint Nicholas's Day, New Year's Day, and Pinkster, a day of June-time picnics, as well as Christmas, Easter, Whitsuntide, Saint Valentine's Day and May Day, and with the coming of the English the gayeties did not diminish.

At William and Mary College, which had its first commencement in 1700, at which not only Virginians and Indians were present, but people who had journeyed from Maryland and Pennsylvania as well, it was necessary to issue an order 'y^t no scholar belonging to any school in ye College, of w^t Age, Rank, or Quality, soever, do keep any race Horse at ye College, in ye Town — or anywhere in the neighborhood — y^t they be not anyway concerned in making races, or in backing or abetting, those made by others, and y^t all Race Horses, kept in ye neighborhood of ye College & belonging to any of ye scholars, be immediately dispatched & sent off, & never again brought back, and all of this under Pain of ye severest Animadversion and Punishment.'

Similar orders forbid cock-fighting, the 'frequenting of ye Ordinaries,' betting, playing at billiards, cards, or dice.

New York was famous for her clubs even early in the eighteenth century. Often they were housed in some tavern or coffee-house, and these were many and good. In Virginia there were stringent laws against gaming in the public houses. Gambling debts were not recoverable; innkeepers who permitted any game of cards or dice except backgammon were subject to a heavy fine besides forfeiting their licenses.

The first American paper mills were started late in the seventeenth century and of course it seems useless to look for American-made playing cards before this time.

Isaiah Thomas, in his 'History of Printing in America,' mentions James Franklin, an older brother of Benjamin, as a Boston printer. He tells how he printed 'upon cards' verses that the youthful Benjamin had written about Blackbeard the pirate. (Benjamin Franklin afterwards alludes to them as 'miserable ditties,' but at the time he sold them on the streets of Boston.) It is possible that James Franklin may have made playing cards as well, because the difficulty of making paper of the proper texture was a considerable one, and the printing of cards, after this was achieved, was comparatively simple. Playing cards were common in New England at this time and life there in the eighteenth century was very different from that of a hundred years before. After all, the bond between the colonies and the mother country was very close, and the Old-World customs were pretty sure to be reflected sooner or later in the New. Cards are often listed in the inventories. In 1720, fifty dozen packs belonged to James Lyndell. A shilling a pack was the price. In 1722, Peter Cutler's shop goods included a round card table, thirteen shillings, a handsome mahogany card table with five legs, etc. In 1733, James Jekyl had one card table at twelve shillings, and another of black walnut, at six pounds. These tables were generally square, but sometimes round or triangular. The Boston clergy seems to have played, for the Reverend Thomas Haward had a mahogany card table in 1736. James Jackson had one of the same rare wood a year earlier. Probably many of these cards were brought from England, but it is just as probable that others were made by local printers, printers of newspapers, bookbinders and stationers. We know that this was true in the middle colonies fifty years later. Makers of wallpaper also made playing cards.

David Gairdner, at his warehouse on Belcher's Wharf, Boston, advertised in the 'Boston Gazette,' October 15, 1751, 'plain and gilded Bibles, common Prayer Books, and Books bound and ruled for Accomptants, playing cards, . . . sand glasses, Leather Breeches, men and women's Gloves, Ivory Combs, etc.'

Following Benjamin Franklin's career as a Philadelphia printer, we find him interested not only in the printing of the paper, but in the paper mill as well, where they made 'fullers pressboard,' and 'glazed fulling paper,' used by bookbinders and makers of cards. It is not surprising that from the beginning there appears the often repeated advertisement in his paper, 'Ready money for old rags may be had by the Printer hereof.'

Other notices giving a hint of his activities are of 'Superfine Crown Soap for sale at the Printing Office'; 'Very good Lamp Black made and sold by the Printer hereof.'

In 1732 he published his first 'Almanach,' and thereafter the notice appears each year, 'Poor Richard's Almanach, Printed and Sold by Benjamin Franklin.' There are also 'Glazed Fulling Papers and Bonnet Papers sold by the Printer hereof'; 'Choice Writing Parchment Sold by the Printer hereof'; 'Very good Chocolate to be sold by the Printer hereof'; in October, 1737, he advertises 'Large Bibles . . . Dictionaries . . . Latin Grammars . . . Religious Courtship . . . Scales, Compasses, Slates . . . Other Stationery Ware — just imported, and to be Sold by the Printer hereof.' In the same year there is also the notice, 'Just Published, Every Man his own Doctor, or the Poor Planter's Physician, Printed and Sold by the Printer hereof.'

These are followed by 'Great Variety of Maps and Prints, sold by B. Franklin'; 'Bookbinding is done reasonably in the best manner': also, 'Made and sold by Robert Barton near the post office in Philadelphia at the most reasonable rates . . . Backgammon tables with men, boxes and dies'; and 'Choice Good Parchment sold by the Printer hereof.'

In 1745 he uses cuts of ships advertising 'Cruising Voyages' for the Barbados, for London, and for South Carolina. There is also a proclamation of the royal governor, Edward Trelawney, asking for volunteers against His Majesty's enemies, the 'cruel and crafty French' and Indians. This is headed by the British coat of arms. This same coat of arms appears on the ace of spades of all English playing cards at the time. In the Philadelphia Library, which Benjamin Franklin founded in 1731, is his machine with which he made his experiments with electricity. It is rather simple. Friction was created by a belt connecting two wheels, over which hung a silk curtain. On a revolving rod at the top are eight discs, and these are cut from old playing cards. There is no watermark discernible, and no clue to the maker's name. But if he was Benjamin Franklin, which seems likely, he could have used the same plate, not only for the king's business, but for his own as well, which thrifty thought would doubtless have appealed to him.

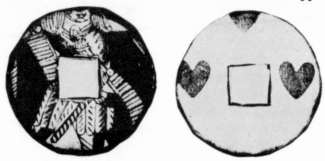

DISCS CUT FROM PLAYING CARDS AND USED BY BENJAMIN FRANKLIN ON HIS MACHINE FOR EXPERIMENTING WITH ELEC-TRICITY IN 1752

At this time he advertises, 'To be sold by the printer hereof, very good sealing wax,' and prints a map of Louisbourg, with news of the campaign. In September of this year he publishes an advertisement, 'Just imported by Hamilton Wallace and Company in the Ship Agnes and Betty, Capt. Brame, & in the ship Mercury, Captain Hargrave from London, the following Goods to be sold very cheap for ready Money or six months credit, viz. Buttons, mohair, bed quilts . . . playing cards, etc.'

At this time Benjamin Franklin was postmaster of Philadelphia. On February 23, 1747, the entire front page of the paper is given over to the lottery whose drawing was held at the State House in the presence of the magistrates. Philadelphia raised money for public improvements, for the paving of its streets, for the building of churches and steeples, by means of lotteries. Yet the same magistrates who presided at the lottery drawing in 1747, two years later suppressed a presentation of Shakespeare by a little company of players. Cock-fighting and bull-baiting were common sports, and playing cards, which had been under the ban in 1703, when all persons found playing them in public were called before the grand jury, were now in popular favor as they were in England. Society was very gay in this largest of American cities, and the first Philadelphia Assembly was held in 1748.

At this time Franklin advertises, 'Stationery of all kinds, to be sold at the Post Office.' 'Stationery' was an elastic term, and often included Bibles, books, and playing cards and 'sundry other things too tedious to mention,' which is a favorite last line in importers' advertisements, and also those of local book shops.

In the 'Pennsylvania Gazette' of February 26, 1750, is the advertisement, 'Just imported & to be sold very cheap for ready money by Thomas White at his house in Market street — almost opposite the sign of the Conestogoe Waggon. Ben Weston's Snuff, glassware . . . playing cards, etc.'

In the same paper for April 11, 1751, 'Walter Dougherty in Chester town, Kent County, Md. has to be sold a fine large brick house completely furnished, likewise a Billiard room. . . . There is a good billiard table.' This is a reminder of how much the homes and lives of the planters in Virginia and Maryland were like those they had left in England.

On May 23, 1751, in Mr. Franklin's paper is the advertisement, 'Just imported, and to be sold wholesale and retail by Joseph Redmond at his store at the dwelling house of Mr. Peter David in Second street, A large assortment of toys. . . . Mogul and Andrew cards, etc.'

On June 6 of the same year he advertises, 'Very good. Temple Spectacles, sold at the Post Office. Ten shillings the pair.'

'The Gentlemen's London and Universal Magazine for months January and February to be sold at the Post Office. Also very good coffee and Padusoy.'

'Trenton Lottery Tickets sold by Joseph Hall.'

In the 'Pennsylvania Gazette' for October 31, 1751, is the advertisement, 'Just imported in the ship Peak Bay, Walter Sterling from London, and to be sold cheap for ready money or short credit by Alexander Hamilton at his store in Water street, Blankets, rugs, . . . playing cards, etc.'

In March of 1752 there are notices of various activities at the printer's office: 'William Franklin has a few lottery tickets to dispose of. Also very good prints without frames to be sold at the printing office.' 'Very good ink sold at the printing office.' 'Ready money for good quills at the Printing Office.' 'To be sold very cheap, A Billiard Table. Enquire at the new printing office.' 'Philadelphia Steeple Lottery Tickets to be sold by David Hall at the new Printing office.' There is also the advertisement of Joseph Preston, 'nearly opposite the Friends' Meeting House,' who has imported cards to sell.

On March 4, 1753, 'David Franks has to sell very reasonable . . . playing cards, etc.' This advertisement does not say that these were imported.

In February of 1757 appears the notice, 'Method and Process of Making Potash equal if not superior to the best foreign potash — to be sold at the printing office.' At this time advertisements for deserting soldiers begin to replace those of runaway slaves which have occupied so much space in the 'Pennsylvania Gazette' from the time of its first issue. Most of us think of eighteenth-century Philadelphia as the shrine of American liberty, centering about the perfect simplicity of Independence Hall and the affixing of the American signatures to the declaration 'that all men are created equal, that they are endowed by their Creator with certain unalienable Rights, that among these are Life, Liberty, and the pursuit of Happiness.' Yet by far the largest number of advertisements in the Philadelphia papers are of slaves trying to escape their masters. There is more than a little pathos in many of these, 'a well set up fellowe,' carrying with him 'a Dutch Bible and a prayer book,' is one of many. The contradictions of the eighteenth century often seem inexplicable.

Meanwhile Benjamin Franklin intrepidly continues his advertisements of articles for sale at the post office: 'Good cartridge papers and Pasteboards for bookbinders to be sold at the Post Office' is one. There are many allusions to 'Our cruel and crafty enemy, the French.' Also, 'Very good shop paper sold at the Post Office, where may be had ready money for clean Linen Rags.' These rags are presumably for the soldiers instead of for the paper mill, for a few days later a proclamation for recruits, signed by Lord Geoffrey Amherst, is followed by an appeal for 'half worn sheets and clean linen for bandages.'

A diversity of goods is to be had at the post office: 'Good stockings fit for soldiers, to be Sold. Enquire at the Post Office.' 'Doctor Cowden's best round high toasted snuff, to be sold by the Bottle at the printing office.' 'Paper hangings, copper plate pieces by the best masters, stationery of all kinds, to be sold at the Post Office.'

There are many notices of the Philadelphia races at this time; also announcements of three different lotteries; and to cap the climax, the advertisement, 'A large Living Lion to be seen in Chestnut Street. The price for men is 18d, women 12d, children 6d,' showing that amusements were many and varied.

The issue of the 'Pennsylvania Gazette,' announcing the passage of the famous Stamp Act of 1765, appears with broad black bands of mourning. This was, of course, but a mild expression of the dismay and indignation that were felt throughout the Colonies. In the Stamp Act are to be found the following paragraphs:

'And for and upon every pack of playing cards and all dice which shall be sold or used within said colonies or plantations, the several stamp duties following,

'For every pack of such cards, the sum of 1 shilling.

'And for every pair of such dice, the sum of ten shillings.

.   .   .   .

'And for the better securing the said duty on playing cards and dice, be it further enacted that from and after the first day of November 1765, no playing cards or dice shall be sold or used in play within said colonies and plantations unless the paper and thread enclosing them shall have been sealed and stamped as provided in pursuance of this act.'

The articles that were taxed under this act were the very things that were known to yield a material revenue, so that playing cards must have been made and used in appreciable quantities at the time.

Of the cards that have come down to us from those days are many on whose plain white backs are written invitations to teas and assemblies and balls. It was the custom to use playing cards as cards of invitation, and often to quarter them and use them as visiting cards. This was a perfectly conventional thing to do, not only in America, but in France as well. The earliest one that we know in America was sent to Mrs. Jeykell in cosmopolitan Philadelphia of 1749. She was the granddaughter of the first mayor of the city, and the wife of Sir Joseph Jeykell, secretary to Queen Anne. The invitation reads, 'The gentlemen of the army present their compliments to Mrs. Jeykell, and beg the favor of her company to a ball at the State house on Monday next.'

In 1765, playing cards were used as admission cards to the classes at the University of Pennsylvania.

Benjamin Franklin, writing to his wife from Paris on September 14, 1767, ends by saying: 'This letter will cost you a shilling, and you may think it cheap when you consider it cost me at least fifty guineas to get into the situation that enables me to write it. Besides I might if I had staid at

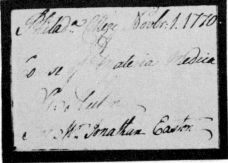

A CARD OF ADMISSION TO ONE OF THE CLASSES AT THE PHILADELPHIA COLLEGE, 1770

AN INVITATION ON THE BACK OF A PLAYING CARD, 1792

home have won perhaps two shillings of you at cribbage. By the way, now I mention cards, let me tell you that quadrille is quite out of fashion and English whist all the mode at Paris and the court.'

When Tench Coxe in 1800 published his Washingtoniana, he prefaced it by saying that 'Everything performed or written by Washington is estimable and ought to be preserved'; and the subsequent addresses, messages, and letters more than bear out this statement. It is emphasized again in the 'George Washington Diaries.' The picture their entries present is of the great Virginian who said, 'Agriculture is the most healthy, the most useful and the most noble employment of man.' And they show him among the woods and fields and streams that he loved. The casual references to cards are many.

'January 16, 1768. At home all day at Cards — it snowing.' Mr. Fitzpatrick's footnote says: 'The entries for gains or losses at cards and other play are as carefully entered in Washington's accounts as all other

AMERICAN PLAYING CARDS IMPORTED FROM ENGLAND, 1765

FOR EXPORTATION, FIFTY
POUNDS PENALTY IF RELAN-
DED, AND TWENTY POUNDS
IF SOLD OR USED IN GREAT
BRITAIN.

AMERICAN PLAYING CARDS IMPORTED FROM ENGLAND, 1765

(289)

income and expenditure.' ('1765, January — By cash set aside for card money, five pounds.') Grouped throughout the years from 1772 to January 1, 1775, for cash won and lost at home, Fredericksburg, Williamsburg, Annapolis, and other places, the entries show a total loss of 78 pounds, 5 shillings, 9 pence, and a corresponding gain of 72 pounds, 2 shillings, 6 pence; a loss at play of 6 pounds, 3 shillings, 3 pence in four years.

'October 11, 1768. Went into the neck and up the creek after Blew Wings.' (Part of this night was spent at cards, at which he lost nineteen shillings.)

'September 5, 1770. At home all day playing cards.'

'March 16, 1770. Went to doeg run and took the hounds with me. Found a fox by the Widow Ashford's and soon lost him. Upon my return home found Colo. Lewis, my Bro. Cho, and Mr. Brooke here. In the Evening Mr. Jno. West and Mr. Stedlar came, also Mr. Whiting.' (At the card game this night Mr. Washington lost 6s., 3d.)

'December 31, 1771. Went up to Alexandria at the request of Messrs. Montgomerie, Wilson and Stewart, to settle with them along with Mr. John (Semple) (as Excr. of Colo. Thomas Colvill) for the Maryland Tract of Land which they had purchased of Mr. Semple. Staid all night.' (Washington played cards this night and lost 2l., 11s., and on this visit to Alexandria he purchased two new packs of cards at a cost of two shillings.)

In all probability these cards were English, similar to some found not long ago in a forgotten corner of an old store in Baltimore. They were made about 1765 by Henry Hart in London, and both the ace of spades and the wrapper are marked 'Exportation.'

A few years later, the following is one of Washington's General Orders at Morristown.

'HEADQUARTERS, MORRISTOWN
'8th May, 1777

'. . . the commander in chief in the most pointed and explicit terms forbids ALL officers and soldiers playing at cards, dice or any games except those of EXERCISE for diversion; being impossible if the practise be allowed at all to discriminate between innocent play for amusement and criminal gaming for pecuniary and sordid purposes.'

There were forty printing presses in the country before the Revolution. Like Caxton, these printers were also stationers and bookbinders and booksellers. That many of them also made playing cards is extremely likely. Hugh Gaine was a well-known printer in New York, who published almanacs, and James Parker had a press at Woodbridge, New Jersey. In 1732, Richard Fry was a stationer, bookseller, paper-maker, and rag merchant of Boston. He was also the earliest account-book manufacturer in the country; while Daniel Henchman, of Milton, was the most enterprising bookseller and printer in America. One of the earliest paper mills was also in Milton. An advertisement in the Boston newspaper in 1733 reads:

'In Milton near the paper mill
A new built house to rent,
Ask of the printer and you will
Know further to content.'

In Milton, too, in 1757, Jazaniah Ford was born, and he is the first American to be designated as card-maker. For more than half a century the Ford playing card manufactory flourished in Milton, one of the important industries of Massachusetts. Thomas Ford, evidently a brother of

COURT CARDS OF JAZANIAH FORD, MILTON, MASSACHUSETTS, c. 1800

Mr. Ford uses his initial, F, as decoration on the king of clubs. The early cards of Samuel Hart in Philadelphia seem to be from these same old blocks

Jazaniah Ford, had a 'paper staining manufactory' in Boston. His advertisements are numerous. In the 'Columbian Centinel' for December 30, 1807, is the notice:

'To Paper Makers.

'For sale, a quantity of White Rags. Inquire of Thomas Ford at his paper staining manufactory, No. 2 Fish Street where is for sale a general assortment of Paper Hangings and Borders, wholesale and retail.'

In the 'Columbian Centinel' of December 11, 1811, he advertises:

'Paper Hangings by the Manufacturer.

'Thomas Ford respectfully informs his friends and the Public at large that they may be supplied with a variety of the above articles upon cheap and liberal terms, by calling at his factory No. 2 Fish street, where they are selling wholesale and retail of various fashionable and pleasing figures

DECATUR CARDS, MADE BY JAZANIAH FORD, MILTON, MASSACHUSETTS, IN 1815

He seems to have used the same court cards for his Lafayette cards of 1824, when a portrait of the
great Frenchman appears on the ace of spades

(292)

from 25 cents to 4 dollars per roll. While in England, he selected the most elegant patterns in the several British factories he visited. His colours he warrants to be of the best kind and durability, being chosen by himself immediately from the manufacturer. All favors gratefully received, and prompt attention paid thereto.'

On December 21, 1811, in the 'Columbian Centinel' is the advertisement:

'Ford and Co.'s Superior Playing Cards.

'Elisha Penniman (a partner in the concern of the Playing Card Manufactory at Milton, conducted by Mr. Ford) has on hand and intends keeping at his store No. 22 Marlboro street Boston —
A regular supply of each kind of CARDS, made at their Factory, for wholesale customers only and at the manufactory prices viz: — best Eagles, Harry 8ths, Eagle do do, Merry Andrew — Eagle Merry Andrews — Highlanders, and Refuse.'

Jazaniah Ford also issued special editions of cards, one evidently in 1814, after Stephen Decatur's victory, when the court cards appear in Algerian costumes, and the ace of spades, in addition to the usual eagle and the maker's name, shows a picture of the great sea fight. Another, ten years later, was in honor of Lafayette's visit to America. The ace of spades is nicely engraved and shows a portrait medallion of General Lafayette, after the Sully portrait. The eagle is above, a bough of bay and another of oak, the flag, cannon, and the maker's name below.

THE ACE OF SPADES OF A PACK OF CARDS MADE BY JAZANIAH FORD, OF MILTON, IN 1824 IN HONOR OF GENERAL LAFAYETTE'S VISIT TO AMERICA

This is supposed to have been engraved by Abel Bowen

Joseph Ford, a nephew, son of Nathan and Waitstill Ford, born in 1799, carried on the card factory after Jazaniah Ford's death in 1832. The design on Joseph Ford's ace of spades is reminiscent of that of the English makers, though the eagle appears in an aura of glory above it. Jazaniah Seth Ford, son of the first card-maker, was also born in 1799, and is also said to have been interested in the card factory.

Amos Whitney, born in 1766, was also a card-maker. His advertisement in the 'Columbian Centinel' of October 30, 1799, reads:

'Playing Cards for sale at the manufactory of Amos Whitney & Co. No. 123 Orange St. & at the Bookstore of William Pelham No. 59 Cornhill. Superfine Columbian, Harry the Eighth and Merry Andrew Playing cards by the groce, dozen or single pack.'

PLAYING CARDS MADE BY JOSEPH FORD, OF MILTON, *c*. 1835

The originals are in the collection of the Society for the Preservation of New England Antiquities
in Boston

The Whitney ace of spades is the most interesting one we know. It shows
in an oval medallion the early official eagle of Paul Revere[1] and Samuel
Hill, with the olive branch in one claw and the arrows in the other, and the
thirteen stars huddled above. In the border at the top is lettered the prim
New England injunction, 'Use but Don't Abuse Me,' while below is the
motto from the arms of Old England, 'Evil be to Him that Evil Thinks.'
Amos Whitney's name appears in the census of 1790, but it is almost certain that he was making cards before this time. According to the genealogy he died in 1804, and his name as card-maker ceases to appear in the

---

[1] "I have been trying vainly to get proof of my statement that Paul Revere engraved plates for
Playing Cards. Some of my friends have heard so, but cannot tell from what source. It may be a family
tradition as my great, great grandfather was a very close friend of Revere. I refer to Captain John
Hayward, who founded the stone quarrying business in Quincy. I have some of his papers now referring
to pre-revolutionary conditions."

From a letter written May 18, 1928, by Walter C. Belcher, Holbrook, Massachusetts.

ACE OF SPADES OF AMOS
WHITNEY, BOSTON, 1799

THE AMERICAN EAGLE ENGRAVED BY PAUL REVERE ON HIS
BUSINESS CARD

THE AMERICAN EAGLE ENGRAVED BY
SAMUEL HILL, BOSTON

(295)

Boston directories. In 1811, the contents of the factory which was evidently his are advertised for sale in the 'Columbian Centinel':

'To Playing Card Manufacturers;
This Day: the 18th Sept.
At No. 124 Orange street,
Will be sold at Auction to the highest bidder in order to close a concern, a complete assortment of UTENSILS for a PLAYING CARD MANUFACTORY, upon a large scale; consisting of the following articles, viz —

'2 sets new Court Blocks; and 8 do partly worn, for English or American Cards; 1 set do for Spanish Cards; 1 set do for French Cards; 1 shew card block; 2 sets Types for printing backs of French or Spanish cards; 1 set Court Blocks in brass, for English; 1 Block and 2 Copperplates for Aces; 10 Blocks for do of various descriptions in metal; 2 Blocks for Counters; 15 sets new Court Stencils, 8 of which from new Blocks; a number sets do in good condition; 1 set do for Shew Cards; 8 sets do for pips or spots, new; 6 sets do for Spanish cards; 2 sets do for French cards; 7 pasting brushes; about 4 doz. Painting do part of them new; 11 Loting do; 4 Glazing machines and Marbles complete; about 4 doz. Flints for polishing, chiefly new; 1 Printing Press; 1 hand do for wrappers; 8 Cutting Machines large and small; about 1200 Poles for hanging paper; about 1500 Hooks for do; about 4700 printed Covers or Wrappers for Cards of different descriptions; and 10 dozen Press boards of maple and pine.

'A Dye Press of a new Construction, for imbossing Message Cards, Paper & from which 900 impressions have been taken within the hour.

'The foregoing articles which cost upwards of 1600 dollars will be sold in one lot precisely at 12 o'clock — the purchaser will be indulged with a credit of 12 months by giving his note with a good endorser.

'Besides the above, there are a great number of other articles, which will be sold for cash, or where the amount exceeds 100 dollars, at 60 days — among which are, a Copper, containing 55 gallons, nearly as good as new; 3 large iron bound Screw Presses; 4 Stoves and Funnels; 1 large and 2 small Scale Beams, Scales and Weights; a quantity of Vermillion; Red Lead; French Berries; Lamp Black, and a very great number of other articles. Sale to begin at ten o'clock.'

From this inventory, it is not hard to reconstruct that early factory, nor to follow the processes that went into the making of the cards of that day.

In the 'American Mechanics' Magazine' of September 17, 1825, the following article on the making of playing cards appears;

September 17, 1825

American
MECHANICS' MAGAZINE,
Museum, Register, Journal & Gazette.

THE MAKING OF COMMON FRENCH PLAYING CARDS

The mode of manufacturing these common articles presents several curious circumstances: the whole process is included in five points.

1. The paper of which cards are made.
2. The mode of forming the cards themselves.
3. The printing and illumination of the figures.
4. The mode of smoothing the cards.
5. The manner of cutting them.

The paper is of three kinds: — a brown hand, which forms the centre of the card. This paper is thin, and two sheets are usually glued together to form the basis of the card. The opaqueness it imparts, and the facility with which it takes paste, are the reasons for using this paper; it is covered on one side with cardmakers' paper, and on the other by pot paper.

The cardmakers' paper, which is used for the back, must be very white; without the slightest speck, lest the card should be known by its back; for the same reason it must have no frame márk, nor the maker's name.

The pot paper is used for the printed face; it must be very white, and be slightly pasted to the belly paper, as it is termed. This paper is furnished by a government board; the sheets are fourteen inches Fr. long, and eleven and a half wide, and form twenty cards of the common size. The frame mark is twenty fleurs de lys, so placed that one of them will appear in the centre of each card when cut.

None of these papers must be folded, for it would be impossible to get rid of the mark made by the fold.

The pasting these papers into cards requires considerable address. The sheets of these papers are first placed in three separate piles before the cardmakers; and after the first of white, two sheets off each pile are taken in succession and placed in a pile on his left hand, the pile being finished by a single sheet of the same as that at bottom; by which means a pile is formed in which the papers required for each card are found in their proper places, but so that the cards are alternately lying on their back and their face. After this the pasting is begun, and is rendered easy to the cardmaker by the single observation that the white paper is not to be spread with the paste unless a sheet of brown is to follow.

When the pasting is finished, the heap is covered with a sheet of paper,

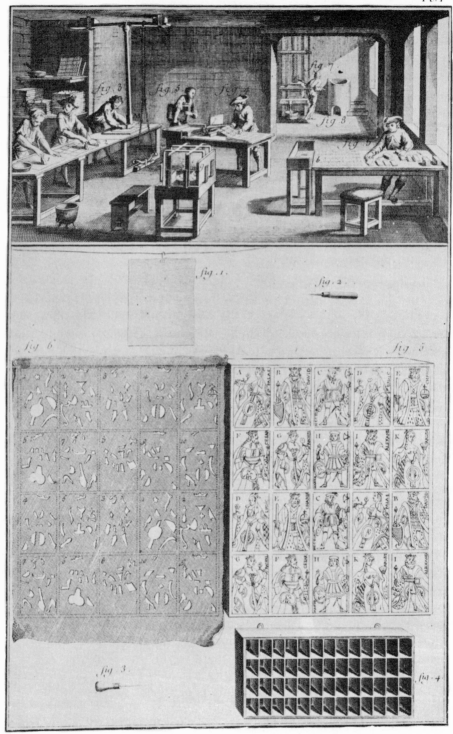

THE MAKING OF PLAYING CARDS IN 1760

From the *Encyclopédie des Arts et Métiers* of Duhamel de Monceau

and placed under a press, which at first is but slightly screwed; but the pressure is increased every quarter of an hour, until the screw refuses to go any farther. The heap being then taken from the press, the edges are washed with a very soft brush dipped in water, to dissolve the paste that may have been squeezed out by the action of the press. The cards are then pasted together in pairs by the edges, with their backs turned to each other, for fear they should get spotted in printing or colouring.

The printing of French playing cards is usually from wooden blocks; they belong, indeed, to the cardmakers, but they are deposited in the government office, and the printing is performed there, on the government pot paper. The figured cards are always printed from two blocks; one containing two sets of the four kings and four queens, along with two knaves of clubs, and as many of spades. The second block prints ten knaves of hearts, and as many of diamonds. This arrangement arises from the circumstance that the figures on the first of these blocks are coloured with five colours, red, yellow, blue, gray, and black; while the figures of the second block have no black in them; and this difference would embarrass the colourer if it were not guarded against in this manner. Of course, they print five impressions of the king block to each single one of the red knave block; and this gives the court cards for ten packs. The plain cards have a block for each suit, each containing the cards for two packs.

The yellow colour used is made from Turkey berries, with about an eighth of alum. The red, of vermilion ground with gum water. The black is made of lamp black, mixed with glue, and left for five or six months before it is used, and frequently stirred. The blue of indigo mixed with size. The gray is merely a dilute blue.

The colours are applied by means of stencils, made of paper, painted on both sides with several coats of oil paints. The king block requires five stencils, that being the number of its colours; the red knave block four, for the same reason. The blocks for the plain cards, as each suit is printed separately, require of course but one stencil each.

The stencils for the figured cards are made by cutting out, with a sharp pointed knife, the space in which each separate colour is to be laid on; but those for the plain cards are cut out with a punch.

The stencil for any colour being placed on the sheet of cards so as to answer correctly to the print, a quantity of colour is taken up with a soft brush, and spread thin on a board; another brush, with short, close, and hard bristles, is first rubbed on the newly coloured board, and then on the stencil; the brush drives the colour through the holes cut in it, and this illumines the card. The stencil being taken off, the sheet of cards is placed in a pile on one side of the illuminer; and when a pile is thus illumined on one face with the colour then in use, it is illumined on the other face, so that the sheet of cards first coloured on one side, becomes the last that is coloured on the other. The other colours are then laid on with their respective stencils.

When the sheets of cards are illumined, or dressed, as it is termed they are separated, and each sheet is heated by itself on a square stove with a flat top; one sheet being placed on each side, and one on the top; they heat very quickly, and are turned, yet so that the back of the card may be heated the most.

As soon as the colours are perfectly dry, and the sheet of cards of a proper heat, they are soaped, which is performed with a rubber made of old hats sewed together. This rubber is about three inches thick and the same size as the sheet of cards; this rubber is passed over a cake of dry soap, and then over the warm sheet, first on the painted side, and then on the back.

After this the sheets of cards are polished, while hot, with a stone; the back is polished with more force, and with a more convex stone rubber than the painted side. The card sheets are then put again under the press for some time, to make them perfectly flat.

The sheets being now finished, there remains only the cutting of them into single cards. This is done on a flat strong plank, placed upright on its side, and having a raised border on the two ends. Parallel to one of these sides, at the exact distance of the length of a card, a knife edge is screwed down; and by means of a screw another knife edge is capable of being brought down in contact with it. At the other end of the table a similar knife edge is placed, parallel to the raised edge and at the exact distance of the breadth of a card.

The workman then taking a sheet of cards, with the illumined side uppermost, first cuts off the rough edge by causing the knife edge to follow the printed border; he then pushes the sheet home to the raised border, and repeats the cut; proceeding in this manner, the sheet is cut into four strips, each of which is then divided across into five equal parts, or single cards.

The cards thus cut are then sorted and examined; the specked cards separated to be sold by the pound, and the perfect cards made up into packs.

This mode of making and colouring common cards may be used for manufacturing cheap illumined cards, for certain branches of education.

Communications for the American Mechanics' Magazine,
Post paid, and addressed to
JAMES V. SEAMAN,
Broadway, New York, will receive due attention.

William Van Norden, Printer.

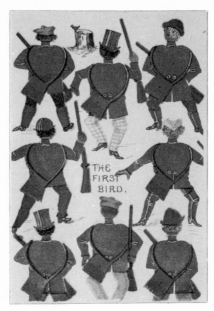

A KNAVE OF SPADES MADE IN AMERICA ABOUT 1800, AND THREE CARDS FROM A
TRANSFORMATION SERIES PUBLISHED BY TIFFANY IN 1879

THE CABALLERO OF ESPADAS, OR SWORDS, THE ACE OF COINS, THE TWO OF
BATONS, AND THE SOTA OF CUPS, FROM AN EDITION OF SPANISH PLAYING
CARDS MADE IN NEW YORK IN 1849 FOR MEXICAN CONSUMPTION

Thomas Crehore, of Dorchester, was a third card-maker. He was born in 1769, and made his playing cards in a factory behind his house in River Street. He was an important member of the community, one of the leaders in the controversy with Dr. Codman, and one of the founders of the

PLAYING CARDS MADE BY THOMAS CREHORE, CARD-MAKER OF DORCHESTER
MASSACHUSETTS, 1801–1846

third religious society in Dorchester. The genealogy mentions an item in his handwriting, which was in the possession of his granddaughter, Miss Edith Crehore, reading, 'Card factory built 1806, dry house built 1821, addition to printing room built 1826, factory burned, 1846.' He is, however, styled 'card-maker' in a deed of 1801, and the last item in an advertisement in the Boston directory of 1820 is, 'Crehore's Best and Common Playing Cards.' These were for sale by 'the administrators of the estate of Edward Cotton at 47 Marlboro street at the corner of Franklin street.'

Thomas Crehore is mentioned in a letter written by Cohen, a New York card-maker, concerning the practice, which he said was common among American card-makers of 1820–30, because of the preference for English goods, of marking the ace of spades 'London' or putting the name of an English maker upon it. The particular cards Cohen mentions are marked 'Reynolds & Sons,' and he says that they were probably made by Thomas Crehore.

HOME-MADE PLAYING CARDS FROM NANTUCKET, IN IMITATION OF MR. CREHORE'S PRODUCT

Another pack, marked 'Jones & Co. London,' are said to have been used by Dolly Madison in the White House. The cards are evidently of that time, but the ace of spades is utterly unlike the English duty ace then in use.

In no other part of the country in these early days was card-making a separate and distinct trade, and it was only in Massachusetts that the manufactories attained a very considerable size and importance.[1]

As in Philadelphia, the earliest cards that have survived are those that were used as invitations. Aside from the invitation cards, we have a series, on each one of which is written the directions for different figures of square dances, with most engaging names. There is the 'Military Assembly,' 'The Success of the Campaign,' 'Defeat of Burgoyne,' 'Lady Buckley's Whim,' and 'The Retreat of Clinton.'

The Marquis de Chastellux, describing an evening in Boston, says: 'For the first time since I have been in America, they made me play Whisk. The cards were English, that is to say much prettier and dearer than ours, and we marked our points with louis or Portugese pieces. As soon as the party was over the losses were not difficult to adjust because they were faithful to the rule established in society since the beginning of the troubles

[1] David H. Gilbert, born May 15, 1805, in Mansfield, Massachusetts, the son of David and Deborah Green Gilbert, worked for a while in the playing card manufactory of Isaac Crehore, the son of Thomas Crehore, in Dorchester. This was about 1840. At that time the paper stock used in making the cardboard was pasted by hand. The slow and expensive method engaged Mr. Gilbert's attention and led him to devise a method of pasting them in a machine which worked successfully. Later the machine was taken to England and patented there by Lawrence, Cohen & Co., of New York.

The mill in Dorchester burned in 1846, and Mr. Gilbert went to Philadelphia and set up another card manufactory there.

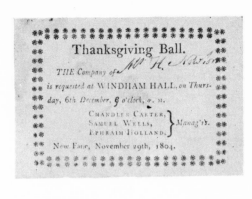

A NEW ENGLAND CARD OF INVITATION, 1804

A WRAPPER FOR PLAYING CARDS MANUFACTURED AT NANTES DURING THE AMERICAN
REVOLUTION

which did not permit playing for money so long as the war lasted. This law however was not scrupulously followed in the clubs nor when men played with each other. Bostonians like high play and perhaps it is fortunate that the war came at this time to moderate a passion whose consequences had begun to be dangerous.' Just before Lafayette left France for the first time, the cause of the struggling Colonies had so laid hold upon the popular imagination of French court circles (where all Americans were indiscriminately called Bostonians) as to displace whist by a new game called 'Boston.' In describing a rainy day at General Nelson's country house, he says: 'It is not useless to observe that on this occasion, when fifteen or twenty people, of whom all were strangers to the family and the land, found themselves assembled in the country and forced by bad weather to remain in the house, there was no question of playing cards. How many parties there have been among us of tric trac, of whisk, of lotto, as a necessary consequence of an abundance of rain!'

Cards for America were made at Nantes during the war years, and shipped to the struggling Colonies.

There is an 'Almanach des Jeux,' published in Paris in 1784, the title-page of which reads, 'augmentée des Jeux du Maryland & du Wisk Bostonien.' An 1802 edition of the rules for playing 'Boston,' published in London, says, 'The Game of Boston was first invented by the officers of the French Army in America, during the late war there and has been

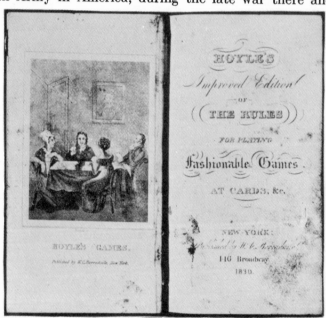

THE FRONTISPIECE AND TITLE-PAGE FROM AN EDITION OF
'HOYLE'S GAMES' PUBLISHED IN NEW YORK IN 1830

introduced into this country by the officers of the Russian ships of war which have lately visited Great Britain.'

A Beaufort edition of 'Hoyle's Games,' published in Philadelphia in 1796 by J. Rice, who also made playing cards, as we know from his advertisements, is said to be the earliest book on gaming published in America. Another edition of 'Hoyle's Games' was published in New York in 1830. There is also an edition of Horatio Smith's 'Festivals, Games and Amusements,' published in New York in 1833. It has an appendix concerning American festivals, games, and amusements, written by Samuel Woodworth, which is not included in the earlier London edition. This is an interesting little essay. In writing about New England he quotes an early Plymouth Colony law which read, 'No one shall keep Christmas, or any saint day, read common prayer, make mince pies, dance, play at cards, or play on any instrument of music, except the drum, trumpet and Jews'-harp.'

In the 'Acts and Laws of the Commonwealth of Massachusetts,' passed by the General Court, A.D. 1785, appears 'An act . . . for the encouragement of agriculture and manufactures and for promoting frugality and economy. That from and after the first day of August next, there shall be paid, in addition to the impost already laid, the following impost on the articles hereinafter enumerated, which shall be brought into this Commonwealth by land or water, viz., . . . for every pack of playing cards, two shillings.' This act is mentioned in the 'Professional and Industrial History of Suffolk County, Massachusetts,' with the observation that the articles named give 'a fair index to the manufactured products of Boston in 1785.' It would also seem to prove that cards were being made in sufficient quantity to supply the very large demand.

In the first report of the Secretary of the Treasury at Washington, in 1789, he mentions important wall-paper manufactories in Boston, New Jersey, and Philadelphia. In the report of 1810, Albert Gallatin says: 'The following branches are finely established, supplying in several instances, and in all a considerable part of the consumption of the United States: Iron and manufactures of iron, manufactures of cotton, wool, flax, hats, paper, printing types, printed books and playing cards. . . . The manufacture of paper hangings and playing cards is extensive.' He enlarges upon this statement with statistics compiled by Tench Coxe:

PLAYING CARDS

Value in dollars

Suffolk County, Massachusetts.	28,000
Norfolk County, Massachusetts.	82,500
Bergen County, New Jersey.	3,750 (3000 packs)
Philadelphia.	42,200 (4 manufactories)

In 1812, the statistics have changed somewhat, the table in the report for that year reading:

PLAYING CARDS
Value in dollars

Massachusetts............................	97,500
New Jersey...............................	3,750 (3000 packs)
Pennsylvania.............................	42,900

After the war there was a great scarcity of material for the paper mills. The following advertisement is repeated many times in the Boston newspapers:

'The Bell Cart will go through Boston before the end of next month to collect Rags for the Paper Mills at Milton when all people that will encourage the Paper Manufacturer may dispose of them.'

Advertisements of playing cards are found in the Boston papers of 1785 and grow more and more numerous with the passing of the years. A perusal of these papers also reveals the amusing fact that the largest and the most frequent advertisements of all are of the many lotteries that were flourishing in Massachusetts — the Harvard College lottery, the Biddeford lottery, the lottery of the Amoskeag Canal, are only a few. Tickets for these could be had at almost any of the shops advertising their wares, according to a familiar paragraph appended to nearly every one. The following is an example:

Playing Cards.

Superfine Columbians and common playing cards per groce, dozen or single pack. Sold by Thayer & Furber. No. 30 Union St.

Tickets and Parts in the Fourth class of the Amoskeag Canal Lottery which will positively commence drawing in three days, may be had as above when the prizes will be paid on demand.

Constant attendance until 8 o'clock in the evening.

('Columbian Centinel,' October 29, 1800.)

The American card-makers advertised their cards as 'Columbians' and 'Eagles' and stoutly invited comparison with the 'Moguls,' 'Merry Andrews,' and 'Harry the Eighths' of their English competitors. A typical advertisement reads:

Winter Evenings Amusement.

Prices of playing cards of a new and superior manufacture, just received for sale by W. Blagrove, No. 61 Cornhill.

	dls.	cts. doz.	cts. single pack.
Superfine Eagles............................	5		50
Eagle Harry VIII..........................	3	50	37½
Merry Andrew.............................	2	50	25
Common Merry Andrew.....................	2	25	25

Purchasers of cards are requested to make a trial of the above, particularly the Eagles and if they are found inferior to any cards now in use, they will be received again and the money returned.

W. B. has also received a fresh supply of Lorillards's Maccoboy Snuff.

('Columbian Centinel,' January 31, 1810.)

Without doubt, sometimes the number of stars on the ace of spades represents the number of states in the union at the time, and may therefore be indicative of the date. But this is not always true. Cohen who made his first cards in 1832 invariably uses the thirteen stars. While Samuel Hart makes use of an ace bearing fifteen at a time when the union numbered twice as many states.

We have two packs of Crehore cards, one with his name and one without, both of which have sixteen stars above the eagle, while the identical eagle on the ace of the New York Card Manufactory's ace, is surmounted by seventeen stars.

In the Boston papers of 1800, Ebenezer Clough advertises his 'paper staining factory.' At the top is a small engraving showing his workroom, surmounted by a spread eagle with a ribbon in its beak like those on the aces of spades of the early American cards. Upon the death of Washington, Clough made a wall-paper in memory of the great President, and on this the same eagle and the symbols familiar on the early aces of spades also appear. Samuel Hill, who advertises in the 'Columbian Centinel' of 1789 as an 'engraver, seal cutter, and copper plate printer,' designed the heading for Mr. Clough's advertisement and may have been responsible for the wall-paper design. One wonders if he also did any of the designs for the card-makers, or if any of them can be attributed to Paul Revere, who did many eagles for both the Provincial money and that of the Continental Congress, and put this same American eagle, with the thirteen stars, on his business card.

The following advertisements of playing cards are to be found in the 'Columbian Centinel':

Playing Cards.
By the gross, dozen or single pack, may be had at No. 50, Cornhill.

(October 1, 1791.)

Winter Evenings' Amusements.
Henry VIII Playing Cards by the groce or dozen to be sold at 64 Long Wharf. Upon reasonable terms for cash or short credit.

(November 29, 1794.)

Playing Cards. Henry VIII and Highlander.
W. P. Blake. Boston Book store. 59 Cornhill.

(December 6, 1794.)

Playing Cards. Best Columbian, Harry the eighth and Merry Andrew playing cards.
W. P. & L. Blake. No. 1 Cornhill.

(November 11, 1797.)

Harry VIIIth & Merry Andrew playing cards for sale.
Thomas Chase. Court street.

(March 1, 1797.)

Playing cards. Harry the eighth & Merry Andrew Playing Cards are kept constantly for sale wholesale and Retail by Thomas Chase. No. 6 Cornhill.

(November 15, 1797.)

Playing Cards.
Columbian, Harry 8th & Merry Andrew Playing Cards of a superior quality may be had at the book store of John West No. 75 Cornhill by the groce, dozen or single pack as cheap as at the manufactory.

(December 2, 1797.)

Writing paper for sale.
By W. P. & L. Blake.
At the Boston Book Store No. 1 Cornhill. An Assortment of the best English letter paper * * * * * * * playing cards, backgammon boards, etc.

(January 30, 1799.)

Playing Cards and Backgammon Boards. Superfine Columbian and Common Playing Cards, best English Henry VIII and Highlanders. do per groce, dozen or single pack. Also Backgammon Boards, various sizes for sale, by Thos. Furber, No. 30 Union Street.

(November 20, 1799.)

No. 5 School street — Playing cards per groce, dozen or single pack from the various manufactories in this state, some of which are of a very superior quality — prices from 2 to 4 dollars per dozen and 25 to 38 cents per pack.

(December 21, 1805.)

Superfine Playing Cards.
Just from the manufactory — and for sale by A. J. Allen No. 66 State Street a quantity of Superfine Eagle Playing Cards; Harry the Eight do do; Merry Andrew do do; Highlanders do do; large and small blanks do; Embossed visiting cards of the first quality; also a good assortment of stationery, charts and Custom House Blanks. Personal attendance from eight in the morning until ten o'clock in the evening. The smallest favors thankfully received.

(December 2, 1805.)

French Cards.

W. Blagrove; has just received & has for sale, a quantity of French Playing Cards of the first quality — wholesale and retail.

(January 3, 1810.)

Variety Book Store. J. W. Burditt & Co.
Books, Stationery, etc.

For sale by James W. Burditt & Co. at the sign of Franklin's Head, Court street, a large collection of books upon various subjects, too many to enumerate in an advertisement — among which are the following — Divinity * * * * * * * Miscellanies, * * * * * * * Law, * * * * * *. Likewise Playing Cards, Backgammon Boards, Battledores and Shuttlecocks.

(February 7, 1810.)

At Whitwell & Bond's Office, Kelly Street. On Friday next, at ten o'Clock. Sale at Auction.

A variety of Piece Goods * * * * * * 20 groce Playing Cards of a good quality.

(February 7, 1810.)

Loo Counters, Playing Cards, etc.

For sale at No. 3 School Street, 50 sets Loo Counters, Playing Cards of the first quality by the groce, dozen or single pack, Chess Men of ivory, etc.

N.B. Every article above enumerated will be sold lower than the going prices to make it worth while for purchasers to step a little out of their way into School street to get furnished. Playing cards and Chess men will come particularly under this arrangement.

(February 7, 1810.)

American Playing Cards.

Just received from the Manufactory, a fresh supply of Playing CARDS which will be sold by the groce, dozen or single pack at A. J. Allen's Stationery Store, No. 66 State street, where dealers in cards and public houses will be supplied through the season on low terms.

(September 28, 1811.)

Playing Cards, &c.

For sale by the Subscribers at their store No. 37 India street, a variety of CARDS, consisting of Moguls, Columbians, Henry Eights, Merry Andrews, Highlanders and Spanish, ALSO A quantity of Message Cards of different sizes — and a few dozen of geographical cards; the whole of which being a consignment — and in order to close a concern will be disposed of for Cash or at a Credit at a discount from the usual prices.

Thomas and Edward Motley.

(December 11, 1811.)

Sale at Auction.

On Saturday next at —— o'clock.

At 71 State street — on a liberal credit.

A number of cases of Playing, Message and Geometrical Cards worthy the attention of dealers in the article.

C. Hayward, Auct. (December 21, 1811.)

Books and Stationery.

For sale at Thomas Wells' book store No. 3 Hanover street, a good assortment of Family and School Bibles * * * * * * * * * * America and British Ink Powder, Playing Cards, etc. Wanted as above, an active LAD as an apprentice where the Book binding business is likewise carried on.

(December 21, 1811.)

Jane Salter.

No. 14 Hanover street. Has for sale

A few Dutch pocket looking glasses * * * * * * * Bowles' Geographical Game of Europe, with Totum and counters, several amusing games; do, Dissected Maps and Pictures, Libraries, Alphabetical, Geographical and Grammar Cards * * * * * * * with a handsome variety of toys.

(December 25, 1811.)

Ann Allen

Has for sale at her variety shop, No. 82 Court Street * * * * * * * Playing and Conversation Cards.

(December 28, 1811.)

The geographical cards of these Boston advertisements may be the ones described by Mrs. Van Rensselaer in her history of playing cards. She says in part: 'This pack is now owned by Dr. Richard Derby, a descendant of the Lloyd who was granted the manor of Lloyd's Neck, one of the original grants held under the English in the Colony of New York. On the back of the knave of diamonds is written in faded ink this inscription,

'To Angelina Lloyd, from her affectionate uncle,
Henry Lloyd.'
February 13th, 1795.

They are evidently similar to the English cards of a century before, but, instead of being disparaging in their descriptions of America and its inhabitants, as the English ones almost invariably were, these bear enthusiastic accounts of localities the author undoubtedly knew well. On the jack of diamonds he states that 'Long Island is 140 miles by ten. The middle is sandy. The place called Lloyd's Neck, from its position and fertility is, or might be made a paradise.' The chief towns of America and their populations are given as follows: Mexico, 150,000; Lima, 60,000; Cuzco, 42,000; Panama and Philadelphia, 42,000; New York, 23,000; Boston, 19,000, and Newport 6000.

You can't help wondering if Thomas Fleet, at his printing house in Pudding Lane in 1719, did not have some little American card games — Æsop's Fables, geography, and alphabet games as well as Mother Goose, for the little children of Boston.

The seafaring days of New England are recalled by the lacquer boxes containing trays and counters for playing 'Pope Joan,' which are occa-

sionally to be found, together with the old willow-ware and sandalwood and ivories that made the long journey around the Horn. Pope Joan was a popular card game in the eighteenth and early nineteenth centuries. According to the rules set forth in Hoyle, you paid one counter to the knave, two to the queen, three to the king, four to the ace, and five to Pope Joan, which was the nine of diamonds. Hence the necessity for the little trays. The counters, which were of mother of pearl or of ivory, were sometimes round, sometimes oval, and sometimes long and narrow so that they looked almost like little fish, and it was by the name of fish that they were called by the players.

This was undoubtedly a corruption of the French word for counter, 'fiche';

THE TOP AND BOTTOM OF A PAINTED IVORY BOX FOR HOLDING THE 'FICHES,' OR COUNTERS, AT QUADRILLE

The inside cover of this delicate and lovely little box is signed 'Mariqual le Jeune à Paris.'

however, from the idea of fish, the English called the little dish in which they put their counters at Quadrille, the pool. The French never made their counters in the form of fish, as the English did. Theirs were round or oval and were kept in delicate and lovely little painted ivory boxes.

In 1796, according to the government records the import duty on playing cards was twenty-five cents a pack, and the excess of the imports over the exports (for the thirteen States) was 1552 packs. Massachusetts was, however, doing more than its share in producing cards, for in the year 1792 Tench Coxe says that one thousand packs were exported from there.[1]

In the records of 1804, we find that John Dorr, merchant of Boston, paid an import duty of $936 on Dutch playing cards brought on the ship Jenny from Antwerp.

In connection with cards from foreign countries, by far the most interesting story comes from Canada. It is recounted in detail in the Canadian Archives, 'Documents Relatifs à la Monnaie, au Change et aux Finances du Canada sous le Régime Français, choisis et édités avec Commentaires et Introduction par Adam Shortt.'

In 1685, Jacques de Meulles, Seigneur of La Source, Knight, Councillor of the King in his Councils, Grand Bailiff of Orléans, Intendant of Justice, Police, and Finance in Canada and the Northern Territories of France, found himself in great straits to provide for the sustenance of the troops. A forced issue of paper currency seemed to afford the most effective remedy. The lack of suitable paper and printing materials led him to resort to the only available substitutes, the packs of playing cards, obviously imported by the merchants to meet a popular demand. He explains his action in the following letter:

QUEBEC, *September 24, 1685*

MY LORD —

    .   .   .   .

I have found myself this year in great straits with regard to the subsistence of the soldiers. You did not provide for funds, My Lord, until January last. I have, notwithstanding, kept them in provisions until September, which makes eight full months. I have drawn from my own funds and from those of my friends, all I have been able to get, but at last finding them without means to render me further assistance, and not knowing to what saint to pay my vows, money being extremely scarce, having distributed considerable sums on every side for the pay of the soldiers, it occurred to me to issue, instead of money, notes on cards, which I have had cut in quarters. I send you My Lord, the three kinds, one is for four francs, another for forty sols, and the third for fifteen sols, because with these

---

[1] *View of the Commerce of the United States*, p. 61, by Timothy Pitkin, a statistician. Statistics showing the number of packs of playing cards exported from the United States:

Year	Number	Year	Number	Year	Number	Year	Number
1792	1000	1801	3828	1805	480	1809	728
1796	200	1802	3410	1806	13501	1810	9036
1798	3230	1803	8994	1807	4889	1811	4256
1799	377	1804	4032	1808	1728	1813	1728

three kinds, I was able to make their exact pay for one month. I have issued an ordinance by which I have obliged all the inhabitants to receive this money in payments, and to give it circulation, at the same time pledging myself, in my own name, to redeem the said notes. No person has refused them, and so good has been the effect that by this means the troops have lived as usual. There were some merchants who, privately, had offered me money at the local rate on condition that I would repay them in money at the rate in France, to which I would not consent as the King would have lost a third; that is, for ten thousand écus he would have paid forty thousand livres; thus personally, by my credit and by my management, I have saved His Majesty thirteen thousand livres.

. . . .

(Signed)   DE MEULLE

QUEBEC, 24th September, 1685

CARD MONEY USED IN THE CANADIAN PROVINCES DURING THE FRENCH RÉGIME

This card money was issued again in 1686, in 1690, and in 1691, under Bochart-Champigny, who succeeded de Meulle, and by 1708 an issue of small cards replaced even copper coins. It was 1719 before the card money was withdrawn and the coinage of France was once more in circulation in the French provinces after an interval of more than thirty years.

On March 2, 1729, because of the dearth of actual money, resort was once more had to card money, this time an issue of 400,000 livres authorized by the French Government. From the following letter it is evident that the cards to be used for this money were purchased from playing card-makers in France, but that because of an accident to these specially ordered cards, which were to be 'blank on both sides,' regular playing cards were again used for most of the issue:

MESSRS DE BEAUHARNOIS AND HOCQUART
CANADA, *October* 25, 1729

MY LORD,

M. Hocquart had the honour to inform you in Paris that he had made a purchase of about 2000 sets of cards, blank on both sides, to provide for the making of the card money ordered by His Majesty. Two thirds of them have been soaked in water and entirely ruined in the wreck of the King's ship. We shall be obliged to use ordinary cards for the making of a part of this money.

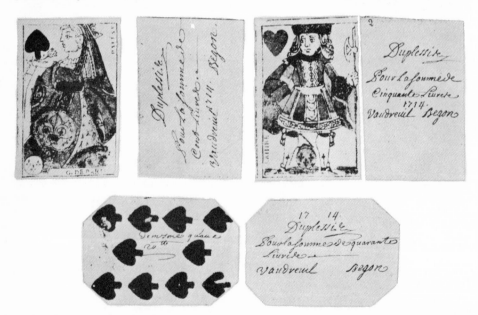

CARD MONEY OF THE HIGHER DENOMINATIONS USED IN THE CANADIAN PROVINCES
DURING THE FRENCH RÉGIME

We beg you, My Lord, to have sent by next year's ship 2,000 sets of 52 cards each, in order that we may be in a position to make new money in case the first be counterfeited, unless you would prefer, My Lord, to give orders in Paris to have the money prepared, observing the precautions set forth in the memorandum herewith: by this means a considerable labour will be avoided by the Controller of the Marine, who would be more usefully employed in working at financial matters, or in relieving M. Hocquart in this part of his service, for which he is so eminently suited.

(Signed)   BEAUHARNOIS.   HOCQUART

QUEBEC, *October* 29, 1729

Herewith attached are seven specimens of the different denominations, from 24 livres to 7*s*. 6*d*., as they have been issued in Canada in 1729.

·   ·   ·   ·   ·   ·   ·   ·   ·   ·   ·   ·   ·   ·

Let there be made the number of 174,334 cards similar to the specimens herewith, on which engrave the name of the Controller, the year, the denominations, and the names of Messrs. Beauharnois and Hocquart also, just as the whole is written in the specimens.

Send three new dies, one with the arms of His Majesty which will be placed at the head, and two others, the first with the arms of M. de Beauharnois and the second with those of Sr. Hocquart, to employ in stamping the said money at Quebec.

These dies must be difficult to counterfeit and well cut.

One might add a vignette on the back of each of said cards.

[Not signed.]

QUEBEC, *October* 25, 1729

The card money circulated at first in the neighborhood of Quebec, but soon afterward extended to Montreal and Three Rivers, later to the growing towns and villages, and finally to the settlements of the *habitants*, and was used until the cession of the provinces to the British.

In New York at the end of the eighteenth century, Dr. Alexander Anderson 'did on wood, designs of all sorts, from sheet ballads, primers, business cards, tobacconists' devices, wrappers of playing cards, diplomas and newspaper cuts of every sort, to magazines, stately scientific treatises and large Bibles.'

Of these card wrappers, one made for John Casenave, a New York cardmaker, bears a brawny Indian smoking a pipe of peace. A second one bears the New Jersey coat of arms, and the name of D. C. Baldwin, who made cards in Bergen County, across the river.

There is also a Henry VIII wrapper bearing the name of Henry Hart, London, and marked, 'For Exportation.' Henry Hart was a well-known

A PLAYING-CARD WRAPPER PRINTED FROM A WOOD BLOCK OF ALEXANDER ANDERSON FOR JOHN CASENAVE, CARD-MAKER IN NEW YORK, 1801–1807

A PLAYING-CARD WRAPPER FROM AN ALEXANDER ANDERSON WOOD BLOCK, FOR D. C. BALDWIN, BERGEN COUNTY, NEW JERSEY

London maker. Thirty years after this time, members of his family were the most important card-makers in America, but there is no record of their making cards before 1832. The conclusion is, therefore, that this wrapper is another instance of an American maker presenting his product as something made in England.

The Bergen County card-maker, D. C. Baldwin, was also a maker of wall-paper. In the first report of the Secretary of the Treasury in 1789, the wall-paper manufactory is mentioned, and it is probable that the playing cards were also being made then.

John Casenave's name appears in the New York City Directory from 1801 to 1807, at 64 Broad Street and 28 Whitehall, with a store at 23 Pearl Street and 65 James Street. In 1809 and 1810 he is described as a 'wine merchant' at 12 and 10 Pearl Street. And from 1811 to 1816 as a 'merchant' at 10 Pearl Street, 34 South Street, 29 Pearl Street, and 38 South Street.

A later wrapper is for 'Decatur Cards' and pictures the famous sea fight. This wrapper also bears the name of David Felt and Company of New York, as makers and distributors. David Felt was a New York stationer, whose name appears in the city directory in 1826, and during the following years. By 1845, he had made a fortune, and he purchased a large tract of land in Union County, New Jersey, and established the model village of Feltville.

In 1815, the New York Card Manufacturing Company was making playing cards at 133 Pearl Street. In 1814, the name is the New York Manufacturing Company at the same address, and in 1813, the New York Manufacturing Company is located at 98 Water Street, according to the city directory. The ace of spades bearing the name, 'New York Card Manufactory,' bears the address 102 John Street, however, though the cards are evidently of about this time.

Another pack of these cards has the same ace of spades, which bears only the name 'Charles Bartlet.' And a third pack, with the identical ace, has upon it only the name 'Boston Card Factory.'

About 1840, there was also a card manufactory at Marblehead, belonging to Samuel Avery.

In the New York City Directory of 1830, Robert Sauzade is listed as a playing card-maker, with a manufactory at 114 Leonard Street, and his name is also in the business directory for 1837.

A PLAYING-CARD WRAPPER, PROBABLY FIRST MADE BY ALEXANDER ANDERSON FOR THE DECATUR CARDS ISSUED IN 1815 BY JAZANIAH FORD OF MILTON

It was later used by David Felt, a card-maker in New York, in 1826

At the Essex Institute in Salem is quite an extraordinary collection of American card games. Many of them were made in Salem by W. &. S. B. Ives, who in 1843 published the famous 'Dr. Busby.' Soon after, their first game of 'Authors' appeared, and was followed by many similar pictorial games, Scripture History, The Game of Beasts, The Game of the States, and Mahomet and Saladin, or The Battle for Palestine. Their first board game, The Mansion of Happiness was the first game of its kind to be published in America, and this was also first brought out in 1843. The Parker Brothers, who shortly succeeded the Iveses, and who, after nearly a century are still making games in Salem, have recently reprinted The Mansion of Happiness from the original blocks, in its original form. The board folds in two neatly, and beneath the flap which fastens it is a convenient pocket holding a spinning indicator and four different colored playing pieces or men, like those of Parchesi, and also the instructions for playing this 'Instructive Moral and Entertaining Amusement.' The board not only

A TYPICAL ENGLISH PLAYING-CARD WRAPPER
FOR VALIANT HIGHLANDER CARDS
Printed from a wood block of Alexander Anderson

A TYPICAL ENGLISH PLAYING-CARD WRAP-
PER FOR HARRY THE EIGHTH CARDS
Printed from a wood block of Alexander
Anderson

THE ACE OF SPADES USED BY DAVID FELT,
CARD-MAKER IN NEW YORK, 1826

AN EARLY AMERICAN ACE OF SPADES
SHOWING THE THIRTEEN STARS

ACE OF SPADES USED BY THE BOSTON CARD FACTORY AND THE NEW YORK CARD MANUFACTORY

The Boston ace has sixteen stars, and the New York one, seventeen. If these stand for the number of States in the Union, as is sometimes true, the Boston card is the earlier

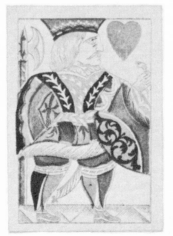

THE SAME ACE OF SPADES, USED BY CHARLES BARTLET

There are only fifteen stars on this ace, so perhaps he was the first card-maker to use it. Two of his court cards are also shown

(319)

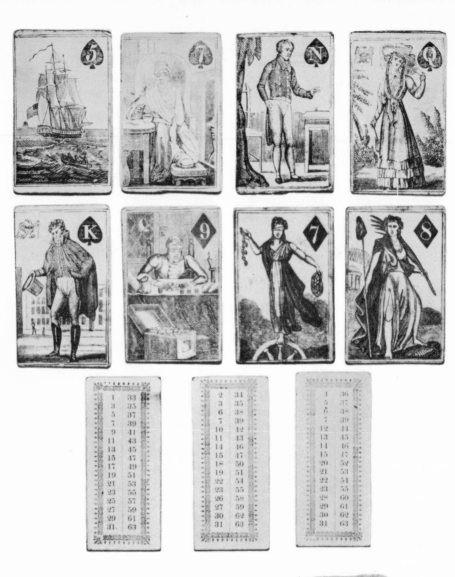

FORTUNE-TELLING CARDS MADE BY TURNER AND FISHER, NEW YORK, *c.* 1822
The court cards are lettered N, Q, and K for Knave, Queen, and King

(320)

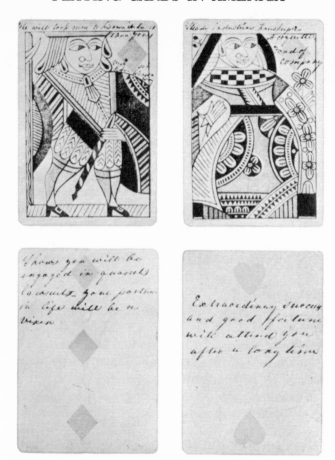

FORTUNE-TELLING CARDS FROM NEW ENGLAND

pictures virtues to be attained, but also vices to be shunned, most luridly portrayed, and the New England punishments for these, the stock, the pillory, the ducking stool and the whipping post. When all of these vicissitudes have been safely passed, the successful player arrives at the Mansion of Happiness in the center, where lovely maidens with rose garlands dance chastely to the music of harp and timbrel. It is all typically New England, and the 'Summit of Dissipation' shows a wildly dancing gentleman, his blue coat tails flying, beside him a decanter of red, red wine and strewn on the floor before him, dice and playing cards.

Yet the eagle of the early American playing card-makers carries the name of the game on a ribbon in his beak. The Mansion of Happiness was invented by Miss Abbott, the daughter of a Beverly, Massachusetts, clergyman. One wonders if she was also responsible for The Magic Ring which is similar in form, but much more sentimental in character, having to do with the adventures of a knight and lady, with adventures in the form of battles and dungeons and mermaids. 'Characteristics, an Original Game by a Lady,' may also have been hers. This is a card game. A sample card reads:

Switzerland   Died 1638

Was distinguished for

Patriotism   Enthusiasm
Bravery   Modesty
Good sense   Paternal affection

It is not hard to guess the name of the hero which is on the card matching this. 'The Strife of Genius, By a Lady' may also have been Miss Abbott's. It was published by William Crosby in Boston. A perfectly delightful card game 'Robinson Crusoe and His Man Friday' was published a little later by Crosby and Nichols in Boston, Santon and Miles in New York, and Samuel Hart in Philadelphia. The pictures on these cards are so precisely a child's idea of this favorite adventure tale, that you wonder why the game isn't being printed to-day.

'Shakespeare, a card Game' was published by C. S. Francis in New York in 1845. 'The Game of Kings' is another published in New York in the same year by Josiah Adams. In 1861 we find the Excelsior Games being published in Boston, and in 1865 there are 'Magic Cards' which are puzzle pictures, published by L. Prang and Company.

A very much earlier Geographical Game, gives interesting statistics concerning the world at large and America in 1810, while an alphabet game on very heavy cardboard has a distinct New England flavor, and was doubtless made for very small Bostonians at about this same time.

There are many advertisements in the Philadelphia newspapers, both of imported cards and those made in America.

In the 'Royal Pennsylvania Gazette' of March 10, 1778, is the following:

John Johnston and Co.

At their store, the corner of Market and Water streets, formerly occupied by John Campbell sells wholesale and Retail, on the most Reasonable terms, The following Goods, . . . Merry Andrews and Harry the Eighth's Playing Cards.

A month later, under the date of April 24, 1778, in the same paper another advertisement is to be found, 'The Kings Patent or Falstaffs Playing cards, so much esteemed and universally used in Polite Companies, may be had of the Printer — also Henry the Eighth and Merry Andrew's.'

This is another instance of the printer of a paper making playing cards. He was James Robertson, a Tory, who had his shop on Front Street, between Chestnut and Walnut, and it is cards with the conventional English names that he advertises. In his paper of May 22, 1778, is the advertisement, 'At Hugh Warden's store corner of Walnut and Front streets, a variety of British and India Goods, . . . Harry and Andrew's playing cards.'

In the 'Pennsylvania Journal' of September 8, 1779, whose printer was a good American, is the advertisement of 'Lester & Poyntell. Playing Cards of the best quality are sold wholesale at Lester and Poyntell's Book and Stationery store in Second street near Market, opposite the Friends' Meeting House.'

Also in the 'Pennsylvania Journal' of March 1, 1783, is the advertisement,

E. Ryves.

CARDS. The subscribers beg leave to offer to the public, a new invented game at cards, called Ortho, designed not only for amusement but instruction in the orthography of the English language. Instead of the four suits of pips in common use, these cards are furnished with four sets of the English alphabet, having such certain powers assigned to the respective letters as to admit of variety, ingenuity, and entertainment in the play, with an additional and important advantage of insinuating a correctness in spelling, and a knowledge in the operation of letters in the formation of words. These cards, neatly ornamented and made up in packs of 104 cards each, with full directions how they are to be played, printed on the wrapping paper, are made and sold by the subscribers, at their paper hanging and card factory, in Walnut street, above the New Gaol, Philadelphia, and may be had at most of the shops.

Price 7s. 6d. by the single pack, with a large allowance to purchasers by the dozen.

E. Ryves, and Co.

The above may be had at T. Bradford's book store.

Very much earlier than these, and probably the very first of this sort of card game in America, were the religious playing cards printed by Christopher Sower on his press in Germantown, in 1744, the year after he printed his American Bible. There are three hundred and eighty-one cards with Scriptural and poetical verses on each. The text is all in German and the title is 'The Lottery of the Pious, or the Spiritual Treasure Casket, whereby one never loses.' The cards are numbered like lottery tickets, and the poetry is all from the works of Gerhard Tersteegen. Sometimes they were in leather cases, and sometimes in little boxes of fancy wood, nicely dovetailed. The good people usually used them on Sunday afternoons. They would draw a card from this little treasury of good and beautiful thoughts and contemplate its meaning. Sometimes, when they felt gloomy or despondent, they would resort to it, feeling confident of drawing a promise of consolation and help.

Almost the same idea was used later in the Scriptural cards attributed to Charles Wesley. Some editions of these have verses of his hymns, many of them long forgotten, on each card, and other editions have Bible verses as well. Some of the cards are in Charles Wesley's writing. The rhymes, rhythms, and metaphors are most unusual. It is doubtful if he had thought of them at the time of his sojourn in America with General Oglethorpe, for the advertisement of them in John Wesley's paper appears in 1786. It reads: 'May be had of Mr. Wesley's booksellers in town or country, Scriptural playing cards which appeared a few years since. Many persons were pleased with them and now wish me to re-print them.'

There are 56 cards in Mr. Wesley's game, and the first and last bear the printer's name, 'James Todd, Bedale.'

'These people called Methodists' after 'a dish of tea' would shuffle these cards and the one drawn would furnish a conversational text. It is amusing to find that they quickly took on the old-time significance of cards as a means of divination. Good men and women believed that Providence spoke through them, and many decisions were made according to the guidance of these little scraps of paper.

Another series of little prints, which may have been part of an educational game in Philadelphia, are 'Various Employments.' They are very similar to the many English pictorial series, and show a merchant, a shipwright, straw hat-makers, basket-makers, a rope-maker, a brazier, a spinner, and a hair-dresser, all of the late eighteenth century.

Other advertisements of cards are, in the 'Pennsylvania Journal,' January 18, 1783;

CARDS.

Playing Cards, of the best Quality, to be sold at the Paper Hanging and Card Manufactory, in Chestnut street, above the new Gaol.

In the 'Pennsylvania Packet,' February 19, 1784: 'Caleb Buglass, near the city Vendue Store, Front street — sells Bibles and Testaments * * * * * * * * * * inkstands, and playing cards.'
In the 'Pennsylvania Evening Herald,' December 17, 1785:

J. RICE

Amusement and Instruction. This day is published by J. Rice, North side of Market street between Second and Third Streets.

The new Impenetrable Secret, or young lady's and gentleman's Polite Puzzle, being an entirely new set of entertaining Cards, neatly printed, consisting of moral and diverting histories of Pamela, Clarissa and Sir

EDUCATIONAL CARDS OF THE LATE EIGHTEENTH CENTURY IN PHILADELPHIA

(325)

Charles Grandison. The whole designed, while they amuse and entertain, to establish principles of virtue and morality in the minds of both sexes * * * * * also bloks, medicines, songs, and musical instrument strings.

On September 8, 1786, is the advertisement: 'Benjamin January takes this method to inform his friends and the public in general that he carries on the bookbinding business in all its branches at his shop in Front street at the sign of the Bible and Dove where merchants, shopkeepers and others may be supplied with all kinds of account books and the following articles of stationery, post paper, fool's cap, wrapping paper, sealing wax wafers, quills, ink powder, playing cards, etc.'

In the 'Federal Gazette' of January 27, 1790 is the notice:

CARD MAKING

Wanted immediately, a Person who is thoroughly acquainted with the principal branches of making Playing Cards, in the true European manner; such a one will meet with very good encouragement. Enquire of the printer. [The printer in this instance was Andrew Brown, an American patriot.]

During the next year, 1791, there are many advertisements of Lester and Poyntell's paper-hanging manufactory, while their previous advertisement in 1779 mentioned only playing cards.

In the 'Federal Gazette' of February 19, 1790, is the advertisement, 'Ryves and Ashmead's Superfine American Manufactured Playing Cards. Sold Wholesale and Retail At Thomas Seddon's Bookstore in Market street.'

Tench Coxe, of Philadelphia, in a 'View of the United States of America,' written at various times between the years 1787 and 1794, says:

'The products, manufactures and exports of Pennsylvania are very many and various . . . [he lists two pages of these, and among them mentions playing cards]. Papers of all kinds form a very beneficial branch, of considerable and increasing extent. The Species made are paper hangings, playing cards, pasteboards, etc. . . .

'A single state, Pennsylvania has upwards of fifty paper mills which work up materials of no value. The manufactures from those mills are computed at $250,000, the persons employed in them do not exceed 150 or 200. The state contains about one ninth of the people of the United States, and their contributions to the expense of the government and the interest on the public debt, are consequently about 400,000 dollars. Their paper mills therefore stand them for five eighths of their quota. It appears to be the duty of the government to encourage the people in all the states to do the same, especially as it can be done by water means and not by men diverted from their farms. * * * * * * * We have exceedingly diminished our imports of coarse linen and woolen goods, cordage, * * * * * * playing cards, etc. 1000 packs of playing cards were exported from Massachusetts in the year from October 1, 1791 to September 30, 1792. * * * * * * * There were imported into the United States, for one year, ending the thirtieth day of September, 1790, 19,066 packs of playing cards. * * * * * * * * * * * The tariff on playing cards of twenty five cents per pack is a great encouragement to local manufacturers. June 30, 1794.'

From the United States Treasury reports we find that in 1814, 400,000 packs of playing cards were manufactured in the United States, and the duty of twenty-five cents a pack was increased to thirty cents by the Tariff Act of April 27, 1816. While in the report of the first session of the eighteenth Congress, 1823–24, the following playing card statistics are given:

PLAYING CARDS

	Packs	Value in dollars
From French European ports on the Atlantic	420 (in foreign vessels)	33
From French European ports on the Mediterranean	12 (in American vessels)	4
56 shipments of imports	156 shipments of exports	

Again, in his 'Brief Examination of Lord Sheffield's Observations on the Commerce of the United States,' which he wrote in 1791, Tench Coxe says: 'From a return made to the Manufacturing Society of Philadelphia, it appears there are forty eight paper mills in Pennsylvania alone and five others are building in one county in that state. * * * * * * * The Treasury of the United States and several banks have paper of the most perfect kind specially made for them; the printing of books has increased to a most astonishing degree and the factories of paper hangings are carried on with great spirit in Boston, New Jersey and Philadelphia. * * * * * * After a very careful estimate of a number of the principal branches of American manufactures the writer of this paper does not hesitate to affirm that the shoes and boots, sadlery and other articles of leather, gunpowder, snuff, paper and paper hangings, playing cards, pasteboard, books, * * * * made in the year past, exceed in value the manufactured goods which Great Britain shipped in the same term to all foreign nations but the United States.'

To continue with the advertisements of playing cards in the Philadelphia papers on March 5, 1795, in the 'Federal Gazette,' is the following: 'Innocent Amusement; or, Polite Conversation Cards, For the Entertainment of Young Ladies and Gentlemen; Just published at No. 41 Chestnut street. Price 50 cents.'

In the 'Federal Gazette' of December 15, 1800, is the advertisement of 'James Humphreys. No. 106 South Side Market Street. In addition to his assortment of the very best English Playing Cards (Received from London) Has just received from Boston an assortment of American playing cards which he will sell wholesale or retail on most reasonable terms.'

PLAYING CARDS SOLD IN PHILADELPHIA ABOUT 1800, BY J. Y. HUMPHREYS
The ace and jack of spades and the court cards of the heart suit are shown

There is a pack of cards bearing the name of J. Y. Humphreys which has survived to the present day. They are nicely engraved and hand-colored. In the heart suit, which is red, the king is George Washington, taken from Gilbert Stuart's Lansdowne portrait; the queen, Venus; and the knave, Red Jacket the Indian.

The diamonds are painted yellow and have John Quincy Adams for the king, Justice for the queen, and for the knave the Indian Gy-ant-wachia; the clubs, which are blue, show Thomas Jefferson as the king, Ceres for the queen, and Joseph Brant for the knave; the spades are also blue, and the king is Andrew Jackson; the queen, Athena; and the knave, a fourth Indian, hard to identify.

These cards are very similar to later special packs made by Jazaniah Ford, of Milton, and perhaps they are the 'American playing cards from Boston' of the advertisement.

Another use of playing cards at this time in Philadelphia was to use their plain backs for mounting silhouettes. A silhouette of Joseph Hopkinson, who wrote 'Hail, Columbia' at the end of the century, is thought to be Peale's work, and is on the back of a playing card.

A SILHOUETTE OF JOSEPH HOPKINSON, ON THE BACK OF A PLAYING CARD
It is supposed to be the work of Charles Wilson Peale.

Charles Fraser, the young Carolinian, in 1798, on the back of a ten of diamonds did a pen-and-ink sketch of George Washington. There is also an invitation, written on the back of a playing card, to a party in honor of the great President's birthday, in 1792.

In Watson's 'Annals of Philadelphia,' he says that there were three playing card manufactories in the city at the end of the eighteenth century.

Yet in the directory of 1806, arranged according to trades and professions, 'in which is comprised the name and abode of all professions and occupations by which the stranger may find the residence of any gentleman with whom he has concerns,' card-makers are not listed, and the names of the men who have advertised cards in the newspapers appear in the lists of stationers, bookbinders, and wall-paper stainers. There seems to be a curious reluctance to name in cold type the lucrative pursuit of card-making.

In the Philadelphia Directory for 1811, the names of Thomas de Silver, bookbinder and playing card-manufacturer, 152 South Sixth Street, and

Joseph Phillips, card-manufacturer, 419 North Fourth Street, are to be found.

In 1816 there are the additional names of C. Buffard, playing card-manufacturer; Eli Fizel, playing card-maker, 93 Sassafras Street; and James Y. Humphreys, card-manufacturer, 95 South Front Street. Also there are listed in the same year, George Crager, card-maker, 137 Cherry Street; Andrew Adams, card-manufacturer, 2 South Third Street; David Wenthing, card-maker, 5 Plum Street; but, because no further records are to be found of their activities, it is impossible to tell whether they made playing cards or the wire cards for carding wool and cotton.

It was in 1832 that Lewis I. Cohen, a young stationer in New York, made his first pack of cards, and founded the business of L. I. Cohen, 71 William Street, New York City. He had already made a name for himself as the first maker of American lead pencils, and his interesting and

THE ACE OF SPADES AND THE COURT CARDS OF THE SUIT OF CLUBS OF AN EDITION OF
PLAYING CARDS PRINTED BY L. I. COHEN IN NEW YORK IN 1838
The court cards are interesting to compare with those made twenty years earlier by Ford and Crehore

genial personality had made his store at 71 William Street the rendezvous, not only of his friends in the stationery business, but also of many of the writers and artists of his day.

His father, Joseph Cohen, had been a soldier in the Revolution and was officer of the day in Philadelphia when the news of Cornwallis's surrender at Yorktown was brought to the city. Lewis I. Cohen was born in Lancaster, Pennsylvania on July 23, 1800. Soon after, the family moved to Charleston, South Carolina, where he lived until his fifteenth year, when he went to London as apprentice to his half-brother, Solomon Cohen, who was a well-known English manufacturer of lead pencils. In the summer of 1819 he returned to the United States on the barque Mary and Susan. As they were docking at Burling Slip, he saw a Florida schooner loaded with cedar logs at the other side of the wharf. Upon landing, he examined these logs and was amazed and delighted to find such great lengths of wood without knots. He promptly bought the shipment for thirty pounds, out of the eighty he brought from England. This price was a fraction per log of what his brother was paying per foot in London. He then arranged with Captain Champlin, of the Mary and Susan, to take the entire cargo back as ballast, without cost. He reserved one log, which he sent to a Fulton Street sawmill to be cut into pencil lengths to use himself, and this day's events laid the foundation of the Cohen fortune. The same energy and decision seem characteristic of the man during his entire career, not only in the interests of his business, but also in his many charitable activities. He is also said to have been the first stationer in America to sell steel pens in place of the old quills. (Metallic writing pens were patented in the United States in 1809 by Peregrine Williamson.)

In 1833, he moved to 122 William Street, where two years later he invented his machine for printing at one impression the four colors on the faces of playing cards. While working on this machine he used part of the building of R. Hoe and Company, on Gold Street, as his factory, and when it was perfected he kept his process a secret for twelve years.

In the New York City Directory of 1832, in which he is listed as a pencil-maker, his address was 71 William Street.

In 1838, he moved to 118 William Street, and in 1844 purchased the building at 134 William Street as a store, and the buildings at 184, 186, 188, and 190 William Street as a factory for making playing cards, to accommodate the growth of this part of his business. In the directory of 1845–46 he is listed as importer of French and English fancy and staple stationery, manufacturer of patent ivory surface playing and business cards, enamelled cards,' etc.

In these early Cohen cards, the ace of spades bears the American eagle, sometimes with the thirteen stars above, and sometimes without them.

The ribbon fluttering from the eagle's beak is sometimes lettered 'E Pluribus Unum,' or 'New York,' instead of the usual 'American Manufacture' used by most card-makers. The maker's name, L. I. Cohen, always appears, after the English manner, and sometimes the street address is given.

An early pack of the 'ivory surface playing cards' are printed in gold, even the suit signs of the numeral cards being heavily bordered with it. In 1850, Lewis I. Cohen sold the stationery end of his business to Jerolamon Motley and Company, keeping only the playing card manufactory, and in 1854 he retired, leaving it in the hands of his son, Solomon L. Cohen, and his nephew, John M. Lawrence, under the firm name of Lawrence and Cohen.

THE ACE OF SPADES USED BY LEWIS I. COHEN IN 1844

Another interesting pack bearing the name of L. I. Cohen has a wrapper picturing a railroad train, and lettered 'Railroad Cards.' To be in keeping with the modern spirit of this title, the cards are double heads — the earliest we know in America, and the backs are printed in an all-over conventional pattern. The wrapper bears the revenue stamp dated 1861.

THE WRAPPER AND ACE OF SPADES OF AN EDITION OF RAILROAD CARDS, 1861

Among his last cards are several packs whose backs are in conventional designs of very genuine taste and merit, indicative of the work of Owen Jones.

The Lawrence and Cohen cards are very much like the English ones of the period. They have typical English wrappers, and they abandon the

American eagle that has always appeared on American aces of spades. They use the Owen Jones designs for their card backs, and mention the fact on both the wrappers and the aces of spades. At first they were at 184 William Street and later at 222–228 West Fourteenth Street.

A WRAPPER FOR EAGLE PLAYING CARDS MADE BY L. I. COHEN IN NEW YORK, 1832

GOLD-EMBOSSED PLAYING CARDS MADE BY L. I. COHEN, *c.* 1845

For a pack of their later cards they use a wrapper picturing a steamboat, a purely American design, and destined to be popular among American makers for many years. These cards are double heads, but this idea is evidently still a novelty in America. Another late pack bearing their name shows an index in the corner of each card, and the Mogul wrapper is let-

ACES OF SPADES USED BY LAWRENCE AND COHEN

A CARD BACK DESIGNED BY OWEN JONES AND USED BY LAWRENCE AND COHEN

A MOGUL WRAPPER, FOR SQUEEZERS, OR AMERICAN INDEXED PLAYING CARDS

EARLY DOUBLE-HEAD PLAYING CARDS MADE BY LAWRENCE AND COHEN

These are Steamboat cards and are not indexed

AN ACE OF SPADES OF JOHN J. LEVY

AN ACE OF SPADES MADE BY SAMUEL HART, PHILADELPHIA AND NEW YORK, *c.* 1850

tered 'Squeezers.' These cards were made as an advertisement for a tobacco company, whose name appears upon their backs.

On December 5, 1871, Lawrence and Cohen turned the business into a stock company, taking in three nephews of Lewis I. Cohen, all of whom had learned their trade in his factory. They were Samuel Hart and Isaac Levy, of Samuel Hart and Company, of Philadelphia, and John J. Levy, of New York. The new corporation was called the New York Consolidated Card Company.

Abraham Hart was a bookseller and Sara Hart a stationer in Philadelphia in 1831. Samuel Hart's name first appears in the directory of 1844 as a stationer at 27 South Fourth Street. In 1849, the name of Samuel Hart and Company, 160 Market Street, importers of staple and fancy station-ery, manufacturers of playing and blank cards, is listed. They are later at 236 South Thirteenth Street, and then at 416 South Thirteenth Street. The wrappers show the American eagle and are lettered 'Hart's Linen Eagle.' A later one is lettered 'Club House' and shows the eagle above a

quartered shield flanked by two soldiers, and the address given is 222–228 West Fourteenth Street, New York, which is the address later used by Lawrence and Cohen. There is a joker in this pack of cards, and the ace of spades is lettered 'London Club Cards.' Other novelties he introduces are round-cornered cards, and 'satin surface' cards which are double heads and come in both the Mogul and Steamboat wrappers. A special edition, whose ace of spades bears the portraits of George and Martha Washington, was reissued later, beautifully engraved by the New York Consoli-dated Card Company in 1871.

A SPECIAL EDITION ACE OF SPADES WITH PORTRAITS OF GEORGE AND MARTHA WASHINGTON, *c.* 1850

These portraits remind us of earlier ones, which may or may not have been made and used by makers of playing cards. There are medallion portraits of George Washington and John Adams, engraved by John Bowen, who worked in Philadelphia between 1810 and 1819, and these appear on a printed background, such as was being introduced for card backs by the makers of the time.

Another portrait of Washington is on a card, the size of a playing card, and its arrangement was evidently inspired by the feeling concerning the Monroe Doctrine.[1]

In one edition of 'Hart's Linen Eagle' the address of the New York office is 560 Broadway, and another has 'Philadelphia Card Manufactory' on the ace of spades, and the address, 48 John Street, New York.

A pack of cards with plaid backs have the Hart name on the ace of spades, which is lettered 'California Poker Deck' and pictures two 'forty-niners.'

It is rather amusing to know that in Shakespeare's time he speaks of a 'deck' of cards, but that nowadays to call a 'pack' a 'deck' is a provin-cialism of the States in the Mississippi and Ohio River valleys, according to the 'Catalogue of Playing Cards,' published by the British Museum in the eighteen-seventies. These Hart cards would seem to prove that the word was also in common use either in the Far West, or in the East, or possibly in both places.

[1] These are lettered, 'Beware of foreign influence.'

A PLAYING-CARD WRAPPER USED BY SAMUEL HART, *c.* 1850

'Paire' and pack seem to have been synonymous terms for a long while, for many an old writer speaks of a 'paire of cards.' In an old play in the Garrick collection called 'The longer thou livest the more foole thou arte,' Idleness desires Moros, the clown, to 'looke at his booke,' and shows him 'a paier of cardes.' In another old play, 'A Woman Killed with Kindness,' a 'paire of cardes and counters' are mentioned. Roger Ascham, discussing the relative merits of archery and playing cards in his 'Toxophilus,' which he published in London in 1545, says: 'A man no shoter, (not longe agoo,) wolde defende playing at cardes & dise, if it were honestly used, to be as honest a pastime as youre shotinge: for he layed for him, that a man might pleye for a little at cardes and dyse, and also a man might shote away all that ever he had. He sayd a payre of cardes cost not past two pence and that they needed not so moche reparation as bowe and shaftes, they wolde never hurte a man his hande, nor never weare his gere. A man shulde never slee a man with shoting wyde at the cardes. In wete and drye, hote and coulde, they woulde never forsake a man, he shewed what great varietie there is in them for everye mans capacitie: if one game were harde, he might easelye learne another: If a man have a good game there is greate pleasure in it: if he have an ill game, the payne is shorte, for he may soone gyve it over, and hope for a better: with many other mo reasons. But at the last he concluded, that betwixt playinge and shoting, well used, or ill used there was no difference: but that there was lesse coste and trouble, and a greate deale more pleasure in playing, than in shotynge.' By the time of Charles II, they are rarely called 'a pair of cards,' though in 'Poor Robin's Almanac' for 1684, under December are the lines:

'Perhaps a pair of cards is going
And that's the chiefest matter doing.'

In Italy, to-day, 'pair' is used in the same way, for they still say 'un paio di carte.'

Mr. W. A. Chatto, a very careful writer, discussing these things, says that in the reign of Queen Elizabeth cards were sometimes called a 'bunch.' But in 'Henry VI,' Shakespeare says

'The king was slily fingered from the deck.'

TRANSFORMATION CARDS, ISSUED BY SAM-
UEL HART IN PHILADELPHIA ABOUT 1860
  These same designs, under the name of Pictorial Cards, were published by William Tegg in London. There are also Viennese and Munich editions of these.

An entry in an account book, kept in Braintree in 1771, reads, 'a sette of cards for playing.' But to come down a century, we find another interesting edition of cards issued by Samuel Hart, a pack of transformation cards after the designs originally published by William Tegg in London, and after-ward copied in Viennese and Munich papers as 'Pictorial Cards.' The ad-dress on the ace of spades is 416 South Thirteenth Street, Philadelphia, and 307 Broadway, New York.

John J. Levy's cards show the old Cohen ace. His address is first 177–179 Grand Street, and later at 184 William Street. A pack of his later cards are double heads, and the wrapper shows a ship with both steam and sails, perhaps a forerunner of the popular steamboat.

The Congress Card Manufactory in New York made a pack of cards for C. R. Hewet, a stationer at 45 Vesey Street, in 1852. The ace of spades shows a picture of the City Hall below the spread eagle. The suit signs are outlined on each card and there is much elaborate detail in the court cards. A second pack with the same ace of spades is lettered only, 'Congress Manufacturing Co.,' and at the bottom, 'Astor House, N. York.' This evidently refers to their address, which is given in the Trow and Wilson Directories of 1853–55 as 2 Astor House and Pitt Street.

Besides these, there are curious little fortune-telling cards made by Turner and Fisher, probably in the eighteen-twenties. 'Dr. Busby' was a popular card game which was published in 1843, and 'Yankee Notions' another, made by T. W. Strong in New York in 1856. There are four suits in this game, eagles, stars, shields, and flags of ten cards each, numbered from 1 to 0, and ten humorous court cards numbered in the same way.

In the mean time another company manufacturing playing cards, with

PORTRAITS OF GEORGE WASHINGTON AND JOHN ADAMS WHICH SEEM TO HAVE BEEN
USED AS CARD BACKS IN PHILADELPHIA EARLY IN THE NINETEENTH CENTURY

A POLITICAL ACE OF SPADES OF
1823

AN ACE OF SPADES OF 1853,
USED BY THE CONGRESS,
MANUFACTURING COMPANY,
NEW YORK

(339)

MRS. SALLY SMITH   THE BABY   AN OLD MAID

From 'Yankee Notions' playing cards, 1856

Andrew Dougherty at its head, was started in New York. His early cards are stenciled and the suit signs are often askew. So, too, are the faces of the court cards, which often have most amusing expressions. It is not until considerably later that he makes cards that compare favorably with those of Mr. Cohen, who, perhaps because of his London apprenticeship, had from the first 'been thoroughly acquainted with the principal branches of making Playing Cards in the true European manner.'

ACES OF SPADES USED BY ANDREW DOUGHERTY FROM 1848 TO 1872

Andrew Dougherty began making his cards in a very primitive way at first in Brooklyn, then at 148 Ann Street, then at 78 Cliff Street, New York. Most of the early Dougherty cards are in wrappers decorated with the familiar eagle, and lettered 'American Cards,' though some of them show the English Moguls and Merry Andrews. The backs are sometimes plain, and sometimes a moiré effect is achieved by wavy lines.

His Small Spanish cards, stenciled in golden yellow, bearing the date 'Ano 1849,' are among the most vivid reminders of those adventurous days of the middle of the century, when many of them doubtless made the long voyage to the California gold fields or found their way up the yellow Mississippi in the path of trade with the great awakening West. A much-used pack of these in the Cincinnati collection has a card in it with 'Hanni-bal, Mo.' scrawled upon its back. Shades of Mark Twain and Huckleberry Finn, and the steamboats on the Mississippi!

About 1858, the Dougherty card-manufactory was moved to 26 Beek-man Street. He uses the same American wrappers with the eagle, varying them only occasionally with the English designs, Moguls and Harry the Eighths. For one edition he uses the old Decatur wrapper used by David Felt in the twenties. This was in all probability originally made for the Decatur cards of Jazaniah Ford, in 1815.

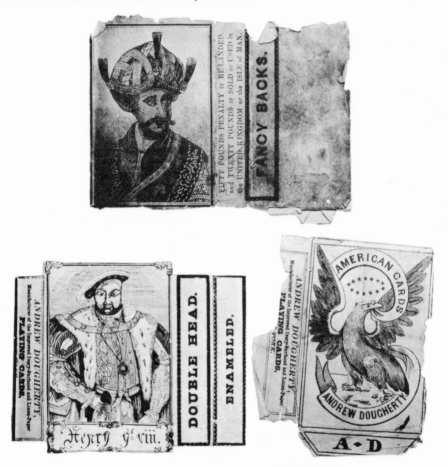

AMERICAN PLAYING CARD WRAPPERS, 1845–1861

KING OF HEARTS AND ACE OF SPADES MADE BY COUGHTRY AND DOUGHERTY
NEW YORK, *c.* 1850

CONFEDERATE PLAYING CARDS PRINTED IN LONDON IN 1862
The backs show the Confederate flags

He makes his cards in two qualities, and uses a new ace of spades, lettered 'Excelsior Cards.' In the better grade, this ace is nicely engraved. Their wrapper bears the one-cent revenue stamp, marked 'A.D. Nov. 1862,' but the cards are from much earlier designs. They may have been printed for use in the army.

Dougherty also made an edition of 'Illuminated Great Moguls' similar to the gold-decorated Cohen cards. An earlier edition of these was brought out under the name of the United States Card Manufactory, Coughtry and Dougherty.

UNION PLAYING CARDS ISSUED IN NEW YORK IN 1862

(343)

In the 'History of American Manufactures,' by J. L. Bishop, the following statistics are given concerning the playing card industry in 1860:

CARDS, PLAYING, PRINTERS', ETC.

	Philadelphia	New York and Brooklyn
Number of establishments...............	4	2
Capital................................	$44,000	$63,000
Cost of raw material...................	$80,000	
Male hands............................	33	51
Female hands..........................	59	49
Value of products......................	$134,600	$154,000

The Civil War was a signal for issuing so-called patriotic and partisan packs of cards. A pack of 'Picture Playing Cards' showing portraits of Union generals was made by M. Nelson in New York in 1863. A Confederate pack was made in London, by Goodall, the backs being decorated with Confederate flags. An American issue, evidently to counteract these, displays the Stars and Stripes as its back design.

ARMY AND NAVY CARDS OF THE CIVIL WAR DAYS
MADE IN NEW YORK IN 1865

The cards shown are the jack and four of zouaves, the ace of drummer boys, and the three of monitors

'Union Playing Cards,' made by the American Card Company, 14 Chambers Street, and 165 William Street, New York, in 1862, have for their red suit signs American flags and stars, and for the blue suit signs, shields and American eagles. The kings are infantry officers in full dress, the queens goddesses of liberty, and the jacks artillery commissioned officers in fatigue uniform.

Andrew Dougherty also made a pack of Civil War cards, which he called 'Army and Navy Cards.' The suit signs are drummer boys and zouaves for the red suits, and the blue suits are the Monitor and the Merrimac. The court cards are caricatures in the costumes of the day. Each blue ace bears the name 'A. Dougherty, Manufacturer, 26 Beekman Street,

New York.' And one of them, in addition, the words 'To Commemorate the greatest event in naval history, the substitution of iron for wood.' These cards were made in 1865.

Another war-time card game is 'The Game of Battles.' It must have run through several editions, as the box is lettered 'Second series. The Game of Battles. North and South. 1861–62–63.' At the top of each of the fifty-two cards is either the Stars and Stripes or the Confederate flag. Below is the name of the battle in which the followers of the flag were victorious, the date and statistics. There are two cards covered with numbers, and one card of 'Improved Directions' for playing the game.

Up to the time of the Civil War it was necessary to keep cards in card presses when not in use, to prevent their curling up. It is said that during the war President Lincoln summoned Andrew Dougherty to Washington and asked his advice in regard to the best and most effective way of raising more revenue for the Government. Mr. Dougherty and the President were in conference for some time. Mr. Dougherty's son William, a boy of ten, accompanied his father. He sat watching Mr. Lincoln while he talked. When the father and son were coming away, Mr. Lincoln put his big hand on the little boy's small one and said, 'I hope you'll live to be as good a man as your father.'

In 1872, Andrew Dougherty built a new factory at 76–80 Centre Street, and it was not until 1896 that he transferred his business to his three sons. The cards from the Centre Street factory are double heads, but at first they seldom have indices. When they do, and when the corners are rounded instead of square, another innovation, both facts are mentioned on the wrapper. The eagle wrapper is still used, as well as the English Moguls and Harrys. The Steamboat wrapper is also used. With the indexed cards, a fifty-third card, the 'Jolly Joker,' is included, but this was also more or less of a novelty. The backs are usually conventional designs, but with none of the merit of the English ones.

It was not until the late seventies that indices came into common use on English and American cards. Indeed, nearly ten years later unindexed cards are still found.

In America, the two large companies, the New York Consolidated Card Company and Andrew Dougherty, issued indexed cards, the former under the name of 'Squeezers,' the latter under the name 'Triplicate.' A tacit understanding between the two about sales territory is commemorated in a card back of 1877, showing two bulldogs straining at their leashes in front of their respective houses. On the collar of one is 'Squeezer'; on the other, 'Trip.'

Andrew Dougherty's Triplicate playing cards have a specially designed ace, and the wrapper shows this design as well as a picture of the factory.

1   2   3

1 AN EARLY VARIETY OF CARD INDICES

From a pack of Triplicate playing cards of 1875

2 A PLAYING CARD BACK OF 1877

Commemorative of a sales agreement between Andrew Dougherty and The New York Consolidated Card Company, makers respectively of Triplicate and Squeezer playing cards, both of which were trade names for indexed cards, which had just been introduced.

3 A PLAYING CARD BACK IN HONOR OF THE CENTENNIAL EXPOSITION IN PHILADELPHIA IN 1876

1   2   3

1 A TYPICAL JOKER OF EUCHRE DAYS

2 AN AMERICAN PLAYING CARD BACK OF 1887 IN HONOR OF QUEEN VICTORIA'S GOLDEN JUBILEE

3 A KNAVE OF CLUBS FROM A PACK OF MEDIEVAL PLAYING CARDS, NEW YORK, 1897

The unindexed cards are still called 'Excelsior.' A pack of these, with round corners, is in a Mogul wrapper, marked 'Jones & Co. London. Exportation.' About 1880, the name 'Triplicate' was changed to 'Indicators,' to mean indexed cards.

Besides the cards exported to London, there is a Spanish edition in 1882, in all respects like those made in Spain at the time, except that they bear the Dougherty name. A later edition, called 'Spanish American Playing Cards,' are the usual American playing cards, with a blue line forming a border around the edge of each card.

An injunction was granted against a 'Dorrity Playing Card Manufacturing Company' for infringement on the Dougherty trade-marks and name.

When the joker is included with the cards not indexed, it is called 'The Best Bower,' the name also used by the New York Consolidated Card Company. Euchre, which had come to America years before with French colonists, was a popular game at the time. In playing it, the knaves of the trump suit and the other suit of the same color were called 'Bowers,' and the joker or 'Best Bower' was the highest card of all. Progressive euchre is said to have first been played in Cincinnati at the Mount Auburn home of Mr. William T. Irwin.

The story of the New York Consolidated Card Company's cards is very similar to that of the Dougherty Company's. They used two types of aces to indicate quality. The most common wrapper is one showing a conventional design of their own and a picture of the factory, though Steamboat wrappers are to be found. Their special back designs are interesting. One shows a portrait of Mary Anderson at the height of her popularity. An edition of 1885 shows a portrait of President Garfield, and one of 1887, in honor of Queen Victoria's Golden Jubilee, has a beautifully lithographed portrait of the Queen at the time of her coronation.

A special edition of 'American Playing Cards,' at the time of the Paris Exposition, have court cards picturing the reigning families in Great Britain, Germany, Austria, and Italy. Their club cards and 'Harmonie Solo Karten' use the old, old designs of the Cohens and Harts. In 1882, there is an edition of 'Gem Squeezers' a supposedly improved index, with a new ace of spades. There is also an issue of cards with 'Patent Suit Signs.' 'Foster's Self Playing Bridge Cards' are another novelty, which were also made by Dougherty. There are also Spanish cards made by the Consolidated Card Company.

At the time of the Civil War there was also an 'American Card Company,' whose name is on their ace of spades, which shows the old eagle. The Great Mogul wrapper is lettered 'Longley Card Company, Cincinnati,' and the five-cent revenue stamp is marked '1862.' The cards are

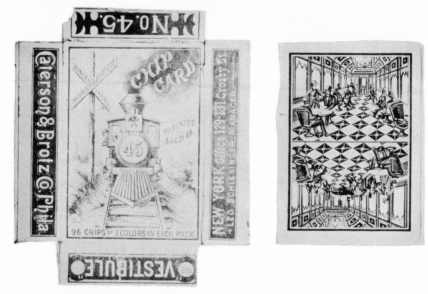

CHIP CARDS OF 1888 HAD NINETY-SIX PAPER CHIPS IN THE BOX WITH THE USUAL
PACK OF FIFTY-TWO CARDS

These cards and chips were designed for travelers, as is evidenced by the wrapper and
the design of the card backs

coarsely printed double heads. A similar pack has a joker, picturing a tiger, and lettered 'The Paper Fabrique Company's Highest Trump Card.'

About ten years later there are cards in a Steamboat wrapper made by the Card Fabrique Company, of Middletown, Ohio. On the back of the wrapper, the name appears as the 'Globe Playing Card Company, Middletown.' The Globe Card Company, manufacturers, No. 78 Hawley Street, Boston, made round playing cards in 1874, the hearts printed in red, clubs in green, spades in black, and diamonds in yellow.

There is also a pack of the usual playing cards of this time, bearing the name of the Eagle Card Company on the ace of spades and the Steamboat wrapper, but the revenue stamp is lettered 'Paper Fabrique Co.' The joker is a 'Heathen Chinee' in color.

Other card-makers of the seventies are the Sterling Card Company, Vesey Street, New York; Victor E. Mauger, of New York, whose designs, in both cards and wrappers, resemble the English; an 1876 edition of his cards is in honor of the Centennial at Philadelphia; the Continental Card Company in Philadelphia; the United States Card Company of New York, whose cards, issued soon after the close of the war, show a portrait of President Lincoln on the ace of spades.

In 1881, Russell, Morgan and Company issued their first pack of cards. An addition had been built to their Printing Factory on Race Street, Cin-

WRAPPER AND ACE OF SPADES OF AMERICAN CARDS OF THE CENTENNIAL
YEAR, 1876

cinnati, and machines installed for the making of cards. This new business flourished, and two years later it was necessary to move to a larger
factory on Lock Street. In 1891, the corporate name of the company was
changed to the United States Printing Company, at which time the
company was engaged in the manufacture of colored show posters, colored
labels, and playing cards. In 1894, the United States Playing Card
Company was incorporated. Their next move in 1900 was to their present
site in Norwood.

They began, in 1881, by making six grades of cards, and the names for
these are interesting because there is an absolute breaking away from the
traditional names that had clung to the English and later to the American
cards for more than a hundred years. These new and purely American
trade names were:

101. Tigers	404. Congress
202. Sportsman's	505. Army and Navy, gold edges
303. Army and Navy	606. Congress, gold edges

BORDER INDEX CARDS OF 1878, SHOWING A KING OF HEARTS AND THE CARD BACK

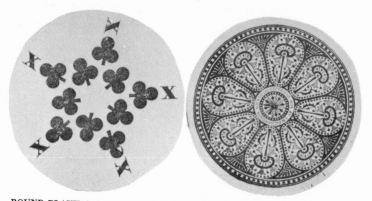

ROUND PLAYING CARDS MADE BY THE GLOBE CARD COMPANY IN 1874

COURT CARDS MADE BY RUSSELL, MORGAN AND COMPANY IN 1881

(350)

THE ACES OF SPADES USED BY RUSSELL, MORGAN AND COMPANY IN 1881

Left to right, above: 101, Tigers; 202, Sportsman's; 303 and 505, Army. Below: 303 and 505, Navy
404 and 606, Congress

A JOKER USED BY RUSSELL, MORGAN AND COMPANY IN 1881

THE FRONT OF A PLAYING-CARD BOX USED BY RUSSELL, MORGAN AND COMPANY IN 1881

THE BICYCLE ACE OF SPADES OF 1885

(351)

FAMILIAR JOKERS AND CARD BACKS OF BICYCLE PLAYING CARDS

In 1885, their competitors in the East brought out two popular brands of cards, the Consolidated calling theirs 'Mascot' and Dougherty naming his 'Tally-ho' for the four in hands that were the acme of smartness in those days.

These were also the days of the high-wheeled bicycles, and, because they were even newer and faster than the high-wheeled carts, the United States Playing Card Company chose the name 'Bicycle' as their emblem and it has remained exclusively theirs, for one of their grades of cards, for more than forty years.

Other American cards characteristic of the eighties are two games of baseball playing cards. One was issued in Boston in 1884. The backs picture a baseball diamond with players and spectators in the costume of the day, while the faces of the cards show balls and players; another series made in New York in 1888, consisting of seventy-two cards, shows a ball player of one of the eight great American teams on each card.

There were also political playing cards published in New York by A. H.

BASEBALL CARDS OF 1884, SHOWING THE CARD BACK AND
ONE OF THE CARDS

BASEBALL PLAYING CARDS OF 1888

Caffee in 1887 and 1888, whose court cards were caricatures of leading political figures. Benjamin Harrison and Grover Cleveland are the kings of hearts and spades. These are very similar to the political playing cards published in England at the same time.

There have also been many series of transformation cards similar to the English ones. 'The Eclipse Comic Playing Cards' were made in 1876 by F. H. Lowerre; in 1879, Tiffany and Company, also in New York, published a delightful series called 'Harlequin Playing Cards' which were designed by C. E. Carryl. During the eighteen-eighties several packs of transformation cards were issued as advertisements.

The United States Playing Card Company have never caricatured men in public office in any country, nor the serious events in any part of the

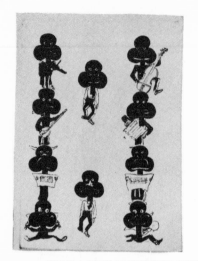

FROM A PACK OF ECLIPSE COMIC PLAYING CARDS, F. H. LOWERRE, 1877

GROVER CLEVELAND AS THE
KING OF HEARTS IN A PACK
OF POLITICAL PLAYING CARDS
PUBLISHED IN 1888

A CARD FROM A PACK OF GEO-
GRAPHICAL EUCHRE PLAYING
CARDS, 1886

(354)

FROM A PACK OF WORLD'S
COLUMBIAN EXPOSITION CARDS
The United States Playing Card
Company, 1893

A RIP VAN WINKLE JOKER OF
THE GAY NINETIES
The United States Playing Card
Company

THE VALET, OR SOTA, OF COINS, OR SUNS, AND THE
REY, OR KING, OF CUPS, OF AN EDITION OF SPANISH
CARDS WHOSE COURT CARDS PICTURE THE INDIANS OF
SOUTH AMERICA
Colombiano cards. The United States Playing Card Com-
pany, 1895

(355)

FROM AN EDITION OF CIRCUS PLAYING CARDS, 1896

world. In 1900, they were awarded the Grand Prix at the Paris Exposition.

The use of special editions of playing cards as advertisements, by manufacturers of other products in America, is a long and interesting story in itself, which had its beginning in the sixties.

A LOVELY STAR OF 1895

Julia Marlowe as the queen of spades in a pack of Stage Playing Cards. The United States Playing Card Company

Another curious edition of the eighties was a pack of playing cards called 'Geographical Euchre,' published in 1886, and giving statistics concerning all of the States and Territories.

At the time of the World's Fair in Chicago, in 1893, several packs of cards were issued picturing the Exposition buildings. There have been many series of fortune-telling cards, the ideas of most of them being borrowed from the old Le Normand cards. Of the cards for foreign countries, some of the packs destined for use in Mexico and South America show the most interesting and original development, and a pack of Japanese-American cards is novel.

Playing cards made of aluminum were an experiment tried in 1901, and Spanish War cards, whose case was in the form of a knapsack with small chips stored in the roll, are of course for the great American game of poker.

Roulette cards and chess cards have also been made in America. The usual packs of fifty-two cards 'for playing' have been made in all sizes — from toy cards one quarter by three eighths inch to the large show cards

HUSTLING JOE PLAYING CARDS MADE BY THE UNITED STATES
PLAYING CARD COMPANY

A KNAPSACK CARD BOX AT THE
TIME OF THE SPANISH WAR
The roll at the top holds small chips

ROOKWOOD INDIAN CARD
BACK, DESIGNED IN 1903 BY
M. A. DALY FOR THE UNITED
STATES PLAYING CARD COM-
PANY

A KNIGHT AND A BISHOP FROM A PACK OF CHESS CARDS

SOUVENIR PLAYING CARDS OF THE UNITED STATES PLAYING CARD COMPANY

CARDS FROM SOME TWENTIETH-CENTURY EDUCATIONAL CARD GAMES

The first is from 'The Flower Game'; the second from 'The Bird Game'; the third from 'The New Testament Game'; and the fourth from 'The Poetry Game'

FROM A PACK OF FORTUNE-TELLING TAROTS DESIGNED IN 1916 AND PUBLISHED IN
AMERICA

(359)

seven and three eighths by ten and three eighths inches, and with infinite variations.

Besides these there are the souvenir cards, picturing different parts of the country in series of photographs. The face of the card is taken up by the picture, only the indices in the corners, marking it as a 'card for playing.' The photographic work is wonderfully well done and the backs often have real merit. In looking at these it is interesting to remember those geographical games of the seventeenth century that were made in France, Germany, Italy, and England. After all, these souvenir cards are only a modern presentation of the old idea, produced with all the resources of to-day. Perhaps in another three hundred years these cards will be as great curiosities as the older ones are to us.

Many pictorial card games have also been made which have as definite a charm for children of to-day as their predecessors probably had for the children of earlier generations and older lands. The first and most famous of the educational cards were the fifteenth-century Italian tarot series. Then came the cards of Thomas Murner in Cracow, and then those of Jean Demarests, which were to interest his young king, Louis Quatorze, in the geography of the world he lived in and its story. These modern games are based on precisely the same idea, and we come back to the conclusion that, in spite of their great variety, 'cards for playing' have changed little in all of these hundreds of years.

AMERICAN PLAYING CARDS IN THE COLLECTION OF THE UNITED STATES PLAYING CARD COMPANY

Playing cards by Henry Hart, London, for export to America, 1765	20 cards
Photographs, cards used on Benjamin Franklin's machine for electrical experimentation, 1752	6 cards
Photograph, ace of hearts, with Joseph Hopkinson silhouette by Charles Wilson Peale on its back	1 card
Photographs of the playing cards in the collection of the University of Pennsylvania, whose backs were used as cards of admission, invitations, and advertisements, 1749–1814	13 cards
Playing cards, Amos Whitney, Boston, c. 1785	3 cards
Photographs, home-made playing cards, Nantucket	8 cards
Various employments, a card game, Philadelphia, 1790	8 cards
Playing cards, early ace with eagle, no name of maker	52 cards
Playing cards, Thomas Crehore, Dorchester, 1801	52 cards
Historical playing cards, J. Y. Humphreys, Philadelphia, 1801	16 cards
Photographs, five card wrappers from wood blocks of Dr. Alexander Anderson, the originals in the print collection at the New York Public Library	
Playing cards, marked London, but probably made in America	52 cards

Fortune-telling cards, Turner and Fisher, 1820	41 cards
Decatur cards, Jazaniah Ford, Milton, Massachusetts, 1815	8 cards
Playing cards, Joseph Ford, 1826	5 cards
Fortune-telling cards	4 cards
La Fayette cards, Jazaniah Ford, Milton, 1824	5 cards
Boston card manufactory, c. 1812?	1 card
New York card manufactory	1 card
L. I. Cohen, New York, c. 1832	1 card
Invitation cards, 1792–1814	2 cards
Monroe Doctrine ace	1 card
Washington and Adams cards	2 cards
Playing cards, David Felt, New York, 1826, and original Decatur wrapper from an Alexander Anderson wood block	52 cards
Invitation cards, 1797–1807	14 cards
Three uncut card sheets from wood blocks, twenty court cards to each sheet, the suit signs in color, by Jazaniah Ford of Milton, 1780–1825	60 cards
Two uncut sheets from wood blocks, twenty court cards to each sheet, uncolored and without suit signs, by Jazaniah Ford of Milton, 1780–1825	
Two uncut sheets, court cards in classical costume, engraved from copper plates, uncolored. By Jazaniah Ford, Milton	34 cards
Court cards by Jazaniah Ford, Milton	12 cards
Court cards in classical costume, hand-colored. By Jazaniah Ford, Milton, 1815	120 cards
La Fayette aces, hand-colored, engraved by Abel Bowen, 1824. By Jazaniah Ford, Milton, 1815	200 cards
Indian gaming sticks from Sitka	
Arizona Apache monte cards painted on sheepskin, Spanish suit signs	35 cards
A mahogany card press	
A mahogany card press mounted in ivory	
A dealing machine for faro	
Playing cards, by L. I. Cohen, c. 1838	52 cards
Playing cards, outlined in gold, L. I. Cohen	52 cards
Early ace of spades, L. I. Cohen	1 card
Playing cards, Mogul wrapper, Lawrence and Cohen, two packs	104 cards
Playing cards, flag back, for Civil War, 1862	52 cards
Railroad cards, Lawrence and Cohen	52 cards
Two packs of playing cards, eagle wrappers	104 cards
Playing cards, Lawrence and Cohen, Steamboat wrapper	52 cards
Three packs of playing cards, Lawrence and Cohen, Owen Jones back designs	156 cards
Harmonie Solo Karten, Lawrence and Cohen	36 cards
Mogul squeezers, Lawrence and Cohen	52 cards
Excelsior playing cards, Lawrence and Cohen, 1861	52 cards
Playing cards, J. J. Levy, cherub back, c. 1850	52 cards
Playing cards, J. J. Levy, Steamboat wrapper	52 cards

Playing cards, Samuel Hart and Company, linen eagle wrapper, 2 packs — 104 cards

Playing cards, Samuel Hart and Company, club house cards with joker, 1857 — 53 cards

Playing cards, Samuel Hart and Company, early, 'Philadelphia Card Manufactory' — 52 cards

*Playing cards, Samuel Hart and Company, 'round-cornered, No. 41' — 52 cards

Transformation cards, Samuel Hart and Company — 52 cards

California poker or faro cards, three packs, Samuel Hart and Company — 156 cards

*Patent playing cards, Samuel Hart and Company, 1864 — 52 cards

Playing cards with joker, the best bower, Samuel Hart and Company — 106 cards

Playing cards, Mogul wrapper, 1868, Samuel Hart and Company — 52 cards

Playing cards, Steamboat wrapper, George and Martha Washington ace of spades — 52 cards

Playing cards, Andrew Dougherty, 1848 — 49 cards

Playing cards, Andrew Dougherty, 1848 — 52 cards

Playing cards, Andrew Dougherty, merry Highlander wrapper — 52 cards

Playing cards, Andrew Dougherty, eagle wrapper — 52 cards

Bird game, *c.* 1865 — 63 cards

Magic cards, *c.* 1840 — 16 cards

Questions and answers, *c.* 1830 — 36 cards

Spanish cards, made by Andrew Dougherty, nine packs, with wrappers, 1850 — 360 cards

Playing cards, moiré backs, Andrew Dougherty, *c.* 1850 — 39 cards

Playing cards, Andrew Dougherty, *c.* 1850 — 36 cards

'American cards,' Andrew Dougherty, eagle wrapper — 52 cards

'Excelsior cards,' Andrew Dougherty, 1850–77, ten packs — *c.* 500 cards

'Illuminated Excelsior cards,' Andrew Dougherty, edged with gold — 52 cards

Playing cards, Andrew Dougherty, *c.* 1855 — 41 cards

Playing cards, Andrew Dougherty, *c.* 1856 — 6 cards

Playing cards, Andrew Dougherty, *c.* 1857 — 3 cards

Playing cards, Andrew Dougherty, *c.* 1850 — 39 cards

Playing cards, Andrew Dougherty, *c.* 1859 — 30 cards

Playing cards, Andrew Dougherty, *c.* 1860 — 2 cards

Playing cards, Andrew Dougherty, *c.* 1861 — 52 cards

Playing cards, Andrew Dougherty, *c.* 1862 — 12 cards

Playing cards, Andrew Dougherty, *c.* 1864 — 15 cards

Army and Navy cards, Andrew Dougherty, eight packs (Monitor and Merrimac) — 416 cards

'American cards,' Andrew Dougherty, 1863–75, three packs — 156 cards

Playing cards with 'best bower,' Andrew Dougherty — 53 cards

'Triplicate playing cards,' Andrew Dougherty, two packs, *c.* 1875 — 106 cards

*From the collection of George Clulow.

*'Great Moguls for exportation,' Andrew Dougherty,
    c. 1875   52 cards

'Mogul Indicators,' Andrew Dougherty, two packs   104 cards

Spanish cards, made for export by Andrew Dougherty,
    c. 1882   48 cards

Spanish-American cards, Andrew Dougherty   52 cards

Advertising transformation cards, Murphy Varnish
    Company, by Andrew Dougherty   52 cards

Playing cards, Coughtry and Dougherty   3 cards

'Yankee Notions,' New York, 1856   45 cards

Union cards, New York, 1862   52 cards

Confederate cards, London   2 cards

Playing cards, Congress Manufacturing Company,
    New York, 1852   52 cards

Playing cards, Congress Card Manufactory, New York,
    C. R. Hewet   52 cards

Game of battles, 1863   49 cards

Round playing cards, Globe Card Company, Boston,
    1874, three packs   156 cards

Playing cards, Longley Card Company, Cincinnati,
    1862   52 cards

Playing cards, Paper Fabrique Company, Middletown,
    Ohio, two packs with jokers   106 cards

Playing cards, Eagle Card Company, three packs   159 cards

Playing cards, border index cards, Eagle Card Company   52 cards

Chess playing cards, hand-colored proofs   49 cards

Playing cards, The United States Card Company   53 cards

Playing cards, The New York Consolidated Card Com-
    pany, Mary Anderson backs   52 cards

Playing cards, The New York Consolidated Card Com-
    pany, joker, 'best bower,' two packs   106 cards

Spanish playing cards, New York Consolidated Card
    Company, 1878   48 cards

Royal playing cards, New York Consolidated Card
    Company, 1879   53 cards

'Patent Gem Squeezers,' New York Consolidated Card
    Company, 1882, two packs   104 cards

*Playing cards, New York Consolidated Card Company,
    1885, President Garfield back   52 cards

Patent suit playing cards, The New York Consolidated
    Card Company, 1886   52 cards

Foster's self-playing bridge cards, The New York Con-
    solidated Card Company, 1889   52 cards

Foster's self-playing bridge cards, A. Dougherty   52 cards

Shakespearian playing cards, The New York Con-
    solidated Card Company, four packs   208 cards

Golden Jubilee cards, The New York Consolidated Card
    Company   53 cards

Medieval playing cards, The New York Consolidated
    Card Company   53 cards

Spanish playing cards, The New York Consolidated
    Card Company, 1900   48 cards

*From the collection of George Clulow.

Wizard fortune-telling cards, The New York Consoli-
dated Card Company, 1900   52 cards
Comic political playing cards, A. H. Caffee, 1887–88   106 cards
Chip cards, Caterson and Brotz, Philadelphia, 1888   53 cards
*Comic playing cards of fortune, E. Gardinier, 1877   52 cards
Playing cards, Joe Koehler, New York, on gold back-
grounds, c. 1880   52 cards
Colonial playing cards, Bay State Card Company   53 cards
*Playing cards, The American Playing Card Company,
New York, 1875, five packs   265 cards
Pictorial game, Educational Playing Card Company,
Indianapolis, c. 1900   52 cards
Faro cards, The Continental Card Company, Phila-
delphia, c. 1874, two packs   106 cards
Playing cards, The Continental Card Company, Phila-
delphia, 1876, for the Exposition   52 cards
'Fleet,' a card game, San Francisco, Bankers' Art Press   52 cards
Playing cards, The Dorrity Playing Card Company,
c. 1875   52 cards
'The Traveler's Companion,' cards and chips, Union
Playing Card Company, 1886   53 cards
Playing cards, steamboats, Columbia Card Company,
St. Louis, 1886   53 cards
Playing cards, steamboats, National Card Company,
Indianapolis, 1886   53 cards
Playing cards, Knickerbocker Playing Card Company,
Albany, 1890   53 cards
Playing cards, by A. Dougherty for Wagner Palace Car
Company, c. 1895   53 cards
'Hummer' playing cards, The Chicago American Card
Company, c. 1896   53 cards
Playing cards by the Globe Card Company for the Rock
Island Railroad, c. 1896   53 cards
Playing cards, The Brooklyn Card Company, c. 1896   53 cards
Playing cards, 'Invincible Whist,' Ellithorpe and Com-
pany, New York, c. 1896   53 cards
'American Beauty Cards,' by the North American
Card Company, Chicago, c. 1897   53 cards
Anheuser Busch cards, by The Gray Lithographing
Company, 1897   53 cards
Playing cards, by The American Playing Card Com-
pany, Kalamazoo, two packs   106 cards
Playing cards, by F. Munguia, La Estrella, Mexico
City, c. 1885, three packs   144 cards
Playing cards, by Emilio Cuenca y Ca., Mexico City,
c. 1899, two packs   96 cards
Playing cards, 'Fair Play,' A. Dougherty, c. 1900   53 cards
Toy cards, Uncle Sam   53 cards
Playing cards, Excelsior Card Company, c. 1900,
steamboats   53 cards
Egyptian astrological cards for fortune-telling, Dick
and Fitzgerald, New York   52 cards

*From the collection of George Clulow.

Pan-American playing cards, made of aluminum, by
The Aluminum Manufacturing Company, Two
Rivers, Wisconsin, 1901 — 52 cards

Niagara Falls souvenir playing cards, Niagara Playing
Card Company, 1901 — 52 cards

Billionitis, a card game, A. E. Giffen, 1905 — 52 cards

Cruiser cards, A. Dougherty, c. 1905 — 53 cards

Kazoo playing cards, American Playing Card Company, Kalamazoo, c. 1905 — 53 cards

Playing cards, Metropolitan Playing Card Company,
c. 1905 — 53 cards

Bridge whist, A. Dougherty, c. 1906 — 53 cards

Buster Brown playing cards, Standard Playing Card
Company, Chicago, 1907 — 53 cards

Hungarian playing cards, A. Dougherty — 36 cards

Playing cards, Tiger Moguls, Eagle Card Company,
Cincinnati, c. 1862 — 53 cards

Playing cards, steamboats, Perfection Card Company,
Philadelphia, 1886 — 52 cards

Rough-back playing cards, Caterson and Brotz, Philadelphia, 1888 — 53 cards

Playing cards, Chicago steamers and four-in-hands,
Bay State Card Company, 1893 — 106 cards

*Eclipse comic playing cards, F. H. Lowerre, 1876 — 52 cards

Roulette cards, W. W. Russell Card Company, New
Jersey, 1905 — 39 cards

Playing cards, Victor Mauger, New York, fourteen
packs, 1871–78 — 642 cards

Playing cards, Victor Mauger, New York, Centennial
cards, 1876 — 53 cards

Pictorial fortune-telling cards, M. L. Hesse, Los An-
geles, 1917 — 50 cards

Playing cards, New York Card Factory, c. 1870 — 52 cards

Pepper playing cards, two suits on each card, E. W. Mc-
Carroll Company, Pittsburgh — 52 cards

French piquet cards, Regenstein and Roesling, New
York, 1876 — 32 cards

New York souvenir cards, The Ad Card Company,
1917 — 52 cards

Playing cards, The Sterling Card Company, Vesey
Street, New York, c. 1870, three packs — 106 cards

Tiny playing cards, Deland, Philadelphia, c. 1914, two
packs — 106 cards

Playing cards, for New Year's greetings, c. 1875 — 14 cards

Touring, a card game, W. J. Roche, 1906 — 52 cards

Playing cards for advertising, for W. S. Kimball,
Rochester, 1878 — 52 cards

Playing cards for advertising, for Lorillard Tobacco
Company, New York, by The New York Consolidated
Card Company — 52 cards

Playing cards for advertising, for Kinney Tobacco
Company — 52 cards

*From the collection of George Clulow.

Playing cards for advertising, for President Suspender Company	52 cards
Harlequin playing cards, C. E. Carryl, Tiffany and Company, New York, 1879, two packs	104 cards
American cards, Liberty Playing Card Corporation, New York, 1915	53 cards
Mlle. le Normand's gypsy fortune-telling cards, Wehmann Brothers, New York, c. 1880	52 cards
Japanese-American playing cards, Lewis Sears Company, Seattle, 1905	53 cards
World's Fair cards, Winter's Art Lithographing Company, Chicago, 1893	52 cards
Lawson's baseball playing cards, Boston, 1884	42 cards
Baseball playing cards, Baseball Card Company, New York, 1888	72 cards
Geographical euchre, Perfection Card Company, Philadelphia, 1880	52 cards
Souvenir cards, National Guards of New York, 1894, Perfection Card Company	52 cards
American playing cards, Olive S. Prouty, 1892	52 cards
Prince Charles playing cards, C. P. H. Cook Company, Hartford, Connecticut, 1897	53 cards
Six-suit playing cards, Hiram Jones, 1895, International Playing Card Company, Chicago, 1895	78 cards
Biblical card game	64 cards

Total: 259 editions, about 12,020 cards

CARDS FROM THE UNITED STATES PLAYING CARD COMPANY

Original designs and first proofs for court cards, aces, jokers, indices, pips, as well as for card backs, which were used for the first cards made in 1881. Also copper plates and dies. From Henry Furste.

A collection of back designs, by Henry Furste, 1881–86.

A collection of back designs, by Matt. A. Daly, 1898–1929.

Playing cards showing varying sizes, qualities, backs and indices, 1881–1929, about 1400 packs, not all complete.

Souvenir cards, World's Columbian Exposition, Chicago, 1893	53 cards
Columbiano Naipes, Spanish playing cards, 1893	48 cards
Los Leones, Spanish playing cards, 1894	48 cards
Monarch Bicycle cards, 1895	53 cards
Hustling Joe, transformation cards, 1895	53 cards
Stage cards, 1895	51 cards
Circus playing cards, 1896	53 cards
Ye Witches' Fortune cards, 1896	53 cards
Stage playing cards, 1896	52 cards
Philitis, whist of the ancients, 1898	52 cards
Cadet patience cards, 1897	53 cards
Fauntleroy patience cards, 1898	53 cards
Vanity Fair transformation cards, 1900	53 cards

Cards with photographs of Cincinnati, private edition,
   1905   53 cards
Fan Craze baseball cards, 1906   55 cards
Little Duke patience cards, 1908   53 cards
German skat cards, 1908   24 cards
Stage playing cards, 65X, 1908   52 cards
Mardi Gras, playing cards 1908   53 cards
Nile fortune cards, 1913   52 cards
Souvenir cards, National Lithographers, 1915   52 cards
Cards with colors of suit signs reversed, 1915   53 cards
Movie souvenir playing cards, 1917   53 cards
Freedom playing cards, 1918   53 cards
Gypsy witch fortune-telling cards of Mlle. le Normand,
   1918   52 cards
'Fortune' cards for export to France, 1920   52 cards
Viennese tarot cards, 1924   54 cards
Playing cards on brown paper, made from cement
   sacks, 1925   53 cards
'Going to Market' advertising cards, 1925   53 cards
Playing cards for the blind, English Braille system,
   made during the war, 1917   53 cards
Souvenir cards, each pack a series of photographs of
   some part of America, forty-four different packs,
   1898–1925
Educational card games, 1896–1912. These were delightful games for children. There are twenty-four
   different titles.
Card backs, jokers, aces of spades, and cases from hundreds of editions, 1881–1930.

Total: about 2074 editions, about 13,700 cards

Total of entire collection: 3,285 editions, about 58,210 cards

BIBLIOGRAPHY

* Books bought from George Clulow, F.R.G.S., London, are starred.

*Recherches Historiques sur les Cartes à Jouer avec des notes critiques & interessantes. Par l'auteur des Mémoires sur la Langue Celtique. À Lyon: Chez J. Deville Libraire & Mercière au grand Hercule. Avec approbation et privilége. 1757
    No author's name on title-page, but dedicated to Monseigneur le Marques de Paulny, par 'Votre très humble & très Obéissant Serviteur, Bullet.'
16mo, French mottled calf.

*Éclaircissements Historiques et critiques sur l'invention des Cartes à jouer. Par M. l'Abbé Rive, tirées de sa notice d'un MS. de la Bibliothèque de M. le Duc de la Vallière, intitulé le Roman d'Artus, Comte de Bretaigne. Imprimée à Paris: Chez Didot l'aine en 1779 in 4to. À Paris: Chez l'auteur, Hôtel de la Vallière, rue de Bac. 16mo, French mottled calf with gold dentelles, by Ramage. 1780

*Versuch den Ursprung der Spielkarten die Einfuhrung des Leinenpapieres und den Anfang der Holzschneide kunst in Europa zu erforschen von John Gottl: Imman Breitkopf. Leipzig: Bey John Gottl: Imman Breitkopf. 1784
    8vo, three quarters French mottled calf, by Ramage. 12 plates.

*An Inquiry into the Origin of Playing Cards, by J. G. Imman Breitkopf, Leipzig, 1784. Translated from the German by I. W. May and transcribed by Charles Bond, Gravesend. 1815
    Folio, vellum binding, gold lettering. Beautifully written manuscript with a number of facsimiles of ancient playing cards and proof impressions on folio paper from 'Singer' on playing cards.

*Researches into the History of Playing Cards, with illustrations of the Origin of Printing and Engraving on Wood, by Samuel Weller Singer. London: Printed by T. Bensley and Son for Robert Triphook, No. 23 Old Bond Street, London. 1816
    4to, full Russian calf, extra gilt, g.e., 19 plates, many of them colored, and a large number of wood cuts and engravings.
    The same. A very handsome copy in full levant red morocco, with gold tooling and inside dentelles, bound by Clarke and Bedford.
    Only 250 copies of this book were printed.

*Geschichte der Holzschneidekunst von den altesten bis auf die neuesten Zeiten nebst zwei Berlagen enthaltend den Ursprung der Spielkarten und ein Berzeichniss de sammelischen xylographischen Werke von Joseph Heller, mit sehr vielen Holzschnitten. Bamberg. 1823
    12mo, contemporary binding of mottled paper. Ex Libris, George Clulow. Fine folding plates.

*Facts and Speculations on the Origin and History of Playing Cards, by William Andrew Chatto.

> Haec mihi charta nuces, haec est mihi charta fritillus. — Martial.
> With cards I while my leisure time away,
> And cheat old Time; yet neither bet nor play.

London: John Russell Smith, 4, Old Compton Street, Soho Square. 1848
    8vo, three quarters calf, bound by Root and Son. Many excellent illustrations, many of them in color. Gold edges.

*On the Origin and Antiquity of Playing Cards, and description of a pack of the time of the commonwealth illustrative of the chief personages and events of that period, by J. T. Pettigrew, Esq., F.R.S., F.S.A., vice-president. London.   1853
    8vo, three quarters green morocco, bound by Ramage.
    2 Plates by R. Cruikshank.

*Les Cartes à Jouer et la Cartomancie. Par P. Boiteau d'Ambly. Ouvrage illustré de 40 bois. Paris: Librairie de L. Hachette et Cie, rue Pierre Sarrazin, No. 14.   1854
    16mo, contemporary binding of half red morocco. Many illustrations.

The same. London: John Camden Hotten, Antiquarian Bookseller, Piccadilly.   1859
    16mo, three quarters morocco, binding by Ramage. Many illustrations.

*The History of Playing Cards, with Anecdotes of their use in Ancient and Modern Games, Conjuring, Fortune Telling and Card Sharping. Edited by the late Rev. Ed. S. Taylor, B.A., and others. London: John Camden Hotten, Piccadilly.   1865
    16mo, three quarters calf, bound by Root and Son, gold edges.

Notice sur un Jeu de Cartes attribué aux premières années du regne de François I, et sur un Jeu de 1760. Par Alphonse Trémeau de Rochebrune.   1867
    8vo, paper cover.

*Origine des Cartes à Jouer, Recherches Nouvelles sur les Naïbis, Les Tarots et sur les autres espèces de Cartes, ouvrage accompagne d'un Album de soixante quatorze planches offrant plus de 600 sujets, la plupart peu connus ou tout a fait nouveaux. Par R. Merlin. Paris: Chez l'Auteur, rue des Écoles 46, chez Rapilly, Quai Mala-quais No. 5 et chez les principaux Marchands d'Estampes. Droit de la traduction réservée. Paris.   1869
    4to, three quarters morocco, gold edges, bound by Alfred Matthews. Seventy-three fine plates.

*Recherches sur les Cartes à Jouer et sur leur fabrication en Belgique depuis l'année 1379 jusqu'à la fin du XVIII Siècle. Par Alexandre Pinchart, chef de section aux archives générales du royaume. Bruxelles.   1870
    8vo, half morocco, bound by Mansell, successor to Hayday.

Mœurs, Usages et Costumes au Moyen Age. Paul Lacroix. Paris: Firmin Didot frères, fils et Cie.   1871
    8vo, first edition, with 15 fine lithographic plates and numerous illustrations in the text. Handsomely bound by Rivière in full morocco extra, the back and sides richly gilt tooled to a Grolieresque design, g.e.

Cartes Numérales à jouer. Par Étienne Charavay. Revue des Documents Historiques. May, 1873, Paris.
    8vo, paper cover.

*The Origin and Manufacture of Playing Cards. By George Clulow, F.R.G.S. A paper read before the Society of Arts, on May 8, 1889, London.
    Folio, three quarters cloth.

Histoire du Jeu de Cartes en Normandie. Par M. L. Chanoine Davranches. Rouen.
    8vo, original paper cover.   1892

The Devil's Picture Books, a history of Playing Cards. By Mrs. John King Van Rensselaer. Illustrated. New York. Dodd, Mead and Company.   1893
    8vo, cloth. Illustrated.

Recherches sur la Fabrication des Cartes à Jouer à Troyes. Par Louis Morin. Troyes: Imprimerie et Lithographie Paul Nouel.   1899
    8vo, original paper wrapper. Autographed, presentation copy from the author. Sixteen lithographed plates in black and white.

Recherches sur la Fabrication des Cartes à Jouer à Troyes. Par Louis Morin.
    8vo, three quarters vellum.

Un Atelier de Peintres Dominotiers à Troyes. Par Louis Morin. Paris.   1899
    8vo, original paper binding, uncut.

Les Cartes à Jouer Lyonnais. H. R. d'Allemagne. Extrait Revue d'Histoire de Lyon.
    8vo, original paper cover, uncut.   1906

Les Cartes à Jouer du Quatorzième au Vingtième Siècle. Par Henry René d'Alle-
    magne. Contenant 3200 réproductions de cartes, dont 956 en couleur, 12 planches
    hors texte coloriées à aquarelle, 25 phototypies, 116 enveloppés illustrées pour jeux de
    cartes et 340 vignettes et vues diverses. Deux tomes. Paris: Librairie Hachette et
    Cie.   1906
    Folio, gold edges.

Histoire de la Carte à Jouer en Guienne. Alexandre Nicolai. Bordeaux: Feret et Fils.
    4to, three quarters vellum. Excellent illustrations. 1 plate in colors. 1911

The Origin and History of Playing Cards. Stanley A. Cohen. New York.   1916
    16mo, three quarters morocco, g.e.

The Game of Ma Jong; its origin and significance. By Stewart Culin. Reprinted from
    The Brooklyn Museum Quarterly, October, 1924.
    This contains illustrations and the history of the Korean and Chinese playing
    cards of earliest times.
    8vo, original paper cover. Autographed.

Prophetical, Educational and Playing Cards by Mrs. John King Van Rensselaer. Phil-
    adelphia: George W. Jacobs & Co.   Illustrated.   1912
    8vo, cloth binding, gold edges.

Von der Spielkarte und von Kartenmacherhandwerke. By A. Bertelsson in Heft 10, Offset
    Buch and Werbe Kunst. Leipzig. Many illustrations, some in color. Also 'Kinder-
    spielkarten' by Siegfried Berg, and 'Maler and Drucktechnik. By Th. Kurth, in the
    same book.   1925
    Folio, original paper cover.

Playing Cards of all Nations. By W. G. Bowdoin, in the Metropolitan Magazine, illus-
    trated.
    8vo, paper.

A Pack of Cards; its Stories, Legends and Romances. The Strand Magazine.
    8vo, illustrated.

The Wood Cut Playing Card. By Cyril G. E. Bunt, in 'The Woodcut. An Annual. No.
    II.' No. 6, Édition de Luxe. London: The Fleuron, Ltd.   1928
    4to, on hand-made paper, uncut, gold top, many illustrations.

CONCERNING COLLECTIONS OF PLAYING CARDS

*Die Aeltesten Deutschen Spielkarten des Koniglichen Kupferstich Cabinets zu Dres-
    den von Max Lehrs, Directorial Assistent am Koniglichen Kupferstich. Cabinet
    mit 29 Tafeln in Lichtdruck. Dresden.   No date
    Folio, three quarters calf, gold lines. Bound by Roger de Coverly and Sons.

*Jeux de Cartes Tarots et de Cartes Numérales, du quatorzième au dix-huitième siècle.
    representés en cent planches d'après les Originaux avec un précis historique et
    explicatif. Publiés par la Société des Bibliophiles Français. À Paris de l'imprimerie
    de Crapelet. Par Jean Duchesne, Aîné.   1844
    Contains hand-illumined reproductions of the seventeen tarot cards in the Li-

brairie Nationale, which were painted by Jacques Grigonneur for Charles VI of France in 1392. Also reproductions of fifty tarots from Italy, the so-called tarots de Mantegna from copper plates, together with facsimiles of other rare cards in the collection at the Librairie Nationale in Paris. Only thirty-two copies of this book with these illustrations were printed.

Folio, three quarters brown morocco. Ex Libris George Clulow.

*Die Spielkarten der Weigel'schen Sammlung, mit 8 facsimile. (Two of these are hand-illumined.) T. O. Weigel. Leipzig. 1865
Folio.

Histoire de l'Imagerie Populaire et des Cartes à Jouer à Chartres. Par J. M. Garnier. Chartres: Imprimerie de Garnier. 1869
12mo, three quarters morocco. Illustrated.

A Catalogue of Playing and Other Cards in the British Museum, accompanied by a concise general history of the subject. By William Hughes Willshire, M.D. Edinburgh: Printed by order of the Trustees. 1876
4to, cloth. Illustrated.

*Die Sammlung der Spielkarten des Bairischen Nationalmuseums von K. A. Bierdimpff. Offizielle Ausgabe. Munchen. 1884
12mo, three quarters calf, bound by Root and Son.

*Playing Cards in Nuremberg. Katalog der im germanischen Museum befindlichen Kartenspiele und Spielkarten. Foreword by A. Essenwein. Nuremberg: Privately printed by the Museum. 1886
4to, three quarters calf, gold lines and edges, bound by Ramage. Forty plates.

*Recherches sur les Cartiers et les Cartes à Jouer à Grenoble. Par Edmond Maignien, Conservateur de la Bibliothèque de Grenoble, correspondant du Ministère de l'instruction publique. Grenoble. 1887
8vo, three quarters calf, gold edges, bound by Ramage. Ten plates, five in color.

Chess and Playing Cards. A catalogue of the games and implements exhibited by the United States National Museum at the exposition at Atlanta, 1895. The Government Printing Office, Washington. 1898
8vo, three quarters crimson morocco. Illustrated.
A second copy in a paper cover.

Playing cards of various ages and countries, selected from the Collection of Lady Charlotte Schreiber. Three volumes, containing 442 plates. Foreword and description by A. Wollaston Franks. London: John Murray, Albemarle Street. 1892–1895
Folio, half red morocco.

A catalogue of the H. D. Phillips Collection of Playing Cards, now in Stationers' Hall, London. Three volumes, typewritten. 1903
4to, paper.

Descriptive catalogue of playing cards exhibited by Mr. George Clulow, illustrative of his lecture before the Bath Literary and Philosophical Association, March 25, 1892
8vo, paper.

'Whitney Collection of Playing Cards,' in the Harvard Alumni Bulletin, Nov. 10, 1927. Cambridge.
8vo, paper, illustrated.

The Worshipful Company of Makers of Playing Cards. List of the Master, Wardens, Court of Assistants, Officers and the Livery of the Company, with preface by the clerk. London. 1927
12mo, paper.

CONCERNING THE MAKING OF PLAYING CARDS

*L'art du Cartier. Explication de six planches, avec quelques details particuliers de l'art, pour servir de supplement à l'article 'Cartes' du Dictionnaire.　　　　1760?
　　This is a section from the 'Encyclopedie des arts et Mètiers' of Duhamel de Monceau, and has an interesting synopsis of the terms used by the card-makers of France of the eighteenth century. The carefully drawn diagrams of the implements used convey an accurate idea of the simplicity of the old methods of manufacture.
　　12mo, three quarters calf, bound by Roger de Coverly and Sons.

The same, unbound.
　　Folio.

*Die Kunst Karten zu Machen von Herrn du Hamel de Monceau. Aus den Franzsischen der Descriptions des arts et metiers uberfetz von Johann Heinrich Gottlob von Justi. Berlin, Stettin und Leipzig: Johann Heinrich Rudigern.　　　　1764
　　8vo, three quarters red mottled calf, bound by Ramage.

*Nouveau Manuel Complet du Cartonnier, du Cartier et du fabricant de Cartonnages ou l'art faire toutes sortes de Cartons, de Cartonnages et de Cartes à Jouer, &c. Par M. Lebrun. Paris.　　　　1845
　　16mo.

Recherches sur la Fabrication des Cartes à Jouer à Angoulême. Par Paul Mourier. Angoulême, Imprimerie L. Coquemard & Cie.　　　　1904
　　12mo, original paper cover. 7 plates of illustrations.

The History of a Success. Copyright, 1896, by the United States Printing Company. Cincinnati. Illustrated.
　　16mo, original paper cover.

CONCERNING DESIGNS FOR PLAYING CARDS AND THEIR BACKS

*Etchings of P. Benner, a miniature painter of South Germany who studied and worked with Isabey in the late 18th and early 19th century. There are impressions each $3\frac{3}{8}'' \times 1\frac{7}{8}''$ on sheets $15'' \times 11''$, of 16 card designs, one numeral and three court cards of each suit. The court cards are full-length figures in the costume of the fifteenth century, and are very Flemish in character. The king of hearts is signed. The whole is in a leather-bound portfolio.
　　Folio.

An article by Walter Morley on English duty stamps, with illustrations of three duty aces, one of Ireland in 1783, one of Hunt and Sons, a Great Mogul with the government stamp on his breast, evidently unique, and a duty ace of 1806.

*Original Designs for the backs of Playing Cards by Owen Jones. An extraordinarily handsome binding by Zaehnsdorf. 'Ex Bibliotheca Chartarum Ludorum — George Clulow — 1885.' There is a box of polished wood to hold the book, with a bronze plate inset upon the lid, inscribed 'Original Designs by Owen Jones.'
　　Folio, full blue morocco with gold lines, lined with full calf, stamped borders, g.e.

Sample Book. 1877–78. De la Rue. London.
　　4to.

Sample Book. 1879. Goodall. London.
　　Small 16mo, original cloth binding.

Sample Book. 1898–99. Goodall. London.
　　8vo, three quarters black morocco.

Scrapbook of card designs, both faces and backs. Many of them artist's proofs. Andrew Dougherty. New York. 1878
 Folio, three quarters black morocco.

Sample Book. A. Dougherty Playing Cards. New York. 1890
 Small 16mo, original cloth binding.

Catalogue of the Standard Playing Card Manufacturing Co. Chicago. 1907
 Small 16mo.

Scrapbook. Samples of National Playing Cards. No date
 8vo, original cloth binding.

Sample Book. United States Playing Cards. Russell, Morgan & Co., Cincinnati.
 Small 16mo, original half cloth binding. 1881

Catalogue, United States and National Playing Cards. Sample Book B. Cincinnati.
 4to, full morocco binding, crimson. 1896

Sample Book. United States Playing Cards and National Playing Cards. Cincinnati.
 Small 16mo, original binding, half cloth. 1897

Catalogue, United States, National Playing Cards. Sample book C. Cincinnati. 1898
 4to, full black morocco, original binding.

Catalogue 5, United States Playing Cards, National Playing Cards. Cincinnati. 1901
 Small 16mo.

Sample Book. The United States Playing Card Company. Cincinnati. 1904
 8vo, three quarters black morocco.

Sample book of Playing Cards manufactured by The United States Playing Card Company. Cincinnati. No date
 8vo.

CONCERNING ANCIENT 'CARDS FOR PLAYING'

*Deutsches Miniertes Kartenspiel 1440–1445. A portfolio containing fifty-two photographic reproductions, $7\frac{1}{2} \times 4\frac{3}{4}''$, of cards painted in Stuttgart. This is a hunting series, the suit signs being stags, dogs, ducks and falcons. The court cards are in the costume of the early fifteenth century and a banner replaces the ten of each suit.
 4to.

*Trappola Cards. Fifteenth Century. Schöngauer.
 A volume containing facsimiles by Ottley of the rare series of German cards No. 28, of the collection of The United States Playing Card Company.
 4to, three quarters red morocco, g.e.

Fascimiles of Rare and Curious Engravings by William Young Ottley. A collection of 129 reprints of early masters of the Italian, German, and Flemish schools, illustrative of the history of engraving. India proof plates, including the set of 47 pomegranate cards of the fifteenth century, a portrait of Virgil Solis, a Game of Chess by the master of 1466, and Two Soldiers playing at Cards by Jacob Binck, c. 1530. London: Longmans, Rees, Orme, etc. 1828
 Folio, uncut, gold top, three quarters vellum.

Proof-sheets of cards of Andreas Benedictus Gobl of Munich. Second half of the eighteenth century. 4 vols. Folio, contemporary binding of marbled paper.

Zeko Cards. Black Forest. A pack of 53 cards, 21 atouts and 32 numeral and court cards, bound in a little book. The cards were made by C. L. Wust in Frankfort. c. 1860
 Ex Libris George Clulow. There is also a bookplate of Sidney Williams, a crest, and his name. Small 16mo, three quarters olive calf.

*Playing Cards.   1862
    A pack of the usual playing cards with backs designed by Owen Jones, made by de
    la Rue in London. Bound in a little book. The bookplate of Sydney Williams is in
    this book.
    Small 16mo, three quarters red calf, full gilt back.

*Cards for the Blind. A pack of Stralsund piquet cards perforated according to the
    Braille system, bound in a little book with an explanatory diagram in manuscript.
    The bookplate of Sydney Williams is in this book; also a small bookplate, G.C. in
    monogram (probably George Clulow).   *c.* 1884
    Small 16mo, three quarters calf.

*Peculiar Playing Cards. By George Clulow. From the Strand Magazine, January and
    February,   1893
    1 vol. 8vo. Illustrated.

Playing cards; past and present. The Stationery Trades' Journal, October,   1909
    Also, interview with Mr. Louis Coffin, United States Playing Card Company.
    8vo, paper.

CONCERNING TAROTS

*Dialogo de Givoche che nelle Vegghie Sanesi si vsano di fare del materiale intronato. All'
    illustrissima et excellentissima Signora Donna Isabella de Medici Orsini, Duchessa
    di Braciano. Appresso Bertano. In Venetia.   1575
    Contains the earliest printed account of the game of Tarocchi.
    Small 16mo, pressed green morocco with gold lines, bound by Root and Son.

The same. In Venetia: Presso Daniel Zanetti.   1598
    Small 16mo, original vellum binding.

*Giuoco di Carte, con nuova forma di Tarrocchini. Intaglio in Roma di Giuseppe Maria
    Mitelli. Dedicato dall' istesso. All' Illustriss: Sig Co: Filippo del gia' Co: Pros-
    pero Bentivoglio Illmo Sig^r Co: mio Sig^r. e Pron Col:^{mo} *c.* 1725
    Folio, three quarters crimson morocco.
    There are seven sheets, one being the dedication page. Each of the other sheets is
    lettered at the top 'Gioco di Carte di Tarocchini,' and at the lower right-hand corner
    is the name of the designer and engraver, Giuseppe Maria Mitelli, Inv: Dis. e Int.
    This is a complete set of the sixty-two cards of the Tarochini of Bologna. (See No. 29,
    The Collection of the United States Playing Card Company.)

*L'Utile col diletto o sia Geographia Intrecciata nel Giuoco de Tarocchi con le insegne
    degl' illustrissimi, et Eccelsi Signori Gonfalonieri ed Anziani de Bologna. Dal 1670,
    fino 1725. Dedicato al Nobil Uono Sig. Marchese Gio: Paolo Pepoli. In Bologna per il
    Bianchi alla Rosa, con licenza de' Superiori.   1725
    Translation of the manuscript note at the end of the book:
    'This little book being very rare must not be separated from the whole pack of
    playing cards engraved by Giuseppe Maria Mitelli. The rarity of both (book and
    cards) consists in this, that in the year 1725, in which year it was printed, it was also
    prohibited the preserving, as the use and sale of it were also prohibited under the
    penalty of from seven to ten years' imprisonment for the people and of five years'
    banishment to the Forte Urbano for the nobility. Observe the work "Memorie" con-
    cerning the history of the calculation by the Commendatore Conte Leopold Cico-
    gnara — Prato Giachetti 1831 in 8 with Atlante — where at page 138 he wishes to
    describe and analyze the Tarocchi of Mitelli and at page 240 is reported the Bando of
    proscription that bears the date of 12 September, 1725, a few months after the publica-
    tion of the incriminated little book in spite of the obtained permission. The Conte Cico-

gnara said that Giuseppe Maria Mitelli engraved with much elegance this game (in our collection signed B) and he put so much taste in it that we may call it one of his best productions. Perhaps il Cicognara did not know that G. M. Mitelli had already engraved another game of Tarocchi completed in 62 cards signed A (in our collection) which for its beauty and invention is much superior to the other above mentioned. In our collection is also to be found another pack of cards numbering 40, called Passatempo, distinguished with the letter C and engraved by the same Giuseppe Maria Mitelli in the year 1690. From the same witty author (and from his father Agostino), the writer possesses ten different books which contain more than a hundred of their engravings. Bologna, 1852. Michelangelo Gualandi.'

Small 16mo, full calf with gold lines, gold dentelles, binding by Ramage.

*Istruzioni Necessario per chi Volesse impare il Giuoco dilettevole delli Tarocchini di Bologna. In Bologna per Ferdinando Pisarri all' Insegna di S. Antonio con licenza de' Superiori.   1754

12mo, three quarters crimson morocco, bound by Tout.

*Jeu des Tarots, ou l'on traite de son origine ou on explique des Allegories & ou l'on fait voir qu'il est la source de nos Cartes modernes à jouer. Par Court de Gebelin. Paris.   1781

8vo, three quarters morocco.

*Le Regole per ben Giocare a Tarocco ossia osservazioni pratiche sopra detto Gioco, opera medita de celebre Autore, ALMANACCO. In Brescia.   per l'anno 1787

16mo, contemporary binding in a pull-off case of morocco.

*Tarok. (Translation from Manuscript of Benner.) In Hungarian. Foreword in French signed Montesquieu.   No date, but about 1820

16mo, three quarters French mottled calf, bound by Ramage.

*Beknopte Handleiding tot het Tarok-Spel. Amsterdam: P. Roos.   1846

16mo, g.e., three quarters French mottled calf, binding by Ramage.

The Key to the Tarot. Oracles behind the Veil. Dr. L. W. de Lawrence. Chicago. Illustrated.   1916

8vo, cloth, g.e.

CONCERNING CARDS FOR DIVINATION AND FORTUNE TELLING

*Le Ingeniose Sorti composte per Francesco Marcolini da Forli, intitulate Giardino di Pensieri. Nouamente Ristampate, e in Nouo et Bellissimo Ordine Riformate MDL (Colophon). In Venetia per Francesco Marcolini da Forli ne glianni del Signore MDL. Del mese di Luglio (sic). Con Privilegio. Venice.   1550

This rare book affords evidence of the elaborate use of playing cards for divinatory purposes early in the sixteenth century. The work is sought by iconophilists for its woodcuts after the designs of Giuseppe Porta, or Salviati, which are ranked among the best examples of the Italian wood engraver of the period. Besides the frontispiece, it contains ninety-nine woodcuts which are emblematic of the virtues and follies of mankind and of the sayings and doctrines of the ancient moralists and philosophers. Under each design there are explanatory verses in triolets. The title-page is copied from a print of Marco di Ravenna with minor alterations in detail, as the tablet, which in the print is quite plain, has in the frontispiece the lettering 'Joseph Porta, Garfagnino,' and the open book, which in the print bears astronomical characters, has in the copy what is intended as a page of Marcolini's book. The cards used by Marcolini are the king, knight, knave, ten, nine, eight, seven, two and ace of denari, and the system of divination is described in the preceding pages.

Folio, full crimson morocco, gold lines, g.e., bound by Root & Son.

*Il Laberinto del Clarissimo Signor Andrea Ghisi. Nel qual si contiene una bellissima & artificiosa tessitura di due milla ducento sessanta Figure, che aprendolo tre volte, con facilita si puo saper qual figura si sia immaginata. Al Serenissimo Don Francesco Gonzaga Prencipe di Mantoua. In Venetia M.DC.VII. Appresso Francesco Rampazetto.   1607

There is the dedication to the Prince of Mantua, and thereafter follows a double page of wood block prints, each two inches square, and each emblematic of some vice or virtue. There is a double page of these prints for each letter of the alphabet, the same prints being repeated at times, but their order changed. There is an epilogue in verse, in praise of the author.

Folio, bound in the original vellum.

*Le Passetemps de la Fortune des Ingénieusements, compilé par Maistre Laurens l'Esprit pour response de vingt questions par plusieurs coustumièrement faites & désirées sçauoir. Les vingt questions sont specifiées en la Roüe de Fortune, au feuillet sequent. À Paris: Chez Charles Sevestre sur le Pont-neuf, vis à vis la Samaritaine.   1634

A bookplate of the arms of the Marquis d'Entragnes. Original binding of contemporary calf, with stamped arms in gold in the center of each side. Many interesting wood engravings. Small 8vo.

*Das Zeit Kurtzende Lust und Spiel Haus in Welchen der Curiose Kunstler &c, &c, &c. Des Galanten Frauenzimmers curioses Jahr Tag Stunden und Traum Buch auf Befehl einer Hohen person gedruckt. Zu Kunstburain Liesin Jahr Kunstberg.   1680

Fourteen parts in one volume, thick 12mo, Gothic letter, curious plates, original stamped hogskin. Ex Libris George Clulow, F.R.G.S.

*Giardino dei Pensieri composta da Francesco Marcolini da Forli. L'anno MDL Ristampato nel MDCCLXXXIV.   1784

Folio, full crimson morocco, gold lines, g.e. Wood engravings.

Prefixed to this reprint of the curious 'Giardino dei Pensieri' of Marcolini da Forli is a portrait of Marcolini and on the reverse of the title-page an eagle with a banner, inscribed 'Copia III.' The portrait is lettered 'Ios Daniotto tot hoc Opus Sculp.' The designs of the cards and the illustrations on each page are copied from the 1550 edition, but are from copper plates, the text being letterpress. There is an epilogue in triolets, eulogistic of 'del gran Daniotto,' from which one gathers there were but thirty-six copies of this reprint.

*Le Bohémien, contenant L'Art de Tirer les Cartes, suivi de L'Art d'Escamoter. Et de l'application des Rêves aux numéros de la Loterie. À Paris: Chez Pigoreau, Libraire, place Saint-Germain-l'Auxerrois. An six de la République.

Le Tireur de Cartes ou Le Cartonomancien, qui démontre toutes les manieres de tirer les cartes usitées par les personnes qui s'amusent à dire la bonne avanture. À Paris: Chez Deroy Libraire, rue du Cimetière — André — des — Arts, No. 15. An cinquième.   1797

Small 16mo, French mottled calf, gold borders and inside dentelles, g.e. and uncut. Frontispiece, wood engraving.

*L'Oracle Parfait, ou Nouvelle Manière de Tirer les Cartes, au moyen de laquelle chacun peut tirer son horoscope. Avec Figures. On a placé à la fin le Traité de marques naturelles du corps, par Melampus, ancien auteur Grec. À Paris: Chez Blanchon, Libraire, rue du Battoir, Nos. 1 et 2.   1802

12mo, three quarters pressed morocco, uncut. Diagrams.

*Aphorismen über den Kuss ein Weihnachtgeschenk für die Kusslustige und Kussgerechte Welt von einem Spiritus Asper. Mit 10 herzlichen Kupfern. Leipzig, gedruckt und verlegt von C. A. Solbrig.   1808

Small 16mo, full pressed brown morocco, gold lines, insides dentelles, bound by Ramage, g.e.

*Manuel des Sorcières ou Cours de Recréations Physiques, Mathématiques, Tours de Cartes et de Gibecière: suivi des Jeux de Société, quatrième édition, mise dans un nouvel ordre, et augmentée de plusieurs Tours, Jeux à gages et pénitences. Avec Figures. A Paris: Chez Ferra jeune, libraire, Rue des Grands Augustins, No. 23; Delaunay, Libraire, Palais Royal Galerie de Bois, No. 243. Fourth edition. 1815
16mo, three quarters mottled French calf, bound by Ramage. Engraved frontispiece.

*Vier Farben. The meaning and symbolism of the German playing cards explained by Susanna Rümpler, Kartenschlagerin. Leipzig. 1829
16mo, mottled calf, bound by Ramage. Inside dentelles. Lithographed frontispiece. Hand-colored illustrations of a pack of German cards.

The Dreamer's Sure Guide, or the Interpretation of Dreams faithfully Revealed. New York: Elton and Harrison. 1837
16mo, numerous wood block illustrations, the frontispiece hand-colored. 62 pages, yellowed and worn. No cover.

*Sibylle, die gewandte Kartenschlagerin, oder neuester Schickfalsprophet, mit 7 lithografirten Tabellen. Nürnberg, 1839
16mo, three quarters calf, bound by Ramage.

*Bibliothèque du Destin, L'Art de tirer les Cartes, révélations complètes sur les destinées au moyen des Cartes et des Tarots après les méthodes les plus certaines, suivé d'un jeu des patiences. Par Johannes Trismegiste, orné de 150 figures. Paris. 1843
In the same volume are (1) L'art d'expliquer les Songes. Par Johannes Trismegiste. Bruxelles. 1844

L'Art de Connaitre l'Avenir, par la Chiromancie, les Horoscopes, les Divinations Anciennes, le marc de café, &c. Par Johannes Trismegiste. Bruxelles. 1845
Small 16mo, red mottled French calf, gold dentelles, bound by Ramage.

*Tales of the Mountains; or Sojourns in Eastern Belgium. The Prophetess of Embourg. Volume the Second. London: William Pickering. 1851
16mo, three quarters French mottled calf, bound by Ramage.

*L'Art et la Manière de se Tirer les Cartes Soimême, les Mystères de la Cartomancie dévoilés par Mlle. Le Normand. Méthode de la plus facile pour connâitre le présent, le passé, l'avenir et la personne qui vous aime. Paris. c. 1850
16mo, three quarters calf. Folded plate with diagrams.

Wahrsage kunst, von Mlle. Le Normand. Wien. 1856
An explanation of the fortune-telling cards No. 223, the collection of The United States Playing Card Company.
Small 16mo, paper.

*Manuel de Cartomancie ou l'Art de Tirer les Cartes, mis à la Portée de tous illustré de 132 figures explicatives par Esmael. Paris: Garnier Frères, Librairies, Editeurs, 6 Rue des Saints Pères. 1875
On the title-page is written, 'À Monsieur Georges Clulow, à Londres, 1878.'
Small 12mo, three quarters calf, contemporary binding, back beautifully tooled. Illustrated.

Fortune Telling by Cards. By I. B. Prangley. Illustrated. London: L. Upcott Gill, 170, Strand, W.C. 1899
16mo, three quarters calf.

*Astaroth. L'avenir dévoilé par les cartes, contenant La Divination par les cartes, etc. Paris: Librairie de Theodore Lefevre et Cie, rue des Poitevins. Illustrated.
Small 12mo, three quarters calf, bound by Ramage. No date

*Mutter Hulda. Die untruglische Wahrsagern und allezeitgertige Kartenschlagerin eine angenehme Winterabenden. Halle, gedruckt und zu haben bei W. Plotz. No date
Small 16mo, French mottled calf, three quarters, bound by Ramage. Engravings.

*Chap Books. The Dreamer's Oracle; Fortune Telling by Cards; Napoleon's Book of Fate.
12mo, three quarters calf, gilt top. No date

*Wahrsagekunst aus den Linien der Hand die kunst des Kartenschlagens, etc. Mit 8 Abbildungen. Leipzig: Friedrich Voigts Buchhandlung. No date
Small 16mo, three quarters calf, bound by Ramage.

Fortune Telling with Playing Cards. Cincinnati. The United States Playing Card Company. 1923
12mo, paper.

Soo Fan, the Oriental fortune-telling game. 1924
12mo, paper.

CONCERNING EDUCATIONAL AND PICTORIAL CARDS

*Murner (T.). Logica memorativa Chartiludium Logice, siue totius dialectice memoria: & novus Petri hyspani textus emendatus: Cum iucundo pictasmatis exercitio: Eruditi viri. f. Thome Murner Argentini. In fine: Argentine Johannes Gruninger impressit. Anno MDIX.
12mo, full straight grain morocco, three line gold fillet border, inside dentelles, g.e., bound by Blaise, 68 rue du Bac. From the Didot library, g.e. Fine copy with large margins. Excessively rare. The work contains 52 full-page woodcuts. Manuscript note on the fly leaf: 'Jeu de Cartes inventé par Thomas Murner, professeur de l'Université de Cracovie, pour servir à l'enseignement de la Logique: Strasbourg, 1509, 2me édition non moins rare que la 1ere, qui est de Cracovie, 1507. Rien de plus bisarre peut-être, et tout fois rien de plus curieuse que cette fantaisie doctorale, dont l'auteur faillit d'être brulé comme sorcier. C'est le plus ancien exemple connu de l'application du jeu de Cartes à l'instruction élémentaire.
Mes Nouvelles Études historiques sur les Cartes à Jouer. Paris, 1842.'

*Murner. Chartiludiu Institute sumarie doctore Thoma Murner memorante et ludente . . . (At the end) Impressum Argentinae per Iohannem Prus, Impensis ac sumptibus circuspecti uiri Iohannis Knoblauch. Anno Salutis nostrae M.D.XVIII. (Strasbourg.)
Small 4to, numerous woodcuts, full red morocco in the Janseniste style, g.e. by Hardy. Fine copy of rare edition from the Didot Collection.

*Das Geistliche Teutsche Carten Spil. Das ist: Ausfuhrliche Erzehlung was massen das Israelitische Volck im Alten Testament so wunderlich vermischt und hin und wieder getrieben worden; Auch was sich mit Demselben und Anderen im Alt und Neuen Testament Merckwurdiges hat zugetragen. In Vier Thail: Das ist in die Herz — Schell — Brun — und Aichel — Farb abgetheilt und mit 32 schonen Kupffern gezieret; Allwo alle Blatter insonderheit ausgelegt und mit beygesetzter Moral — oder Sitten Lehr durch Geist und Weltliche Historien und Geschichten Spruch — und Reim — Verfassungen explicirt und geziert; Auch so wol unter als nach dem Essen auf dem Tisch oder auf der Cantz konnen aufgelegt werden den himmlischen Groschen zu gewinnen. Durch den Viel — Ehrwurdigen und Wolgelehrten Herrn Andream Strobl Des Hoch Lobl. U.L.F. Collegiat Stifft Lauffen investirten Chor-Herrn und Seniorem, zusammen gemischt &c. Zu besserem Gebrauch der Herren

Prediger ist ein eignes Register und Predig — Buchl hinzugesetzt worden. Der I.
Thail oder die Hertz Farb. Zum andernmal gedruckt. Sultzbach. In Verlegung
Peter Paul Bleuel Kunst und Buchhandlern Und zu finden bey Johann Ziegern.

Anno 1603

After the preface, which ends, 'Omnia ad majorem DEI Deiparaeque gloriam,'
there is a page:

'Ex Mandato Reverendissimi Archi-Episcopalis Consistorii Salisburgensis
Spiritualem Lusum Cartifoliorum quadripartitum ab Andrea Strobl Canonico
Curato in Laussen, Germanico Idiomate conscriptum, diligenter per legi, & in eo nihil
Orthodoxe fidei aut bonis moribus contrarium reperi, proinde illum non tantum ut
typis mandetur, sed etiam ut saepius Ecclesiasticorn & Saecularium manibus teratur
dignum censeo. Datum Hallinae, 5 Februarii 1685.

Nicolaus Daval,
I.U. Licentiatus Cellsissimi Reverendissimi
Principis & Archi-Episcopi Salisburgens.
Consiliarius Consistorialis.'

The thirty-two illustrations, which are finely engraved from copper, are of Bible
stories, with the suit sign unobtrusively but unfailingly shown.

Small 8vo, very thick, beautiful early paper, contemporary binding of oak boards
covered with pig-skin, the sides with center panels and stamped borders. Two clasps.
Title-page in red black, Gothic type.

*Chartiludium Logicae seu Logica Poetica vel Memorativa. R–P. Th: Murner Ar-
gent ord: Minorum. Opus quod centum amplius annos in tenebris latuit Erutum
& in appertam faculi huiusce curiosi lucem productum. Opera, Notis, & Conjecturis.
Joan. Balesdens in Senatu Gal. Ad. Paris, Apud Tussanum du Bray, via Jacobaea,
sub Spicis maturis. Cum Privilegio Regis. M.D.C. XXIX.

This is a reprint of the original text of the Strasbourg edition of 1509 with the notes
of Balesdens, the curious woodcuts being reproduced in smaller size.

16mo, g.e., full pressed morocco, inside dentelles in gold. Foliated wreath in gold in
center of each side.

*Cartes des Rois de France. Jeu des Reynes Renommées. Paris: Chez Henry le Gras,
Libraire, au 3e pilier de la grande Salle du Palais.   1644

The 52 cards of each set with title card, are bound together in a little book.

16mo, contemporary binding of French mottled calf, gilt floriated back.

*Géographie. A set of proofs of the fifty-two cards in the first state of the plates before the
suit signs were added. Bound in a little book.

16mo, contemporary binding of French mottled calf, gilt floriated back and edges.

*Jeux Historiques des Rois de France, Reines Renommées, Géographie et métamor-
phose. Par seu Mr J. Desmarests Conseiller, Secretaire & Contrôlleur Général de
l'Extraordinaire des Guerres. Et gravez par Do la Bella. Ces mêmes Jeux sont ac-
commodés en cartes faciles à jouer, & se vendront séparément. À Paris: Chez Nicolas
le Clerc sur le Quay des Augustins, à la descente du Pont S. Michel, près l'hôtel de
Luynes, à l'image S. Lambert, et chez Florent le Comte, rue S. Jacques, près la Fon-
taine S. Benoist, au Chiffre Royal. Avec Privilége du Roy.   1698

16mo, contemporary binding of mottled French calf, floriated gilt back.

There are two bookplates, one of George Clulow, the other an unknown crest, with
the motto 'Sitio Justitiam.' Like the two preceding books, this one also contains
the cards of two of the games devised by Desmarests to interest the young Louis XIV
in his lessons, and which were illustrated by della Bella, the Florentine engraver.
This book contains the pages of 'Avis au Lecteur,' followed by the title card and the
other 52 of the series of the Jeu des Fables, and likewise the title card and the other
52 of the Jeu de Géographie.

England exactly described, or a Guide to Travellers in a compleat sette of mapps of counties of England. 44 tables and maps engraved by Richard Blome, according to Mr. Ogilby's survey. London.   *c.* 1650
    Narrow 8vo, covered with Anatolic embroidery in colored silks and gold and silver threads.

*Das Astronomische Kartenspiel. Nürnberg.   1656
    A little book explaining the astronomical cards (No. 741, the collection of The United States Playing Card Company).
    There is one engraving, two separate little engraved discs, one representing the earth and the other its orbit, loosely sewed to the page in the space left for it.
    Small 16mo, in full red levant morocco, with inside dentelles in gold, g.e.

*Jeu d'Armoiries de l'Europe; pour apprendre le Blason, la Géographie, et l'Histoire curieuse. Par C. F. de Brianville Mont-Dauphin. Dédié à Monsieur d'Hozier. À Lyon: Chez Benoist Coral, Libraire en rue Merciéré à la Victoire. Avec Priviége du Roy.   1659
    Small 16mo, full red morocco, gold lines, g.e., bound by Root & Son. Engraved frontispiece. This is a description of the cards No. 801, the collection of The United States Playing Card Company.

*Jeu d'Armoiries des Souverains et etats d'Europe, pour apprendre le Blason, la Géographie, & l'Histoire curieuse. Dédié à son Altesse Royale de Savoye. Par C. Oronce Finé, dit de Brianville, Conseiller & Aumônier du Roy. Troisième édition, revue, corrigée & augmentée. À Lyon: Chez Benoist Coral, rue Merciere, à la Victoire. Avec Privilége du Roy.   1665
    Small 16mo, full blue morocco, gold lines and edges. Engraved frontispiece and explanatory plate. This book also describes the cards No. 801.

*Jeu d'Armoiries des Souverains & etats d'Europe, pour apprendre le Blason, la Géographie, & l'Histoire curieuse. Dédié à Son Altesse Royale de Savoye. Par C. Oronce Finé, dit de Brianville, Conseiller et Aumônier du Roi. Huitième édition, revue, corrigée & augmentèe. À Lyon: Chez B. Coral; se vend à Amsterdam, chez Pierre Mortier, Libraire sur le Vygendam, à la ville de Paris.
    Small 16mo, contemporary binding of vellum. Engraved frontispiece and explanatory plate. This also relates to the cards No. 801.

Libro y Baraja Nuevos, e Inseparables, para la Academia, y Juego de Armerías, de los Escudos de Armas de las quatro Monarquías mayores, con sus Provincias, Reyes, Principes, Estados, Republicas, Islas, y Casas Soberanas de Europa: para aprender el Blason, la Geographía, y la Historia, muy util, y essential para toda la Nobleza: Dispuesto y recopilado de varios Authores por D. Francisco Gazán, Empleado por S. M. en la Corte. Segunda Impression, corregida y enmendada. Con Licencia y Privilegio. En Madrid. En la Imprenta de Antonio Marin.   Año de 1748
    16mo, contemporary mottled Spanish calf. Two folding plates. The frontispiece, five card players, the others the usual plate of heraldic emblems, common to all the books descriptive of the de Brianville heraldry, of which this is the Spanish edition.
    With this is a complete pack of the cards in a mottled calf case, matching the book. The cards have the Spanish suit signs, cups for the arms of Germany, swords for Spain, batons for France, and coins for Italy. El Rey de Oros carries the papal arms of Clemente XII.

*Explanatory Notes of a pack of Cavalier Playing Cards, Temp. Charles II. Forming a complete political satire of the Commonwealth, by Edmund Goldsmid, F.R.H.S. F.S.A. (Scot). Edinburgh: E. &. G. Goldsmid.   1886
    8vo, reproductions and descriptions of the cards in our series No. 35.

*Het Gheestelijck Kaertspel met Herten Troef oft t'Spel der Liefde door den Eerw. Pater F. Ioseph a S. Barbara Carmelit Discals. t'Antwerpen. By P. J. Rymers op de groote Merckt in de Pauw. The third edition. 1666

(The Spiritual Card game with hearts trumps, or the Game of Love, by Father Joseph of Saint Barbara, a Barefoot Carmelite.) We are indebted to the Reverend Father Bronsgeest of Saint Xavier's for a translation of much of this book. There is a dedication dated June 10, 1666, and six ecclesiastical approvals throughout the same year.

Engraved frontispiece and illustrations of these Biblical cards.

16mo, French mottled calf, inside dentelles in gold, bound by Ramage.

*Le Jeu des Nations. À Paris 1674

Without name or address of publisher, the 'Extrait du Privilége du Roy' gives the exclusive right of publication 'au Sieur D., en considération des ses services,' for ten years; probably Jean Desmarests was the licensee. At the end of the book is 'À Paris, chez Hubert Jailliot, joignant les grands Augustins, au bout du Pont-neuf, aux deux Globes.' 1675

Avec Privilége du Roy. The book contains also Le Jeu du Tourtable.

Small 16mo, full calf, inside dentelles of gold, g.e., bound by Ramage.

*Instructions pour un jeu de Cartes nouvellement inventé. Le Jeu des Cartes Militaires. Dédié à son altesse Monseigneur le Duc du Maine, Colonel Général des Suisses, par le Sr. D.M. À Paris: Rue du Bouloy, près Saint Honoré, à l'Hostel du Saint Ésprit. Avec Privilége du Roy. 1676

The dedication is signed C. H. F. Desmartins. The book also contains the rules for Hombre, Trionfe, Beste, and Brelan.

16mo, mottled French calf, inside dentelles in gold, by Ramage.

*A collection of prints in illustration of the several transactions of the Popish Plot. 1678

The cards (No. 14, of the Collection of The United States Playing Card Company) are of this same series, but are later prints. In a number there are changes in the detail of the illustrations, and often the lettering of the title is not the same, though the subject is.

Small 16mo, containing 41 very coarse engravings. Bound in full calf, gold lines, full gilt back, by Tout.

*Giuoco d'Armi dei Sovrani e stati d'Europa per apprendere l'Armi, la Geografia, e l'Historia loro curiosa. Di C. Oronce Fine, detto di Brianville. Tradotto dal Francese in Italiano, & accresciuto di molte aggiunte nesessarie per la perfetta cognitione della Storia da Bernardo Giustiniani Veneto. In Napoli: Appresso Antonio Bulison All' Insegna della Sirena. Con lic. e Privil. 1677

Small 16mo, contemporary vellum binding. This is an Italian edition of the French heraldic series of 1655, of de Brianville. The book contains hand-illumined copies of the fifty-two cards of the series, with explanations of the cards and directions for their use.

*Giuoco d'Armi dei Sovrani e gli stati d'Europa per apprendere l'Armi, la Geograpfia, e la Storia loro curiosa. Di C. Oronce Fine, detto di Brianville. Tradotto dal Francese in Italiano & accresciuto di molte notizie necessarie per la perfetta cognizion della Storia da Bernardo Giustiniani Veneto. In Napoli: Presso Antonio Bulison, All' Insegna della Sirena. Con lic. e Privil. 1681

16mo, contemporary binding in ivory, silver clasp, red velvet back. This is a later Italian edition of the de Brianville heraldry, containing uncolored engravings of the cards, and the usual text. The frontispiece is the arms of Sig. D. Antonio Miroballo, to whom the edition is dedicated.

La Méthode du Blason. Par P. C. F. Menestrier. Lyon. Thomas Almaury. 1689
16mo, full calf, gilt back, gilt lines on sides with the arms of Count Hoym gilt tooled in center. This is a description of the arms of Europe and of the playing cards from these designs edited by this same publisher.

*Heraldic Playing Cards. German. 1691
Forty-three prints evidently from the original copper plates of the Nürnberg heraldic series of cards, No. 55, the Collection of The United States Playing Card Company. They are on a heavy hand-made paper and bound in a book. 12mo, half calf.

*The Use of the Astronomical Playing Cards. Teaching any ordinary capacity by them to be acquainted with all the Stars in Heaven, to know their place in Heaven, colour, nature, and bigness. As also the Poetical Reasons for every Constellation, very useful, pleasant and delightful for all lovers of Ingeniety. By Joseph Moxon, Hydrographer to the Kings most Excellent Majesty. London: The Playing Cards, and these Books are sold by James Moxon in Warwick Lane at the Sign of Atlas.
1692
16mo, full French mottled calf with gold lines, uncut, bound by Root & Son.

*A Second edition of Camden's Description of Scotland, containing a supplement of these Peers, or Lords of Parliament, who were mentioned in the First Edition; and an account of these since Raised to, and further advanced in the Degrees of Peerage, until the year 1694. Edinburgh, Printed by the Heirs and Successors of Andrew Anderson, Printer to his most excellent majesty. 1695
The Cards Armorial referred to in the supplement, 'The Blazoning of the Ensignes Armorial of the Kingdoms of Scotland, England, France and Ireland and of the Coats of Arms of the Nobility of Scotland, as they are illustrated upon the Cards Armorial' are No. 103 in the collection of The United States Playing Card Company and are of the greatest rarity.
12mo, half morocco, gilt edges.

*Playing Cards. Meal Tub Plot — South Sea Bubble. From the Proceedings of the Society of Antiquaries, by A. W. Franks, Esq., C. B. Litt. London. 1892
The latter are cards No. 57 in the collection of The United States Playing Card Company. The book gives a description of each card in these two series.

*The Secret History of the Rye House Plot: and of Monmouth's Rebellion. Written by Ford Lord Grey, in MDCLXXXV. Now first published from a Manuscript signed by himself, before the Earl of Sunderland. The Second Edition. London: Printed for Andrew Millar, in the Strand. 1754
Small 8vo, three quarters calf. The cards No. 104 of the collection of The United States Playing Card Company tell this story in a series of illustrations.

*A series of fifty-two pencil drawings by Zuccarelli for Biblical playing cards. 1748
These are the original drawings. Zuccarelli was a member of the Royal Academy, living in England from 1752–1773. The cards made from these are No. 38, The United States Playing Card Company Collection.
16mo, full black morocco, gold lines, and edges.

*The Beggar's Opera, A Comic Opera by John Gay. Adapted for Theatrical representation as performed at the Theatre Royal, Drury Lane. Regulated from the prompt book, by permission of the Managers. London, Printed for the Proprietors, under the Direction of John Bell, British Library, Strand Bookseller to his Royal Highness the Prince of Wales. 1791
There is a preface about John Gay, an introduction and the casts at the Drury Lane and the Covent Garden, as well as the entire book of the opera. The songs,

with music are given on the pack of musical cards, No. 37 of The United States Playing Card Company Collection.
16mo, French mottled calf, gold border and dentelles, by Ramage.

*French Playing Cards. A scrapbook, containing packs 720, 721, 722, 723, 724, 725, 726, 727, 728, 729, 730, 731, 732, 733, 734, 735, 736, 737 of the collection of The United States Playing Card Company. These cards are delightful little French color prints of the early nineteenth century.
Folio, tan cloth, gold lettering.   c. 1800

*Taschenbuch für 1801. Herausgegeben von Freidrich Genz, Jean Paul und Johann Heinrich Voss. Braunschweig von Freidrich Vieweg.   1801
There is an engraved frontispiece signed Cl. Kohl, Vienna, 1799. This is one of many pocket almanachs published as New Year's gifts, at this time. It contains a number of prettily engraved copies of famous pictures, sentimental anecdotes and poems, and 12 pages for a diary with an engraved heading for each month. It has also reproductions of 8 cards of the heart suit of Butler's Hudibras. These are done in the manner of Hogarth, and are prefaced by a biography of Hogarth and a translation of the poem.
Small 16mo in original red morocco, g.e., in a later slip case of morocco.

*Taschenbuch für freunde des Scherzes und der Satire, Angefangen von J. D. Falk, fortgesezt von Janus Eremita, mit 12 Satirischen Kupfern. Leipzig, in der Commerschen. The illustrations are twelve playing cards, 'Bout-Rimes Pittoresques' delicately engraved from copper. A number of them are signed de Heller. These are perhaps the most interesting of the transformation cards. The drawing is excellent and the subjects are whimsical and varied.   1804
16mo, full pressed red morocco, gold lines and inside dentelles, by Ramage.

The History of England in cards, by way of Question and Answer. A book giving directions for playing with the cards, No. 885 and containing the fifty questions whose answers are on the cards. This book is in the case which originally contained it and the cards. Printed for Darton and Harvey. London.   1807
Small 16mo, paper.

*Karten-Almanach. Tübingen, in der J. G. Cottaschen Buchhandlung.   1810
This shows the engravings of the Cotta series of playing cards for 1810, and contains descriptions of each card, sometimes in verse, sometimes in prose.
16mo, three quarters red morocco, gold lines, by Root & Son.

*Pictorial Cards in thirteen plates, each containing four subjects, partly designed from the subjoined tale of Beatrice; or, the Fracas. London: Published by R. Ackermann, 101, Strand. Printed by L. Harrison, 373, Strand.   1819
This is the description of part of the series No. 41 of the collection of The United States Playing Card Company which, with the cards, appeared originally in Ackermann's Repository.
12mo, half red morocco.

*Rules and Directions for Playing Magna Charta or Knight Errantry, a new game for young persons: to which is appended a synopsis of Chivalry, by a lady. Greenwich: Printed for M. Landry, Fancy repository, No. 6, Stockwell Street.   1820
16mo, three quarters French mottled calf.

*A Brief explanation of the Countries, &c, represented by the new Geographical Cards. London: Published by C. Hodges, Stationer, 27 Portman Street, Portman Square, and sold by all booksellers in town and country.   1827
Small 16mo. This is an explanation of the cards No. 413, the collection of The United States Playing Card Company. Bound in cherry colored moiré silk.

The Orphan of Pimlico and other Sketches. Fragments and Drawings by William Makepeace Thackeray. (Including twenty-one playing cards.) London: Smith Elder & Co.
Folio, half morocco, gold top. 1876

The Game of Logic. By Lewis Carroll. London: Macmillan & Co. New York: The Macmillan Company. 1887
12mo, original cloth binding.

Education by Play. Second edition, illustrated. The Cincinnati Game Co. Cincinnati.
16mo, paper. 1900

CONCERNING THE MORALITY OF GAMING

Sermones de Ludo cum Aliis. Manuscript. SAEC. M.D.
A treatise on many subjects, largely theology, 433 folios, in Latin with many
marginal notes in Italian. Illuminated capitals. From folio 205–209 it treats of cards
and card games. Those games are permissible which do not keep people from mass,
and which encourage the heart to good works. The atouts of a tarot series are listed
in the following order:

1. El Bagatella
2. Imperatrice
3. Imperator
4. La papessa (note referring to those
   who deny the Christian faith)
5. El papa
6. La tempetia (Temperantia?)
7. L'Amore
8. Lo caro triumphale
9. La Fortez
10. La rotta
11. El gobbo
12. Lo impichato (the Hangèd)
13. La morte
14. El diavolo
15. La sagitta (in place of La Maison
    Dieu?)
16. La stella
17. La luna
18. El sole
19. Lo angelo
20. La justicia
21. El mondo ave dio padre
22. El mato

Part of this treatise is on vellum and part on paper, some folios of which are reën-
forced around the edges with vellum strips; all available spaces in margins and on the
first and last pages are used for medicinal and other recipes. This is bound in oak
boards covered with calf and once had clasps. It is in a slip cover of full morocco.
There is a bookplate, a crest, lettered 'From the Library of Robert Steele, Wands-
worth Common.' Double columns, initial strokes in red, capitals in red and blue,
underscoring in red.

*Tractatus Duo: Primus de Amicitia Christiana. Secundus de ludo Aleae. Recens excusi.
L. Danaeo, autore. Genevae, apud Eustathium Vignon. 1579
16mo, French mottled calf, inside dentelles in gold, by Ramage. Marginal notes.

*Commentarius pro re. Domestica et nummaria saluteque. Animarum in primis Con-
servanda ad Christiani Orbis Uniuersitatem a Fr. Angelo Roccha Episcopo Tag-
astensi & Apostolici Sacrarii Praefecto Directus contra ludum alearum chartarum
scilicet ac taxillorum, &c, &c. Romae apud Guillelmum Facciottum. Superiorum
Permissu. Anno Domini. 1616
Small 8vo, three quarters calf, g.e. There is an engraved title-page showing figures
of Theologia and Philosophia.

*Trattato di Fr. Angelo Roccha, Vescovo e Prefetto della Sacristia Apostolica per la
salute dell' anime e per la conservatione della robba, e del denaro contra I. Giuochi
delle carte, &c. In Roma Appresso Guglielmo Facciotto. Con licenza de Superiori.
Anno Domini. 1617

The same engraved title-page as in the previous volume of 1616, and the text is presented in a similar form.

8vo, vellum.

A Defence of the Lawfulnesse of Lots in Gaming against the Arguments of N.N. Oxford: Printed by J.L. for E.F. 1633

12mo, without binding. A manuscript note on the paper cover gives the name of the author. By the Rev. John Downe, Rector of Instow, Devon; see Madan's Early Oxford Press.

*Pascasii Justi de Alea, Libro duo. Amsterdami. Apud Ludovic Elzivirium. 1642

Pascasii Justi Elzoviensis Philosophiae & Medicinae Doctoris Alea, Sive de curanda ludendi in pecuniam cupiditate.

Small 16mo, French mottled calf, full gilt back, borders and dentelles, by Root & Son. Engraved frontispiece, C. V. Dalen.

Paradoxaechartulaelusoriae of Bewys dat het Kaartspel, &c, Zeer Vorderlyk is tot voortplanting van den Christelyken Godsdienst onder de Christenen, &c. Te Amsterdam, by F. H. Demter, Boekverkoper. No date

16mo, calf.

*An index or abridgement of the Acts of Parliament and Convention from the reign of King James the First including the former index or abridgement and containing the same to the ninth session of the Current Parliament digested into Heads in the order of the alphabet by Sir James Stewart of Gutters, Her Majesty's Advocat. Edinburgh: Printed by George Mossman and are to be sold in Parliament Closs, Anno Domini.

Vide page 48 for the statute against playing cards and dice. 1702

16mo, full calf, inside dentelles in gold, by Root and Son. Uncut.

Traité du Jeu, où l'on examine les principales Questions de droit naturel et de morale qui ont du rapport à cette Matière. Par Jean Barbeyrac. À Amsterdam: Chez Pierre Humbert. 1709

2 vols. 16mo, contemporary calf, full gilt backs. Engraved frontispiece.

*An Essay upon Gaming in a dialogue between Callimachus and Dolomedes. By Jeremy Collier, M.A. London: Printed for J. Morphew, near Stationers' Hall, 1713

Bound also in the same volume:

On Card Playing in a letter from Monsieur de Pinto to Monsieur Diderot. Autographed 'From the author, T.F.' Also a translation from the original and observations by the translator. London: Printed for J. Walter, at Charing Cross; J. Almon, in Piccadilly; E. and C. Dilly, in the Poultry; and W. Griffen in Catherine Street, Strand. 1768

16mo, three quarters morocco, blue, gold lines, uncut.

*An account of the Endeavours that have been used to suppress Gaming Houses, and of the discouragements that have been met with. In a Letter to a Noble Lord. London: Printed in the year 1722

12mo, three quarters calf, by Ramage.

*The Third Charge of Whitlocke Bulstrode, Esq.; to the Grand Jury, and other Juries of the county of Middlesex, at Westminster, October 4, 1722

London: Printed for D. Brown at the Black Swan and Bible without Temple Bar, and R. Gosling at the Middle Temple Gate, Fleet Street. 1723

12mo, three quarters red morocco, gold lines, bound by Root and Son.

*Traité du Jeu, où l'on examine les principales Questions de droit naturel et de morale qui ont du rapport à cette Matière. Par Jean Barbeyrac, Professeur en droit à Groningue. Seconde edition, revue & augmentée. Amsterdam: Chez Pierre Humbert. 1737

3 vols. 16mo, three quarters calf, bound by Ramage. Engraved frontispiece in each

volume, by L. F. du Bourg. 'La Vertu accompagnée de la Justice, de la Prudence et de la Sagesse dirigent le Jeu pendant que l'Avarice est foulée aux pieds.'

*A Letter to a Lady on Card Playing on the Lord's Day. London: Printed for J. Leake, at Bath; and sold by M. Cooper, in Paternoster Row and R. Dodsley in Pall Mall. 12mo, half morocco.   1748

*Some thoughts on the Nature and Use of a Lot, shewing the immorality of Playing at Cards, and dissuading from it. By a Protestant. London: Printed for R. Hett, at the Bible and Crown in the Poultry.   1750
    Small 8vo, three quarters calf, by Ramage.

*A Letter to the Club at White's. In which are set forth the great Expediency of Repealing the Laws now in force against excessive gaming, etc. By Erasmus Mumford, Esq. London: Printed for W. Owen, at Homer's Head, near Temple Bar. 1750
    Bound with this:
    A Modest Defense of Gaming. London: Printed for R. and J. Dodsley, in Pall Mall, and sold by M. Cooper, in Paternoster Row.   1754
    12mo, three quarters blue morocco, gold lines.

*Acts of Parliament. Laying several duties upon certain stocks of cards and dice, among many other articles.   1711–1756
    Folio, three quarters calf, gold lines.

Reflexions on Gaming; and Observations on the Laws relating thereto. In which is considered, The Mischiefs that are occasioned by Gaming Houses being Encouraged by Persons of Rank and Distinction. And A Remedy proposed for the same. London: Printed for J. Barnes, at Charing Cross; and sold by C. Corbett, in Fleet street.
    12mo, three quarters blue calf.   c. 1750

*Serious Reflections on the Dangerous Tendency of the Common Practice of Card Playing; especially of the Game of All Fours as it hath been Publickly play'd at Oxford in this present year of our Lord,   1754
    In a letter from Mr. Gyles Smith, to his Friend, Abraham Nixon, Esq; of the Inner Temple. (Manuscript note: 'By Dr. Benj. Buckler.') London: Printed for W. Owen, at Homer's Head near Temple Bar.
    12mo, three quarters French mottled calf, by Ramage.

*A Modest Defense of Gaming. First printed in the year   1754
    Evidently from a volume of tracts. The pages begin at 173 and run to 193.
    16mo, half morocco.

*Pamphlets against card playing:
    A Plain and Candid address to all lovers of the Game at Cards. London: Printed in the year   1756
    Observations on card playing with an address to the Clergy. London: Printed for R. Baldwin, in Paternoster Row.   1758
    An address to Persons of Fashion, containing some particulars relating to Balls, and a few occasional Hints concerning play houses, card tables, &c, in which is introduced the character of Lucinda, a Lady of the very best fashion and of most extraordinary Piety. By a Gentleman of the University of Oxford. London: Printed for George Keith, at the Bible and Crown in Gracechurch street: and sold by J. Robson in New Bond street.   1761
    Hints for a Reform, particularly in the Gambling Clubs. By a Member of Parliament. London: Printed for R. Baldwin, No. 47 Paternoster Row.   1784
    A Disswasive from Gaming. By Josiah Woodward, D.D. Late Minister of Poplar. The Fourth edition, corrected. London: Printed for J. F. and C. Rivington, Book-

sellers to the Society for Promoting Christian Knowledge, No. 62 St. Paul's Churchyard.

12mo, three quarters French mottled calf, by Ramage.

Trattato de' Giochi e de' Divertimenti, permessi o prohibiti ai Cristiani. In Roma: Presso Michel Angelo Barbiellini alla Minerva. Con Licenza de' Superiori. 1768

16mo, original vellum. Slightly wormed.

*Lettre et Reflexions sur la Fureur du Jeu, auxquelles on a joint une autre Lettre morale. Par M. Dusaulx, Ancien Commissaire de la Gendarmerie, de l'Académie Royale des Inscriptions & Belles Lettres, & celle de Nancy. À Paris: Chez Lacombe, Libraire, rue Christine, près la rue Dauphine. 1775

12mo, full French mottled calf, gold lines and inside dentelles, by Ramage.

*De la Passion du Jeu, depuis les temps anciens jusqu'à nos jours; par M. Dusaulx, Ancien Commissaire de la Gendarmerie, de l'Académie Royale des Inscriptions & Belles Lettres, & de celle de Nancy. Dédié à Monsieur. À Paris de l'imprimerie de Monsieur. Se trouve à Paris chez N. L. Moutard, Libraire Imprimeur de la Reine, rue des Mathurins, hôtel de Cluny. Avec approbation et privilége du Roi. 1779

2 vols. 12mo, contemporary calf, full gilt back, three line border and inside dentelles. Title printed in red and black.

*A Dissertation on the Pernicious Effects of Gaming. Published by appointment, as having won a prize (June, 1783) in the University of Cambridge. By Richard Hey, LL.D. Fellow of Magdalen College. The second edition. Cambridge: Printed by J. Archdeacon, Printer to the University. 1784

There is a letter from the Registry of the University at Cambridge, dated 27 May, 1893, written to George Clulow, bound with this book, which says, 'In the years 1783, 1784, & 1785, a gentleman who desired that his name might be concealed gave fifty guineas successively for the best English essays on the pernicious effects of gaming, duelling and suicide, which were gained each year by Richard Hey, fellow of Magdalen college.'

Small 8vo, three quarters blue morocco, gold lines.

*An Essay on Gaming. By William Green, A.B. London: Printed for the author, by Sammells & Ritchie, Albion Buildings, Bartholomew Close; and sold by C. Forster, No. 41 Poultry. 1788

16mo, three quarters red morocco, by Ramage.

*Ueber das Kartenspiel von J. E. F. Witting, pastor zu Ellensen bei Einbeck. Leipzig, bey Johann Ambrosius Barth. 1791

16mo, mottled French calf, gold dentelles, by Ramage.

*Gaming:

The Consequences of the vice of Gaming as they affect the welfare of individuals, and the stability of civil government, considered. A Sermon preached in the Cathedral Church of Winchester, by Thomas Rennell, A.M., Prebendary of Winton and Rector of St. Magnus, London Bridge. London: Printed for Rivingtons, Elmsley, Paine, Cadell, Egertons, and Debrett. Dedication to the Marquis of Buckingham. 1794

A Letter from Colonel Venault de Charmilly, Knight of the Royal and Military Order of St. Louis, to Lieut. General B. Tarleton, Colonel of the Twenty-first Light Dragoons and Governor of Berwick. London. 1810

An Exposure of the system of Gaming, practised at the gaming houses of London and Paris: By Scrutator. London. 1835

8vo, three quarters calf, by Ramage.

*A Disswassive from Gaming. By Josiah Woodward, D.D. Late Minister of Poplar. The fifth edition, corrected. London: Printed for F. and C. Rivington, &c. 1803

A Dissuasive from the sin of Drunkenness. By Josiah Woodward, D.D., late Minister of Poplar. A new edition corrected. London. 1808
The Baseness and Perniciousness of the sin of Slandering and Backbiting, by Josiah Woodward, D.D., late Minister of Poplar. The Ninth edition. London. 1787
16mo, half morocco; there is a bookplate, a crest, with the name of Cornelius Walford, F.S.S., below.

*An essay on Card Playing. By Simon Simple, Rochdale: Printed by J. Hartley in the Market place. 1807
12mo, half morocco.

*The Confessions of a Gamester. 'The end of these things is death.' London: Printed for J. Hatchard and Son, 187, Piccadilly. 1824
12mo, three quarters French mottled calf, by Ramage.

*Gambling in High Life. Extracts from the London newspapers, consisting of paragraphs and letters under the above designation — published in various daily and weekly papers from the 26th of November, 1826, to the 13th of January. 1827
Title-page and fourteen folios of text, in script.
8vo, three quarters calf, gold lines, by Root and Son.

Secret Band of Brothers. By J. H. Green. Philadelphia: T. B. Peterson & Bro. 1858
12mo, original cloth binding, Darley illustrations.

*Influence de l'esprit aléatoire sur l'économie politique et sociale Trente et Quarante, dévoilé par J. Jouet de Lanciduais. Paris: Chez E. Dentu, Libraire éditeur, galerie d'Orléans, 13, Palais Royal. 1859
8vo, three quarters French mottled calf, by Ramage.

*The Gaming Table: its votaries and victims, in all Times and Countries, especially in England and France. By Andrew Steinmetz, Esq. London: Tinsley Brothers, 18 Catherine St. Strand. 1870
2 vols. 8vo, three quarters red morocco, gold lines, by Zaehnsdorf, g.e.

*Das Spiel seine Entwicklung und Bedeutung im deutschen Recht. von Dr. Heinrich M. Schuster. Wien. 1878
8vo, three quarters morocco.

*Zerfreutes und Erneutes — Von Freidrich B. Ebeling. Berlin. 1890
16mo, three quarters French mottled calf, by Ramage.

Betting and Gambling. By Major Seton Churchill. Second edition, fourth thousand. London: James Nisbet & Co., 21 Berners Street. 1894
16mo, cloth.

Rien ne va plus. Par Carle des Perrières. Nouvelle édition. Paris: Jules Rouff, éditeur, 14 Cloitre Saint Honoré. No date
16mo, three quarters blue morocco.

Cartes à Jouer. Décret présidentiel du 31 Décember 1895
16mo, original paper cover.

PROCLAMATIONS AND BROADSIDES AND PRINTS

*By the King. A Proclamation concerning playing cards and Dice. Given at our Court at Greenwich, the eighteenth day of June in the fourteenth year of Our Reign. Imprinted at London by Robert Barker, printer to The King's Most Excellent Majestie, and by the Assignes of John Bill. 1628

*By the King. A Proclamation prohibiting the Importation of Foreign Cards, and for seizing such as are or shall be Imported. Given at our Court at Whitehall the seventh day of November 1684 in the sixth and thirtieth year of Our Reign. London: Printed by the Assignes of John Bill deceased: and by Henry Hills and Thomas Newcomb, printers to the King's Most Excellent Majesty.   1684

A Royal Mandate forbidding 'Hazard' and all games of chance and betting with dice, charts, etc. Dresden.   1776
  Folio, 12 pages.

Certificate of the Mayor and Alderman of Valence, attesting the poverty and helplessness of the old card-maker Guillaume Braun. January 17   1775
  The seal of Valence is at the lower left-hand corner.

A print, mezzotint $13\frac{3}{4} \times 9\frac{3}{4}''$, A. Krause, Pinxt. James Wilson, fecit. 'Flemish Amusement. The Boorish Family invent Contrivances for Merriment.' London: Printed for Robert Sayer.   1771

An etching $3\frac{1}{4} \times 3''$, 'Card Playing,' after van Ostade.

A color print $8\frac{3}{8} \times 12\frac{1}{2}''$, 'All Fours.' James Gilray.

A color print $8\frac{3}{8} \times 12\frac{1}{2}''$, 'Two Penny Whist.' H. Bunbury, Esq., a caricaturist, son of Sir W. Bunbury of Suffolk (1750–1811). Exhibited at the Royal Academy. Contributed to Boydell's Shakespeare. His 'Hints to Bad Horsemen' obtained him great popularity and the praise of Sir Joshua Reynolds.

An engraving $11\frac{1}{2} \times 9\frac{1}{4}''$, 'Die Waecht die Wind,' by Franz de Wit.

Card Playing, an etching $8\frac{1}{4} \times 6''$, after D. Teniers, by H. Krafft.

Card Players, an etching $5 \times 3''$, after Adriaen Brouwer.   c. 1630

Card Players, an engraving by P. Molyn, after W. C. Akersloot. Two Latin Quatrains below. Size $9 \times 12\frac{3}{4}''$.   1626

CONCERNING DOCTRINES OF CHANCE

*Essai d'Analyse sur les Jeux de Hazard. À Paris: Chez Jacque Quillau, Imprimeur-Jure Libraire de l'Université, rue Galande. Avec approbation et privilége du Roy. Engraved headings to preface and first chapter.   1708
  Small 4to, contemporary binding in full calf, fillet border and inside dentelles in gold, full gold back.

*Christiani Hugenii Libellus de Ratiociniis in Ludo Aleae. Or, The Value of all Chances in Games of Fortune; Cards, dice wagers, lotteries &c. Mathematically Demonstrated. London: Printed by S. Keimer, for T. Woodward, near the Inner Temple Gate in Fleet Street.   1714
  12mo, three quarters French mottled calf. (Manuscript note.) Translation by William Browne from the original edition of 1658. Dedicated to Dr. Richard Mead, Physician to St. Thomas's Hospital, and Fellow of the Royal Society.

*The Doctrine of Chances, or a Method of Calculating the Probability of Events in Play, by A. de Moivre, F.R.S. London: Printed by W. Pearson for the Author.   1718
  Dedicated to Sir Isaac Newton, Kt. President of the Royal Society.
  4to, three quarters calf, by Ramage.

*The Laws of Chance: or, a mathematical investigation of the probabilities arising from any proposed Circumstance of Play. Applied to The Solution of a great Variety of Problems relating to Cards, Bowls, Dice, Lotteries, &c. By Samuel Clark, Teacher of Mathematics. London: Printed for T. Payne, in Castle street, next the Upper Mews Gate, Charing Cross.   1758
  Small 8vo, original binding full calf, gold lines.

*An Essay towards making the Doctrine of Chances Easy to those who understand

Vulgar Arithmetic only. By Mr. Hoyle. A new edition corrected. London: Printed for T. Osborne, in Gray's Inn, and R. Baldwin, at the Rose in Paternoster Row.
                                                                                1764
    No copies of this book are genuine but those that are signed by the Proprietors on the back of this title. Signed in autograph. Thos. Osborne. R. Baldwin.
    12mo, three quarters red morocco, bound by Root and Son.

*The Sportsman's Sure Guide, or the Gamester's Vade-Mecum; shewing the exact odds at horse racing, lotteries, raffles, cock fighting, cards, &c, &c. With a table shewing the odds of the variety of chances of throwing any number of points with dice, from One to Ten inclusive; Also odds of backgammon, bowls, coits, &c. The whole forming a complete guide to the Turf, the Cock pit, the Card table, and other species of Public Diversion, either in the parlour or the field. By Henry Proctor, at Woodhouse, near Masham, in Yorkshire.

> Would ye wish to read of matters
> Long concealed from vulgar eyes,
> Harry Proctor for ye caters,
> Buy the Book and win the Prize.

London: Printed for R. Mariner, in Compton Street, Soho.   1773
    16mo, three quarters calf, gold lines, g.e., bound by Root and Son.

*A Guide to the Lottery; or, the Laws of Chance. Price two shillings. Entered at Stationers' Hall. No date, but   c. 1780
    12mo, three quarters calf, by Root and Son. Containing tables of calculations for the odds at cards.

La Théorie des Jeux de Hasard, ou Analyse du Krabs, du Passe dix, de la Roulette, du Trente et Quarante, du Pharaon, du Biribi et du Lotto. Par P. Huyn. À Amsterdam: Chez G. Van Gulik et Changuion, Libraires.   1803
    8vo, calf.

Des Jeux de Hasard au Commencement du 19ème Siècle. Par J. Lablée de l'Athénée de Lyon. Paris: Chez Petit Libraire, Palais du Tribunat, Galerie vitrée No. 229. An. XI.
    Engraved title-page.   1803
    16mo, half calf, original binding.

*Tactique des Jeux de Hasard. Recherches sur les meilleurs manières d'y jouer et de jouer avec assurance de gain, &c. Par James Smyll, Ingénieur. Leipzig: À la Commission de la libraire de J. C. Hinrichs.   1820
    12mo, three quarters French mottled calf, by Ramage.

*Atlas de la Tactique des Jeux de Hasard, consistant en 16 planches coloriées et 40 Tableaux de calcul spéculatifs et démonstratifs. Par James Smyll, Ingénieur. Leipzig: En Commission de la libraire de J. C. Hinrichs.   1820
    8vo, three quarters calf, by Ramage.

*Rouge et Noir. The Academicians of 1823; or the Greeks of the Palais Royal, and the Clubs of St. James's. By Charles Persius, Esq. London: Published by Lawler and Quick, 9 Old Broad Street and Stephen Couchman, 10 Throgmorton Street.   1823
    12mo, three quarters red mottled calf. Frontispiece, colored print, 'La Roulette.'

*Manuel des Jeux de Calcul et de Hasard, ou Nouvelle Académie des jeux; &c. Par M. Lebrun, de plusieurs académies. Paris: Roret Libraire, rue Hautefeuille, au coin de celle du Battoir.   1828
    16mo, three quarters French mottled calf by Ramage.

*Traité des Jeux de la Roulette et du Trente-un ou de la Rouge et Noire. Par J. J.

Weih. À Bade (grand-duché): Chez l'auteur et chez les marchands libraires et de nouveautes. 1829

16mo, full mottled calf, gold lines and dentelles by Ramage. Engraved frontispiece, and numerous plates.

*How to win at Écarté: the scientific game, with illustrative exercises and mathematical demonstrations of the only sure mode of play. By Reuben Roy, with an engraving (frontispiece). London: Henry Kent Causton, Birchin Lane. No year, but preface is dated Jan. 29.

16mo, full calf, gold lines and inside dentelles, g.e., engraved frontispiece. Bound by Ramage.

*The Doctrine of Chance, or the Theory of Gaming made easy to every person acquainted with common Arithmetic so as to enable them to calculate the Probabilities of Events in Lotteries, Cards, Horse racing, Dice, etc., with tables on Chance never before published, which from mere inspection will solve a great variety of Questions. By William Rouse. London: Printed by Gye & Balne, Gracechurch street, for the Author. No date

An illustration on the title-page, drawn and engraved by J. Mitan.
8vo, original binding of full calf, gold border and floriated back.

L'art de Gagner à Tous les Jeux. Tricheries des Grecs dévoileés avec vignettes explicatives. Robert Houdin. Paris: Calmann Lévy, éditeur, ancienne maison Michel Lévy Frères. 1879

12mo, three quarters red morocco.

Felix P. Monaco. Assurance contre toutes les pertes que l'on fera dans l'établissement de Monte Carlo remboursement immédiat. Combinaison ouverte et parfaitement expliquée à la portée de tous, pour gagner à coup sur une pièce par tour de roulette. Étude Sérieuse sur le Casino de Monte Carlo. 1884

12mo, three quarters morocco.

L'art de bien Jouer La Roulette, indiquant La Maturité, La Limite des Chances et les Règles pour les attaquer sur le champ et avec succès, avec des Tables de Mises et des Nouvelles Cartes à marquer suivi d'un aperçu sur la meilleur manière de jouer Le Trente Un. Par un ancien employé de 113. Dix huitième édition. Anvers & Aix la Chapelle: Max Kornicker, Libraire de la Cour. No date

At the back is a magazine clipping in Italian, reviewing a book published in Gratz by Rudolfo Bergner, written by a former croupier at Monte Carlo, revealing many secrets and showing how in the end the bank must always win.
8vo, full calf.

Calcul des Probabilités. Par J. Bertrand, de l'académie Française, secrétaire perpetuel de l'Académie des Sciences. Paris: Gauthier Villars et Fils, Imprimeurs Libraires du Bureau des Longitudes, de l'école Polytechnique. 1888

8vo, three quarters green morocco.

Théorie des Jeux de Hasard. Par H. Laurent, examinateur d'admission à l'École Polytechnique, Professeur à l'Institut national Agronomique. Paris: Gauthier Villars et Fils. Encyclopédie Scientifique des Aide Mémoire publiée sous la direction de M. Léauté, Membre de l'Institut. No date

16mo, three quarters red morocco.

The Gambling World. Anecdotic Memories and Stories of personal experience in the temples of hazard and speculation, with some mysteries and iniquities of stock exchange affairs by Rouge et Noir, with an appendix by 'Blue Gown' on turf gambling and bookmakers' practices; also portrait of the author and sketches at Monte Carlo drawn by Paul Renouard. New York: Dodd, Mead & Company. 1898

8vo, cloth, gold top, uncut.

Chance and Luck: a discussion of the laws of luck, coincidences, wagers, lotteries and the fallacies of gambling; with notes on poker and martingales. By Richard A. Proctor. New impression. Longmans, Green and Co., 39 Paternoster Row, London, New York and Bombay. 1902
12mo, cloth.

CONCERNING DECEITS AND DECEPTIONS PRACTICED BY SHARPERS

*Do no Right, Take no Wrong; or The Way of the World Displayed; In several Profitable Essays, serious and comical:
I. The Treachery of False Friends.
II. The tricks and cheats usually imposed on the Unthinking and Ignorant, by the Town Sharpers.
III. The Deceits us'd in particular Trades and Professions.
The whole intermixt with Pleasant Relations, Comical Descriptions, and Satyrical Characters; being very Delightful and Instructive, for the Diversion of the Wise, and the Information of the Otherwise. By S. H. Misodolus. London: Printed for Robert Gifford, in Old Bedlam, without Bishopgate. 1711
16mo, original binding in full calf. Engraved frontispiece.

*Memoirs of the Lives, Intrigues and Comical Adventures of the most Famous Gamesters and Celebrated Sharpers in the Reigns of Charles II, James II, William III and Queen Anne, &c, &c. By Theophilus Lucas, Esq.; London: Printed for Jonas Brown without Temple Bar and Ferdinando Burleigh in Amen Corner. 1714
16mo, full calf, gold border and inside dentelles and floriated back, by Root and Son.

*L'Antidote ou le Contrepoison des Chevaliers d'Industrie, ou Jouers de Profession. Démontré par un Vénétien dans les Lettres qu'il écrit à un de ses Amis pendant ses Voyages en Europe, &c, &c. À Venise: Aux Dépens de l'Auteur. 1768
12mo, three quarters French mottled calf.

Die aufgebechten und verrathenen Geheimnisse der Falschen Spieler. Aachen und Spaa. 1793
16mo, original paper binding.

*The Sharper Detected and Exposed. By Robert Houdin. London: Chapman and Hall, 193 Piccadilly. 1863
12mo, three quarters calf, by Ramage.

Card Sharpers. Their Tricks Exposed, or the art of always winning. Translated from the French of Robert Houdin by Joseph Forster with explanatory diagrams. London: Spencer Blackett, 35 St. Bride Street, Ludgate Circus, E.C. 1891
12mo, cloth.

*Gambling Sharps and Their Tools. By Champion Bissell. From the Cosmopolitan Magazine, February. 1891
8vo, three quarters French mottled calf, gold lines and back, by Root and Son. Illustrated.

Card Sharping Exposed. By Robert Houdin. Translated and edited, with notes by Professor Hoffmann. London: George Routledge and Sons, Limited. Broadway, Ludgate Hill. No date
12mo, cloth.

CONCERNING CARD TRICKS

*Nova Ghirlanda di Bellissimi Giochi di Carte, e di Mano. Con altri bellissimi Gioch d'Intertenimento. Data in Luce da me Benedetto Siuiero da Cento detto il Carbonaro. Venetia, Fiorenza, Bologna, Oruiero, Padoa, e Macerata, Perugia & in Roma, appresso Bernardino Tani. Con licenza de' Superiori. 1638
16mo, French mottled calf, gold filet border and inside dentelles, by Ramage.

Sammlung auserlefener, und ganz neu erfundener rarer Kartenkunste, Zeitvertreib in langen Winterabenden. Zusammengetravgen von J.H.G. Wien. 1769
  16mo, original paper binding.

*Physical Amusements and diverting experiments. Composed and performed in different capitals of Europe, and in London. By Signor Giuseppe Pinetti, de Wildalle, &c, &c. London: Printed in the year 1784
  12mo, three quarters calf, by the Co-operative Bookbinders, 17 Bury Street, London, W.C. Engraved frontispiece.

*Gale's Cabinet of Knowledge; or, Miscellaneous Recreations. Containing Moral and Philosophical essays, &c, &c. including the most celebrated Card Deceptions ever exhibited. &c. Illustrated with copper plate engravings. London: Printed for the Proprietors by W. Kemmish. The preface is dated November first, 1796
  12mo, three quarters calf, gold lines, by Root and Son.

Curiositatenkabinet, Eine Sammlung der besten und auserlesensten Kartenkunste, etc. Gratz: bei Christian Friedrich Trotscher. 1797
  16mo, original binding of three quarters calf.

Allerhand Kartenkunststude gesammelt und herausgegeben von A. R. Shepper. Ravensburg: Verlag Otto Maier. No date
  12mo, original paper binding.

Deutliche Unweisung zur leichten Erlernung Kartenkunststucke. Der Unterhaltung und Belustigung frohlicher Gesellschaftreife geweiht. Third edition. 1829
  12mo, original paper binding.

*Almanach Manuel de l'Amateur de Tours de Cartes, contenant l'Explication de tous les Tours de Cartes Anciens et Nouveaux. Recueillis par Bonneveine. Paris: De la Rue, Libraire-Éditeur, 3 rue des Grands-Augustins. No date. c. 1873
  16mo, three quarters French mottled calf, by Ramage.

Tours de Cartes. Recueil complet par Tissot. Paris: De la Rue, Libraire-Éditeur, 5 rue des Grands-Augustins. No date
  16mo, half calf, original binding.

*Cards and Card Tricks, containing a brief History of playing cards; full instructions with illustrated hands for playing nearly all known games of chance or skill; and directions for performing a number of amusing tricks. Illustrated. By H. E. Heather. London: L. Upcott Gill, 'The Bazaar' office, 170, Strand, W.C. No date
  12mo, full mottled calf, gold borders, dentelles and floriated back, by Ramage.

The Book of Card Tricks. Principles of Sleight of Hand. By R. Kunard. New edition, illustrated. Chicago: Alhambra Book Co., Publishers. No date
  16mo.

Card Tricks, How to Do Them, and Sleight of Hand. By A. Roterberg. Chicago: Frederick J. Drake & Co. Publishers. 1902
  16mo, cloth.

Petite Bibliothèque Universelle. Tours de Cartes Anciens et Nouveaux. Par Eugène Durand. Nouvelle édition, illustrée de gravures explicatives. Paris: Librairie des Publications à 5 centimes. 34 rue de la Montagne Sainte Geneviève. No date
  16mo, three quarters calf.

Tours de Cartes Anciens et Nouveaux. Par Eugène Durand. Paris. No date
  16mo, uncut, three quarters morocco, bound by Sand.

Nouvelle Collection de Tours de Cartes. Ouvrage complet. Par H. Felix. Paris: Bernardin Béchet & Fils, Libraires-Éditeurs, 53 Quai des Augustins. No date
  16mo, three quarters calf.

Card Tricks, Fortune Telling, and Dream Book. Chicago, The Advertising Playing Card Company.
16mo, paper.

Card Tricks for the Amateur Magician. Cincinnati, The United States Playing Card Company. 1923
12mo, paper.

Hart's Card Language; a method of communicating thought by means of ordinary playing cards. By Robert M. Hart, third edition. Honesdale, Pa. 1902
12mo, paper.

PLAYS, POEMS AND SATIRES ON GAMING

*Shufling, Cutting and Dealing, in A Game at Pickquet: Being Acted from the Year 1653 to 1658. By O.P. and others; With great Applause. Tempora mutantur et nos. Printed in the Year 1659
12mo, three quarters morocco, by Zaehnsdorf.
This is one of the political tracts of the time, in the form of a dialogue between Oliver Cromwell and some of his officers.

*The Rape of the Lock. An Heroi-Comical Poem. Written in the Year 1712

> Nolueram Belinda, tuos violare capillos;
> Sed juvat hoc precibus me tribuisse tuis.
> *Martial*

Dedicated to Mrs. Arabella Fermor by 'Your Most Obedient, Humble Servant, A. Pope.'
12mo, three quarters morocco, gold lines. Engraved head and tail pieces.

The Rape of the Lock. An heroi-comical Poem in Five Cantos. The second edition. Six plates engraved by du Guernier after du Bose. Title-page in red and black. London: Bernard Lentott at the Cross Keys in Fleet Street. 1714
12mo, three quarters calf.

*The Humours of Whist. A Dramatic Satire. As Acted every Day at White's and other Coffee Houses and Assemblies. London: Printed for J. Roberts, in Warwick Lane. 1743
12mo, three quarters calf, by Ramage. Title-page lettered in red and black.
A satire on gambling, burlesquing Hoyle, whose treatise on Whist had just appeared.

*Herrn Alexander Popens Lockenraub ein scherzhafter Heldengedicht aus dem Englischen in Deutsche Verse ubersetzt von Luisen Adelgunden Victorien Gottschedinn. Nebst einem Anhange freyen Uebersetzungen aus dem Franzosischen. Leipzig, in Bernhard Christoph Breitkopfs Verlag. Mit Kupfern. 1744
8vo, full morocco, paneled in brown and black, gold lines and inside dentelles, blind tooling, g.e., by Root and Son. The delightful illustrations are by A. Vernerin.

*The Polite Gamester: or, The Humours of Whist. A Dramatic Satire, as Acted every Day at White's, and other Coffee Houses and Assemblies. London: Printed for M. Cooper, in Paternoster Row; W. Reeve, Fleet-street; and C. Sympson, Chancerylane. 1753
12mo, three quarters morocco, gold lines.

*The Card.

> Quicquid agunt Homines, Votum, Timor, Ira, Voluptas,
> Gaudia, Discurcus, nostri Farrago Libelli.
> *Juvenal*

London: Printed for the Maker, and Sold by J. Newbery, at the Bible and Sun, in St. Paul's Church-Yard.   1755

2 vols. 12mo, three quarters mottled French calf, gold lines and full gold backs, by Root and Son, gold tops, uncut. The frontispiece is a knave of clubs in color.

A letter inserted in Vol. II, dated March 5, 1913, from George Clulow, encloses a catalogue description of this book, as follows: 'Kidgell (John) The Card, coloured frontispiece, rare. The existence of this curious book seems entirely unknown to bibliographers; it was the author of this rare work who fraudulently obtained the proof sheets of Wilks' Essay on Woman, and issued a pamphlet upon it, as bad as the work itself.' The book is a series of tales, largely in the form of letters.

*Calculations, Cautions and Observations; relating to the Various Games Played with Cards: Addresses to the Ladies. By E. Hoyle, jun. London: Printed for R. Griffiths, in the Strand.   1761

16mo, French mottled calf, gold lines and dentelles, by Ramage.

*The Gamblers, a Poem: with notes critical and explanatory. London: Printed for the Author, and sold by Samuel Hooper, Ludgate Hill.   1777

4to, three quarters calf, gold lines, by Tout and Sons.

*Casino; a mock heroic poem. Dedicated, by permission, to her grace The Duchess of Bolton. To which is added an appendix, containing the Laws of the Game of Casino, and Rules and Directions for Playing It. Printed at the Salisbury Press, by Collins; and sold by J. Bell Bookseller, at No. 148 Oxford street. No date, but   c. 1794

8vo, full calf, gold lines and inside dentelles, by Ramage, g.e.

*Il Giuoco delle Carte, Poemetto dell' Abbate Saverio Bettinelli con Annotazioni. In Venetia: Appresso Pietro Savioni.   1778

12mo, full mottled calf, gold lines and dentelles, by Ramage, uncut, gold top.

*Whist, a Poem in twelve cantos. London: Printed for J. and F. Bell, No. 148 Oxford Street.   1791

This is by Alexander Thomson, though the author's name is not given. Rare. First edition.

12mo, three quarters pressed red morocco, by Ramage.

*Whist: A Poem in twelve cantos. By Alexander Thomson, Esq. Second edition. London: Printed for T. Cadell in the Strand; and sold by J. and F. Bell, No. 148 Oxford Street.   1792

12mo, original binding of mottled calf, gilt back, rare.

*The Rape of the Lock, an heroi-comical poem, by A. Pope. Adorned with plates. London: Printed for W. Bulmer and Co.   1801

Six engravings (two by Bartolozzi) after Hamilton, Burney, Stothard, and Fuseli. A re-issue of the edition of 1798 which was printed by C. Bensley.

12mo, full brown morocco, gold lines, by Root and Son, uncut, and gold top.

*The Faro Table; or, the Gambling Mothers. A Fashionable Fable. In two volumes. (Bound together.) London: Printed by J. Dean, 57 Wardour Street, Soho, for J. F. Hughes, Wigmore Street, Cavendish Square.   1808

12mo, three quarters calf, by Ramage, gold top, uncut.

*Le Boston, poème didactique en deux chants précédé des Règles de ce Jeu, et du Tableau de ses Paiements. À Bordeaux de l'imprimerie et fonderie de Racle, rue Sainte-Catherine No. 74.   1810

12mo, full calf.

*Rouge et Noir, in six cantos.

The Game

The Palais Royal	The Salon
Frescati	The Sharper
Versailles	The Guillotine

and other Poems. (Manuscript.) By Sir John Dean Paul. London: C. and J. Ollier, Vere Street. Bond street. 1821
　16mo, three quarters red pressed morocco, by Ramage.

*The Four Knaves: A Series of Satirical Tracts. By Samuel Rowlands. Edited, with an introduction and notes, by E. F. Rimbault, Esq., Ph.D., F.S.A. London: Reprinted for the Percy Society by T. Richards, 100 St. Martin's Lane. No. XXXIV.
June, 1843
　The Knave of Clubbs. Tis merry when knaves meete. Printed at London by E. A. dwelling nere Christ church. 1611.
　The Knave of Harts. Haile Fellow, well met. London: Printed for John Bache and are to be sold at his shop at the entring in of the Royall Exchange. 1613.
　More Knaves yet? The Knaves of Spades and Diamonds. London: Printed for John Tap, dwelling at Saint Magnus.
　12mo, half morocco. Engraved frontispiece to each of the three tracts, which are in the form of poems.

Comic Whist: Its History and Practice. By an Amateur. Its illustrations designed by Kenny Meadows, and engraved by Orrin Smith and W. Linton. London: Bell and Wood, Fleet Street. 1843
　16mo, original cloth binding.

Comic Backgammon: Its History and Practice. By the author of 'Whist.' With illustrations by Kenny Meadows, and engraved by W. Linton. London: D. Bogue, 86 Fleet Street. 1844
　16mo, original cloth binding.

*Backgammon: its History and Practice. By the author of 'Whist.' With illustrations designed by Kenny Meadows, and engraved by W. Linton. London: D. Bogue, 86 Fleet Street. 1844
　16mo, three quarters calf, by Root and Son, g.e.

*Whist: Its History and Practice. By an Amateur. Its illustrations designed by Kenny Meadows, and engraved by Orrin Smith and W. Linton. New edition. London: D. Bogue, 86 Fleet Street. 1854
　16mo, three quarters mottled calf, gold lines, by Root and Son.

Backgammon: Its Theory and Practice. With something of its history. By Captain Crawley. Illustrated by Kenny Meadows. London: C. H. Clarke, 13 Paternoster Row. Preface dated 1860
　16mo, original cloth binding, g.e. Manuscript note, first edition, scarce.

Musical Whist with Living Cards. Introduction, historical and descriptive notes by Cavendish. London: Thos. de la Rue & Co. Dublin: William McGee, 18 Nassau Street. 1892
　Autographed, 'William Pole, F.R.S. A present from the Author. 1894.'
　12mo, full calf.

Spielkarte und Kartenspielin Wort und Bild von Dr. Timon Schroeter. Leipzig. 1883
　Folio. Illustrations of German cards in color.

The Game of Bridge. Ten cards in a folder, each a sepia drawing humorously illustrating a term at bridge. Life Publishing Co. 1905
　16mo, paper.

Cupid's Pack of Cards. An epigram for every card, a saw for every chip. By Walter
    Pulitzer. Illustrations by Theo Aulmann. Boston: Luce and Company.   1908
    12mo, paper.

Scrapbook of clippings collected by George Clulow, F.R.G.S. 1698–1891. In a portfolio.
    Folio, three quarters red morocco.

Bridge Whist. By George Fitch. Reprinted from Collier's for August 1. Illustration by
    C. D. Gibson. New York.   1908
    16mo, paper.

What I Know About Poker. By Richard Carle. Chicago: The Darrow Publishing Co.
    16mo, paper.

CONCERNING PLAYING CARDS IN AMERICA

Massachusetts Gazettes and Centinels, 1786–1790, containing advertisements of play-
    ing cards. In a portfolio.
    Folio, half morocco.

Travels in North America, in the years 1780, 1781, & 1782, by the Marquis de Chastellux.
    Translated from the French by an English Gentleman. London: G. G. J. and J.
    Robinson.   1787
    2 vols. 8vo, boards. Two maps of America and a chart and two engravings of
    Natural Bridge. Bookplates of James Lord Lifford.

Industrial and Commercial Correspondence of Alexander Hamilton Anticipating His
    Report on Manufactures. Edited by Arthur Harrison Cole, Ph.D. With a preface
    by Professor Edwin F. Gay. Published under the auspices of the Business Historical
    Society, Inc. Chicago: A. W. Shaw Company.   1928
    1 vol. 8vo, cloth, five plates.

Early American Trade Cards, from the collection of Bella C. Landauer, with critical
    notes by Adele Jenny. New York: William Edwin Rudge.   1927
    1 vol. 4to, cloth, 44 plates.

Some Eighteenth Century Invitations. By Howard M. Chapin. An article in An-
    tiques, 683 Atlantic Avenue, Boston, June,   1926
    1 vol. 4to, paper. Many illustrations.

Bureau des Publications Historiques Archives de Canada. Documents relatifs à La
    Monnaie au Change et aux Finances du Canada sous le Régime Français. Choisis et
    édités avec Commentaires et Introduction par Adam Shortt. Ottawa: F. A. Acland.
    2 vols. 8vo, paper, 8 plates.   1926

A photographic copy of an article in the Superior Printer, published in Cincinnati June,
    1887, Vol. I. No. 2, telling the history of the Russell & Morgan Printing Company.

A photograph, 16 × 13, of the Russel and Morgan factory, Cincinnati.   1894

A scrapbook containing clippings concerning playing cards and games. Portfolio.
    Folio, cloth.

Photographs of the Andrew Dougherty Card Company, 80 Center Street, New York.

Stereopticon photographs of the Andrew Dougherty Card Company, 80 Center
    Street, New York.

Scrapbook. The World War in the annals of The United States Playing Card Company.
    4to, black morocco.

Cincinnati, the Queen City of the West. Her principal men and institutions. Bio-
    graphical Sketches and Portraits of leading citizens. Descriptive Accounts of her

Enterprises. Halftone engravings of private and public edifices. Edited by George Mortimer Roe. Published by the Cincinnati Times Star Co. Cincinnati, U.S.A.: Press of C. J. Krehbiel Company.   1895
    Folio, full morocco, g.e.

The Tenth Annual 'Congress' of the Bicycle Pushers. At a dinner at the Country Club, Cincinnati. Verses to Mr. Omwake and the other officers of The United States Playing Card Company, by Mr. J. B. Ferris. Autographed.   1906
    8vo, paper, uncut.

Martins. An account of the martins, and fourteen photographs of the factory and grounds of The United States Playing Card Company, Cincinnati, and the martin houses.   1920
    8vo, paper.

The Arts and Crafts in New England, 1704–1775. Gleanings from Boston newspapers. By George Francis Dow. Topsfield, Massachusetts: The Wayside Press. Illustrated.   1927
    4to.

Dictionary of American Painters, Sculptors and Engravers. By Mantle Fielding. Printed for the subscribers in Philadelphia.
    4to. Illustrated, uncut. Bound in blue cloth.

The Playing Cards of Puritan New England. Old Time New England, April   1928
    8vo, paper.

A History of American Life. Edited by Arthur M. Schlesinger:
The First Americans, 1607–1690. By Thomas Jefferson Wertenbaker. Illustrated. New York: The Macmillan Company.   1927
    8vo, original cloth.

Provincial Society, 1690–1763. By J. T. Adams. Illustrated. New York: The Macmillan Company.   1927
    8vo, original cloth.

The Rise of the Common Man, 1830–1850. By C. R. Fish. Illustrated. New York: The Macmillan Company.   1927
    8vo, original cloth.

The Emergence of Modern America, 1865–1878. By Allan Nevins. New York: The Macmillan Company.   1927
    8vo, original cloth.

BIBLIOGRAPHIES OF PLAYING CARDS

A Bibliography of Card Games and of the History of Playing Cards. Compiled by Norton T. Horr, B.S. Cleveland, O.: Printed for Charles Orr.   1892
    8vo, green cloth, uncut.

Playing Cards and Gaming, a Bibliography of Works in English. Compiled by Frederic Jessel. Longmans, Green and Co., 39 Paternoster Row, London, New York, and Bombay.   1905
    All rights reserved. 8vo, black cloth, uncut.

A Catalogue of a Selected Portion of the Library of the late G. Clulow, Esq. With other rare and beautiful books to be sold by auction by Messrs. Hodgson & Co., at their rooms 115 Chancery Lane, London, W.C. 2, on Wednesday July 7, 1920.
    8vo, three quarters red morocco.

CONCERNING GAMES

*De Ludis Orientalibus Libri Duo, quorum prior est duabus partibus, viz. 1, Historia Shahiludii Latinè: deinde 2, Historia Shahiludii Heb. Lat. per tres Judeos. Liber posterior continet Historiam Reliquorum Ludorum Orientis. Olim Congessit Thomas Hyde S.T.D. Linguae Arabicae Professor Publicus in Universitate Oxon. Protobibliothecarius Bodlejanus. Oxonii.   1694
   16mo, original vellum, gold lettering. Engraved folding plates.

A book written in Chinese characters, describing games played with American playing cards. The United States Playing Card Company.   No date
   12mo, paper, frontispiece in color.

A book written in Japanese, describing games with American playing cards.
   16mo, paper.   No date

Hana-Awase. The Game of Japanese Cards. Tokio: Kamigataya Honten. Ginza, Kyobashi, Japan.   No date
   16mo, paper, illustrated.

How to play Hachi-hachi, in six lessons. K. Okata. New York.   1927
   8vo, paper.

The Gambling Games of the Chinese in America. Vol. I, No. 4, in the series of Philology, Literature and Archæology, Publications of the University of Pennsylvania. By Stewart Culin.   1891
   8vo, paper.

Cento Giuochi Liberali, et D'Ingegno, nuovamente da M. Innocentio Ringhiere, gentil'huomo Bolognese ritruovati, et in dieci libri descritti. In Venezia per Giovan' Maria Bonelli.   1553
   A manuscript note on the flyleaf says that this, which is the second edition, is better and more rare than the first edition, published in Bologna in 1551.
   8vo, original vellum.

Itali ed altri Strumenti Lusori degli Antichi Romani descritti da Francesco de Ficoroni Socio della Reale Accademia di Parigi e dedicati All' Em.mo, Rev.mo Principe, Il Signor Cardinale Nicolo Maria Lercari. In Roma: Nella Stamperia di Antonio de' Rossi.   1734
   8vo, original vellum.

*Giochi Numerici Fatti Arcani Palesati da Giuseppe Antonio Alberti Bolognese. In Bologna: Nella Stamperia di Bartolomeo Borghi. Sotto il Volto de' Polaroli.   1747
   Con licenza de' Superiori. Bound with this is:
   Osservazioni all' appendice de' Giuochi Numerici pubblicati da Giuseppe Antonio Alberti Autore de' detti Giuochi.
   16mo, full mottled calf, paneled sides, gold fillet border and dentelles, full gilt back, by Root and Son, g.e. Engraved illustrations of games and tricks.

*Giochi delle Minchiate, Ombre, Scacchi, ed altri d'ingegno, dedicati alla Illma Signora la Signora Principessa Donna Giulia Albani Ghigi da D. Francesco Saverio Brunetti da Corinaldo. In Roma, per il Bernabò, e Lazzarini. Con licenza de' Superiori.
   16mo, full calf, paneled sides, inside dentelles in gold, by Ramage.   1747

Monumenta Latina Postuma Josephi Averani J. C. Florentini in Pisano Athenaeo Antecessoris nunc primum edita. Florentiae: Ex Typographia Albizziniana Praesidum approbatione, Aere Venantii Monaldini Bibliopolae Romani in Via Cursus.   1769
   8vo, original paper binding, uncut.

Trattato teroico-pratico dei Giuochi. Tresette, &cartè, Mercante in Fiera e Giccahetto. Macerata: Presso Cius. Mancini Cortesi. Con approvazione.   1832
   16mo, original paper cover, uncut.

*Italian Games at Cards and Oriental Games. Arranged by Aquarius. London: Fredc.
C. Mathieson & Sons, 10 Old Broad Street. 1890
Small 16mo, black morocco, lettering and inside dentelles in gold, by Ramage.

Pietro Gori. Il Giuoco del Calcio con vignette.

> Al Prato, al Calcio su; giovani assai;
> Hor che le palle balzan più che mai.
>
> *Canti Carnasiateschi*

Firenze: R. Bemporad & Figlio. Cessionari della Libreria editrice Felice Paggi.
Via del Proconsolo, 7. 1898
16mo, full calf.

*Games most in Use, in England, France, and Spain, viz. Basset, Picquet, Primero,
L'Ombre, Chess, Billiards, Grand Tricktrack, Verquere, &c. Some of which were
never before printed in any Language. All Regulated by the most Experienced
Masters, with a Table to the Whole. London: Printed, and Sold by J. Morphew, near
Stationers' Hall; and by the Booksellers. No date
16mo, French mottled calf, gold borders and dentelles, by Root and Son.

The Academy of Play; Containing a full Description of And the Laws of Play, Now
observed in the several Academies of Paris, Relative to the following Games, viz.
Piquet, Quadril, Ombre, Quintill, etc. . . . From the French of the Abbé Bellecour.
London: Printed for F. Newbery, the Corner of St. Paul's Church-Yard, Ludgate
Street. No date. *c.* 1755
16mo, original calf.

An Inquiry into the Antient Greek Game supposed to have been invented by Palamedes
Antecedent to the Seige of Troy; with reasons for believing the same to have been
known from remote antiquity in China, and progressively improved into the Chi-
nese, Indian, Persian and European chess. Also two dissertations:
I. On the Athenian Skirophoria.
II. On the mystical meaning of the bough and umbrella, in the Skiran rites.
London: Printed by W. Bulmer and Co. Cleveland Row, St. James's, for T. Becket,
Pall Mall. 1801
4to, three quarters brown morocco. Engraved illustrations.

*Festivals, Games and Amusements, Ancient and Modern. By Horatio Smith, Esq.
London: Henry Colburn and Richard Bentley, New Burlington Street. 1831
16mo, three quarters calf, uncut, bound by Ramage. Engraved frontispiece and
folding plates. Frontispiece, Wouverman's 'The Hawking Party,' engraved by Dean.

Festivals, Games and Amusements. Ancient and Modern. By Horatio Smith, Esq.
With additions by Samuel Woodworth, Esq., of New York. Printed and published
by J. and J. Harper, No. 82 Cliff Street, and sold by the principal booksellers throughout the United States. 1833
16mo, original paper binding. Frontispiece, Wouverman's 'The Hawking Party,'
engraved by Schoyer. The other plates the same as in the London edition.

The Philidorian; a Magazine of Chess and other Scientific Games; edited by George
Walker. Complete in one volume. London: G. Walker and Son, No. 17 Soho Square,
Sherwood and Co., Paternoster Row, and Simpkin and Marshall, Stationers' Court.
8vo, three quarters blue morocco. 1838

The Hand Book of Games comprising new and carefully revised treatises on whist,
piquet, etc., etc. Written or compiled by professors and amateurs. Edited by
Henry G. Bohn. London: York street, Covent Garden. 1850
16mo, thick, original cloth binding.

*Games at Cards. 1861–1887
Nine articles by Pole, Proctor, and others, appearing in the various English magazines.
8vo, three quarters red morocco, by Ramage.

*The Card Player; comprising Concise Directions for Playing Cribbage, Écarté, Piquet, All-Fours, Quadrille, Vingt et un, Loo, Speculation, Pope Joan, and all the best round games. By George Frederick Pardon. London: George Routledge and Sons. The Broadway, Ludgate. New York: 416 Broome street. 1862
Small 16mo, mottled calf, gold borders and dentelles, by Ramage.

Social Games, a collection of Thirty-one Games with cards. By Mrs. E. D. Cheney. Boston: Lee and Shepard. New York: Lee, Shepard, and Dillingham. 1871
16mo, cloth.

*Round Games at Cards by Cavendish. London: Thomas de la Rue & Co. 1875
16mo, three quarters calf, by Ramage.

Card Essays, Clay's Decisions and Card Table Talk, by Cavendish. London: Thos. de la Rue & Co., 110 Bunhill Row. 1879
12mo, original cloth binding.

*Trumps' New Card Games, containing directions and rules for playing Hearts, Boodle, Newmarket, Five or Nine, Domino Whist, Cayenne Whist, Solo and Heart Jack Pot. By Trumps. New York: Dick & Fitzgerald, Publishers, 18 Ann Street. Copyright 1886
16mo, three quarters mottled calf, by Ramage.

The Handbook of Games. Enlarged edition, with contributions by Dr. William Pole, F.R.S.; Major General Drayson; Robert F. Green; and Berkeley. In Two Volumes. Vol. I. Table Games. London: George Bell & Sons, York Street, Covent Garden. 1890
12mo, original cloth binding.

*The King's Book of Sports. A History of the Declaration of King James I and King Charles I as to the use of lawful sports on Sundays, with a reprint of the declarations and a description of the sports then popular. By L. A. Govett, M.A., New College, Oxford. London: Elliott Stock, 62 Paternoster Row. 1890
12mo, cloth.

Encyclopedia of Games. By R. F. Foster. New York: F. A. Stokes. Eighth edition. 1897
12mo, three quarters morocco, bound by Sand.

The Book of Games, with directions how to play them. By Mary White. Ninth edition New York. Charles Scribner's Sons. 1898
16mo, original paper binding.

Outdoor Sports and Pastimes. Correct Rules for Athletics, Baseball, &c, &c. Eighth edition. Union Pacific Railroad, Omaha, Nebraska. 1900
12mo.

The Card Players' Companion. Fifth edition. Cincinnati: The Russell & Morgan Printing Company. 1891
16mo, paper.

Card Parties. Chicago: Armour & Co. 1905
Small 16mo, paper.

Solstice, deck and rules of the Game illustrated and explained. C. G. Van Fleet. 1893
16mo, three quarters morocco.

Rules and Regulations of a new and interesting game of cards known as Repple, by George A. Repple, St. Louis. 1906
 16mo, paper.

Sixteen hundred, a game. Cincinnati: The Church Printing Company. 1910
 16mo, paper.

How to Entertain with Cards. Cincinnati: The United States Playing Card Company.
 12mo, paper. 1921

Card Stunts for Kiddies. Cincinnati: The United States Playing Card Company. 1923

Six popular card games. Second edition. Cincinnati: The United States Playing Card Company. 1921
 12mo, paper.

Popular Games of Cards. How to Play Them. Third edition. Cincinnati: The Russell and Morgan Printing Company. 1889
 16mo, original paper cover.

Book of Card Rules. Kalamazoo, Mich.: American Playing Card Company. 1909
 12mo, three quarters morocco.

The Official Rules of Card Games. Hoyle up to date. Fifteenth edition. Cincinnati: The United States Playing Card Company. 1911
 Small 12mo, original paper cover.

The Official Rules of Card Games. Hoyle up to date. Seventeenth edition. Cincinnati: The United States Playing Card Company. 1913
 Small 12mo, original paper cover.

The Official Rules of Card Games. Hoyle up to date. Twentieth edition. Cincinnati: The United States Playing Card Company. 1915
 Small 12mo, original paper cover.

The Official Rules of Card Games. Hoyle up to date. Twenty-second edition. Cincinnati: The United States Playing Card Company. 1917
 Small 12mo, original paper cover.

The Official Rules of Card Games. Hoyle up to date. Twenty-third edition. Cincinnati: The United States Playing Card Company. 1918
 Small 12mo, original paper cover.

The Official Rules of Card games. Hoyle up to date. Twenty-fourth edition. Cincinnati: The United States Playing Card Company. 1919
 Small 12mo, original paper cover.

The Official Rules of Card Games. Hoyle up to date. Twenty-fifth edition. Cincinnati: The United States Playing Card Company. 1920
 Small 12mo, original paper cover.

The Official Rules of Card Games. Hoyle up to date. Twenty-seventh edition. Cincinnati: The United States Playing Card Company.
 Small 12mo, original paper cover. 1923

The Official Rules of Card Games. Hoyle up to date. Twenty-eighth edition. Cincinnati: The United States Playing Card Company. 1924
 Small 12mo, original paper cover.

The Official Rules of Card Games. Hoyle up to date. Twenty-ninth edition. Cincinnati: The United States Playing Card Company. 1926
 12mo, paper.

The Official Rules of Card Games. Hoyle up to date. Thirtieth edition. Cincinnati: The United States Playing Card Company. 1928
Small 12mo, original paper cover.

Illustrerad Spelbok. En handledning I de Flesta I sverige och Utlandet Brukliga Spel sasom Schack, Biljard, Domino, Bradspel, Vira, Whist, &c, &c. Utarbetad af Tom Wilson. Stockholm. Loostrom & Komp: s Forlag. 1888
12mo, three quarters blue morocco.

*Handboekje voor hen die zich willen oefenen in het Lomber-, Quadrille-, trekjes-en cinquille spel. Te Amsterdam, bij N. Geysbeek, no date, but about 1810
16mo, three quarters mottled calf, bound by Ramage.

*Onderwijs in het Whist, Omber, Quadrille, &c, &c. Naar Hoyle en Payne. Tweede Verbeterde Druk. Amsterdam. Bij Gartman, Vermandel en Holtrop. 1810
16mo, three quarters mottled calf, by Ramage.

*Het Kaartspelen Gemakkelijk Gemaakt, of Handleiding om de vermakelijkste Spellen als Lomberen, piketten, reversie, &c, &c. Naar den Vijftienden Druk uit het Hoogduitsch vertaald. Tweede Druk. Te Amsterdam, bij J. C. Van Kesteren.
16mo, full calf, gold lines and inside dentelles, by Ramage. 1821

*Kort en Grondig Onderwys van het alom vermaard en zeer vermakelyk Volte Spel. Alsmede van het zeer geestryk spel, genaamd a l'Hombre. Te Amsterdam, Gedrukt by de Erve de Weduwe J. Van Egmont: op de Reguliers Breestraat. No date
16mo, full mottled calf, gold lines and inside dentelles, by Ramage.

*De Regelen van het Ombre en Quadrille spel Gemakkelijk Gemaakt en Verklaard. Leyden D. Noothoven van Goor. No date
Small 16mo, full calf, gold lines inside dentelles, by Ramage.

*Handleiding en Regelen voor de Spelers van Wist, Boston, Ombre, &c, &c. Met Platen. Amsterdam. G. Theod. Bom.
16mo, three quarters pressed morocco. By Ramage.

*Kaartspelen:
Verklaring van het ombre en quadrille-spel. Te Amsterdam bij J. Bekouw & Zoon. No date
Nieuwe Beschrijving der meest gebruikelijke Kaartspelen. Amsterdam G. Theod. Bom. No date
Beknopt Overzicht van het Piket en Whistspel. Leiden, D. Noothoven van Goor. No date
16mo, three quarters calf, gold lines, by Root and Son.

*Spanish Games at Cards by Aquarius. London: Fredc. C. Mathieson & Sons, 10 Old Broad Street. 1890
Small 16mo, full calf, gold lines and inside dentelles, by Ramage.

Divertissemens innocens, contenant les Régles du Jeu des Échets, du Billiard, de la Paume, du Palle-Mail et du Trictrac. À La Haye: Chez Adrian Moetjens, Marchand Libraire, près de la Cour, à la Librairie Françoise. 1696
Small 16mo, thick, original binding of calf. Rare. Title-page in red and black.

A second copy of the above, original calf binding, with an engraved frontispiece by A. Schoonebeck.

*Encyclopédie Méthodique. Dictionnaire des Jeux, faisant suite au Tome III des Mathématiques. À Paris: Chez Panckoucke, Hôtel de Thou, rue des Poitevains. 1792
8vo, three quarters French mottled calf, by Ramage. Engraved plates of eighteenth-century games.

Des Jeux de Hasard au Commencement du 19ème Siècle. Par J. Lablée de l'Athénée de Lyon. Paris: Chez Petit Libraire, Palais du Tribunat, Galerie vitrée No. 229. An XI
16mo, half calf, original binding. Engraved title-page.   1803

Nouveaux Jeux de Société, suivis d'un Moule de Vers, etc. Par C. J. R. (de D). Paris: Ménard et Desenne, Fils, Libraires, rue Git le Cœur No. 8.   1817
12mo, uncut, original binding, paper.

Le Nouveau Savant de Société ou Encyclopédie des Jeux de Société. Quatrième édition, avec Figures et Planches. À Paris: Chez J. N. Barba, Libraire, Éditeur des Œuvres de M. Picar et de M. Alexandre Duval.   1825
4 vol. 16mo, uncut. Engraved frontispiece, Jeu de la Chouette.

*Nouveau Manuel des Jeux et Amusemens de Société, à l'usage de la jeunesse des deux sexes. Par M. H. Raisson. Paris: Au Dépôt des Nouveaux Manuels, rue de Battoir, 3.   1883
Small 16mo, three quarters calf, by Ramage. Engraved frontispiece, 'Les Jeux Innocens.'

Manuels-Roret. Nouveau Manuel Complet des Jeux de Calcul et de Hasard, ou Nouvelle Académie des Jeux. Par Mm. Lasserre, Lebrun et Leroy. Nouvelle édition. Paris: À la Librairie Encyclopédique de Roret, Rue Hautefeuille No. 12.   1853
16mo, half morocco.

Musée Rétrospectif de la Classe 100 Jeux à l'exposition Universelle Internationale de 1900, à Paris. Rapport présenté par M. Henry d'Allemagne, archiviste-paléographe.
2 vols. 4to, three quarters blue morocco. Many fine full-page illustrations, a number in color.

Jean Boussac. Encyclopédie des Jeux de Cartes. Jeux de Combinaisons de ruse, de hasard; patiences, etc. Paris: Libraire Ernst Kolb. Léon Chailley, Successeur, 8 rue Saint-Joseph.   No date
16mo, three quarters red morocco.

Règles des Jeux. Billiard, Dames, Domino, etc. Librairie des Villes et des Campagnes. Paris, 13, rue Cujas.   No date
16mo, full calf.

*Zwei und Dreysig Neue Kartenkunste zu einem angenehmen Zeitvertreibe in Gesellschaften achte durchaus Verbesserte und vermehrte Auflage. Frankfurt und Leipzig.
16mo, three quarters mottled calf, by Ramage.   1772

Der Whist und Bostonspieler wie er sein soll, oder: Grundliche Anweisung das Whist und Boston Spiel, etc. 27 belustigenden Kartenkunststucken von F. v. H. Quedlinburg und Leipzig.   No date
16mo, original paper binding.

Ganz neues allgemeinnutziges Unterhaltungsbuch für muntere Gesellschaften, etc. Gratz: Bey Christian Friedrich Trotscher.   1799
12mo, uncut.

*Neuester Spielalmanach für das Jahr   1800
Von Julius Casar. Engraved frontispiece.
Small 16mo, full mottled calf, gold lines and inside dentelles, by Ramage.

Neuestes Spielbuch, nebst einer grundlichen Anweisung zu einer leichten Erlernung des L'Hombre, Quadrille, etc. Wien: Bey Johann Georg Edlen von Mosle.   1802
16mo, original paper binding. Engraved frontispiece.

Berliner Almanach für Karten Schach un Pharospieler auf das Jahr   1804
Berlin: Bey Wilhelm Dehmigle, dem Jungern.
Small 16mo, original paper binding. Engraved frontispiece.

Der Meister in allen Kartenspielen, etc. Hamburg und Altona: Bei Gottfried Vollmer. No date, but about 1810
    12mo, uncut, original paper binding.

Das Whist, Boston, Casino und Imperial spiel, etc. Abgedrucht aus Julius Cäsar's Spielalmanach. Durchaus verbessert von G. W. von Abenstein, Berlin. 1810
    16mo, original paper binding.

Spielalmanach für Karten, Schach, Bret, etc., von Julius Cäsar. Nach den grundlichsten Regeln, etc., von G. W. von Abenstein. Berlin: G. Hayn. 1815
    16mo, three quarters green morocco.

Das Whist, Boston, Casino und Imperial Spiel, etc. Abgedrucht aus G. W. von Abenstein, Berlin. 1819
    16mo, three quarters mottled French calf.

Talisman des Glucks oder der Selbstlehrer für alle Karten, Schach, etc., von C.G.F. von Duben, second edition. Berlin. 1819
    16mo, three quarters blue morocco, thick. Engraved frontispiece.

*Das Ganze der Kartenspiele, oder Anweisung die üblichsten Deutschen, Franzosischen und Englischen Kartenspiele, als Boston, Whist, etc., von G. U. Enther. Quedlinburg und Leipzig. No date
    12mo, three quarters pressed morocco.

Neuester Spielalmanach für Karten, Schach, Brett, Billiard, Kegel und Ball Spieler; von G. W. von Abenstein. Berlin: Bei G. Hayn. 1820
    16mo, original binding, three quarters calf.

Neuestes Allgemeines Spielbuch enthaltend Der vollkommene Kartenspieler, . . . Der allezeit fertige Brettspieler, . . . Der willkommene Gesellschafter. Wien. 1829
    12mo, original cloth binding.

Neuestes Spiel Taschenbuch, oder grundlicher Unterricht zur pratichen Erlernung der Karten, Billiard, Schach und anderer Spiele, von T. F. Muller. Ulm. 1830
    16mo, original binding, half morocco.

Neuestes Spielbuch, etc., nebst den Regeln und Gesetzen von Georg Grimm. Leipzig. 1840
    16mo, three quarters red morocco.

Allgemeines Karten Spielbuch. Eine Anleitung alle besannten Conversations-Kartenspiele. Wien: Verlag von Franz Tendler. 1846
    16mo, three quarters blue morocco.

Neuester Spiel Almanach, von Carl Konig. Berlin. No date
    Small 16mo.

Encyclopädie der Spiele von L. von Alvensleben. Second edition. Leipzig: Verlag von Otto Wigand. 1855
    16mo, thick, original paper binding.

*Zwei und siebenzig, deutsche, französische, und englische Kartenspiele, als Skat, l'Hombre, etc., von Posert. Quedlinburg und Leipzig. 1864
    16mo, three quarters calf.

Deutsche, französische und englische Kartenspiele von v. Posert. Third edition. Quedlinburg und Leipzig. 1873
    16mo.

Encyclopädie der Spiele, von Freidrich Anton. Fifth edition. Leipzig: Verlag von Otto Wigand. 1889
    12mo, cloth.

Das Grosse Buch der Kartenspiele, etc., von Ernst Lange. Berlin.   No date
    12mo, three quarters blue morocco.

Deutsche, französische, und englische Kartenspiele, von F. von Posert. Ninth edition.
    Leipzig.   No date
    12mo, three quarters blue morocco.

Der perfecte Kartenspieler, etc., von Baron F. von Thalberg. Berlin.   No date
    12mo.

THE GAMESTERS
1674–1776

*The Compleat Gamester: or, Instructions How to play at Billiards, Trucks, Bowls
and Chess. Together with all manner of usual and most Gentile Games either on
Cards or Dice. To which is added The Arts and Mysteries of Riding, Racing, Archery, and Cock-fighting. London: Printed by A.M. for R. Cutler, and to be sold by
Henry Brome at the Gun at the West end of St. Paul's.   1674
    16mo, full French mottled calf, gold border and inside dentelles, and full gold back,
by Root and Son.

*The Compleat Gamester, etc., as above. The second edition. London: Printed for
Henry Brome at the Gun at the West end of St. Paul's.   1676
    16mo, full calf, paneled sides with gold tooling and inside dentelles, and full gilt
back, g.e. (probably by Zaehnsdorf). Engraved frontispiece, picturing a game of
billiards, of trictrac, dice, cock fighting and cards.

*The Compleat Gamester, etc. The second edition, as above.   1680
    Below the frontispiece is lettered 'Printed for Hen: Brome.'
    16mo, full calf, paneled sides with gold tooling and inside dentelles, and full gilt back,
g.e., by Zaehnsdorf.

*The Compleat Gamester: or Instructions How To Play at all manner of usual, and
most Gentile Games, either on Cards, Dice, Billiards, Trucks, Bowls, Chess. Also
The Arts and Misteries of Riding, Racing, Archery, Cock fighting. To which is added,
The Game at Basset, never before Printed in English. All Regulated by the most
Experienced Masters. London: Printed for Charles Brome, at the Gun, the West end
of St. Paul's Church.   1709
    16mo, full calf, gold lines and inside dentelles and full gilt back, by Root and Son.

*The Court Gamester: or, full and easy instructions for Playing the Games now in
Vogue, after the best Method; as they are play'd at Court, and in the Assemblies, viz.
Ombre, Picquet, and the Royal Game of Chess. Wherein The Frauds in Play are
detected, and the Laws of each Game annex'd, to prevent Disputes. Written for the
Use of the Young Princesses. By Richard Seymour, Esq; London: Printed for E.
Curll in Fleet-street.   1719
    16mo, full calf, paneled sides, gold borders and inside dentelles and full gold back,
g.e., by Ramage.
    *A second copy, identical in all respects, bound by Root and Son.

*The Court Gamester: or, full and easy instructions, etc., as above. The second edition,
corrected. London: Printed for E. Curll next the Temple Coffee House in Fleet-street.   1720
    16mo, full calf, paneled sides, inside dentelles in gold, by Ramage.
    *A second copy, identical in all respects, bound in mottled calf, by Ramage.

*The Court Gamester, etc., as above. The third edition, corrected. London: Printed
for E. Curll at the Dial and Bible over against Catherine Street in the Strand, 1722
    16mo, French mottled calf, gold lines and dentelles, by Ramage.
    Also a copy of this same edition in the original calf binding.

*The Compleat Gamester: Or, Full and Easy Instructions For Playing at above Twenty several Games Upon the Cards; with Variety of diverting Fancies and Tricks upon the same, now first added. As likewise at All the Games on the Tables. Together with The Royal Game of Chess and Billiards. To which is added The Gentleman's Diversion in the Arts and Mysteries of Riding, Racing, Archery, Cock-Fighting, and Bowling. The fifth edition, with Additions. London: Printed for J. Wilford at the Three Golden Flower de Luces in Little Britain. 1725

16mo, mottled calf, gold border and dentelles, and full gold back, g.e., by Zaehns-dorf. Engraved frontispiece, as in the second edition.

The Court Gamester: Or, Full and Easy Instructions for Playing the Games now in Vogue after the best Method; as they are played at Court, and in the Assemblies, viz. Ombre, in all its Branches. Picquet. And, The Royal Game of Chess. Wherein The Frauds in Play are detected, and the Laws of each Game annexed to prevent Dis-putes. Written for the Use of the Young Princesses. By Richard Seymour, Esq; The Fourth Edition Improved. London: Printed for E. Curll, against Catherine Street in the Strand. 1728

16mo, original binding of half calf.

*The Court Gamester. In Two Parts. Part I. Containing, Full and Easy Instructions for Playing the Games now in Vogue after the best Method; as they are played at Court, and in the Assemblées, viz. Ombre, in all its Branches, Picquet. And, the Royal Game of Chess. Part II. Containing, The Knowledge of Play, written for Publick Benefit, and the Entertainment of all Fair Players, wherein the Frauds in Play are detected, and the Chances of the Games of Hazard, Pharao, and Basset, are calculated and determined. To which is added, The Journal of a Gameing Lady of Quality, a Tale. In a Letter to a Friend. By Dr. Swift. London: Printed, and sold by J. Wilford, behind the Chapter House, near St. Paul's. 1732

16mo, full calf, paneled sides, gold borders and dentelles, by Ramage, g.e.

*The Compleat Gamester: In Three Parts. viz. I. Full and Easy Instructions for playing the Games, chiefly used at Court, and in the Assemblées, viz. Ombre, Qua-drille, Quintille, Picquet, Basset, Faro, and the Royal Game of Chess. II. The true manner of playing the most usual Games at Cards, viz. Whist, All Fours, Cribbidge, Put, Lue, Brag, &c. With several diverting Tricks upon the Cards. III. Rules for playing at all the Games both Within and Without the Tables; likewise at English and French Billiards. Also the Laws of each Game annexed to prevent Disputes. Written for the Use of the Young Princesses, By Richard Seymour, Esq; The Fifth Edition. London: Printed for E. Curll in Rose Street Covent Garden; and J. Wilford, behind the Chapter House in St. Paul's Church Yard. 1734

16mo, full calf, paneled sides, gold borders and dentelles, full gold back by Zaehns-dorf, g.e. Engraved frontispiece after Hogarth.
Also a copy bound in the original calf.
A third copy in original calf, blind tooled.

*The Compleat Gamester: In Three Parts. Containing, I. The Court Gamester: Or, Full and Easy Instructions for playing the Games of Ombre, Quadrille, Quintille, Picquet, Basset, Faro, and the Royal Game of Chess. II. The City Gamester: Or, True Manner of playing the most usual Games at Cards, viz. Whist, All Fours, Cribbidge, Put, Lue, Brag, &c. With several diverting Tricks upon the Cards. Also Rules for playing at all the Games both Within and Without the Tables; and at English and French Billiards: With the Laws of each Game annexed, to prevent Dis-putes. III. The Gentleman's Diversion: Or, The Arts of Riding, Racing, Archery, Cocking, and Bowling. Written for the Use of the Young Princesses, By Richard Sey-mour, Esq.; The Sixth Edition. London: Printed for E. Curll, at Pope's Head, in

Rose Street, Covent Garden; and J. Hodges at the Looking Glass, on London Bridge.
1739
    16mo, mottled French calf, gold border, dentelles and back, by Root and Son.
A second copy bound in the original calf with full gilt back.

*The Accurate Gamester's Companion: Containing Infallible Rules for playing The Game of Whist to Perfection In all its Branches. Treated in an easy manner, and illustrated with Variety of Cases. Also the Laws of the Game, Calculations relative to it, &c. The Ninth Edition improv'd. To which are added, The Game of Quadrille, Piquet, Chess and Backgammon, fully explained. Likewise a Dictionary for Whist, And an artificial Memory. The whole founded on the Experience of Edmond Hoyle, Gent. London: Printed for Tho. Osborne: And Sold by W. Reeve, at Shakespear's Head, near Serjeant's Inn Gate in Fleet Street.   1748
    16mo, full calf, gold lines and inside dentelles. Title-page in red and black.
Autographed, Edmond Hoyle.

*The Accurate Gamester's Companion: as above. But containing the tenth edition of the treatise on Whist, published in 1750, instead of the eighth of 1748, as in the previous volume.   1748
    16mo, French mottled calf, paneled sides, gold lines, full gold back and inside dentelles, g.e. Autographed, Edmond Hoyle and Tho. Osborne.

*The Polite Gamester: containing Short Treatises on the games of Whist, Quadrille, Back-gammon, Piquet and Chess. Together with an Artificial Memory, or an Easy Method of assisting the Memory of those that play at the Game of Whist. By Edmund Hoyle, Gent. Dublin: Printed for Peter Wilson, in Dame Street.   1752
    This contains the fifth edition of the treatise on whist.
    16mo, French mottled calf, gold lines, and inside dentelles, by Ramage.

*The Polite Gamester: as above, but with a New Addition, with great Additions to the Game of Whist; among which are, A Dictionary of Whist, which resolves almost all the critical Cases that may happen at the Game. Also a whole chapter of thirteen new Cases, never before published. Dublin: Printed for G. and A. Ewing, at the Angel and Bible in Dame Street.   1752
    This contains the thirteenth edition of the treatise on whist.
    16mo, three quarters French mottled calf.

*The Compleat Gamester: In Three Parts. Containing, I. The Court Gamester: Or, Full and Easy Instructions for playing the Games of Whist, Ombre, Quadrille, Quintille, Picquet, and the Royal Game of Chess. II. The City Gamester: Or, True Manner of Playing the most usual Games at Cards viz. All-Fours, Cribbidge, Put, Lue, Brag, Lottery, &c. With several divertting Tricks upon the Cards: also Rules for playing at all the Games both Within and Without the Tables; and at English and French Billiards: With the Laws of each Game annexed, to prevent disputes. III. The Gentleman's Diversion: Or, The Arts of Riding, Racing, Archery, Cocking, and Bowling. First written for the Use of the Young Princesses, By Richard Seymour, Esq; And now carefully revised, very much enlarged and improved, agreeable to the present Method of playing the several Games, By Charles Johnson, Esq.; The Eighth Edition. London: Printed for J. Hodges, at the Looking Glass, facing St. Magnus Church, London Bridge,   1754
    Engraved frontispiece after Hogarth.
    16mo, full calf, gold back and fillet border and inside dentelles.

*The Polite Gamester: containing Short Treatises on the Games of Whist, with an Artificial Memory, Quadrille, Back-gammon, Piquet and Chess. Together with an Essay Towards making the Doctrine of Chances Easy to those who understand Vulgar Arithmetick only. To which are added, Some Useful Tables on Annuities for

Lives, &c. &c. &c. By Edmund Hoyle, Gent. Dublin: Printed for George and
Alexander Ewing. 1761
   16mo, full calf, gold lines and inside dentelles.

*The Polite Gamester: as above, but printed for T. Ewing in Capel Street. 1772
   16mo, full calf, inside dentelles in gold, by Ramage.

*The Polite Gamester: as above, but printed by James Hoey at the Mercury in Parlia-
   ment Street (No. 19) 1776
   16mo, full calf, gold lines and inside dentelles, by Ramage.

ACADÉMIES DES JEUX

*La Maison des Jeux. Où se trouvent les Divertissemens d'une Compagnie, par des
   Narrations agreablès, & par des Jeux d'Esprit, & autres Entretiens d'une honneste
   conversation. Dernière édition. Revue, Corrigée & Augmentée. À Paris: Chez Antoine de Sommaville, au Palais sur le deuxième Perron, allant à la Sainte Chapelle, à
   l'Escu de France. Avec Privilége du Roy. 1657
   2 vols. 16mo, full calf, gold lines and inside dentelles, by Ramage, g.e. (par
C.D.M. Sorel).

*La Maison Académique, contenant les Jeux:

Du Piquet,	Des 4 parties du Monde,
Du Hoc,	De la cronologie,
Du Tric-trac,	Des Villes de France,
Du Hoca,	De cupidon,
De la guerre,	De la chouette,
De la Paulme,	Du Regnard & de la Poulle,
Du Billard,	De Loye,
Du palle mail,	Des Eschets,
Divers Jeux des cartes,	Des Blasons & Armoiries,
Qui se jouent en differentes facons,	Des proverbes,

& autres Jeux facessieux & divertissans.

À Paris: Chez Estienne Loyson, Marchand Libraire au Palais, dans la Galerie des
Brisonniers, au Nom de Jésus. Avec Privilége du Roy. 1659
   16mo, mottled calf, gold lines and dentelles, by Root & Son. Engraved frontispiece.

La Maison des Jeux Académiques, contenant un Recueil Général de tous les Jeux
divertissans pour se réjouir, & passer le temps agréablement. À Paris: Chez Estienne
Loyson, au Palais, à l'entrée de la Galerie des Prisonniers au Nom de Jésus. (Par E.L.)
Avec Privilége du Roy. 1665
   16mo, original calf, gilt back and edges. Engraved frontispiece.

*A second copy of the above, beautifully bound in blue morocco, gold lines, inside den-
   telles and full gilt back, by Chambulle-Duru, g.e.

*La Maison des Jeux Académiques, etc., as above, et augmentée de la˙ Loterie
   Plaisante. 1668
   16mo, full brown morocco, gold lines, by Root and Son, g.e.

*A second copy of the above, bound in French mottled calf, gold lines and dentelles,
   g.e., by Root and Son.

*La Maison Académique, contenant les Jeux, etc. Divisée en Deux Parties. À la
   Haye: Chez Jacob van Elinckhuysen, Marchand Libraire dans le Halstraet, au
   Dauphin. 1702
   16mo, pressed brown morocco, gold lines and dentelles, g.e., by Ramage.

*Académie Universelle des Jeux, contenant les Règles des Jeux de Cartes permis; du Tric-trac, des Échecs, de la Paulme, du Mail, du Billard, & autres. Avec des Instructions faciles pour apprendre à les bien jouer. À Paris: Chez Le Gras, Libraire, Grande Salle du Palais, à l'L Couronnée. Avec Approbation & Privilége du Roy.   1718
   16mo, French mottled calf, gold border and dentelles, by Ramage. Engraved frontispiece.

*Académie des Jeux Historiques, contenant les Jeux de l'Histoire de France, de l'Histoire Romaine, de la Fable, du Blason, et de la Géographie, & les Règles pour les jouer. Avec les Élemens de ces Sciences pour y servir d'introduction. Dédiée au Roy. Ouvrage très utile aux toutes sortes de personnes, & enrichi de Planches gravées exprès. À Paris: Chez le Gras, Libraire, Grande Salle du Palais, à l'L Couronnée. Avec Approbation & Privilége du Roy.   1718
   16mo, French mottled calf, gold lines and dentelles, by Ramage. Engraved frontispiece.

*La Plus Nouvelle Académie Universelle des Jeux, ou divertissemens Innocens, contenant, Les Règles des Jeux de Cartes permis; des Echecs, etc. Divisées en deux Tomes. À Leide: Chez Pierre vander Aa, Marchand, Libraire, Imprimeur de la Ville & de l'Université.   1721
   2 vols. 16mo, French mottled calf, inside dentelles in gold, by Ramage. Title-pages in red and black. Engraved frontispiece in each.

*La Plus Nouvelle Académie Universelle des Jeux, etc. À Amsterdam: Chez J. Cóvens & C. Mortier, Marchands Libraires sur le Vygendam.   1728
   2 vols. 16mo, three quarters mottled calf, by Ramage. Engraved frontispiece, title-pages in red and black.

La Plus Nouvelle Académie Universelle des Jeux, Tome II, as above,   1728
   16mo, original binding, full calf, full gilt back, containing 400 pages instead of the 190, as in the previous copy.

Académie Universelle, des Jeux, contenant les Règles des Jeux de Quadrille & Quintille, de l'Hombre à trois, du Piquet, du Reversis, des Echecs, du Trictrac; & de tous les autres Jeux. Avec des Instructions Faciles pour apprendre à les bien jouer. À Paris: Au Palais, chez Theodore le Gras, Libraire, Grande Salle du Palais, à l'L Couronnée. Avec Approbation & Privilége du Roy.   1730
   16mo, original calf, gilt floriated back. Engraved frontispiece. 345 pages.

*Académie Universelle des Jeux, etc., as above, but containing 710 pages.   1730
   16mo, French mottled calf, gold lines, dentelles and back, by Root and Son, g.e.

*Académie Universelle des Jeux, as above. Nouvelle édition. 588 pages.   1739
   16mo, original calf, full gilt back.

Académie Universelle des Jeux, etc., as above. 600 pages.   1739
   16mo, original calf, full gilt back.

*Académie Universelle des Jeux. Contenant les Règles de tous les Jeux. Avec des Instructions Faciles pour apprendre à les bien jouer. Première Partie. À Paris: Au Palais, chez Theodore le Gras, Libraire, Grand Salle, à l'L Couronnée. Avec Approbation et Privilége du Roy.   1743
   16mo, full calf, gold lines and dentelles, by Ramage.

Académie Universelle des Jeux, Seconde Partie, as above.   1743
   16mo, original calf, gilt back. Some of this book is contained in the first volume.

*La Plus Nouvelle Académie Universelle des Jeux, etc. Nouvelle édition revue, corrigée, & augmentée des Jeux qui ne se trouvent dans aucune édition précédente, &

enrichie de Figures en tailles-douces. À Amsterdam et à Leipzig: Chez Arkste'e &
Merkus. 1752
    3 vols. 16mo, original calf, gold lines and backs. Engraved frontispiece. Title-
pages in red and black.

*Académie Universelle des Jeux, avec des Instructions faciles pour apprendre à les bien
jouer. Nouvelle édition. Augmentée & mise en meilleur ordre. Deux parties
(bound together). À Amsterdam. 1758
    16mo, French mottled calf, gold lines, dentelles and back, by Ramage. Title-page
in red and black.

*Académie Universelle des Jeux, avec des Instructions faciles pour apprendre à les bien
jouer. Nouvelle édition. Augmentée & mise en meilleur ordre. Amsterdam. 1760
    2 vols. 16mo, mottled calf, gold lines, dentelles, by Ramage. Title-pages in red and
black.

*Académie Universelle des Jeux, etc., as above. Two parts, bound together. À Amster-
dam. 1763
    16mo, calf, inside dentelles.

Académie Universelle des Jeux, contenant les Règles de tous les Jeux, avec des In-
structions Faciles pour apprendre à les bien jouer, augmentée du Jeu de Whisk.
Première Partie. À Paris: Chez la Veuve Savoye, rue Saint-Jacques, à l'Espérance.
Avec Approbation & Privilége du Roi. 1765
    16mo, original binding of mottled calf, full gilt back.

Académie Universelle des Jeux. Les Règles du Jeu de Piquet, etc. Index in manuscript at the end of the book. À Paris: Chez Savoye, rue Saint-Jacques. 1765
    Probably the second part of the above.
    16mo, mottled calf, dentelles and gilt back.

*Académie Universelle des Jeux contenant les Règles de tous les Jeux, avec des In-
structions Faciles pour apprendre à les bien jouer, augmentée du Jeu de Whisk.
Première & Seconde Partie. À Paris: Au Palais, chez Leclerc, Libraire à la Prudence.
Avec Approbation & Privilége du Roi. 1765
    2 vols. 16mo, French mottled calf, gold lines and dentelles, by Ramage.

*Académie Universelle des Jeux, contenant les Règles de tous les Jeux, avec des In-
structions faciles pour apprendre à les bien jouer. Nouvelle édition, augmentée du
Jeu des Échecs, par Philidor, & du Jeu de Whisk, par Edmond Hoyle, traduit de
l'Anglois. Deux parties bound together. À Amsterdam, aux dépens de la Compagnie.
    16mo, original calf, gold floriated back. 1770

*Académie Universelle des Jeux, as above. Two parts in one volume. À Amsterdam. 1773
    16mo, French mottled calf, gold lines and dentelles, by Root and Son.

*Académie Universelle des Jeux, etc., as above. À Amsterdam. 1777
    2 vols. 16mo, original binding of calf, mottled, with gold border and dentelles and
back, g.e.

Almanach des Jeux, ou Académie Portative, contenant les Règles du Reversis, du
Wisk, du Tré-Sette, du Piquet, et du Trictrac. Nouvelle édition, augmentée des Jeux
du Maryland & du Wisk Bostonien. À Paris: Chez Fournier, Libraire, rue du Hurepoix, près du Pont S. Michel, à la Providence. Avec Approbation & Privilége du Roi.
    Small 16mo, French mottled calf, original binding. 1784

Almanach des Jeux ou Académie Portative, contenant les Règles du Wischt, du Reversis, du Tré-Sette et du Piquet. Avec Perte & Gain. À Paris: Chez Fournier,
Libraire, rue du Hurepoix. 1779
    Small 16mo, original calf binding, gold back.

*Académie Universelle des Jeux; contenant les règles des jeux de Cartes permis: celles du Billard, du Mail, du Trictrac, du Revertier, &c., &c. Avec des Instructions faciles pour apprendre à les bien jouer. Nouvelle édition. Augmentée du Jeu des Échecs, par Philidor; du Jeu de Whist, par Edmond Hoyle, traduit de l'Anglois; du Jeu de Tré-sette; du Jeu de Domino, &c., &c. Avec figures. À Amsterdam: Chez D. J. Changuion & T. van Harrevelt.   1786
   3 vols. 16mo, French mottled calf, gold lines and dentelles, by Ramage. Engraved frontispiece. Title-pages in red and black.

Académie Universelle des Jeux, etc., as above. Tome I. À Amsterdam.   1786
   16mo, three quarters French mottled calf, by Ramage. Engraved frontispiece, title-page in red and black.

Académie Universelle des Jeux, etc., as above. À Amsterdam.   1786
   3 vols. 12mo, half calf, original bindings.

Académie Universelle des Jeux, etc., as above. Tome second. À Amsterdam.   1789
   16mo, uncut.

*Académie Universelle des Jeux, etc., as above. À Lyon: Chez B. Cormon et Blanc, Libraires. An 13,   1805
   3 vols. 16mo, three quarters calf, by Ramage.

*Académie Universelle des Jeux, etc., as above. À Paris: Chez Amable Costes, Libraire, quai des Augustins, No. 29. À Lyon: Amable Leroy, Imprimeur-Libraire.
   3 vols. 16mo, three quarters calf, mottled, by Ramage.   1806

Académie Universelle des Jeux, etc., as above. À Lyon: Chez Amable Leroy, Imprimeur-Libraire.   1810
   3 vols, 16mo, three quarters red morocco.

*Académie des Jeux. Nouvelle édition, revue, corrigée, augmentée et acceptée par toutes les Académies de Paris: contenant le Piquet; l'Impériale; la Triomphe; l'Écarté; le Reversis; la Mouche; le Whisk; le Boston; la Bouillotte et le Quinze. Avec les Décisions des Jouers les plus consommés sur les coups les plus difficiles. À Paris: Chez Guyot et.De Pelafol, rue des Grands Augustins, No. 21.   1816
   Small 16mo, full mottled calf, gold border and dentelles, by Ramage.

*Petite Académie des Jeux, contenant les règles des principaux Jeux de Cartes, d'Adresse et de Hasard, tels que: Billard, Biribi, Boston, etc. À Paris: Chez tous les Marchands de Nouveautés.   1817
   16mo, three quarters calf, by Ramage, uncut, gold top.

*Académie des Jeux, contenant les Principaux Jeux de Cartes et de Combinaisons. Nouvelle édition, augmentée d'un Traité complet de l'Écarté, et de l'Abrégé du Jeu des Échecs. Par Philidor. Paris: Guillaume et Compagnie, Libraires, rue Haute-feuille, No. 14.   1821
   Small 16mo, three quarters calf, by Ramage, gilt top.

*Académie Portative, contenant les Règles du Reversis, Whist, Piquet, etc. Nouvelle édition, augmentée des Jeux de Maryland, Impériale et Échecs. Par M. Philidor. À Paris: Chez la veuve Fournier, Libraire, rue Neuve Notre Dame.   No date
   16mo, full calf, gold lines and dentelles, by Ramage.

*Académie des Jeux. Nouvelle édition, revue, corrigée, augmentée, et acceptée par toutes les académies de Paris; contenant le Piquet, etc. À Paris: Chez De Pelafol, rue des Grands Augustins, No. 21.   1821
   16mo, French mottled calf, gold border and dentelles, by Ramage. Engraved plates of cards and games.

Académie Universelle des Jeux, ou Dictionnaire méthodique et raisonné de tous les

jeux. Par L. C*****, Amateur. Paris: Chez Corbet Ainé Libraire, Quai des Augustins, No. 61.   1824
    12mo, three quarters calf, uncut.

Académie Universelle des Jeux, as above. Paris.   1825
    16mo, original calf binding.

*Académie Universelle des Jeux, contenant leurs règles fondamentales et additionnelles, etc., etc. Par L. D****, Amateur. Deuxième édition. Paris: Chez Corbet Ainé, libraire.   1833
    16mo, three quarters calf, gilt floriated back, by Ramage.

*Nouvelle Académie des Jeux, contenant la règle des jeux d'écarté, piquet, etc., etc., les principes et règles des jeux d'échecs, trictrac, dames et domino, suivi d'un traité du Jeu de Billard. Paris: Masson et Duprey, Libraires, rue Hautefeuille, No. 14. 1835
    16mo, three quarters calf, by Ramage.

Académie des Jeux, contenant la manière de jouer les principaux jeux de cartes, etc., précédé d'une introduction. Par Horace Raisson. Paris: Edme et Alexandre Picard, Libraires, rue Hautefeuille, No. 14.   1835
    16mo, uncut.

*Académie Universelle des Jeux, contenant leurs règles fondamentelles et additionnelles, etc. Et un nouveau Traité complet de l'écarté; précédé d'un coup d'œil général sur le jeu, tant dans les temps anciene que modernes. Par L. D****, Amateur. Troisième édition. Paris: Corbet Ainé, Libraire, 20, rue Dauphine.   1842
    12mo, three quarters calf, by Ramage.

Petite Académie des Jeux, contenant les règles et descriptions de tous les jeux de Cartes, etc. Par J. A. Burger. Paris: Librairie de Théodore Lefèvre & Cie, Emile Guérin, Éditeur, 2, rue des Poitevins.   No date
    16mo, calf. Engraved frontispiece, Tableau du Nain jaune.

Nouvelle Académie des Jeux, règles, principes, finesses, combinaisons, etc.; édition approuvée par les Jouers les plus émerités de Paris et augmentée du jeu de l'ane Portugais Récemment importé de Crimée. Par Halbert (d'Angers). Paris: Bernardin Bechet, Libraire-éditeur, 31, Quai des Grands Augustins. No date.   c. 1860
    16mo, calf. Frontispiece.

Nouvelle Académie des Jeux, etc., etc., as above, et augmentée du Jeu de la Manille. Par Halbert (d'Angers). Paris: Bernardin Béchet & Fils, Libraires-éditeurs. 53, Quai des Grands Augustins.   No date
    16mo, calf. Frontispiece.

Académie des Jeux de cartes de combinaison et d'exercice, avec un traité du jeu de whist entièrement nouveau publiè. Par Hilaire le Gai. Paris: Passard, Libraire-éditeur, rue des grands Augustins, 7.   1861
    16mo, calf.

*Nouvelle Académie des Jeux, contenant un dictionnaire des jeux anciens, le nouveau jeu de croquet, le Bésigue Chinois, et une étude sur les Jeux et Paris de Courses. Par Jean Quinola. Paris: Garnier Frères, Libraires-éditeurs, 6, rue des Saints Pères.
    12mo, three quarters morocco. Engraved frontispiece.   No date

*Académie des Jeux, contenant la règle de chacun des principaux jeux, soit de cartes, billard, etc. Nouvelle édition mise en ordre par Richard. Paris: De la Rue, Libraire-éditeur, rue des Grands Augustins, No. 3.   No date
    16mo, three quarters calf, by Ramage. Engraved frontispiece.

Académie des Jeux. Par Richard. Paris: De la Rue, Libraire.   No date
    12mo, uncut, three quarters morocco, bound by Sand.

Académie des Jeux, contenant l'Historique la Marche, les Règles, conventions et maximes des Jeux, etc. Par Van Tenac. Paris: Garnier Frères, Libraires, 6, rue des Saints Pères et Palais Royal. No date
    Small 16mo, thick, original cloth binding.

Académie des Jeux, contenant les règles des Jeux de Piquet, Whist, Manille, etc. Paris: De la Rue, Libraire-éditeur, 5, rue des Grands-Augustins. No date
    16mo.

Le Salon des Jeux, ou règles et descriptions des jeux de cartes, etc., orné de planches. Paris: J. Lamglumé Libraire, rue des Poitevins, 2. No date.   _c._ 1830
    16mo, three quarters morocco, pressed, uncut.

HOYLE'S GAMES

*A Short Treatise on the Game of Whist. Containing the Laws of the Game: and also Some Rules, whereby a Beginner may, with due Attention to them, attain to the Playing it well. Calculations for those who will Bet the Odds on any Point of the Score of the Game then playing and depending.
    Cases stated, to shew what may be effected by a very good Player in Critical Parts of the Game.
    References to Cases, viz. at the End of the Rule you are directed how to find them.
    Calculations, directing with moral Certainty, how to play well any hand or Game, shewing the Chances of your Partner's having 1, 2 or 3 Certain Cards.
    With Variety of Cases added in the Appendix. By a Gentleman. Bath, printed, and London, reprinted for W. Webster, near St. Paul's, and sold by all the Booksellers and Pamphlet Shops in Town and Country.   1743
    Small 12mo, full mottled calf, gold borders and dentelles, by Root and Son.
    This is the first London edition of Hoyle's Treatise on the Game of Whist, and the title-page is followed by an advertisement, quoting a letter from 'a gentleman of Bath to a friend.'

A second copy of the above, in the original binding, three quarters calf. These are piracies of the first edition Hoyle, and are not autographed.

Hoyle's Games. A Short Treatise on the Game of Whist. Sixth edition. Autographed. With folding plate for framing, listing the rules of the game. Also A Short Treatise on Piquet. Second edition. Autographed. And A Short treatise on the game of Backgammon. Autographed. Also Some Rules and Observations for Playing Well at Chess. London: Printed for T. Osborne at Gray's Inn. Thomas Salnvey book-plate.   1746
    16mo, original calf, gold lines.

A Short Treatise on the Game of Quadrille shewing The Odds of winning or losing most Games that are commonly played; either by calling a King, or by playing Sans Prendre. To which are added The Laws of the Game. The second edition. By Edmond Hoyle, Gent. London: Printed for T. Osborne, at Gray's Inn; J. Hildyard at York; M. Bryson at Newcastle; and J. Leake at Bath. Autographed, Edmond Hoyle.   16mo, three quarters morocco.   1746
    In this volume are also treatises on Backgammon (1745), piquet (second edition, 1746), whist (seventh edition, 1747, autographed, Edmond Hoyle), each with a title-page of its own.

Pigott's New Hoyle; or, the General Repository of Games: containing Rules and Instructions for Playing Whist, Piquet, Quinze, etc. . . . With Tables of Odds, etc., . . . as established at Brooke's, White's, The Union, Cocoa Tree, etc. . . . By Charles Pigott, Esq. The ninth edition, corrected and enlarged. etc. . . . London: Printed

for J. Ridgway, St. James's Square. By T. Sutton, Britannia Street, Gray's Inn Lane Road.   No date
    16mo, original calf, blind tooled.

*A Short Treatise on the Game of Whist, etc. . . . By Edmond Hoyle, Gent. The tenth edition with great additions. . . . London: Printed for T. Osborne, at Gray's Inn. Autographed, Edmond Hoyle, Tho. Osborne.   1750
    16mo, mottled calf, gold lines and dentelles, by Ramage. The book also treats of quadrille, piquet, chess, backgammon.

*Mr. Hoyle's Games of Whist, Quadrille, Piquet, Chess and Backgammon, complete. . . . The eleventh edition. London: Printed for Thomas Osborne, at Gray's Inn; James Hodges near London Bridge; and Richard Baldwin, in Paternoster Row. Autographed, Edmond Hoyle, and Tho. Osborne.   No date
    16mo, French mottled calf, gold lines, dentelles and edges, by Root and Son. Interesting marginal notes (in manuscript).

*A second copy of the above. Autographed, Edmond Hoyle, Tho. Osborne. Eleventh edition.
    16mo, three quarters calf, by Ramage.

Mr. Hoyle's Games of Whist, Quadrille, Piquet, Chess and Backgammon. Complete. . . . The twelfth edition. London: Printed for Thomas Osborne in Gray's Inn; Stanley Crowder at the Looking Glass, and Richard Baldwin at the Rose, in Paternoster Row.   No date
    16mo, original calf.

*A Short Treatise on the Game of Whist, etc. . . . By Edmond Hoyle, Gent. The thirteenth edition with great additions. Dublin: Printed for G. and A. Ewing, at the Angel and Bible in Dame Street.   1752
    16mo, three quarters calf, by Ramage.
    This book treats also of backgammon, quadrille, piquet, chess, and contains 'An Artificial Memory' for those that play at whist.

*Mr. Hoyle's Games of Whist, Quadrille, Piquet, Chess and Backgammon. Etc. . . . The fourteenth edition. London: Printed for Thomas Osborne in Gray's Inn; Henry Woodfall and Richard Baldwin, both in Paternoster Row. Autographed, Edmond Hoyle.   No date
    16mo, mottled calf, full gilt back, gold lines and dentelles, by Root and Son.

Mr. Hoyle's Games of Whist, Quadrille, Piquet, Chess and Backgammon. . . . The fourteenth edition. London: Printed for Thomas Osborne, in Gray's Inn; Henry Woodfall, and Richard Baldwin, both in Paternoster Row. Autographed, Edmond Hoyle.   No date
    16mo, original calf.

*Mr. Hoyle's Games of Whist, Quadrille, Piquet, Chess and Backgammon. The fifteenth edition. London: Printed by Assignment from T. Osborne of Gray's Inn for S. Crowder, R. Baldwin, and S. Bladon, etc. . . .   No date
    16mo, three quarters calf, by Ramage.

*Mr. Hoyle's Games, as above. . . . The fifteenth edition, as above.
    16mo, full calf, paneled sides, gold lines and dentelles.

*Mr. Hoyle's Games of Whist, Quadrille, Piquet, Chess and Backgammon, etc. . . . The sixteenth edition. London: Printed by Assignment from T. Osborne; for J. Rivington and J. Wilkie, etc.   No date
    16mo, three quarters calf, by Ramage.

*Hoyle's Games, improved: being Practical Treatises on the following Fashionable Games, viz. Whist, Quadrille, Piquet, Backgammon, Chess, Billiards and Tennis,

with the established rules of each Game. By James Beaufort, Esq., of Cavendish Square. London: Printed for S. Bladon, No. 16 Paternoster Row.   1775
16mo, original calf.

*Hoyle's Games, improved: being Practical Treatises on the following Fashionable Games, viz. Whist, Quadrille, Piquet, Chess, Backgammon, Billiards, Cricket, Tennis, Quinze, Hazard, and Lansquenet. . . . Revised and corrected by Charles Jones, Esq. London: Printed for J. Rivington and J. Wilkie, etc.   1775
16mo, three quarters calf, by Ramage.

Hoyle's Games improved: being Practical Treatises on the following Fashionable Games, viz., etc. Revised and corrected by Thomas Jones, Esq. London: Printed for W. Wood, in Fleet Street; and sold by all Booksellers.   1778
16mo, original calf.

Hoyle's Games improved: etc., as above.   1778
A second copy, 16mo, in the original calf.

*Hoyle's Games, improved: being Practical Treatises on the following Fashionable Games, viz. . . . Revised and corrected by Charles Jones, Esq. London: Printed for J. F. and C. Rivington, etc.   1779
16mo, three quarters calf, by Ramage.

*Hoyle's Games, improved: being Practical Treatises on the following Fashionable Games, viz. Revised and corrected by Charles Jones, Esq. A new edition, enlarged. London: Printed for J. F. and C. Rivington, etc.   1786
16mo, three quarters calf, by Ramage.

*Hoyle's Games, improved, as above.   1786
16mo, full mottled calf, gold lines and dentelles, by Ramage.

*Hoyle's Games, improved: being Practical Treatises on the following Fashionable Games, viz. Whist, Quadrille, Piquet, Backgammon, Chess, Billiards and Tennis, with the established Rules of each Game. By James Beaufort, Esq., of Cavendish Square. London: Printed for Osborne and Griffin; and H. Mozley, Gainsbrough.   1788
16mo, full calf, gilt back, lines and dentelles, by Root and Son.

*Hoyle's Games, improved: being Practical Treatises on Whist, Quadrille, Piquet, Chess, Backgammon, Draughts, Cricket, Tennis, Quinze, Hazard, Lansquenet, Billiards, and Goff or Golf; . . . Revised and corrected by Charles Jones, Esq. A new edition, enlarged. London: Printed for J. F. and C. Rivington, T. Payne and Son, etc.
16mo, mottled calf, gold lines and dentelles, by Ramage.   1790

Traité du jeu de Whist. Traduit de l'Anglois d'Edmond Hoyle. Nouvelle édition augmentée; suivi du jeu de trois sept, du jeu de piquet, du jeu de dez Anglois ou crabs, avec ses Chances & Différences, & du jeu de billard. À Liège: Chez J. F. Desoer, Imprimeur-Libraire, à la Croix d'or, sur le Pont d'Ile.   1794
16mo, original paper cover, uncut.

*Hoyle's Games, improved: being Practical Treatises on Whist, Quadrille, Piquet, Chess, etc. . . . Revised and corrected by Charles Jones, Esq. A new edition, enlarged. London: Printed for R. Baldwin, B. Law, etc. . . .   1796
16mo, three quarters calf, by Ramage.

Hoyle's Games, improved, etc., as above. A second copy. London.   1796
16mo, original calf.

*Hoyle's Games, improved, etc. . . . With an essay on Game Cocks. . . . Revised and corrected by Charles Jones, Esq. A new edition, considerably enlarged. London: Printed by M. Ritchie, Middle Street, Cloth Fair, for R. Baldwin, T. Payne, etc. . . .
16mo, full mottled calf, gold lines and dentelles, by Ramage.   1800

*The New Pocket Hoyle, containing the Games of Whist, Quadrille, Piquet, Quinze, Lansquenet, . . . Accurately displaying the Rules and Practice as admitted and established by the first Players in the Kingdom. London: Printed for T. Bensley, Bolt Court, Fleet Street; for Wynne and Scholey, 45; and J. Wallis, 46 Paternoster Row. Small 16mo, full mottled calf, gold lines and dentelles, by Ramage. 1802

Hoyle's Games, improved: consisting of Practical Treatises on Whist, Quadrille, Piquet, etc. . . . By Charles Jones, Esq. London: Printed for R. Baldwin, T. Payne, etc. . . . 16mo, full calf. 1803

The New Pocket Hoyle, containing the Games of Whist, Quadrille, Piquet, Quinze, etc. . . . Fourth edition. London: Printed for P. and W. Wynne, Paternoster Row; etc. . . . 1807
Small 16mo, calf.

*Hoyle's Games, improved and selected as a companion to the Card Table . . . London: Printed for R. Baldwin; W. Lowndes; etc. . . . 1808
Small 16mo, original paper cover in original paper slip case.

The New Pocket Hoyle. Part II, consisting of Gentlemen's Games; viz. Billiards, Chess, Cricket, Tennis, Cocking, Backgammon, Draughts, Hazard, Goff, Horse Racing. Accurately displaying the Rules and Practice as admitted and established by the first players of the Kingdom. . . . Charles Jackson, Esq. This, with the card games forms a complete and improved edition of Hoyle. London: Printed by T. Davison, Whitefriars; For R. Scholey, etc. 1808
Small 16mo, calf.

*Hoyle's Games, improved and selected as a Companion to the Card Table, etc. . . . By Charles Jones, Esq. . . . London: Printed for W. Lowndes . . . 1813
16mo, three quarters calf, uncut, gold top.

Hoyle's Games, improved, consisting of Practical Treatises on Whist, etc. . . . By Charles Jones, Esq. . . . London: Printed for W. Lowndes; etc. . . . 1814
16mo, thick, three quarters blue morocco.

*Hoyle's Games, improved. A new edition with additions. London: Printed for G. Walker. 1816
A second title-page, The New Hoyle, containing easy rules for playing the Games of Whist, etc. . . . London: Printed for G. Walker, and sold by all Booksellers. 1817
16mo, calf, gold dentelles, by Ramage. Engraved frontispiece by E. Stalker, after J. Thurston.

*Hoyle, abridged. Short rules for short memories at the Game of Whist, with the Laws of the Game. Adapted either for the head or the pocket, with the last new Rules as established at Bath and London by Bob Short. Derby: Published by Thomas Richardson.
Small 16mo, full pressed morocco, inside dentelles in gold, by Ramage.

Hoyle's Games: being a Companion to the Card Table: containing Rules and Directions for playing the games of Whist, etc. . . . London: Printed for William Clarke, 92, Royal Exchange. 1820
Small 16mo, calf.

*Hoyle's Games, improved, consisting of Practical Treatises on Whist, etc. . . . By Charles Jones, Esq. London: Printed for W. Lowndes, etc. . . . 1820
16mo, full calf, gold lines and dentelles, by Root and Son.

The New Pocket Hoyle, consisting of Gentlemen's Games; viz. Billiards, etc. . . . By Charles Jackson, Esq. London: Printed for W. Taylor, Russel Court, Bridges Street, Covent Garden. 1820
16mo, three quarters morocco. Engraved plates.

Hoyle's Games, improved, consisting of Practical Treatises on Whist, etc. . . . By Charles Jones, Esq. . . . London: Printed for George B. Whittaker; etc. . . .   1826
16mo, original binding, half cloth, uncut.

Hoyle's Improved Edition of the Rules for Playing Fashionable Games at Cards, &c. New York: Published by W. C. Borradaile, 146 Broadway.   1830
16mo, calf. Engraved frontispiece.

Hoyle's Games, improved and enlarged by new and practical treatises, etc. . . . By G. H.****, Esq. London: Printed for Longman, Rees and Co. . . .   1835
16mo, original calf.

Hoyle's Games, improved and enlarged, etc., as above. By G. H****   New edition. London: Longman & Co. . . .   No date
16mo, original cloth binding.

Hoyle Made Familiar, containing an accurate description of whist, etc. . . . By Eidrah Trebor, Esq. .Edinburgh: Published by Stirling and Kenney.   1836.
Small 16mo, calf. Engraved frontispiece and two title-pages.

Hoyle made Familiar, as above. By Eidrah Trebor, Esq. Edinburgh: Published by Stirling, Kenney & Co. London: Wm. S. Orr & Co. Amen Corner, Paternoster Row. Tenth edition. Engraved frontispiece.   No date
Small 16mo, original cloth binding, g.e.

Hoyle Made Familiar, etc. . . . as above. By Eidrah Trebor, Esq. London: Ward and Lock, 158 Fleet Street. Thirteenth edition.   No date
Small 16mo, original cloth binding, g.e.

An improved miniature edition of Hoyle's Games, containing rules and directions, etc. . . . London: Henry Lea, 22 Warwick Lane.   No date
Small 16mo, cloth, original binding.

Hoyle's improved edition of the rules for playing Fashionable Games . . . Philadelphia: Thomas Cowperthwait & Co. 253 Market Street.   1841
16mo, full crossgrained morocco, original binding, gold lines.

Hoyle's Games, improved and enlarged . . . By G. H****, Esq. London: Longman, Brown & Co. . . .   1842
16mo, original cloth binding.

Hoyle's Games: containing the established rules . . . Philadelphia: Henry F. Anners. Small 16mo, original cloth binding.   1845

Hoyle's Games, improved and enlarged . . . By G. H****, Esq. New edition. London: Longman and Co.   1847
16mo, original cloth binding.

*Hoyle's Games, improved and enlarged . . . By G. H****, Esq. New edition. London: Longman and Co. . . .   1853
16mo, mottled calf, gold lines and dentelles, by Ramage.

Hoyle's Games. Illustrated edition. Embracing all the most modern modes of play, . . . By Thomas Frere. New York: T. W. Strong, 98 Nassau Street.   1857
16mo, original cloth.

Hoyle's Games, as above. . . . By Thomas Frere.   Boston: G. W. Cottrell, 36 Cornhill. New York: T. W. Strong, 599 Broadway.   1857
16mo, original cloth binding.

Hoyle's Games. Illustrated edition, as above. . . . By Thomas Frere. New York: Lee, Shepard & Dillingham, 49 Greene street.   1857
16mo, original cloth binding.

Hoyle's Games, improved and enlarged . . . By G. H****, Esq. New edition. London: Longman & Co. . . .
 16mo, original cloth binding.

The American Hoyle; or Gentleman's Handbook of Games: . . . By Trumps . . . Seventh edition. . . . New York: Dick & Fitzgerald, publishers.
 12mo, original cloth binding.

Hoyle's Games. Containing all the modern methods of playing the latest and most fashionable games. By Thomas Frere. Improved edition. Boston: J. S. Locke & Co.   1876
 16mo, original cloth binding.

The Modern Pocket Hoyle; containing all the Games of Skill and Chance as played in this country at the present time. . . . By Trumps. Tenth edition, revised and corrected. New York: Dick & Fitzgerald, publishers.   1880
 16mo, original cloth binding.

Hoyle's Games. A Complete Guide and reliable authority upon all games of chance. . . . New York: Excelsior Publishing House.   1887
 16mo, three quarters red morocco.

Wehman's edition of Hoyle's Card Games, containing all the standard rules for . . . playing in America. Published by Henry J. Wehman, song and handbook publisher, Park Row, New York.   1894
 16mo, three quarters calf.

Hoyle. An Encyclopedia of Indoor Games. . . . By R. F. Foster . . . Illustrated with numerous diagrams and engravings. Eighth edition. New York: Frederick A. Stokes Company, publishers.   1897
 12mo, original binding, half cloth.

The American Hoyle; or Gentleman's Handbook of Games . . . By Trumps. . . . Fifteenth edition. . . . New York: Dick & Fitzgerald, publishers.   1904
 12mo, original cloth binding.

The Standard Hoyle. A Complete Guide. . . . New and revised edition. Boston: The Mutual Book Company, publishers.   1906
 16mo, original cloth binding.

Hoyle's Games. Autograph edition. Revised, enlarged and brought up to date. New York: The McClure Company.   1907
 16mo, original cloth binding.

CONCERNING BACCARAT

Traité Théorique et Pratique du Baccarat, contenant la règle du jeu examen des probabilités, du tirage règle et théorie du Baccarat en banque Grecs et Tricheries. Par Laun. Paris: H. De la Rue et Cie, Libraires-éditeurs, 5, rue des Grands-Augustins.   No date
 Small 8vo, calf.

Baccarat Fair and Foul, being an explanation of the game, and a warning against its dangers by Professor Hoffmann. . . . London. George Routledge and Sons, Limited. Broadway, Ludgate Hill, Manchester, Glasgow and New York.   1891
 16mo, original cloth binding.

CONCERNING BACKGAMMON

*A Short Treatise on the Game of Backgammon. By Edmond Hoyle, Gent. Autographed, Edmond Hoyle. Containing an advertisement of the fourth edition of the Treatise on Whist. London.   No date
 16mo, mottled calf, gold lines and dentelles, by Ramage.

CONCERNING BASSET

*Calcolo sopra I Giuochi della Bassetta e del Faraone. Aggiuntovi un Estratto di Lettera sopra il Giuoco publico di Venezia. In Venezia: Presso Giambatista Pasquali, con licenza de' superiori.   1777
  12mo, three quarters calf, by Ramage.

CONCERNING BEZIQUE

The Game of Bezique. By Cavendish. . . . London: Thos. de la Rue & Co.   1870
  16mo, original cloth binding.

Bezique, Euchre, Écarté, All Fours, Napoleon, and all round games now played on the card table. By Captain Crawley. London: Ward, Lock and Tyler, Warwick House, Paternoster Row. Preface dated   1876
  16mo, three quarters morocco.

The Laws of Rubicon Bezique, adopted by the Portland and Turf Clubs, with a guide to the Game, by Cavendish. Third edition. London: Thomas de la Rue & Co. 1895
  16mo, original cloth binding, g.e.

Bezique and Cribbage. By Berkeley. With illustrations. London: George Bell & Sons, York St., Covent Garden and New York.   1901
  16mo, original cloth binding.

Règle Complète du Jeu de Cartes Le Bésigue. Par M. Bercheville. Paris: Le Bailly.
  12mo, three quarters morocco, uncut.   No date

Jeux de Bésigue. Bésigue Chinois. Bésigue Japonais. Par Van Tenac et Laun. Paris.
  12mo, three quarters morocco, bound by Sand.

The Pocket Guide to Bezique. By Cavendish. Sixteenth edition. London: De la Rue.
  Small 16mo, g.e., full morocco, bound by Sand.   1905

CONCERNING BOSTON

*Rules for the Game of Cards, called Boston. Second edition. Gravesend: Printed by R. Pocock, and sold by Messrs. Robinsons, Paternoster Row, and all other booksellers.   1802
  Small 16mo, mottled calf, gold lines and dentelles.

Das Bostonspiel . . . herausgegeben von T. F. Kuhn. Quedlinburg und Leipzig: Verlag von Gottfr. Basse.   1828
  16mo, original paper cover.

Der Boston Spieler . . . nebst 26 belustigenden Kartenkunststucken von F. v. H. Second edition. Quedlinburg und Leipzig.   No date
  16mo, calf.

Boston Rules and Tables.   No date
  8vo, full morocco.

CONCERNING CALABRASELLA

The Pocket Guide to Calabrasella. By Cavendish. Second edition. London: De la Rue.
  Small 16mo, paper, g.e.   1872

CONCERNING CINCH

The Laws and Etiquette of Cinch. Compiled and edited by the Chicago Cinch Club, Chicago.   1890
  16mo, original cloth binding.

CONCERNING COMÈTE

*Règles du Nouveau Jeu de la Comète, avec des Observations sur les différentes manières de le jouer. À Paris au Palais: Chez Theodore le Gras, Grand Salle du Palais, à l'L Couronnée. 1748
    12mo, mottled calf, gold borders and dentelles, by Ramage.

CONCERNING CRIBBAGE

The Cribbage Player's Text Book: being a new and complete treatise on the game, in all its varieties; including the whole of Anthony Pasquin's Scientific Work on Five Card Cribbage. By George Walker. London: Sherwood, Gilbert & Piper, Paternoster Row. 1837
    16mo, original cloth binding. Frontispiece in color.

Dick's Hand Book of Cribbage, containing full directions for playing all the varieties of the game and the laws which govern them. William B. Dick. New York: Dick & Fitzgerald, publishers. 1885
    16mo, original cloth binding.

Cribbage Made Easy: being a new and complete treatise, etc., as above. By George Walker. New York: Dick & Fitzgerald, publishers. No date
    16mo, original binding, half cloth.

CONCERNING DOMINOES

The People's Domino Book. John Leng & Co., Ltd., Dundee, and 186 Fleet Street, London. No date
    8vo, paper.

CONCERNING ÉCARTÉ

Traité de l'Écarté à écrire, par M.B.**** À Paris: Chez Urbain Canel, libraire, rue St. Germain des Prés; etc. . . . À Orléans: Chez Darnault Maurant, imprimeur-libraire. 1826
    8vo, original paper cover.

The Laws of Écarté, adopted by the Turf and Portland clubs, with a treatise on the game by Cavendish. Fourth edition, revised and greatly enlarged. London: Thos. de la Rue & Co., Ltd. 1897
    16mo, original cloth binding.

Écarté and Euchre. By Berkeley. Illustrated. London: George Bell & Sons. 1905
    16mo, original cloth binding.

CONCERNING EUCHRE

The Game of Euchre by John W. Keller. Including treatises on French euchre, setback euchre, etc., and progressive euchre. . . . New York: Frederick A. Stokes Company, publishers. 1887
    16mo, original binding, half cloth.

The Pocket Guide to Euchre. By Cavendish. Fourth edition. London: Thos. de la Rue & Co., Ltd. 1890
    Small 16mo, g.e.

Progressive Euchre. Cincinnati: Joseph E. Church.
    16mo, paper.

Call Ace Euchre. By R. F. Foster. New York: Brentano's. 1905
    16mo, original cloth binding, g.e. Title-page in red and black.

CONCERNING FIVE HUNDRED

The Game of Five Hundred and How to Play It. Vest pocket edition. Cincinnati, U.S.A.: The United States Playing Card Company. 1899
Original cloth cover, small 16mo.

Rules of the Game of Five Hundred, as adopted by the Binghamton Club. Binghamton: The Outing Publishing Company. 1908
Small 16mo, paper.

Foster's Laws of Five Hundred, with hints to beginners. By R. F. Foster. Philadelphia. 16mo, paper. 1908

Five Hundred. How to Play It. Cincinnati: The United States Playing Card Company. 16mo, paper. 1909

CONCERNING GAIGLE

Gaigle. Laws and Rules, How to Play the Game. By Ellis E. Pressler. First edition. Williamsport, Pa. 1895

CONCERNING HEARTS

Foster on Hearts. A description of the game, with suggestions for good play and a code of laws. By R. F. Foster. . . . New York and London: Frederick A. Stokes Company, publishers. 1895
16mo, original cloth binding.

The Game of Hearts. Cincinnati: The United States Playing Card Company. 1900
16mo, paper.

CONCERNING HOMBRE

Le Jeu de l'Hombre comme on le joue présentement à la Cour & à Paris. Avec les Pertintailles. Enrichy de cartes figurées, qui représentent les Jeux qui se jouent. Cinquième édition. À Paris: Chez la Veuve de Claude Barbin, au Palais, sur le second Perron de la Sainte-Chapelle. Avec privilége du Roy. 1705
16mo, original calf, full gilt back, engraved frontispiece, A. Clouzier.

*Le Jeu de l'Hombre, augmenté des décisions nouvelles sur les difficultés et incidens de ce Jeu. À Paris: Chez Pierre Ribou, à la Descente du Pont Neuf, sur le Quay des Augustins, à l'Image S. Louis. Avec approbation et privilége du Roy. 1709
12mo, mottled calf, paneled sides, gold lines and dentelles, uncut, gold top and back, by Root and Son. Engraved frontispiece by Jean Batiste Bonnart.

*Il Nobile Giuoco dell' Ombre spiegato a quelli che vogliono entrare nelle più civili Radunanze per un onesto divertimento. In Venezia: Presso Leonardo Pittoni, con licenza de' Superiori. Engraved frontispiece and title-page. 1725
16mo, red pressed morocco, gold edges and dentelles, by Ramage.

Das Neue Konigliche l'Hombre Spiel. . . . Hamburg. 1726
16mo, original paper cover.

Das l'Hombre Cabinet, oder grundliche Anweisung das l'Hombre, Quadrille und Cinquille Spiel. . . . Frankfurt an der Oder: Bey Carl Gottlieb Strauss. 1785
12mo, original paper binding.

Das neue Koniglische l'Hombre nebst einer grundlichen Anweisung wie Quadrille, etc. Hamburg: In der Heroldschen Buchhandlung. 1788
16mo, original paper binding.

*Das neue Königliche l'Hombre nebst einer grundlichen Anweisung wie Piquet, etc. Funfzehnte verbesserte und vermehrte Auflage. Luneburg: Bey Herold und Wahlstab.
1808

    16mo, three quarters calf, by Ramage.

*L'Hombre royal, oder vollstanidge theoretisch praktische unleitung zur grundlichen Erlernung des Koniglichen oder Franzosischen L'Hombres. . . . Wien und Prag: Im Verlage der G. Haasschen Buchhandlung.
1824

    16mo, three quarters mottled calf, by Ramage.

Geschichte des L'Hombre. Halle.
No date

    12mo, uncut, three quarters morocco, by Sand.

The Game of Hombre. Second edition. London: Printed for private circulation. 1878

    8vo, original cloth binding, gold lines and top, uncut. Frontispiece after Hogarth.

CONCERNING GAMES OF PATIENCE

Patiencen. Gesammelt und herausgegeben von M.***h. Zweite durchgesehene Auflage. Wien: Verlag von H. F. Müller, Kunsthandler.
No date

    16mo, calf.

*Illustrated Games of Patience. By Lady Adelaide Cadogan. Dedicated by permission to His Royal Highness Prince Leopold, K.G. London: Sampson, Low, Marston, Low and Searle, Crown Buildings, 188 Fleet Street.
1784

    8vo, original cloth binding. Ex Libris, George Clulow.

Illustriertes Buch, Patiencen. Neue Folge. 60 Patience Spiele. Breslau: J. U. Kern's Verlag.

    12mo, cloth. Engraved title-page in red and black.

Le Livre Illustré des Patiences. 60 Jeux de Patience avec figures indiquant la place des cartes. Seconde édition. Breslau: J. U. Kern (Max Müller) éditeur.

    12mo, original cloth binding. Engraved title-page in red and black.

Games of Patience for one or more players. Second series. By Miss Whitmore Jones. Illustrated. London: L. Upcott Gill, 170, Strand, W.C.
No date

    16mo, three quarters calf.

Games of Patience, as above. Third series.
No date

    16mo, three quarters calf.

Games of Patience, as above. Fourth series.
No date

    16mo, three quarters calf.

Patience Games. By Professor Hoffmann. London: Chas. Goodall & Son, Ltd. 1900

    Small 16mo, g.e., full morocco, by Sand.

Patience. Anleitung zum legen von Patiencen. Verfasst von Max Weiss. Verlag von Otto Maier in Ravensburg.
No date

    12mo, original paper cover.

CONCERNING PHARAO

*Die ganze Kunst des Pharao Spiels; . . . Leipzig.
1807

    16mo, French mottled calf, gold lines and dentelles, by Ramage.

Betrachtungen über das Spiel besonders über das Pharao von Gerhard Ulrich Anton Vieth. Elberfeld: Gedruckt bei Heinrich Buschler.
1815

    16mo, original paper binding. Engraved frontispiece.

Die wichtigsten Momente aus dem Leben eines Pharaospielers . . . Von Benjamin Feige. Altenburg: Bei Julius Helbig. No date
  Small 8vo, original paper binding.

CONCERNING PIQUET

*Theodor Engelmanns Unterricht im Piquet, etc. Neue stark Verhehrtre Auflage. Berlin: Bei Wilhelm Dehmiate dem Jugern. 1798
  16mo, uncut, three quarters mottled calf, by Ramage.

*The Fashionable Piquet Player: explaining the modern game of Piquet as played in the clubs and most select societies . . . London: Published by Hunt and Sons, card-makers to Her Majesty, 20 Piccadilly. 1838
  Small 16mo, calf, gold tooling and dentelles.

Goyer Lavalette. L'Arbitre du Joueur de Piquet. En Vente: 38, Rue de Peinthièvre, Paris, et chez tous les Libraires. No date
  8vo, original paper binding.

The Laws of Piquet, adopted by the Portland Club. Edited by Cavendish. London: Thomas de la Rue & Co. Printed for private circulation. 1873
  16mo, original cloth binding, g.e.

The Laws of Piquet. Edited by Cavendish and adopted by the Portland and Turf Clubs, with a treatise on the game by Cavendish. Sixth edition. London: Thomas de la Rue & Co. 1889
  16mo, original cloth binding, g.e. Title-page in red and black.

Piquet and Rubicon Piquet. By Berkeley, with illustrations. London: George Bell & Sons. 1898
  16mo, original cloth binding.

The Laws of Piquet, adopted by the Portland and Turf Clubs, with a Treatise on the game by Cavendish. Ninth edition: London: De la Rue & Co., Ltd. 1901
  16mo, original cloth binding, g.e. Title-page in red and black.

CONCERNING POKER

*The Complete Poker Player. A practical guide book to the American national game: containing mathematical and experimental analysis of the probabilities of Draw Poker, also the laws of play and all the decisions upon disputed points in Wilkes Spirit, since 1870. By John Blackbridge, actuary and counsellor at law. New York: Advance Publishing Company, 152 Worth Street. 1875
  16mo, three quarters calf, by Ramage.

*The Poker-Players' Pocket Companion. Compiled from the best authorities. Boston: engraved, printed and copyrighted by John A. Lowell & Co. 1886
  Small 16mo, full pressed red morocco, gold dentelles, g.e., by Ramage.

The Game of Draw Poker. By John W. Keller, including the treatise by R. C. Schenck and rules for the new game of progressive poker. New York and London: Frederick A. Stokes Company, publishers. 1887
  16mo, original binding, half cloth.

Poker: How to Play It. A sketch of the great American game, with its laws and rules and some of its amusing incidents, by one of its victims. Fourth thousand (revised). London: Griffith, Farran, Okeden & Welsh, successors to Newbery & Harris, West Corner St. Paul's Churchyard. No date
  16mo, original cloth binding.

The Poker Book: How to Play the Fascinating Game of Draw Poker with Success. Together with the authentic laws of the game and notes and explanations thereon. With
illustrative hands. By Richard Guerndale. London: L. Upcott Gill, 170 Strand, W.C.
1889
    16mo, three quarters calf.

The Gentlemen's Hand Book on Poker. By 'Florence.' London, Glasgow, and Manchester: George Routledge & Sons, Ltd. New York: 9 Lafayette Place.   1892
    16mo, original cloth binding. Engraved frontispiece.

Poker Rules in Rhyme, with the chances to improve the hand by drawing. Illustrated.
Copyrighted.   1895
    Small 16mo, original binding of half cloth.

Poker Rules and Principles. Cincinnati, The United States Playing Card Company.
1907
    Small 16mo, paper.

CONCERNING POKER PATIENCE

Poker Patience. The International Card Company, 2 Bury Street, London, E.C.
No date
    Small 16mo, original paper cover, g.e.

Poker Patience and Progressive Poker Patience. Charles Vidal Diehl. Published by
Edward Mortimer, Halifax, Yorkshire, and 34 Paternoster Row, London, E.C.
No date
    12mo, original paper cover.

Poker Patience, as above. Second edition. London: The Advance Publishing Company,
146 Fleet Street, E.C.   No date
    12mo, original paper cover.

Poker Patience. By Charles Vidal Diehl. London.   1908
    12mo, paper.

The Pocket Guide to Poker Patience. By W. Dalton. London: De la Rue, Ltd.   1909
    16mo, paper, g.e.

CONCERNING QUADRILLE

The Game of Quadrille, or ombre by four, with its established rules as it is now played at
the French Court. Done from the French. To which is added the game of Quintille,
or ombre by five, both after the old and new manner. To this edition is likewise
added directions for playing the game of ombre by three. The third edition.
London: Printed for R. Francklin in Russel Street, Covent Garden.   1732
    16mo, three quarters pressed morocco, gold lines.

*A New Treatise upon real Quadrille, translated into English from the original French
of Mons. Martin, Master of a licensed Gaming House in Paris. . . . London: Printed
for G. Burnet, at Bishop Burnet's Head, in the Strand.   1764
    16mo, French mottled calf, gold borders and dentelles, by Ramage. The entire
book, from the title-page to the end, is printed in both English and French, the
French on the left-hand page and the English on the right.

Régole del' Giuoco de'l Quintilio trátte da un códice che si conserváva anticamente
nela librería dei Signóri Patrizi' Torriáni in Cherso e che è ora proprietà de'l Sigr.
Anníbale P******i ******** per cura del Abbáte dai due BB. Venezia: Stab. Naz.
di G. Grimaldo.   1868
    16mo, calf.

CONCERNING RIVERSI

*Régole del Riversino . . . Raccolta dal Signor N. N. Nuova edizione correttissima.
Napoli: Dai Torchi di Luca Marotta, Strada S. Biagio de' Libraj, No. 119. A di
II Gennajo.   1821
    8vo, paper binding.

Reversi and Go Bang. By Berkeley. Authorized by Lewis Waterman, with numerous illustrations. New York: Frederick A. Stokes Company. 1890
16mo, original binding, half cloth.

CONCERNING ROUGE ET NOIR

Rouge et Noir oder die Geschichte von den vier Konigen. Aus den Papieren des Staatstanzlers Rolichon von Starklof. Mit einer illuminirten tafel. Mainz: Bei Florian Kupferberg. 1829
16mo, three quarters pressed morocco, full gilt back, original binding.

CONCERNING ROULETTE

Explication des Jeux de la Roulette et du Trente et Quarante. Baden Baden. 1866
16mo, three quarters morocco.

Story of Roulette Cards. New York: The W. W. Russel Card Company. 1905
16mo, paper.

CONCERNING SKAT

Das Skat Spiel . . . von Max Merz. Berlin: Verlag Siegfried Cronbach. No date
16mo, three quarters blue morocco.

Lehrbuch des Schach und Scatspiels von B. C. Richard Schurig. Leipzig: Verlag von Otto Wigand. 1879
16mo, calf.

Illustriertes Lehrbuch des Skakspieles . . . von K. Buhle. Leipzig. 1885
16mo, original cloth binding.

*An Illustrated Grammar of Skat, the German Game of Cards . . . By Ernst Eduard Lemcke. Second edition, revised and greatly enlarged. London: H. Grevel & Co.
12mo, half calf, double frontispiece. 1887

An Illustrated Grammar of Skat . . . as above. New York: B. Westermann & Co.
12mo, original cloth binding. 1887

Skat. By Louis Vidal Diehl. London: George Bell & Sons, 4 York Street, Covent Garden, W.C. 1891
16mo, original cloth binding.

The Game of Skat in Theory and Practice. By A. Hertefeld. Translated and edited by Professor Hoffmann. With numerous illustrations. London: George Routledge & Sons, Ltd., Broadway, Ludgate Hill, Manchester and New York. 1893
8vo, original cloth binding.

Illustriertes Lehrbuch des Skatspiels. Von K. Buhle. Leipzig: Verlag von Ernst Keil's Nachfolger. 1895
12mo, original cloth binding.

Constitution and By-Laws of the North American Skat League. St. Louis. 1898
Small 16mo, original paper cover.

Allgemeine Deutsche Skatordnung von K. Buhle. Third edition. Leipzig: Verlag von Ernst Keil's Nachfolger. No date
16mo, original paper cover.

Skat Congress, Milwaukee. 1888
16mo, paper.

Das Skatspiel. Leipzig: Verlag Albert Otto Paul. 1905
16mo, paper.

Foster's Skat Manual. By R. F. Foster. New York: McClure, Phillips & Co. 1906
16mo, original cloth binding, g.e.

American Skat, or the Game of Skat Defined. A descriptive and comprehensive Guide
. . . By Charles Eichhorn, Detroit, Michigan, 1898. Edition of 1908
8vo, original cloth binding, g.e.

The Game of Skat: Its Origin, History and Development. . . . By Henry Kortjohn,
President of the North American Skat League. St. Louis: Printed by J. W. Steele &
Co., printers, 18 North Third Street. 1903
8vo, original paper cover.

Skat Pointers. Rules and Regulations. Copyrighted by L. Biersach, Freeport, Illinois.
Small 16mo, black morocco. 1903

CONCERNING TRICTRAC

Le Jeu du Trictrac comme on le joue aujourd'huy. Enrichy de Figures. Et d'une
Méthode très-aisée, pour apprendre de soy-même à jouer ce Jeu en perfection. À
Paris: Chez Henry Charpentier, dans la Grand' Salle du Palais, au bon Charpentier.
Avec Privilége du Roy. 1698
16mo, original calf, full gilt back.

Le Grand Trictrac ou Méthode Facile pour apprendre sans Maître la marche, les
termes, les règles & une grande partie des finesses de ce Jeu. Seconde édition. Revue,
corrigée & considérablement augmentée. Par M. L'Abbé S*****, Correspondant des
Académies Royales des Sciences de Paris & de Toulouse. À Avignon: Chez Alexandre
Giroud, seul Imprimeur de la Sainteté. Avec permission des Supérieurs. 1756
16mo, original calf, full gilt back. Engraved frontispiece. Enrichi de Figures.

CONCERNING WHIST

*Maxims for Playing the Game of Whist; with necessary Calculations, and the Laws of
the Games. A new edition. London: Printed for T. Payne and Son, next the Mews
Gate, St. Martins. 1778
16mo, three quarters calf, by Ramage.

Traité du Jeu de Whist, Traduit de l'Anglois d'Edmond Hoyle. Augmenté du Jeu de
l'Anti-Whist ou le Francion, et de celui de Trois Sept. Nouvelle édition. À la Haye:
Chez F. Staatman. 1779
16mo, original calf, full gilt back.

Traité du Jeu du Whist en forme de vocabulaire raisonné indiquant les Lois et les
Règles . . . Suivi d'une ancienne Boutade contre ce Jeu, et d'une Chanson. À Paris:
Chez Léopold Collin, libraire, rue Git-le Cœur, No. 4. 1809
16mo, three quarters green morocco.

Theoretisch-praktische Anleitung zum Whistspiele, . . . Wien. 1825
16mo, calf.

Der vollkommene Whistspieler oder die Kunst Whist zu spielen nach Hoyle's und
Payne's Grundsatzen, . . . Berlin. 1837
16mo, original cloth binding.

Manuel complet du Jeu de Whist. Troisième édition. Paris: Allouard, Libraire Commis-
sionaire. 1847
Small 16mo, full calf.

Whist en Province. Quelques préceptes sur le whist. Sébastopol: Imprimerie Impériale.
1856

Excessively rare. First edition. Didactic verses in French incorporating the twenty precepts for a game of whist as subsequently laid down by John Brunton. This was the only book published by this press, which was established to print proclamations and army orders.

Tableau Synoptique du Whist d'après Hoyle, Payne et Mathews.	No date
Meulan: Imprimerie de A. Hiard. Lemoine, 24 Place Vendôme et chez les principaux libraires.

12mo. A large folding table, mounted on linen. In slip case, half morocco, by Sand.

*The Quarterly Review.	1871
Containing reprints of 'A Short Treatise on the Game of Whist.' By Edmond Hoyle	1743
The Principles of Whist, Stated and Explained. By Cavendish.	1862
A Treatise on Short Whist. By James Clay, M.P.	1864
The Theory of the Modern Scientific Game of Whist. By William Pole, F.R.S. Mus. Doc. Oxon.	1865
8vo, full calf, gold lines and dentelles, full gilt back.

The Whist Players' Companion. Compiled from the best Authorities. Boston. No date
Small 16mo, full morocco, bound by Sand.

Modern Whist. The Whist Players' Pocket Companion. Boston.	1894
Small 16mo, full morocco, bound by Sand.

Whist and Duplicate Whist. Tenth edition. Cincinnati, U.S.A.: The United States Playing Card Company.	1897
16mo, original paper binding.

Fisher Ames

A Practical Guide to Whist by the Latest Scientific Methods, by Fisher Ames, with the Laws of the Game. Second edition. New York: Charles Scribner's Sons. 1891
16mo, original cloth binding.

A Practical Guide to Whist, as above. Ninth edition, revised and enlarged, with the laws of whist as adopted by the American Whist League.	1901
16mo, original cloth binding.

Aquarius (L. D. A. Jackson)

Easy Whist. By Aquarius. London: Chapman & Hall, Ltd.	1884
16mo, original cloth binding.

*Advanced Whist. By Aquarius, as above.	1884
16mo, original cloth binding.

The Hands at Whist. By Aquarius, as above.	1884
16mo, full morocco, inside dentelles in gold, by Ramage.

E. M. Arnaud

*An Epitome of the Game of Whist, Long and Short; consisting of an introduction to the mode of playing and scoring; the Laws of the Game essentially reformed; and maxims for playing, arranged on a new and simple plan, calculated to give rapid proficiency to a player of the dullest perception and worst memory: with definitions of the terms used, and a table of odds. By E. N. Arnaud. Edinburgh: Published by Oliver & Boyd, Tweeddale Court; and Simpkin & Marshall, London.	1829

16mo, uncut, mottled calf, gold lines and dentelles, by Ramage. Engraved frontispiece.

*An Epitome of the Game of Whist, as above. 1829
 16mo, three quarters calf, by Ramage.

Bernard

Traité Elémentaire du Jeu de Whist, contenant les principes de ce jeu, etc. . . . Résumé de traites anciens et modernes. Par Bernard. Paris: De la Rue, Libraire-éditeur, 3 rue des Grands-Augustins. No date
 16mo, original cloth binding.

Ferdinand Frhrn. v. Biedenfeld

Portative Whistbuchlein enthaltend die hauptregeln und maximen des Whist . . . von Ferdinand Frhrn. v. Biedenfeld. . . . Weimar: Verlag und Druct von Bernhard Friedrich Voigt. 1846
 16mo, original paper cover.

Lucy Blackburn

Helps on Modern American Whist. Compiled by Lucy Blackburn, Covington, Ky. Second edition. Copyright. 1900
 16mo, original paper cover.

Standard Leads in Whist in 1900. By Lucy Blackburn, Covington, Ky. 1902
 16mo, paper.

Emery Boardman

Winning Whist. A Harmonious System of Combined Long Suit and Short Suit Play of the Game of Whist. By Emery Boardman. New York: Charles Scribner's Sons. 1896
 16mo, original cloth binding, g.e.

J. Brunton

Les Quarante Préceptes du Whist en distiques rimés français et anglais, suivis de commentaires par J. Brunton. Paris: Libraire Nouvelle, Boulevard des Italiens, 15, en face de la Maison Dorée. 1856
 16mo, calf.

Les Quarante Préceptes du Whist, as above. Deuxième édition. Paris: Libraire de L. Hachette et Cie, Boulevard Saint-Germain, 77. 1866
 16mo, original cloth binding. Title-page in red and black.

Admiral James Burney

A Treatise on the Game of Whist. By the late Admiral James Burney, author of Voyages and Discoveries in the Pacific, etc. Second edition. London: Printed for Thomas and William Boone, 480, Strand. 1823
 16mo, calf.

William Mill Butler

The Whist Reference Book, wherein information is presented concerning the Noble Game, in all its aspects, after the manner of a Cyclopedia, Dictionary, and Digest. All combined in one by William Mill Butler. Illustrated. Philadelphia: Printed and published by the John C. Yorston Publishing Company. 1899
 8vo, original binding of half morocco, uncut. Frontispiece and title-page in red and black.

Caelebs (E. A. Carlyon)

The Laws and Practice of Whist. By Caelebs, M.A. London: Saunders and Otley, Conduit Street, 1851
12mo, original cloth. First edition, g.e.

The Laws and Practice of Whist. By Caelebs. As played at the Portland Club. Second edition. London: Robert Hardwicke, 26, Duke Street, Piccadilly; and all booksellers. Preface is dated 1856. No date
12mo, three quarters calf, by Ramage.

The Laws and Practice of Whist. By Caelebs. Third edition, greatly revised. London: Robert Hardwicke, 192, Piccadilly; and all booksellers. Preface dated, January, 1858. No date
16mo, original cloth binding. Frontispiece in color, g.e.

The Laws and Practice of Whist, as above. Sixth edition. Preface dated April, 1858
16mo, original cloth binding, g.e.

Major Campbell-Walker

The Correct Card, or How to Play at Whist. A Whist Catechism. By Capt. Arthur Campbell-Walker, F.R.G.S. . . . Fourth edition. London: Longmans, Green and Co.
16mo, original cloth binding, g.e. 1877

The Correct Card, or How to Play at Whist, as above. Fifth edition. 1878
16mo, original cloth binding, g.e.

The Correct Card, etc., as above. By Major Arthur Campbell-Walker, F.R.G.S. The thirteenth thousand. New York: D. Appleton and Company. 1885
16mo, original cloth binding, g.e.

Cavendish (Henry Jones)

The Principles of Whist stated and explained, and its practice illustrated. On an original system, by means of hands played completely through. By Cavendish. London: Bancks Brothers, card-makers to Her Majesty and to the principal club-houses, 20 Piccadilly. Manuscript note, 'First edition, extremely rare.' Bookplate of the Army and Navy Club with the inscription, 'This book was presented by the author.' No date (but 1862)
16mo, original cloth binding.

The Laws and Principles of Whist, etc., as above. Seventh edition. London: Bancks Brothers, card-makers to Her Majesty, to H.R.H. the Prince of Wales, and to the Principal club-houses. 12, Glasshouse street, Regent Street, W. 1864
16mo, original cloth binding, g.e.

The Laws and Principles of Whist, as above. Eighth edition with numerous additions. London: Thos. de la Rue & Co. 1868
16mo, original cloth binding, g.e.

*The Laws and Principles of Whist, as above. Ninth edition. 1868
16mo, three quarters calf, by Ramage.

*The Laws and Principles of Whist, as above. Ninth edition. 1870
With this is bound the first edition of Whist Developments, Cavendish, London.
16mo, full calf, gold lines and dentelles, by Ramage. 1885

The Laws and Principles of Whist, as above. Ninth edition. 1872
16mo, original cloth binding, g.e.

The Laws and Principles of Whist, as above. Tenth edition, revised and greatly enlarged. 1874

16mo, original cloth binding, g.e. Engraved frontispiece from the Compleat Gamester of 1680. On the back of the dedication page to James Clay, Esq., M.P., is a black-rimmed card, 'To the Memory of James Clay.'

The Laws and Principles of Whist, as above. Tenth edition.   1875
16mo, original cloth binding, g.e. Engraved frontispiece as above. Also dedication.

The Laws and Principles of Whist, as above. Eleventh edition.   1876
16mo, original cloth binding, g.e. and frontispiece. Also dedication.

The Laws and Principles of Whist, as above. Thirteenth edition.   1881
16mo, original cloth binding, g.e. Engraved frontispiece, as above. Also dedication.

The Laws and Principles of Whist, as above. Fifteenth edition.   1885
16mo, original cloth binding, g.e. Engraved frontispiece. Also dedication.

The Laws and Principles of Whist, as above. Sixteenth edition.
16mo, original cloth binding, g.e. Engraved frontispiece. Also dedication. 1886

The Laws and Principles of Whist, as above. Twenty-second edition. Seventy-fifth thousand.   1895
16mo, original cloth binding, g.e. Engraved frontispiece.

*Whist Developments. American Leads and the Plain Suit Echo. By Cavendish, author of 'The Laws and Principles of Whist,' etc., etc. London: Thos. de la Rue & Co. Dedicated to Nicholas Browse Trist. Bound with the ninth edition of Laws and Principles of Whist, as above.   1884
16mo, full calf, gold lines and dentelles, by Ramage.

Whist Developments, as above. Third edition.   1887
16mo, original cloth binding, g.e.

Whist Developments, as above. Fifth edition.   1891
16mo, original cloth binding.

Whist With and Without Perception. Illustrated by B.W.D. (Believer in Whist Developments) and Cavendish. London: Thos. de la Rue & Co.   1889
16mo, original cloth binding, g.e.

The Laws and Principles of Whist, Stated and Explained and its Practice Illustrated. On an original system, by means of hands played completely through. By Cavendish. Fifth edition. New York: D. Appleton and Company, 549, 551 Broadway.
16mo, original cloth binding.   1875

The Laws and Principles of Whist, as above. Fifth edition. New York: D. Appleton and Company, 1, 3, and 5 Bond Street.   1881
16mo, original cloth binding.

The Laws and Principles of Whist, as above. Seventeenth edition. New York: Frederick A. Stokes and Brother.   1890
16mo, original binding of half cloth.

The Laws and Principles of Whist, as above. Eighteenth edition.   1891
16mo, original binding of half cloth.

Coeckelberghe-Dutzle

Das rationelle Whist oder das Whistspiel . . . von Ritter Ludwig von Coeckelberghe-Dutzle. Wien.   1843
16mo, original cloth binding. Engraved title-page.

Charles Emmet Coffin

The Gist of Whist. Being a Concise Guide to the Modern American Game . . . By Charles Emmet Coffin . . . Seventh edition. New York: Brentano's, copyright. 1893
16mo, original cloth binding.

William Cusack-Smith

Encyclopedia of the Game of Whist, prefaced with words of advice to young players. By Sir William Cusack-Smith, Bart. New York: Brentano's.   1891
16mo, original cloth, g.e.

Hippolyte Demanet

Règles du Whist & du Boston d'après les Meilleurs Practiciens et les Méthodes Américaine et Anglaise . . . Suivies de la Règle du Jeu de Trente et Un. Par Hippolyte Demanet. Paris: Se trouve chez Durand, 10 rue Jacques de Brosse.
12mo, uncut, three fourths morocco, by Sand. No date.   *c.* 1845

M. Deschapelles

Traité du Whiste. Par M. Deschapelles. Paris: Perrotin, Éditeur-Libraire, 1 rue des Filles St. Thomas, place de la Bourse.   1840
16mo, original binding of half morocco.

Traité du Whiste. Par M. Deschapelles. IIᵉ Partie. La Législation. Paris: Librairie de Furne et Cie, rue Saint André des Arts, 55.   1859
12mo, three quarters morocco, original binding, uncut.

W. B. Dick (Trumps)

Dick's Hand Book of Whist. Containing Pole's and Clay's Rules for playing the modern scientific game . . . New York: Dick and Fitzgerald, publishers.   No date
16mo, original paper cover.

Modern Whist, with complete rules for playing, containing American leads . . . Compiled from the latest works of Cavendish . . . By Trumps. New York: Dick & Fitzgerald, publishers.   1892
16mo, three quarters morocco, by Sand.

Colonel A. W. Drayson, R.A.F.R.A.S.

The Art of Practical Whist. Being a series of letters descriptive of every part of the game . . . By Col. A. W. Drayson, R.A.F.R.A.S. Dedicated, by permission, to his Royal Highness, the Duke of Connaught. London: George Routledge and Sons, Broadway, Ludgate Hill. New York: 416 Broome Street.   1879
12mo, original cloth binding.

The Art of Practical Whist, as above. George Routledge and Sons. New York: 9 Lafayette Place. London, Glasgow, and Manchester. No date, but the preface to the fourth edition is dated   1885
16mo, original cloth binding.

The Art of Practical Whist, as above. Fifth edition. London: George Routledge and Sons, Ltd. Broadway, Ludgate Hill. Manchester and New York.   1892
12mo, original cloth binding.

R. F. Foster

Foster's Whist Manual. A Complete System of Instruction in the Game. By R. F. Foster (of New York). Brentano's, New York, Chicago, Washington.   1890
16mo, original cloth binding, autographed, g.e.

Foster's American Leads and How to Learn Them. New York: Brentano's.   1894
    16mo, paper.

Whist Tactics. A complete course of instruction in the methods adopted by the best
    players, illustrated by 112 hands played by correspondence between sixteen of the best
    players in the American Whist League. By R. F. Foster. New York and London:
    Frederick A. Stokes Company, publishers. Copyright, 1895.   No date
    16mo, original cloth binding, g.e. Title-page in red and black.

Whist Tactics, as above. London: Frederick Warne & Co., Bedford Street, W.C., Mudie
    & Sons, 15 Coventry Street, W.   1901
    16mo, original cloth binding, g.e.

Foster's Common Sense Leads and How to Learn Them. By the author of Foster's
    Whist Manual. New York: Brentano's. Copyright, 1898.   No date

C. D. P. Hamilton

Modern Scientific Whist. The Principles of the Modern Game analyzed and ex-
    tended. Illustrated by over Sixty Critical Endings and Annotated Games from Ac-
    tual Play. By C. D. P. Hamilton. London: Lawrence & Bullen, Ltd., 16 Henrietta
    Street, Covent Garden, W.C.   1902
    12mo, original cloth binding.

Modern Scientific Whist, as above. New York: Brentano's.   1904
    12mo, original cloth binding. Title-page in red and black.

Edwin C. Howell

Whist Openings. A Systematic Treatment of the Short Suit Game. By Edwin C.
    Howell. Boston.   1896
    16mo, original cloth binding.

Carl Konig

Das Whist und Boston spiel. Von Carl Konig. Berlin: Verlag von T. Grobe.
    One volume, small 16mo, paper.   c. 1860

Mary d'I. Levick

A Whist Catechism. Compiled by M. d'I. L. Second edition, revised. Philadelphia:
    J. B. Lippincott Company.   1897
    16mo, original cloth binding.

Lieutenant Colonel B. Lowsley

Whist of the Future. Being a forecast, submitting defects in existing whist laws . . .
    By Lieutenant Colonel B. Lowsley. London: Swan, Sonnenschein & Co., Ltd.,
    Paternoster Square.   1898
    16mo, original cloth binding, g.e.

T. Mathews, Esq.

*Advice to the Young Whist Player. Containing most of the maxims of the old
    school, with the author's observations on those he thinks erroneous . . . The tenth
    edition, with additions. By T. Matthews, Esq. Printed at the Bath Herald Office
    by Meyer and Son. Sold in London by Sherwood, Neely and Jones . . .   1816
    16mo, mottled calf, gold borders and dentelles, by Ramage.

*Advice to the Young Whist Player, as above. The sixteenth edition. Bath:

Printed by Mary Meyler, at the Herald Office. Sold in London by Baldwin, Cradock, and Joy . . .   1825
    16mo, three quarters calf, gold lines, by Root and Son, g.e.

Whist. By T. Mathews, Esq., and Major A****. Paris: A. and W. Galignani and Company.   1837
    16mo, original cloth binding, g.e

Instructions sur le Jeu de Whist. Par T. Mathews, en Anglais et en Français . . . Traduit par F. Gardera. Publié par M. Commecy. À Paris: Chez l'éditeur, au Cercle Français, 18 rue Vivienne.   1838
    16mo, calf. Engraved frontispiece.

C. J. Melrose

Modern Scientific Whist: with Reasons why. . . . By C. J. Melrose. London: L. Upcott Gill, 170, Strand, W.C.   1898
    12mo, original cloth binding.

H. F. Morgan

The Whist Player's Guide. By H. F. Morgan, late Captain 28th Regiment. London: Marcus, Ward & Co., 67 Chandos Street; and Royal Ulster Works, Belfast.   1881
    Small 16mo, original cloth binding.

C. S. Nichols   1902

Whist at a Glance. By C. S. Nichols.
    12mo, three quarters morocco, bound by Sand.

George Frederick Pardon

A Handbook of Whist, on the text of Hoyle. By George Frederick Pardon. New edition. London: George Routledge and Sons, The Broadway, Ludgate. New York: 416 Broome Street.   1868
    16mo, three quarters mottled calf.

Pembridge

Whist; or Bumblepuppy? Ten lectures addressed to children. By Pembridge. Third edition. London: G. E. Waters, 97 Westbourne Grove.   1887
    16mo, original cloth binding.

The Decline and Fall of Whist. An old-fashioned view of new-fangled play. By the author of 'Whist; or Bumblepuppy.' London: G. E. Waters, 97 Westbourne Grove.
    16mo, original cloth binding.   1884

G. W. Pettes

Whist Universal. An Analysis of the Game as improved by the introduction of American leads and adapted to all methods of play. By G. W. P. Boston: Ticknor and Company, 211 Tremont street. Copyright, 1887.   No date
    12mo, original cloth binding.

American Whist Illustrated. Containing the laws and principles of the Game, the analysis of the new play and American leads, and a series of hands in diagram, and combining Whist Universal and American Whist. By G.W.P. Boston and New York: Houghton, Mifflin and Company. The Riverside Press, Cambridge.   1890
    16mo, full morocco.

American Whist, as above. Eighth edition. 1893
16mo, full morocco.

American Whist, as above. Ninth edition 1894
16mo, full morocco.

J. G. Pohlman

Whist Rendered Familiar by a New and Easy Introduction to the Game. Deduced from the best authorities. By J. G. Pohlman. Second edition. London: Printed for R. Baldwin, Cradock and Joy. 1827
16mo, three quarters morocco.

William Pole

The Theory of the Modern Scientific Game of Whist. By William Pole, F.R.S. Mus. Doc. Oxon. Second edition. London: Longmans, Green and Co. 1871
16mo, original cloth binding.

The Theory of the Modern Scientific Game, as above. Fifth edition, enlarged.
16mo, original cloth binding. 1873

The Theory of the Modern Scientific Game, as above. Seventh edition. 1874
16mo, original cloth binding.

The Theory of the Modern Scientific Game, as above. Eleventh edition. 1879
16mo, original cloth binding.

The Theory of the Modern Scientific Game, as above. Thirteenth edition. 1882
16mo, original cloth binding, g.e.

The Theory of the Modern Scientific Game, as above. Fourteenth edition. 1883
16mo, original cloth binding.

The Theory of the Modern Scientific Game, as above. Twentieth edition. 1901
16mo, original cloth binding, g.e.

The Theory, etc., as above. From the last London edition, to which is added The Laws and Rules of Whist, from the Portland Club code. New York: copyright 1879, by G. W. Carleton & Co., publishers. London: Longman & Co. 1880
16mo, original cloth binding.

The Theory, etc., as above. 1884
16mo, original cloth binding.

The Theory, etc., as above. 1885
16mo, original cloth binding.

The Theory, etc., as above, together with the laws of whist as revised by the Portland and Arlington Clubs. New York: Frederick A. Stokes. 1887
16mo, original cloth binding.

The Philosophy of Whist. An essay on the scientific and intellectual aspects of the modern game. In two parts. Part I. The Philosophy of Whist Play. Part II. The Philosophy of Whist Probabilities. By William Pole, Mus. Doc. Oxon. . . . Second edition. London: Thos. de la Rue & Co., 110 Bunhill Row. 1884
16mo, original cloth binding, g.e.

The Philosophy of Whist, as above. Third edition. 1884
16mo, original cloth binding, g.e.

The Philosophy of Whist, as above. Fourth edition. 1886
16mo, original cloth binding, g.e.

The Philosophy of Whist, as above. Seventh edition. Revised and augmented.
16mo, original cloth binding, g.e. 1900

Whist. Reprinted from the new edition of Bohn's Handbook of Games. By William
Pole, F.R.S. London. George Bell & Sons. And New York. 1898
16mo, original cloth binding.

Portland (*James Hogg*)

The Whist Table. A Treasury of Notes on the Royal Game by Cavendish, C.
Mossop, A. C. Ewald, Charles Hervey and other distinguished players.... To
which is added Solo Whist and its rules by Abraham S. Wilks. The whole edited by
Portland. With portraits, etc. London: John Hogg, 13, Paternoster Row.
12mo, original cloth binding, uncut. No date

Richard A. Proctor (*Five of Clubs*)

*How to Play Whist. With the laws and etiquette of Whist. Whist-Whittlings, and
forty fully annotated games. By Five of Clubs. (Richard A. Proctor.) London:
Longmans & Co., Paternoster Row. 1885
12mo, three quarters calf, by Ramage. Frontispiece.

*Home Whist. An easy guide to correct play, according to the latest developments.
By Five of Clubs. (Richard A. Proctor.) London: Longmans, Green & Co. 1886
16mo, three quarters mottled calf, by Ramage.

Home Whist, as above. London and New York, 15 East 16th Street. 1889
16mo, full red morocco, original binding, g.e.

Rudolf H. Rheinhardt

Whist Scores and Card Table Talk with a Bibliography of Whist. By Rudolf Rhein-
hardt. Chicago: A. C. McClurg and Company. 1887
16mo, original cloth binding. Title-page in red and black.

G. P. Rishel

Whist Made Easier. By G. P. Rishel. Hornellsville, New York 1895
12mo, three quarters morocco, bound by Sand.

General Scott

A Compendium of Easy Rules of Whist, with Maxims and the Laws of the Game. Dedicated to the Duke of Wellington. By General Scott. Tenth edition. London: Printed
for D. Cox, Ball Alley, Lombard Street. 1814
16mo, calf. Engraved frontispiece, portrait of General Scott.

J. Spencer-Smith (*Un Amateur Anglais, et quelquefois, Un Amateur*)

Le Jeu du Whist. Traité élémentaire des lois, règles, maximes et calculs de ce Jeu . . .
depuis Hoyle jusqu'à Matthews, suivi d'observations sur le petit whist . . . Par Un
Amateur Anglais. Nouvelle édition. Caën: Chez P. Chalopin, rue Froide-Rue. 1820
16mo, calf.

Le Whist. Traité méthodique des règles, maximes, et calculs de ce jeu, tirées des meil-
leures autorités anglaises, tant de la vielle école de Hoyle, que de la nouvelle de
Mathews. Suivi d'observations sur le nouveau jeu de petit whist, compilé et traduit
de l'Anglais. Par J. Spencer-Smith. Caën: Chalopin Fils, Imprimeur Libraire, rue
Froide Rue, No. 2. 1825
12mo, original paper cover, uncut.

Le Jeu du Whist. Traité élémentaire des lois, règles, maximes, et calculs de ce jeu
... Par Un Amateur Anglais. Bruxelles: Société Typographique Belge. 1837
  16mo, calf.

Whist. Traité Méthodique des règles, maximes, et calculs de ce jeu ... Par J.
Spencer-Smith. Troisième édition. Caën: Imprimerie de A. Hardel, Successeur de T.
Chalopin. 1838
  16mo, calf.

Le Whist, rendu facile. Suivi de Traités du Whist de Gand du Boston de Fontaine-
bleau et du Boston Russe. Par Un Amateur. Paris: Arthus Bertrand, Libraire, rue
Hautefeuille. 1851
  16mo, three quarters morocco.

Le Whist, as above. Deuxième édition revue en partie et refondue. Paris: Garnier
Frères Libraires-Éditeurs, 6 rue des Saint Pères. 1855
  16mo, original cloth binding.

H. B. T.

Conventional Whist Leads. When to lead each card of the thirteen originally, and
which card of the remaining twelve to lead on second round ... By H. B. T.
Philadelphia: J. B. Lippincott Company. 1891
  Small 16mo, original cloth binding.

The United States Playing Card Company

Simple Whist. Cincinnati: The United States Playing Card Company. 1901
  16mo, paper.

Charles Van Tenac

Album des Jeux. Traité du Jeu de Whist. Lois, règles, conventions et maximes pour
le bien jouer. Par Charles Van Tenac. Paris: Passard, Libraire-Éditeur, 9 rue des
Grands-Augustins. 1863
  16mo, calf.

Kate Wheelock

Whist Rules. By Kate Wheelock. Copyrighted by the Author. 1896
  8vo, original paper cover, uncut.

Milton G. Work

Whist of Today. Tenth edition. Milton G. Work. Autographed. Philadelphia:
Dreka. 1903
  16mo, cloth.

CONCERNING SHORT WHIST

Major A. (Charles Barham Coles)

*Short Whist: Its Rise, Progress and Laws. Together with Maxims for Beginners and
Observations to Make Any One a Card Player. By Major A****** London: Printed
for Longman, Rees, Orme, Brown, Green and Longman, Paternoster Row. 1835
  16mo, full calf, gold borders and dentelles, by Ramage. Engraved frontispiece.

*Short Whist, as above. 1836
  16mo, three quarters calf, by Root and Son, gold lines, and edges. Engraved
frontispiece.

Short Whist, as above. . . . To which are added Precepts for Tyros. By Mrs. B******
16mo, original cloth binding, g.e. Engraved frontispiece.   1839

Short Whist, as above. Seventh edition.   1840
16mo, original cloth binding, g.e. Engraved frontispiece.

Short Whist, as above. Eighth edition. Printed for Longman, Brown, Green and
Longman.   1843
16mo, original cloth binding, g.e. Engraved frontispiece.

Short Whist, as above. Tenth edition.   1849
16mo, original cloth binding, g.e. Engraved frontispiece.

Short Whist, as above. Eleventh edition.   1850
16mo, original cloth binding, g.e. Engraved frontispiece.

Short Whist, as above. Twelfth edition.   1852
16mo, original cloth binding, g.e. Engraved frontispiece.

Short Whist, as above. Thirteenth edition.   1855
16mo, original cloth binding, g.e. Engraved frontispiece.

Short Whist, as above. Fifteenth edition. London: Longman, Green, Longman and
Roberts.   1862
16mo, full calf, gold borders and dentelles, by Ramage. Engraved frontispiece.

Short Whist. By Major A****** Sixteenth edition, . . . with an essay on the theory
of the modern scientific game by Professor P****** London: Longman, Green, Longman, Roberts, and Green.   1865
16mo, original cloth binding, g.e. A new engraved frontispiece entitled '1865.
Express and expeditious.'

J. L. Baldwin

The Laws of Short Whist. Edited by J. L. Baldwin. Adopted by the following clubs:
Albemarle, Allied University, Arlington, etc., . . . and A Treatise on the Game, by
James Clay. Second edition, with alterations and additions. London: Harrison, 59,
Pall Mall, Bookseller to the Queen and H.R.H. the Prince of Wales.   No date
16mo, full calf inside dentelles in gold, by Ramage, g.e.

The Laws of Short Whist. Edited by J. L. Baldwin, as above.   1864
16mo, original cloth binding, g.e.

The Laws of Short Whist, as above.   1865
16mo, original cloth binding, g.e.

The Laws of Short Whist, as above.   1866
16mo, original cloth binding, g.e.

The Laws of Short Whist. Edited by J. L. Baldwin. And A Treatise on the Game, by
James Clay. A new and improved edition. London: Thos. de la Rue & Co., 110 Bunhill Row.   1881
16mo, original cloth binding, g.e.

Lieutenant Colonel A. F. Blyth (Lieutenant Colonel B***)

The Whist Player. The Laws and Practice of Short Whist. Explained and Illustrated. By Lieutenant Colonel B******. London: Addey and Co., Henrietta Street,
Covent Garden.   1856
12mo, original cloth binding, g.e. Frontispiece in color.

*The Whist Player, as above. Second edition. London: Chapman and Hall, 193
Piccadilly. 1858
   12mo, three quarters calf, by Ramage.

The Whist Player, as above. Third edition. 1866
   12mo, original cloth binding.

Val. W. Starnes

Short Suit Whist. By Val W. Starnes. Brentano's: New York, Chicago, Washington.
   16mo, original cloth binding. 1896

E. P. Watson, Esq.

Short Whist. By F. P. Watson, Esq. To which is added Long Whist, with instructions for young players, by Admiral James Burney. Fourth edition. Revised by
F. P. Watson. London: T. & W. Boone, New Bond Street. 1848
   16mo, full mottled calf, gold dots and dentelles, by Ramage.

CONCERNING SOLO WHIST

Robert Frederick Green

Solo Whist. By Robert Frederick Green, editor of the British Chess Magazine. New
York: Frederick A. Stokes Company. 1891
   16mo, original cloth binding.

Abraham S. Wilks

How to Play Solo Whist. Its Methods and Principles Explained . . . By Abraham S.
Wilks and Charles F. Pardon. London: Chatto & Windus, Piccadilly. 1888
   16mo, original cloth binding.

The Handbook of Solo Whist, containing a general explanation of its methods . . .
By A. S. Wilks. London: John Hogg, 13 Paternoster Row. Preface dated 1898
   12mo, original cloth binding.

The Handbook of Solo Whist, as above. Second edition, revised and enlarged. 1899
   12mo, original cloth binding.

The United States Playing Card Company

Solo, the Greatest American Game. Cincinnati: The United States Printing Company. 1891
   16mo, paper.

CONCERNING DUPLICATE WHIST

American Whist League

Laws of Duplicate Whist, as adopted by the American Whist League. 1898
   16mo, three quarters calf, bound by Sand.

R. F. Foster

Foster's Duplicate Whist. A Complete System of Instruction in Whist Strategy. By
R. F. Foster. Brentano's: New York, Chicago, Washington. Copyright 1894
   16mo, original cloth binding.

Foster's Duplicate Whist. To eliminate luck from whist competition. Three cloth
folders.

John T. Mitchell

Duplicate Whist. Its Rules and Methods of Play ... By John T. Mitchell ... Chicago: A. C. McClurg and Company.   1891
  16mo, original cloth binding.

Duplicate Whist. By John T. Mitchell. An entirely new edition. Containing full explanation of the various methods ... as adopted by the American Whist League. Kalamazoo, Michigan: Ihling Bros. & Everard.   1897
  12mo, original cloth binding.

Cassius M. Paine

Duplicate Whist, National Method. By Cassius M. Paine. Second edition, revised. Kalamazoo, Michigan.   1891
  16mo, paper.

Duplicate Whist, Kalamazoo method.
  16mo, paper.

J. P. Torney

The Laws of Duplicate Whist, as suggested by the chairman of the Committee on Laws. By J. P. Torney. San Francisco.   1898
  12mo, paper.

The United States Playing Card Company

National Duplicate Whist. Cincinnati, U.S.A.: The United States Playing Card Company. Copyrighted   1897
  8vo, original paper cover.

CONCERNING TRIPLICATE WHIST

Charles Lahure

*Le Whist à Trois, ou Mort. Par Ch. Lahure. Paris: A. Lahure, Imprimeur-Éditeur, 9 rue de Fleurus.   1886
  16mo, full mottled calf, gold borders and dentelles, by Ramage. Title-page in red and black.

H. J. Noyes

Triplicate Whist. The Rules and Suggestions for Playing. By J. J. Noyes. Port Chester, New York.   1903
  16mo, original cloth binding. Title-page in red and black.

CONCERNING HANDICAP WHIST

V. R. Coxe

Handicap Whist. By V. R. Coxe.   1903
  12mo, three quarters morocco, bound by Sand.

CONCERNING BRIDGE

George E. Atherton

Bridge up to Date. By George E. Atherton. London.   1905
  16mo, paper.

G. Y. Atchison and A. J. G. Lindsell

The Why and Wherefore of Bridge. By G. T. Atchison and A. J. G. Lindsell. Longmans, Green and Co., 39 Paternoster Row, London, New York and Bombay. 1905
12mo, original cloth binding.

Lucy Blackburn

Helps on the Popular Game Bridge Whist. By Lucy Blackburn, Associate Member of the American Whist League, Author of Whist Helps, and The United States Playing Card Company's Correspondence Whist Lessons. Cincinnati: The Armstrong News and Stationery Company. 1906
16mo, original paper cover. Autographed.

Boaz, or Badsworth (Allan, Lindsay, Lister)

The Laws of Bridge, adopted by the Portland and Turf Clubs and A Guide to the Game. By 'Boaz.' Second edition. London: Thomas de la Rue & Co. 1895
16mo, original cloth binding, g.e.

Modern Bridge. By Slam (E. Chittenden). With the laws of bridge as approved by the Portland and Turf Clubs by Boaz. Longmans, Green and Company, 39 Paternoster Row, London, New York and Bombay. 1901
16mo, original cloth binding.

L. J. Bruck

The House of Lords' Book on Bridge. By L. J. Bruck. New York. 1907
Small 16mo, full morocco.

Herbert Campbell

Bridge for Bridgettes. By Herbert Campbell. Black and White Publishing Company, Ltd., 63 Fleet Street, London, E.C. Preface dated 1909
12mo, original paper cover.

W. Dalton

The Laws of Bridge, revised 1904, with cases and decisions by the Committee of the Portland Club. Edited by W. Dalton. London: Thomas de la Rue & Co., Ltd. 1907
16mo, original cloth binding.

Andrew Dougherty

A Primer of Bridge. By Andrew Dougherty. New York. 1906
16mo, limp leather.

Archibald Dunn

Bridge and How to Play It. By Archibald Dunn. Thirteenth edition. London: George Routledge and Sons, Ltd. New York: E. P. Dutton and Co. 1904
16mo, three quarters morocco.

J. B. Elwell

Bridge. Its Principles and Rules of Play. By J. B. Elwell. With illustrative hands and the club code of bridge laws adopted November, 1902. New York: Charles Scribner's Sons. 1904
16mo, original cloth binding, g.e. Title-page in red and black.

The Analysis and Complete Play of the Bridge Tournament Hands. (Evening Telegram.) By J. B. Elwell. New York: Charles Scribner's Sons.   1904
12mo, original cloth binding.

R. F. Foster

Foster's Bridge Manual. A Complete System of Instruction in the Game, to which is added Dummy Bridge and Duplicate Bridge. By R. F. Foster. New York: Brentano's.   1904
16mo, original cloth binding, g.e. Title-page in red and black.

Bridge Maxims. By R. F. Foster. New York: Brentano's.   1905
16mo, original cloth binding, g.e. Title-page in red and black.

Foster's Laws of Bridge, with Hints to Beginners. By R. F. Foster. Philadelphia.
Small 16mo, full morocco, bound by Sand.   1908

M. S. Hess

Correct Bridge. Its Laws and Principles Fully Explained. By M. S. Hess. Illustrative Hands. Chicago, New York: Rand, McNally & Co., publishers. Copyright   1906
16mo, original binding, full red morocco, g.e.

Professor Hoffman

Bridge. By Professor Hoffman. Eleventh edition. London.   1905
Small 16mo, full morocco, bound by Sand.

Lennard Leigh

Bridge Whist. How to Play It. With full directions, . . . By Lennard Leigh.
Philadelphia: Henry T. Coates and Company.   1901
16mo, original cloth binding, gold top.

Leikeze (Grace Ezekiel)

Kindergarten Bridge Whist. By Leikeze. Copyright, Springfield, Massachusetts.
16mo, uncut, original paper cover.   1906

Virginia M. Meyer

Small Talks on Bridge. By Virginia M. Meyer. San Francisco: Paul Elder and Company.   1911
12mo, paper.

Paul E. Mottelay

The Bridge Blue Book. A compilation of opinions of the leading bridge authorities . . . By Paul F. Mottelay. New York: Charles Scribner's Sons.   1906
12mo, original cloth binding.

Edmund Robertson and A. Hyde-Wollaston

Bridge Developments from the Higher Grammar of Bridge. By Edmund Robertson and A. Hyde Wollaston. New York: Brentano's.   1904
16mo, original cloth binding, g.e. Title-page in red and black.

Annie Blanche Shelby

Bridge Abridged. A comprehensive and concise statement of the maxims, rules and

principles governing the game of bridge. By Annie Blanche Shelby . . . New York:
Duffield and Company. 1906
    16mo, original cloth binding.

K. N. Steele

Simple Rules for Bridge. By K. N. Steele. New York. 1904
    16mo, paper.

Charles Stuart Street

Sixty Bridge Hands. By Charles Stuart Street. New York: Dodd, Mead and Company. 1903
    16mo, original binding, full morocco, gold top.

Eleanor A. Tennant

Bridge up to Date, Including Auction Bridge and the Rules and Laws of the Game. By
Eleanor A. Tennant. London: Hutchison & Co., Paternoster Row. 1909
    16mo, original cloth binding.

The United States Playing Card Company

Bridge Whist, and How to Play It. Cincinnati: The United States Playing Card
Company. 1900
    16mo, paper.

W. H. Whitfield

The Pocket Laws of Bridge. By W. H. Whitfield. London: Thos. de la Rue &
Co., Ltd. 1904
    Small 16mo, g.e., full morocco, bound by Sand.

THE LAWS OF BRIDGE

The Laws of Bridge, as adopted by The Whist Club. Also the Etiquette of the Game
with Hints for Play. Second edition. 11 West 36th Street, New York. 1899
    12mo, original cloth binding, gold top.

The American Laws of Bridge. Adopted November, 1902. Authorized edition. New
York: Charles Scribner's Sons. 1903
    16mo, original cloth binding. Title-page in red and black.

The Laws of Bridge, as adopted by The Whist Club. Also the Etiquette of the
Game. 13 West 36th Street, New York. 1905
    16mo, original cloth binding.

The Laws of Bridge, as adopted by The Whist Club of New York. Also the Etiquette of the Game. Published by the New York Consolidated Card Company.
222–228 West 14th Street, New York. 1905
    16mo, original paper cover.

CONCERNING AUCTION

S. S. Carvalho

Complete Auction Bridge for 1922. The Game. The Bidding. The Play. The Laws.
Current Book Company, Inc. 140 Cedar Street, New York. 1922
    12mo, original cloth binding.

H. P. Clark

Auction Bridge, Condensed. By H. P. Clark. New York.   1911
12mo, paper.

Wynne Ferguson

The 1920 Rules and Laws of Auction Bridge. By Wynne Ferguson, New York City.
16mo, original paper cover. Autographed.   1920

One Hundred Bridge Lessons. By Wynne Ferguson. New York: Bristol Press.   1925
16mo, paper. Autographed.

Practical Auction Bridge. By Wynne Ferguson. New York: George H. Doran. 1926
12mo, cloth. Autographed.

The 1928 Rules and Laws of Auction Bridge. By Wynne Ferguson. New York.   1928
16mo, paper. Autographed.

The Laws of Contract Bridge. By Wynne Ferguson. New York.   1928
16mo, paper. Autographed.

R. F. Foster

Auction at a Glance. By R. F. Foster. Cincinnati: The United States Playing Card
Company.   1920
16mo, original paper cover.

Florence Irwin

"Nullos." The New Call at Royal Auction Bridge. By Florence Irwin. The Strand
Magazine.
8vo, paper.

Sidney S. Lenz

Lenz on Bridge. By Sidney S. Lenz. New York: Simon and Schuster.   1927
2 vols. 12mo, cloth. Autographed.

Virginia M. Meyer

Royal or Lily Auction. By Virginia M. Meyer. San Francisco.   1910
12mo, paper.

Edwin Oliver and G. Edward Atherton

The A B C of Auction Bridge and Other Bridge Variations. By Edwin Oliver. Revised
for American Players by G. Edward Atherton, of the Philadelphia Racquet Club.
Philadelphia: David McKay, publisher, 604–608 South Washington Square. Copyright   1912
16mo, original cloth binding.

Vane Pennell

Auction Bridge. By Vane Pennell. London: Brown, Langham & Co., Ltd. Philadelphia: J. B. Lippincott Co.   1908
16mo, original cloth binding, g.e.

E. V. Shepard

Auction to Win. A textbook demonstrating the highest type of game . . . By E. V.
Shepard. New York: Reynolds Publishing Company, Inc. Copyright   1923
16mo, original cloth binding.

Win at Bridge. Auction Bridge Made Simpler, More Definite: Easier to Win Contract Bridge Introduced. By E. V. Shepard. New York: Reynolds Publishing Company, Inc.

12mo, cloth. Autographed.

Kate Wheelock

Auction Bridge Suggestions, Including the Royal Count. Also the Latest Laws on the Game, by permission of the New York Whist Club. By Kate Wheelock. Copyrighted by the Author. 1912

8vo, original paper cover. Autographed.

Auction High Spade Bids and Nullo Suggestions. By Kate Wheelock. New York. 1913

12mo, paper. Autographed.

Wilbur G. Whitehead

Whitehead's Auction Bridge for Beginners. Wilbur G. Whitehead. New York: Frederick A. Stokes Company. 1928

16mo, cloth. Autographed.

Milton C. Work.

Auction Declarations. By Milton C. Work. With the laws of auction adopted by the Whist Club of New York, effective January 1, 1917. Philadelphia: The John C. Winston Company. 1917

16mo, limp leather, gold edges. Autographed: 'For the United States Playing Card Company, with appreciation for many favors during my Red Cross Auction Tourney. Milton C. Work. January 9, 1918.'

Auction Bridge Complete. By Milton G. Work. Philadelphia: John C. Winston Company. 1926

12mo, cloth. Autographed.

Bridge Pointers and Tests. By Milton G. Work. Philadelphia: John C. Winston Company. 1927

12mo, cloth. Autographed.

Contract Bridge. By Milton G. Work. Philadelphia: John G. Winston Company. 1927

12mo, cloth. Autographed.

THE LAWS OF AUCTION BRIDGE

The Laws of Auction Bridge as Played at the Bath Club. London: Thos. de la Rue & Co., Ltd. 1908

Small 16mo, full morocco, g.e., bound by Sand.

The Laws of Auction Bridge as adopted by The Whist Club. New York: The Consolidated Card Company. 1911

16mo, paper.

PERIODICALS ON GAMING

The Westminster Papers. A monthly journal of Chess, Whist, Games of Skill and the Drama. London: W. Kent & Co. Edinburgh: J. Menzies & Co. Dublin: McGlashan & Gill.

Ten volumes. Vol. II (1869–1870)–Vol. XI (1878–1879).

Each, 8vo, cloth binding.

Whist. A monthly journal devoted to the interests of the Game. Milwaukee.

Six volumes. Vol. 4 (1895)–Vol. II (1900).

Each, folio, cloth binding.

Whist Faces. By the Editor of Whist. Illustrated. 1897
    Small 16mo, full Morocco. Bound by Sand.

Whist. Published monthly in the interest of Whist and Bridge. H. H. Ward and R. F.
    Foster, Editors. R. G. Badger, publisher. New York.
    Volumes I and II, bound together. (1906–1908.)
    8vo, three quarters calf.

Bridge. A monthly magazine published for lovers and students of the game. L. J. Bruck,
    publisher, New York.
    Volumes I and II, bound together. (1906–1907.)
    8vo, three quarters calf.

Whist Sketches. Review and Sketches of the First American Whist Congress. Held in
    Milwaukee, April, 1891. By C. S. B. The Free Press Publishing House, Easton,
    Pennsylvania. 1892
    12mo, original cloth binding. Frontispiece. Title-page in red and black.

Proceedings of the American Whist Congress. Sixteen volumes. From the First (1891)
    through the Sixteenth (1906).
    Each, 8vo, original cloth binding.

Autographs of Players at the American Whist League Convention, Milwaukee. Also
    clippings about this convention. 1901
    8vo, three quarters morocco.

Ninth Annual Congress of the Woman's Whist League. To be held at the Southern
    Hotel, St. Louis. April, 1906
    12mo, original paper cover.

Historical Sketch of the Knickerbocker Whist Club. New York: Privately printed.
    16mo, paper. 1926

ADDITIONAL BIBLIOGRAPHY FOR THE AMERICAN CARDS

Old Virginia and Her Neighbours. John Fiske.
The Dutch and Quaker Colonies in America. John Fiske.
The History of Printing in America. Isaiah Thomas.
The Furniture of Our Forefathers. Esther Singleton.
Watson's Annals of Philadelphia.
Historical Collections of the State of New Jersey. J. W. Barber and H. Howe.
The George Washington Diaries. Edited. By J. C. Fitzpatrick.
The Life of Colonel Paul Revere. Elbridge Henry Goss.
The Professional and Industrial History of Suffolk County, Massachusetts.
Reports of the Secretary of the Treasury at Washington, 1787–1823.
Observations on the Agriculture, Manufactures and Commerce of the United States. In
    a letter to a member of Congress. Tench Coxe. New York, 1789.
A View of the United States of America, written at various times between the years 1787–
    1794. Tench Coxe.
A Brief Examination of Lord Sheffield's Observations on the Commerce of the United
    States. Tench Coxe.
The Colonial Merchants and the American Revolution (1763–1776). Arthur M. Schles-
    inger.
Memorial of Alexander Anderson. B. J. Lossing.
The Colonial Laws of New York. Albany, 1894.
The Social History of Flatbush. Vanderbilt.
History of American Manufactures from 1608 to 1860. J. L. Bishop.

INDEX OF MAKERS OF PLAYING CARDS

GENERAL INDEX

Horse, 6, 27, 99, 129, 134, 146, 177, 217, 234, 267, 277, 279, 281, 282
Hoyle, Edmond, 208
Hoyle's Games, 166, 206, 208, 304, 305
Hungary, playing cards of, 31, 146, 156, 234
Hunting series of playing cards, 89, 90, 91, 125, 129, 142, 153, 157
Hyde, Thomas, 3, 209

Importation of playing cards, 169, 180, 181, 182, 184, 245, 285, 289, 312, 327
Impressionist playing cards, 155
Index marks on playing cards, 8, 188, 189, 251, 252, 333, 334, 345, 346, 347
India, playing cards of, 3, 20–30, 31, 169
Indian costume, 74, 83, 115, 214, 222
Innsbruck, playing cards of, 114, 141, 153, 264
    Card-makers of:
        Heinrich Hauk, 1586
        T. Albrecht, 1750
Institute Summarie, Thomas Murner, 105, 153
Interlaken, playing cards of, 157, 264
Invitation cards, 287, 302, 303, 329, 360
Iron playing cards, 142, 157
Italy, playing cards of, 31, 34, 38, 39, 78, 98, 99, 110, 146, 148, 151, 153, 154, 157, 223–246, 252

Jack-a-napes, 170, 257
Jackson, Andrew, 328
James II, 191
James II, Reign of, 194, 197, 220
Japanese playing cards, 6, 13, 14, 15, 16, 17, 18, 19
Japanese American playing cards, 356, 366
Jeanne d'Arc, 145, 154
Jeanne de Brabant, 159, 257
Jefferson, Thomas, 328
Jena, playing cards of, 119, 120, 121, 155
    German Arms Cards, Dr. T. Schroeter
Jeu d'Allouette, 70, 82
Jeu d'Armoiries des Souverains et états d'Europe, de Brianville, 60, 61, 82
Jeu de Cartes du Blason, 61, 62, 82
Jeu de Drapeaux, 75, 83
Jeu de Fables, 59, 82
Jeu de la Guerre, 63, 65, 82
Jeu de la Sybelle des Salons, 79, 83
Jeu de l'Hymen, 65
Jeu de l'Oie, 65
Jeu de Mappe Monde, 65
Jeu de Marine, 65
Jeu de Reines Renommées, 57, 58, 82, 153
Jeu de Société, 87
Jeu de Whist Indienne, 74, 83
Jeu des Cartes Militaires, 65
Jeu des Nations, 65
Jeu des Roys de France, 56, 58, 59
Jeu du Lindor ou du Naine Jaune, 65, 153
Jeu Français et Allemand et Italien, 68, 82
Jeu Français et Anglais et Portugais, 67, 82
Jeu Français et Espagnol et Hollandais, 68, 82
Jeu Français et Russe et Polonais, 68, 82
Jeu Géographique et Mythologique, 66, 67, 82
Jeu Louis XV, 83, 137, 190
Jeu Héraldique, Daumont, 62, 82
Jeu Impériale, 50, 57, 85
Jeu Mythologique, 59, 82
Jeux, Dictionnaire des, 65
Jeux des Cartes Historiques, 65, 82
Johannes, 257
Jokers, 11, 12, 189, 336, 345, 346, 347, 348, 351, 352, 355
Jones, Owen, 188, 332, 333, 334
Jonson, Ben, 209
Jubilee cards, 157, 190, 222, 346

Juno, 39, 262
Jupiter, 39, 262

Kaiser tarots, 142, 157
Kalmar, playing cards of, 270
Kille, 151, 267, 269
Kings of England playing cards, 211, 221
Klerksdorp, card-maker of, H. M. Guest, 167, 168
Knave, 167, 170
Knaves, The Four, 171
Knightly Orders, transformation cards, 146, 154
Kolibri cards, 81, 83
Korea, playing cards of, 1, 2, 6, 8
Kuntsburg, 148

Lafayette, Marquis de, 148, 292, 304
La Haye, 166
Lansquenet, 100
La Rochelle, card-maker of, La Veuve Pavie, 84
Launcelot, 43, 49, 171
Law, John, 164, 165
Leaves, 7, 100, 113, 119, 121, 248, 279
Le Chariot, 148, 161
Le Clerc, Sebastien, 61
Leger-de-main cards, 71, 83
Le Normand, Mlle, 149, 155, 356
Leipzig, playing cards of, 124, 131, 132, 133, 134, 135, 136, 149, 154, 155
    Musical tarots, 1780
    Battle of Leipzig playing cards, two editions, 1813
    Oval playing cards, historical court cards, 1865
    Mediæval playing cards, 1885
    Card-makers of,
        P. F. Ulrich
        F. Gunthel
        A. Tweitmeyer
        E. Burger
Leyden, 166
Libro y Baraja, Don Francisco Gazan, de Brianville heraldry, 253, 255
Liège, 160, 161, 166
Lille, playing cards of, 65
    Jeux Historiques, four editions, designed by E. Jouy, published by Vanackers
Limoges, 248, 249
Lincoln, President, 345, 348
Lion, 25, 27, 103, 113, 119, 232, 263
Lion and the unicorn, 85, 186, 187
Lithographs 72, 74, 79, 121, 124, 137, 144, 155, 212, 232, 254, 255, 256, 264, 267, 270, 347
Little Saints, 152
Littlebury, playing cards of, 178, 179, 220
    Principall Nations of the World, H. Winstanley, 1660
Logica Memorativa, 102, 103, 104, 105, 153
Lohengrin, 71, 83
London, playing cards of, 160, 170, 175, 177, 190, 192, 198, 205, 206, 214, 215, 284, 315, 342
    Card-makers of:
        Bancks Brothers, c. 1830, 187, 188, 209, 221
        Richard Blome, 1675, 173, 174, 220
        Carington Bowles, 1720, 197, 221
        I. L. Cowell, 1825, 217, 221
        Alfred Crowquill, 1850, 217, 221
        Darton and Harvey, 1807, 221
        William Darton, 1822, 1823, 221, 222
        Deakin and Company, 1880, 189, 222
        De la Rue, 1850, 187, 188, 209, 221, 222
        Count d'Orsay, 1820, 215, 222
        C. E. Eads, 1870, 214, 222
        James English, 1880, 189, 222
        William Faithorne, 1679, 193, 220
        F. Jackson, 1656, 173, 220
        Gibson and Osborne, 1765, 187, 220